Anna Seward and the End
of the Eighteenth Century

Anna Seward and the End of the Eighteenth Century

৪১

CLAUDIA THOMAS KAIROFF

The Johns Hopkins University Press
Baltimore

© 2012 The Johns Hopkins University Press
All rights reserved. Published 2012
Printed in the United States of America on acid-free paper
2 4 6 8 9 7 5 3 1

The Johns Hopkins University Press
2715 North Charles Street
Baltimore, Maryland 21218-4363
www.press.jhu.edu

Library of Congress Cataloging-in-Publication Data
Kairoff, Claudia Thomas.
Anna Seward and the end of the eighteenth century /
Claudia Thomas Kairoff.
p. cm.
Includes bibliographical references and index.
ISBN-13: 978-1-4214-0328-1 (acid-free paper)
ISBN-10: 1-4214-0328-5 (acid-free paper)
1. Seward, Anna, 1742–1809—Criticism and interpretation.
2. England—Intellectual life—18th century. I. Title.
PR3671.S7Z74 2012
821'.6—dc22   2011019914

A catalog record for this book is available from the British Library.

"Anna Seward and the Sonnet: Milton's Champion" was originally
published in *Aphra Behn Online* 1 (2011) and is reprinted here
with permission of the editors.

Special discounts are available for bulk purchases of this book.
For more information, please contact Special Sales at 410-516-6936
or specialsales@press.jhu.edu.

The Johns Hopkins University Press uses environmentally friendly book
materials, including recycled text paper that is composed of at least
30 percent post-consumer waste, whenever possible.

For Peter D. Kairoff
Elizabeth T. and David J. Butler
Robyn L. and John J. Thomas III
and
Holly D. Thomas

Contents

Preface

When I began working on this study in 2004, I thought I had chosen — to borrow the phrase from Jane Austen — "a heroine whom no one but myself will much like" (*Letters* 209). Anna Seward (1742–1809) had been the subject of curiously pejorative biographies, had been overlooked by most scholars of the later eighteenth century, and was being dropped from both eighteenth-century and Romantic-era literary anthologies. While thanks to editors like Paula R. Feldman and writers like Stuart Curran, she is now included in studies of early Romantic-era women writers, she fits among them rather uneasily.[1] Her sonnets, collected and published in 1799, marked her participation in a revival of that verse form that was among the harbingers of what we now call the Romantic era. But most of Seward's writings adhere to traditions established much earlier and practiced by writers like John Milton and Alexander Pope. Even Seward's sonnets, owing to her championship of Miltonic style and subjects, differ widely from sequences such as Charlotte Smith's, which focus nearly exclusively on mysterious, irreparable grief. Seward, trained as a child to recite Milton and as a young poet to emulate Pope, was essentially an eighteenth-century poet, albeit a very late inheritor in that line of succession. Welcome recognition of her status is her recent inclusion in *British Women Poets of the Long Eighteenth Century*, the important anthology edited by Paula Backscheider and Catherine Ingrassia.

To state that a poet born in 1742, whose last important work was published in 1804, was an eighteenth-century writer will seem laughably obvious to readers outside the academy. But any literary specialist will recognize that because 1780, the year of Seward's first publication, marks the inauguration of the Romantic era, she is likely to be grouped with writers such as Smith, Helen Maria Williams, and Mary Wollstonecraft, whose early productions are now considered integral to the development of Romanticism. That Seward was primarily a writer of the late-eighteenth century in fact increases her importance to students of the ensuing period. Seward participated eloquently in the literary, cultural, and political debates of her lifetime. She is a transitional figure—a writer who matured during mid-century but emerged into public view just as many tenets widely held during her youth, such as patriotic pride in Britain's expanding empire, were being tested—and as such her opinions are critical to understanding the spectrum of responses to contemporary issues. Although she was a writer grounded in late-seventeenth and early eighteenth-century principles, she nevertheless incorporated sensibility into her conception of literary greatness and later extolled the late-century "discovery" of an "ancient" British epic, James MacPherson's *Ossian* and of the authentic "medieval" poems of Thomas Rowley, aka Thomas Chatterton, and championed the Scottish dialect poems of Robert Burns as well as the ballads collected by her protégé Walter Scott. She is thus an invaluable guide to the trajectory of British poetry in her century, of developmental continuities sometimes overlooked in our emphasis on the revolutionary. Like her near contemporaries Anna Laetitia Barbauld (1743–1825) and Hannah More (1745–1833), Seward is important because she culminated certain eighteenth-century trends, adapted to new circumstances, and attempted to transmit her values into the next century.

As my familiarity with Seward and her work progressed, a second theme emerged when I began organizing my study around the question of the chief reasons for her disappearance from literary history. Seward had a reputation as a provincial, amateur poet, but what I encountered instead was a strong-willed woman who chose to make her debut in Bath not because she was afraid to subject herself to the London critics but because she wished to control her entrance into the literary marketplace. She first assured herself of a discriminating readership and then began publishing verse and criticism. Likewise, after scrutinizing Seward's modern image as a retired, domestic muse, I discovered a woman proud of her national reputation as the voice, not of retired feminine sentiments, but of robust patriotic prophecy. Instead of finding *Louisa* an endorsement of self-abnegation, I detected a subtext of anger toward the patriarch who nearly destroys the hero's and heroine's lives. Wherever I looked, Seward materialized as a poet determined to establish her critical authority and to wrest some control over her personal circumstances. I hope I have succeeded in re-presenting Seward as an eighteenth-century poet worthy of study and as a personality far more attractive to twenty-first century readers than her former characterizations made her to nineteenth- and twentieth-century readers.

As I concluded this study, Seward was once again becoming the subject of critical appraisal. First, the passionate nature of her poems about her beloved foster sister, Honora Sneyd, has led to speculation about her sexual orientation. Another topic has been Seward's writings about the fine arts. A music lover, Seward also admired painting and landscaping. All these arts are celebrated in her verse, and she also created her own works in embroidery and netting. Most recently, Seward's poems about Coalbrookdale, the site where she deplored early industry's banishment of the muses from a formerly pristine valley, have drawn attention from eco-critics. Seward is emerging as an informed if conservative commentator on the scientific activities of Erasmus Darwin and his circle. While completing my final chapter I had the pleasure of reading two new articles, one by David Wheeler arguing that Seward's invocation of "the genius of the place" in "Colebrook Dale" marks her as an eighteenth-century poet and one by Melissa Bailes explaining Seward's critique of Darwin's theories and her creation of a Linnaean classification of poets that deplores stylistic hybridity in favor of distinct categories. Bailes, like Wheeler, concludes that Seward is not to be mistaken for a Romantic-era poet; her insistence on poetic order in fact helps to explain her resistance to poets like Smith and William Wordsworth.

A crucial new resource for Seward scholars has just been published: the first new biography of Seward since Margaret Ashmun's *The Singing Swan* (1931). Teresa Barnard's *Anna Seward: A Constructed Life* uses previously neglected sources to answer many questions about Seward's life that have become objects of speculation, such as her sexual orientation. Two sets of unedited manuscript letters record Seward's life during the 1770s, a decade made turbulent by her commitment to a chaste but devoted relationship with a vicar choral of Lichfield Cathedral, John Saville. As Barnard describes them, those letters enable a more precise understanding of the context of Seward's published writings. In particular, they force scholars to seek an explanation for the perplexing Honora elegies other than erotic attraction. Barnard's general thesis, that Seward "constructed" herself for posterity through her epistolary journals, private letters, edited correspondence, and will, corrects many aspects of Ashmun's biography and provides scholars with a firmer basis for interpretation.

Many writers would cringe rather than welcome the appearance of a new biography when close to completing a critical study. I am gratified that while I could not take the fullest advantage of Barnard's study, her material supports my conclusions and I have incorporated her facts and insights where they are most helpful. Because I am not a psychologist, for example, I have been circumspect about defining Seward's struggles to control her life, career, and reputation. Barnard confidently—and with ample evidence—describes Seward's writings as an effort to control her life, image, and reputation, whether battling her parents over her commitment to Saville or attempting to construct her will in such a way that her property would descend through female lines and to manage her correspondence so that it would be presented in such as way as to secure her literary eminence. I hope that this book, which is more a formal study of Seward's writings, will complement Barnard's and that together they will renew scholarly appreciation for the writer Barnard describes as "one of the most significant and compelling figures in the history of writing women" (8). Seward's writings provide ample material: I have inevitably left out many poems and much prose that merit attention. I hope that by focusing on writings that establish Seward as an ambitious professional seeking national status, an experimenter who attempts stylistic hybridity in her verse novel, a leading figure in the sonnet revival, and an outspoken literary critic, I will contribute to our growing interest in this significant figure. My chief hope is to inspire further studies of Seward's writings, both those I include and those I regretfully omit.

Six years of concentration on a literary study inevitably accrue large debts of friendship and support. First among my metaphorical creditors is Jennifer Keith of University of North Carolina, Greensboro, a gentle but exacting critic who read several drafts of each chapter as my work progressed. In the larger community of eighteenth-century specialists, I am grateful to Catherine Ingrassia, Peggy Thompson, and Linda Zionkowski for support and to Paula Backscheider for rigorous critiques whenever I presented work-in-progress at American Society for Eighteenth-Century Studies and Southeastern American Society for Eighteenth-Century Studies meetings. Isobel Grundy, likewise, asked crucial questions and made important suggestions, even confirming the correct pronunciation of Seward's name. Zanna Beswick provided insight and support when I visited the UK, especially during a memorable visit to Lichfield. I must also thank Jessica Richard and Andrew Burkett, my colleagues in eighteenth-century and Romantic-era studies, respectively, at Wake Forest University, for astute comments on my drafts. I thank all my colleagues in English, especially Mrs. Connie Green and Mrs. Peggy Barrett, our extraordinary staff who made it possible for me to complete this study while I was chairing a large and busy department. Graduate students Elizabeth Johnson and Bethany Chafin helped at critical times. Dean Lynn Sutton and her staff at the Z. Smith Reynolds Library, too, deserve effusive thanks, especially Mrs. Renate Adler, who patiently renewed *The Singing Swan* and dozens of other books for me each year before her recent retirement; Ellen Daugman, our departmental liaison, and Sharon Snow, our retired rare book librarian, for ordering crucial books such as a first edition of Seward's poems. I was also treated with special courtesy by the librarians at the Davidson College Library in North Carolina and at the Johnson Birthplace Museum in Lichfield, UK. Wake Forest University itself deserves my sincerest thanks, especially Provost Jill Tiefenthaler and Dean

Jacquelyn Fetrow; I began work on this book during an R. J. Reynolds Research Leave in 2004–5. Most recently, the anonymous reader who reviewed my manuscript for the Johns Hopkins University Press gave bracing advice that substantially improved both the structure and argument of this book. Matt McAdam, the humanities editor at the press, has been consistently supportive of this study, and my copy editor, MJ Devaney, has clarified my prose, which sometimes developed "Sewardian" prolixity.

Finally, there are personal debts that can never adequately be repaid. My husband, Peter Kairoff, nurtured me and my project throughout each chapter: more precisely, he shared every inspiration and sustained me through each loss of concentration. My siblings and I have suffered the loss of both our parents while this book was in progress. Together we have emerged from what Seward called "the wither'd, wan, forlorn,/And limping Winter" (*Original Sonnets* 50, ll. 5–6), thanks to mutual support throughout many challenges. I dedicate this book to Peter and to them.

Anna Seward and the End
of the Eighteenth Century

Introduction

Anthologies of both eighteenth-century and Romantic-era British poetry are beginning to include Anna Seward (1742–1809), who is attracting renewed scholarly attention after nearly two hundred years of critical neglect.[1] Her poems have been cited recently as precursors of queer and environmental writing; she has been described as a provincial writer and as a domestic muse.[2] None of these descriptors fits comfortably, however. Seward remains difficult to place: her sexuality is debatable, her environmental awareness is prophetic but limited, her fame is national despite her provincial residence, and her domesticity encompasses not only household management and care of an aging father but also leadership of the most prominent Lichfield salon. Seward's chief claim to renown, her verse, is likewise hard to define. Was she a poet of the eighteenth century or of the early Romantic era? Being unable to decide whether she was one or the other, some editors chose to omit Seward from their anthologies, but the most recent—and I think, correct—opinion is that she was both.

Anna Seward was an eighteenth-century poet whose writings exemplify most trends of her century while anticipating some early Romantic styles and techniques. Her writings illuminate the turn to Romanticism, often by recording how a gifted poet might choose to follow traditional principles or to develop those principles differently than did contemporaries such as Charlotte Smith and Mary Robinson. I intend this book to show how Seward's poems chiefly embody the Augustan poetic values, such as attention to metrical regularity and harmony (still reigning in her childhood along with the taste for satire), the midcentury experimentation with poetic meter, and tastes such as the sentimental, patriotic, and sublime. As Jerome McGann has observed in *Poetics of Sensibility*, Romantic-era poetry grew out of the poetry of sensibility and is therefore more often different in degree than in kind. But Seward's devotion to stylistic refinement combined with her predilection for passionate expression led early nineteenth-century readers to dismiss her style as artificial and overwrought. Her conception of the poet's public function, perfectly understandable to her generation, proved less congenial to her successors. Schooled early to admire Alexander Pope and John Milton, Seward was also influenced by James Thomson, William Collins, Mark Akenside, and numerous valued contemporaries such as William Hayley, William Cowper, and Robert Southey. Like those contemporaries, Seward's verse expressed the norms of the period she lived in, as well, in her case, as the lifelong study of British verse, while intimating the direction of future poetry. But although some of the sonnets she published in 1799 emphasized the private over the public purposes of poetry and experimented with accentual as opposed to metrical prosody, Seward largely maintained her allegiance to the harmony as well as to the sociable emphases of eighteenth-century poetry. As David Wheeler concludes after comparing Seward's invocation of "the genius of the place" in "Colebrook Dale" with Romantic-era poets' use of place, Seward's "place" in literary history "is right on the cusp of the shift from the prevailing Enlightenment ideology to a Romantic one" (38).[3] Because she beautifully exemplifies so many of the century's practices, Seward richly deserves the attention she is only now beginning to be paid, along with Smith, Robinson, Anna Laetitia Barbauld, Helen Maria Williams, Joanna Baillie, and other women poets who influenced national discussions of poetry at the end of the eighteenth century.

Seward entertained a complicated relationship to the period when her career unfolded. I describe that period as "the end of the eighteenth century" rather than referring to it using the less cumbersome "Romantic era" because Seward fits somewhat uneasily amid her peers of that revolutionary period. Writers like Mary Wollstonecraft and Helen Maria Williams boldly contributed to national debates about the French Revolution and ensuing Napoleonic wars during the 1790s, but Seward published little on them. And the little she did publish belied her opposition to official national policies. Beginning her publishing career at thirty-seven, Seward approached late-century political and literary-critical controversies from a perspective quite different from that of the younger writers, such as Robinson, Williams, and Baillie, with whom she is now classed. Raised to emulate Milton and Pope, growing up in the heyday of sensibility, Seward adhered to the poetic principles instilled in her by her father and Erasmus Darwin. Sensibility, likewise, remained her gauge of genius as well as moral excellence. But while the succeeding generation departed from her poetic models and reworked the concept of sensibility almost beyond recognition, Seward has not therefore become irrelevant. On the contrary, she had strong opinions about the early Romantic era that are still worth our attention. Seward's poetry and prose elucidate the eighteenth-century roots of many Romantic-era trends. They also define the British literary tradition that she and her peers inherited and that she defended from perceived challenges. That hers became the "road not taken" does not lessen her importance. Seward remains a major writer, her verse and criticism among the most lucid examples of eighteenth-century ideals applied to the literary and political challenges of the next epoch.

It is tempting to describe Seward as marginal owing to her liminal status at the close of one literary period as another opened. If she is marginal, however, that marginality increases her significance. Rooted in earlier beliefs and practices, she articulated her encounters with those of the revolutionary decades. Her writings are pertinent to ongoing debates among current scholars as they distinguish eighteenth-century cultural, political, and literary beliefs from their Romantic-era counterparts. Although my principal concern in this study is how Seward's eighteenth-century contexts explain many aspects of her literary productions and career, I illustrate her pertinence to Romantic-era studies by rereading a poem that is more "Romantic" than most of her verse. "Lichfield, an Elegy, Written in May 1781" suggests how Seward's eighteenth-century practices can illuminate Romanticist debates over transcendence, historicism, ecocriticism, and feminism in the era's poetry.

Since Seward's poetry brought her to the threshold of the Romantic era, it is instructive to observe how a poem composed within eighteenth-century boundaries might anticipate work by poets who claimed to have escaped those bounds. "Lichfield, an Elegy" (*Poetical Works* 1:89–99) illustrates how Seward worked within the poetic genres of her time but also transcended them to create a metaphor of lingering resonance. Devoid of the floridity and gush that critics have claimed typical of her poetry, the 219-line elegy in heroic couplets contains elements that can be found in the poetry of her immediate successors. Stuart Curran has described "Lichfield, an Elegy" as the climax of a series of poems Seward wrote over the course of a period of time during which her foster sister battled consumption, married and departed from Lichfield, and then died at age thirty ("Dynamics" 228). He observes that the poem "begins deceptively as a . . . loco-descriptive poem" before diverging into elegy ("Dynamics" 228). Indeed, the poem seems at first a confusing mixture of locodescriptive and elegiac. Locodescriptive, topographic, and peripatetic poems were popular throughout the century. William Wordsworth, for example, began his career writing locodescriptive poems ("The Vale of Esthwaite" and "An Evening Walk," for example). Topographic poems included descriptive views from a fixed standpoint, like John Denham's prototypical *Cooper's Hill* (1642), which "read" the surrounding landscape as emblematic of national political significance. Such poems often endowed the landscape with political affinities similar to those of their owners.[4] Another genre, appropriate for urban locales, was the "tour" of a town describing and celebrating important landmarks: Mary Chandler's *Description of Bath* (1733) was an enduring favorite. These poems entertained armchair travelers, but they were also sold to tourists who might carry them along on a literal tour. The urban tours, like the fixed landscape views, usually appealed to local patriotism and pride in historic as well as cultural achievements.[5] Elegiac poetry was popular throughout the century but especially after Thomas Gray's "Elegy Written in a Country Church-Yard" (1751) made it seem the perfect vehicle for expressions of sensibility and morality.[6] "Lichfield, an Elegy" is also reminiscent of the "graveyard poems" that became popular after Thomas Parnell's "Night-Piece on Death" (1722) and, especially, Edward Young's *Night Thoughts* (1742–45). Such poems inspired a fascination with burial places as sites of spiritual meditation that encouraged fearful speculation leading, in most cases, to moral consolation.[7] Seward weaves pieces of these various genres together into a poem that is greater than the sum of its disparate parts.

"Lichfield, an Elegy" commences as a typical descriptive celebration of a place, in this case Seward's native town. She alludes to Lichfield's historic and cultural past and to its distinctive beauty, which is in part a subjective impression grounded in personal memories but also in part objectively embodied in the "blended charms / Of city stateliness, and rural dale" (ll. 13–14). Its cathedral, on her itinerary, is Lichfield's most striking landmark. Seward pauses to admire the rare spectacle of such a building unmarred by encroaching "mansions" or "cells" (ll. 17, 19). Instead, the magnificent structure appears to the viewer "adorn'd, yet simple, though majestic, light; / While . . . / Full on its breast the spiral shadows tall, / Unbroken, and in solemn beauty, fall" (ll. 23–24, 26–27). Seward elaborates on the cathedral as a unique treasure, spared by the city's growth and allowed to appear in serene glory while most such churches have long been crowded from distinct view, their meditative solemnity erased by the sounds of traffic and trade (ll. 28–41). She next shifts her gaze to other churches and to the cottages and villas nestled amid the spring landscape of hills and lake. But mention of the season seems to deflect her attention from the tour at hand to memories of youthful seasons yet more beautiful. Sadly, the lives of both her sister and of Sneyd, the subject of this elegy, ended in their youth, destroying the season's illusion of renewed life (ll. 76–95). Seward confesses that other landscapes might be lovelier, but she will always prefer Lichfield's environs owing to her memories of those beloved but lost companions (ll. 76–79). Her evocation of Honora culminates in a passionate, even angry, challenge to her deceased foster sister: "Why paused you not in Lichfield's bloomy shade?" (l. 111). It is as if her initial celebration of Lichfield has only embittered her, because the town's loveliness was insufficient to sustain Honora's life.

Seward next recalls a visit to Honora's grave in nearby Weston. Having escorted readers on a virtual tour of Lichfield, she now places them beside her while she journeys uphill with "wearied steeds" past the church porch where Honora lies in an unmarked grave (ll. 114–39). The sight of the church precipitates an agonized response, illustrating Seward's eighteenth-century sensibility. The horses slowly pass the church; "swift-rushing tears" glaze Seward's "straining eye-balls" (l. 138) as she struggles to keep the building in view, lamenting the waste of Honora's youthful beauty and excellence (ll. 140–77). The spring day seems to mock her sorrow: she struggles to repress tears while the carriage returns to her native valley (ll. 178–81). An instructive comparison is, once again, found in a poem by Wordsworth; this time, the "There Was a Boy" passage incorporated into both *Lyrical Ballads* (1799) and *The Prelude*. Wordsworth's narrative recalls a playful child now buried in the graveyard of a hillside church described as a "thronèd lady."[8] The boy's grave inspires a "long half-hour" meditation, presumably—as Paul de Man concludes—about the correspondence between adult consciousness, which the boy had barely reached, and awareness of death (53–54). Seward's emphasis on her automatic response to the visual stimulus of the church denotes her tears as the response of sensibility, a spontaneous overflow preempting any effort to achieve philosophical calm. Back in Lichfield, Honora's image still dominates Seward's thoughts, leading her to reproach herself when social pleasures intermittently diminish her grief (ll. 186–89). She concludes the elegy with the recognition that Lichfield itself will always provide her chief consolation as the locale of her most treasured memories. She brings her poem to closure by commanding the cathedral and its environs to preserve all the images of Honora that linger throughout the seasons: "Ye choral turrets, and ye arching shades! / Waft her remember'd voice in every gale! / Wear her ethereal smile, thou lovely vale" (ll. 197–99). Even if tempted to depart Lichfield for more pleasurable or professionally rewarding environs, Seward will remain in this beautiful, even enchanted, town that glows for her because of the "luster . . . / reflected from the fairer past" (ll. 218–19). What began as a picturesque tour of a literal city concludes with the evocation of a place so haunted by Honora's spirit, so imbued with the vestiges of her youthful brilliance, that it commands the poet's devoted residence.

"Lichfield, an Elegy" is explicable in terms of several seventeenth- and eighteenth-century poetic trends, but in fusing them Seward stretches beyond their boundaries. First, Seward blends a descriptive tour and a graveyard meditation, with each aspect of the poem illuminating the other. Early in the elegy, she questions whether Lichfield is uniquely beautiful or whether "remember'd days . . ./ To my thrill'd spirit emulously bring/Illusions brighter than the shining spring?" (ll. 7, 9–10). At the poem's conclusion, she pleads with her memories, inseparable from the city: "Ye shades of Lichfield, will ye always bring/Illusions brighter than the shining spring?" (ll. 189–90). Lichfield is indeed beautiful, but the vivid memories infused into its visible charms transform the cathedral city into a kind of shrine or temple to the lost Honora and Seward into its priestess. Seward acknowledges the literal landscape but charges it with a significance she can describe for her reader as an integral part of the city's allure, an allure that, however, no reader can fully share because the past binding Seward to Lichfield must always remain invisible, personal, "illusions brighter than the shining spring." Seward's reproach to Honora for deserting "Lichfield's bloomy shade" is partly explicable by her concluding acknowledgment that although she might dream of moving to a more amenable city, she cannot bring herself to desert this town inhabited by "the spirit of departed joy" (l. 214). Although Honora is not buried in Lichfield but in a village church she describes as "rustic" and rude (ll. 120, 141), the sunlit cathedral town is haunted by her youthful image and thus binds the poet to its environs. The environment is saturated with, and even for Seward transformed by, powerful memories of Honora. The poet in turn is transformed by this landscape as if by enchantment: she will not pursue joy or professional satisfaction elsewhere lest she break the spell binding her to the past. Curran deems this the triumph of the dead over the living (229). He confirms Seward's success in conveying her despair as well as her apparent determination to preserve the raw sensations of bereavement. Like Thomas Gray in his "Elegy" and "Sonnet on the Death of Mr. Richard West" (1775), Seward places herself in an environment that recalls the dead. In Gray's poems, however, the dead are inaccessible. Seward in contrast implies that she cooperates with the landscape in producing intimations of Honora's continuing if illusory presence. Wordsworth later defined his environment as "both what [his senses] half create/And what [they] perceive"(*Lyrical Ballads*, 119). In "Lichfield, an Elegy," Seward anticipates his theory that the poet "half creates" her surroundings based on imaginative engagement with what she perceives. To glance toward an even later poet, Earl Wasserman has suggested that in "Mont Blanc," Percy Bysshe Shelley eliminates "the distinction between thought and thing," thus justifying "faith in the imagination's visions" (237). Seward by no means proposes such a relationship between the mind and the physical world, but Shelley's philosophy is thus seen to evolve not only from classical precedents but also from poets of sensibility like herself.

A second way that "Lichfield, an Elegy" anticipates poetry to come is in Seward's use of metaphor. At her poem's outset, Seward devotes thirteen lines to praise of the cathedral's unchanged loveliness. Centuries of civic development have miraculously left the cathedral untouched: "One free and perfect whole it meets the sight" (l. 22). The din of vehicles, market vendors, laborers, and other urban noises somehow fail to intrude on the cathedral's services. The only sounds heard in the close are the devotional tones of choir and organ. The poem's conclusion exhorts Lichfield itself to preserve each "consecrated trace" of Honora (l. 193), just as it has saved the cathedral from encroachment. The same breezes that carry the organ's notes will "waft her remember'd voice" (l. 197). The cathedral, meeting the sight as "free and perfect" as when it was constructed, is a metaphor for Honora, whose image the poet desperately wishes to preserve in memory as "free and perfect" as in life. Since Lichfield has been uniquely able to maintain the past in its loveliness, as embodied in its cathedral, Seward commands the city to likewise guard all traces of the young woman whose charm, like the striking cathedral as a public monument, "gives [Lichfield its] exclusive grace" (l. 194). Seward's invocation of the cathedral, a site to be cherished lest the town lose its character, parallels and supports her plea that all sites associated with Honora should be retained lest not only the town but the poet's life lose its value. The cathedral laden with personal significance is different more in degree than in kind from the landscape that inspires Wordsworth in "Tintern Abbey" (1800) (although, of course, the abbey itself never appears in that poem) or the ruined bower that chastens him in "Nutting" (1798–99). It is also reminiscent of imagery in some slightly later poems, such as Ann Yearsley's "Clifton Hill" (1785), William Cowper's The Task (1785), and Charlotte Smith's sonnets (1784), which infuse particular places with metaphoric significance. Seward here explores the power of recollection to transform an object or a place and for the transformed object or place to assume metaphoric power. Wordsworth would develop from such instances his belief in crucial "spots of time"; as Geoffrey Hartman explains the phenomena, they "(1) prophesy the independence from nature of his imaginative powers, *and* (2) impress nature ineradicably on them" (218). Seward similarly acknowledges her imaginative power to transform Lichfield into Honora's shrine, while the city in turn gives her life meaning. She did not always use metaphor in this way, but sensitivity to her environment made her capable of fusing emotion and landscape in this poem as well as in "Colebrook Dale," *Louisa*, and sonnets such as "To the Poppy." When critics have mocked her "sensibility," they have ignored the extent to which sensibility led her to anticipate later poetic developments.

"Lichfield, an Elegy" suggests that Honora Sneyd became Seward's muse: the *genius loci* of a particular place, the guiding spirit of verse rooted in particular memories. Although Seward often used a traditional poetic idiom that conferred enchantment on British locales by invoking personified seasons and classical deities, in this poem she eschewed such devices. She is not proposing Lichfield as the successor to ancient inspired sites, as Pope did with his native region in "Windsor-Forest" (1713). She was not chiefly directing her poem to readers who required a place to be filtered through the classics before it could properly be considered inspirational. In this aspect of the poem, too, she anticipates Wordsworth: his "Lucy" poems announce the speaker's dedication to rural England because its fields and springs witnessed the brief life of his beloved. Late twentieth-century critics countered earlier discussions of the Romantic-era poets' quest for transcendence with historicized readings emphasizing writers' awareness of political events even when they are not mentioned in their poems.[9] Another recent critical trend, ecocriticism, challenges new historicism at the same time that it reinstates the poets' emphasis on nature. As Karl Kroeber explains, "In their finest poetry it is the natural world to which they turn in trying to understand and correct their capacity to deceive themselves and distort their profoundest idealisms" (12). Wordsworth's Lucy may have been fictional, but he conveys a sense of unbearable personal loss by comparing Lucy to such natural phenomena as a half-hidden violet and a solitary star in the night sky, rarely noticed but doubly precious for their obscurity. Seward resembles her Romantic-era peers here in her insistence on naming Lichfield as the unique site of her attachment.[10] Seward is not primarily interested, however, in presenting Honora as a treasure destined in any case to have lived and died unknown. In fact, the only historic references in her poem compare Honora to Lucretia, Cornelia, and Anne L'Enclos, all aristocrats renowned for their beauty and the latter two for their learning. She does not therefore memorialize her beloved foster sister through the image of a violet or a personal token such as her spinning wheel but through the city's grandest and most striking monument. The cathedral metaphor expresses not only Honora's potential achievements or her civic status but also her colossal importance in the poet's life. For Seward's life to retain meaning, she must keep Honora's image as vivid as possible, at all costs. Those costs include residence in Lichfield, not as the home of classical muses but as the seat of her personal memories.

Wordsworth's "Lucy" cycle and Seward's elegy are both daring, his for insisting on the significance of such a humble, solitary life and hers for practically demanding that a city freeze in time rather than lose any trace of a promising but deceased young woman. Both poets identify their muses with specific locales owing little or nothing to classical associations and almost everything to memories of personal attachment. On the other hand, Seward's choice of a locodescriptive frame and of a large, public building to represent her loss and her dramatization of sensibility all link her elegy to earlier eighteenth-century models. Lichfield Cathedral probably held an even more potent significance for Seward because Honora had loved its spires, according to John André in one of his letters that Seward published with her *Monody* on his death (1781): "I remember she called them the *Ladies of the Valley*. . . . Oh! how I loved them from that instant. . . . [E]very object that has a pyramidal form, recalls them to my recollection, with a sensation, that brings the tear of pleasure to my eyes" (30). "Lichfield, an Elegy" thus enshrines two lost presences by reenacting André's original gesture of association. By perpetuating André's involuntary identification of Honora with the cathedral, Seward doubly haunted her poem. André's sentimental tears forever mingle with her own, their response to the "Ladies of the Valley" in suggestive contrast to Wordsworth's contemplative posture beneath the "thronèd lady" of Winander.

"Lichfield, an Elegy" additionally benefits from, and enriches, the insights of feminist Romanticists. Anne K. Mellor has argued forcefully for the expansion of Romantic-era studies to include the period's women writers. She observes that, contrary to misguided assumptions, women participated fully in the era's public sphere, their emphases on "moral virtue and an ethic of care" dominating its agenda (*Mothers* 11).[11] While male poets thought in terms of polarities, imaged often as the male and female, to be encompassed by the mind of the poet (often entailing the destruction of his feminine "other"), women poets sought to create communities. While male poets asserted "an autonomous self" (*Mothers* 86), women cherished relationships. "Lichfield, an Elegy" is thus typically feminine in its yearning for the profound bonds Seward shared with her sister and with Honora. Seward's recollection of Honora, however, also complicates such generalizations as Mellor's. Her apostrophes to Honora recall Wordsworth's turn to Dorothy at the conclusion of "Tintern Abbey," where he addresses his sister partly as the recollection of his younger self (her "wild eyes" reflect "gleams/Of past existence"). Seward likewise regards Honora, at some level, as the ghost of her own youth and her memory as "beams reflected from the fairer past" (l. 218). But the imagery Seward associates with Honora, Lichfield cathedral, grants her foster sister an identity distinct from the poet's. As Hartman remarks, Wordsworth intends his poem's conclusion as "an inscription for Dorothy's heart, an intimation of how this moment can survive the speaker's death" (28). Seward has apparently inscribed her memories of Honora on the town of Lichfield and its environs, bringing to mind Jonathan Bate's ecocritical praise for poems that metaphorically engrave the names of loved ones on places, which recognizes that we can be "lord of that which we do not possess" (9). The conclusion of Seward's poem acknowledges the sacrifice entailed by Seward's devotion to the city's past, including her fear that if she leaves, Honora's spirit will disappear. She is finally less confident than Wordsworth about the poet's ability to preserve the past within her mind. Seward's humility when she confesses the fragility of memories dependent on continual residence in Honora's birthplace, which Honora herself left after her marriage and to which she returned only to die, recalls Mellor's observation of women's perplexity over men's preoccupation with transcendence (*Mothers* 86). Her "inscription" is consciously precarious, engraving a "tour" of a city that was certainly changing even during Seward's lifetime.

Many of Seward's poems epitomize eighteenth-century poetry while stretching the boundaries of available poetic kinds, techniques, and values, as the best writing always does. One example of an eighteenth-century value espoused yet modified by Seward in poems like "Lichfield, an Elegy" is the cultivation of sensibility, which flourished during Seward's early maturity. In *Poetics of Sensibility*, Jerome McGann remarks that New Criticism's abhorrence of sentimentalism ensured that "entire orders of poetical writing went virtually unread," consequently impoverishing "our knowledge and understanding of poetry" (8–9). McGann regards sensibility as the very foundation of Romanticism; he deems Wordsworth's preface to the *Lyrical Ballads* as "a sentimental manifesto in the strictest sense" (121). In his view, we continue ignoring or devaluing the poetry of sensibility at our critical peril. Because the theory of sensibility, or what he calls sentimentalism, informed Romantic theory, McGann argues, we have lost the key to understanding Romantic verse along with the ability to appreciate the poetry from which it evolved. This critical amnesia was especially devastating for late eighteenth- and early nineteenth-century women poets, whose sentimental verse was dismissed when noticed but otherwise ignored. McGann includes chapters on Frances Greville, Ann Yearsley, Mary Robinson, L. E. L., and Felicia Hemans in *Poetics of*

Sensibility to restore both their contexts and credibility. Since McGann's study, monographs by Janet Todd, Markman Ellis, Thomas McCarthy, and others have extended our recognition of the central role played by sensibility throughout British culture as the eighteenth century evolved into the Romantic era.[12] I intend this book as a comparable effort to recognize Anna Seward in her cultural context, but at the same time I make larger claims for her value as one of the—in a literal sense—ultimate eighteenth-century poets: writers in whose work we might trace the century's evolving trends in such a way that poetry's direction becomes apparent.

If Romanticism, as McGann understands it, grew from the theory that sense perceptions, carried through the nerves to the brain, produced emotional responses in sensitive individuals (ultimately inspiring poetry when, as Wordsworth stated, those emotions were recreated or "recollected in tranquility" [*Lyrical Ballads* 756]), we have already observed how "Lichfield, an Elegy" anticipates the Wordsworthian refinement that a person's mind does not simply respond emotionally to an environment but "half creates" the emotion-laden environment itself. Why then is Seward not a more prominent member of the group we call Romantic-era poets? We have recognized that the term "Romantic" applies not just to Wordsworth and a small number of male poets in his and the succeeding generation. The Romantic era encompassed many writers, artists, and thinkers of both genders working mainly in the last decade of the eighteenth century and in the first three decades of the next. Seward, who first published in 1780 and whose influential sonnets appeared in 1799, was familiar with the writings of contemporaries such as Charlotte Smith, Robert Southey, Walter Scott, and Joanna Baillie, all of whom are considered Romantic-era poets. In *British Romanticism and the Science of the Mind*, Alan Richardson includes Seward among the women poets who "despite their unequal education, were by no means insulated from the scientific culture of the era" (37). Yet Seward figures only briefly in his and many recent studies of the Romantic period.[13] In his introduction to the Oxford guide to Romanticism, Nicholas Roe lists some concerns of the time as "imagination, egotism, the particular, the remote, Greek antiquity, the primitive, the medieval, the East, irrational experiences (including dreams and drugs), an awareness of process . . . and a longing for the infinite, encountered through intense experiences of sublime nature" (5). When Seward's poetry speaks to these interests, it does so in ways reflective of Romanticism's roots rather than of its later expressions—or rather it does so in ways reflective of the full-blown expression of earlier eighteenth-century poetic values. If, for example, sensibility became problematic after the Reign of Terror commenced in 1793, as Adela Pinch observes, Seward's verse continued to manifest her passionate responses to experience ("Sensibility" 84). If many Romantic-era poets experimented with accentual meter to express emotions or achieve dramatic effects, as Susan Stewart observes, Seward was less likely to stray from syllabic regularity, rhymed or unrhymed (67–69). And whereas, as Simon Jarvis has discussed, Shelley defended artful prosody against Byron's dismissal of such "mechanical contrivances," Seward placed central importance on the poet's craft (99–101). In each case, Seward is not different in kind but varies greatly in degree from her Romantic-era counterparts. Seward is overdue for a study that explains how and why she wrote and how she conducted her career. Hers was an important voice at the outset of one of the most influential eras in literary history. While her choices differed from those of many contemporaries, they were compelling in context and deserve recognition as part of the late-century critical debate.

Seward's relation to, and sometimes rejection of, the governing trends of her era shape this study's chapters. I have selected topics pursued before but to conclusions that diminished Seward. I propose that fresh readings, in a richer context, can reestablish Seward's importance. My first chapter reconstructs the biographical and critical traditions that have made revisionist work like Teresa Barnard's crucial to understanding Seward's writings. My second and third chapters address Seward's amateur status, rethinking what it might have meant for a mature late eighteenth-century woman to commence a career as publishing poet. I construe her debut in the late 1770s at Batheaston rather than in the pages of a London journal not as an effort to avoid London critics but as a calculated move to build an audience first in manuscript publication before embarking on print publication. A theme that emerges in these chapters is Seward's persistence, throughout her maturity, in asserting control over her life and writings despite the constrictions of her gender in pursuit of what we recognize as a professional literary career. My fourth chapter reviews the "provincial" epithet, so often applied to Seward, in the context of recent studies of British identity and British patriotism throughout the century. Here and in my fifth chapter I observe both Seward's confidence in assuming the role of "British muse" from her provincial locale in the 1780s and her agony when, throughout the 1790s, hatred of the wars against France stifled her patriotic expression. My readings identify Seward not as a retiring domestic muse but as a visionary poet, self-defined in epic or prophetic terms, rallying her compatriots. Again, Seward's persona counters recent generalizations about women's concentration on domestic rather than on "public" issues, extending our conception of the possibilities open to late-century women poets.

I turn next to another of Seward's bids for cultural prominence, her interventions in the increasingly popular novel and, especially, in the sentimental character of contemporary fictional heroines. My sixth and seventh chapters, on Seward's verse novel *Louisa* (1784), examine Seward's diction of sentiment, observing both its exemplary and its experimental dimensions, particularly in her characterization of the hero's well-intentioned but misguided father. I detect a muted but palpable indictment of the aged father in this poem, which may express Seward's resentment of her own father, who thwarted her adolescent pursuit of poetry and, later, her tentative love affairs. Seward's portrait of a sensible but principled heroine is also distinct from the self-abnegating characters typical of the era's sentimental fiction. Here Seward's characterizations support Mellor's claim that late-century women "used their writings not only to advocate . . . more egalitarian marriages for women but also to condemn the abuses of patriarchy and the bad construction of masculinity" (*Mothers* 91).

My eighth through tenth chapters focus on Seward's sonnets (1799), addressing her campaign to assert the "Miltonic" pattern against that of Charlotte Smith, her rival, and her mysteriously passionate laments for Honora Sneyd. My eighth chapter proposes that Seward's vendetta against Charlotte Smith was not purely mean spirited, as many critics believe, but was rather an assertion of poetic and critical authority based on a view of the sonnet she claimed to derive from learned mentors. Since the sonnet was a crucial battleground for late-century poets, Seward's context, motives, and principles must be understood before her sonnets' excellence can be fully appreciated. My ninth chapter explores how Seward's personal correspondence provided the "occasions" for many of her sonnets. My tenth chapter argues that Seward's Honora sonnets, although occasional, can be read coherently as her record of losing a quasi-maternal bond rather than of an erotic obsession, which is what many have detected in these poems. If I am correct, Seward's grief, after her fruitless interference when Honora's illness became fatal, was exacerbated by resentment at having lost control of the young woman she had nurtured and educated. Set in their biographical and aesthetic contexts, the "Honora" poems, with their striking language of sentiment, can be read quite differently than they have been by Backscheider, Curran, and others.

My final chapters reexamine Seward's critical writings, especially her published analyses of Erasmus Darwin's verse and of James Boswell's biographical studies of Samuel Johnson. These chapters complete my thematic study of Seward's efforts to assert control over her career and of her resentment of those, usually men, who denied her even limited authority. Thinking about Seward's criticism from this perspective helps explain her quixotic (and often condemned) effort to undermine Boswell's version of Johnson. Seward's criticism not only demonstrates her poetic principles but also confirms her position as exemplar of eighteenth-century verse. The poetic "daughter" of Erasmus Darwin and Samuel Johnson, and therefore the resentful "sister" of Boswell, Seward was the product of her times in several metaphorical senses. As "child" of such influential figures, Seward absorbed the century's chief literary values as well as her generation's preferences. Her poetic style therefore fuses Milton's practices with those of her Augustan precursors and more contemporaneous sentimental models. As such, Seward's verse epitomizes eighteenth-century poetry; her canon exemplifies both Popeian wit and Akenside-like sensibility, often within single poems. I hope that restoring the contexts in which she wrote will return her poems to view and even to admiration, not like the dusty contents of a neglected *wunderkammer* but as distinguished examples of a rich poetic tradition. The following chapters address selected aspects of her writing in contexts that establish her prominence. The circumstances of her previous disregard are suspicious, commencing with her first biographer's reluctance, shared by his successors, to situate Seward properly within the period in which she wrote.

CHAPTER ONE

Under Suspicious Circumstances

The (Critical) Disappearance of Anna Seward

When she died in 1809, Anna Seward was arguably "the most prominent and formidable woman writer" in Britain (Lonsdale 313). She had produced poetry that, when collected into three volumes, spanned genres from the ode to the sonnet to a novel in verse. Her critical opinions were frequently published in the *Gentleman's Magazine*. She had been the first biographer of Dr. Erasmus Darwin (grandfather of Charles, the famous naturalist), her former neighbor and mentor. She had championed writers such as Thomas Chatterton and Robert Burns and received homage from protégés such as Helen Maria Williams, Robert Southey, Samuel T. Coleridge, and Walter Scott, among the many who paid their respects to her in Lichfield. In the *Gentleman's Magazine*, a biographical notice by Sylvanus Urban published the month after her death concludes that "as an Authoress, few women have exhibited more strength of intellect, or more genuine delicacy of taste, than Miss Seward. Her poetry is particularly distinguished by beauty of imagery, and vigour of sentiment" (379). Yet by the late twentieth century, even renowned feminist critic Germaine Greer challenged readers "to struggle through the great drift of indifferent verse [Seward] . . . wrote" (58). Although Seward's acid tongue and pen had offended some—when, for example, she refused to acquiesce in the national reverence for Samuel Johnson's character following his death in 1784—Greer pronounced Seward desperately shy and "deadly afraid of . . . the brutality and hardness of men" (58–59). How did Anna Seward decline from a poet of national stature, a critical force to be reckoned with, to a timorous poetaster sheltering herself in Lichfield from the rigors of literary competition?

To a large extent, the very qualities that made Seward enchanting to contemporaries rendered her invisible to later readers. Growing up during the heyday of sensibility, she nevertheless formed her poetics by carrying out stringent analyses of earlier models. The *Gentleman's Magazine* accurately described the resulting verse as exhibiting both "strength of intellect" and "vigour of sentiment" (Urban 379) but that combination has made Seward's writings fit uneasily into collections of either eighteenth-century or Romantic-era poems. While her first readers appreciated Seward's ability to combine the rhetorical emphasis of poets like Pope with emotional responsiveness, later readers have found her impossible to categorize. Her poetics seemed old fashioned soon after her death, but not old fashioned enough for many current editors to include her in eighteenth-century anthologies. Unfortunately, she has also been excluded from many anthologies of Romantic poetry, partly because of her adamant dislike of certain poems, such as Charlotte Smith's sonnets, that are today considered exemplars of an emerging Romantic style. Because Seward's poetry does not quite fit the stylistic paradigms of Augustan or Romantic verse, or even of the verse that has until recently been called "pre-Romantic," she has simply been excluded from most critical discussions except as a name in lists of late-century women poets.[1]

My goal in this study is to extricate Seward from those lists and place her again among important late-century poets. Making her case requires if not rewriting, then refining many recent studies of eighteenth-century and Romantic-era culture and literary history. Seward's neglect indicates some rigidity in our accounts of literary professionalism, provincialism, the public sphere, patriotism, and sensibility, to name but a few topics that have merited extensive study in the past two decades. Luckily, some recent monographs position us to understand Seward in her context, expanding our ideas about her culture. Anne K. Mellor's *Mothers of the Nation*, for example, has turned upside-down the concept of a male-dominated Romanticism. Her argument recovers the context in which Seward gained national prominence. Sonia Hofkosh's *Sexual Politics and the Romantic Author* undertakes "to discern other voices and other visions" besides Wordsworth's as exemplary of Romanticism (8). She suggests that Jane Austen's heroines, and by extension all women, "occupying the ambivalent thresholds between personal pleasure and public spectacle," "embody the deep self of the romantic author" (139). Hofkosh's analysis gives us the means to acknowledge both Seward's affinities with her Romantic peers and her differing conceptions of the poetic persona and the literary career. Another intriguing recent book, Susan J. Wolfson's *Borderlines: The Shiftings of Gender in British Romanticism*, counters older theories about the era's polarized gender roles by observing instances of relative fluidity in

Romantic-era writing about masculinity and femininity. Wolfson's refreshing study helps to retrieve the context in which the decorous Seward could, for example, masquerade as "Benvolio" to conduct a published critical debate without raising much comment on her disguise. On the other hand, Seward's decision to adopt a masculine pen name reflects anxieties about the gendered nature of criticism typical of the earlier eighteenth century. I propose that what we have learned about such topics can elucidate Seward and in turn be enriched by consideration of Seward and her poetry. The following chapters take up the issues of Seward's professionalism, her status as national poet, her contribution to the literature of sensibility, her participation in the sonnet revival, her obsession with Honora Sneyd, and her critical practices. All these topics have been studied before, some by distinguished scholars, but by applying recent scholarship about Seward's contexts and paying careful attention to her poetic principles, we can come to a more accurate understanding of her. Some recent studies, for example, render her inexplicable by failing to account for how a Lichfield gentlewoman might have appeared, unironically, a "British muse" despite living an almost entirely provincial existence and having mostly provincial connections. In some instances, such as her quest for national recognition, Seward pushed beyond the boundaries designated for her location, status, and gender. In most cases, Seward could be termed the missing link between Augustan and Romantic writing, combining a sophisticated knowledge of prosody with her ability to dramatize sensibility. Her preference for musical verse and rhetorical effects was derived from Pope; her passionate responses were typical of a generation enthralled (and sometimes appalled) by Rousseau. Restoring Seward will enrich our canon and adjust cultural and literary-historical accounts.

As reflected in the works by Mellor, Hofkosh, Wolfson, and others I have mentioned, the past thirty years have witnessed a remarkable willingness to reevaluate the writings of many women whose poems, plays, and novels disappeared from view while works by their male peers were reprinted. The studies of Aphra Behn that have led to her canonization are only the most spectacular of numerous studies that have taught us to appreciate, for example, Katherine Philips's poems and Charlotte Smith's sonnets.[2] Mary Leapor, the Brackley cook maid, and Ann Yearsley, the Clifton milk woman, have received fine critical biographies, as has even a poet whom Seward herself considered minor, Mary Whateley Darwall.[3] Yet some recent anthologies fail to include any poem by Seward, who was arguably a better poet and certainly a more prominent figure in her lifetime than Leapor, Yearsley, or Darwall.[4] When Seward's poetry is discussed at all, it is often in the context of queer or lesbian writing owing to the passionate elegies she wrote after the death of

Honora Sneyd. This perspective informs important studies by Paula Backscheider and Stuart Curran. While such discussions suggest the relevance of Seward's verse to twentieth-century readers, they do so while overlooking some important contemporary contexts of her work. Another influential view of Seward's writing is John Brewer's. In *The Pleasures of the Imagination* (1997), his important survey of eighteenth-century English culture, Brewer ponders not why Seward disappeared from view but how such an "amateur versifier" achieved prominence in the first place (573–612). He concludes that Seward represented a concept of poetry as the avocation of genteel provincial poets, often women, and that this view became discredited soon after her lifetime. Yet Brewer's explanation is in some ways self-contradictory, since his book argues that by the end of the century London no longer monopolized British culture and that all kinds of provincial contributions were gaining, not losing, influence. More recently, Jenny Uglow, in *Lunar Men*, has demonstrated the national significance of thinkers, writers, and manufacturers centered around Lichfield, headed by Seward's early mentor Erasmus Darwin. While Seward was not a member of the Lunar Society, the perspective she shared with the group would have led her to consider the Birmingham region not as a backwater but as the locus of several important cultural movements.

More than any other woman writer except, perhaps, Aphra Behn, Seward was systematically undermined until recently. If Seward's critical disappearance were a whodunit, her earliest posthumous commentators would be the culprits. How did Germaine Greer, for example, form the impression that Seward had composed a "great drift of indifferent verse"? Greer consulted Walter Scott's three-volume edition of Seward's poetry with his biographical preface (443n58). Scott had been among the many promising young writers Seward championed during her career. She had a taste for Scottish verse that was sufficiently refined (such as Burns's) and for "authentic" antique works (such as Ossian's and Chatterton's), which meant she was destined to appreciate Scott's poetry in volumes such as *The Lay of the Last Minstrel* (1805). At the time of Seward's death, Scott was a popular poet but not yet the great novelist who later commanded public adulation. In fact, he had embarked on a publishing career and had taken on many editorial projects.[5] Seward evidently entrusted her collected poems to his editorial supervision with the confidence of a mentor confirming her approval of a most promising protégé. Scott was at that time editing the works of Dryden and Swift, so her request that he act as her literary executor must have seemed, at least to Seward herself, quite logical. Her selection indicated self-assurance regarding her status among living poets and her ensuing legacy. Given the contemporary appreciation of her verse, and the established nature and duration of her career compared with Scott's, Seward's choice of posthumous editor was not egregious but appropriate.

Scott consented and, faithful to his trust, swiftly published Seward's collected works with a biographical preface. But for various reasons, Seward had not foreseen the degree to which the bequest disobliged her executor. Perhaps one reason it did is that editing her poems was a burdensome addition to the workload of a young publisher who had already taken on more projects than he could comfortably handle. Seward imagined a reading public for her collected poems and letters that would benefit her executor and his firm, while Scott correctly foresaw the unprofitable nature of his task. By 1809, Scott might also have been embarrassed by his connection with Seward. Her career resembled those of many respected eighteenth-century poets, gentlemen and ladies who devoted themselves to belles lettres but who had no practical need to earn a living by their pens. Scott epitomized the competing modern attitude characterized by Samuel Johnson's pronouncement that "no man but a blockhead ever wrote, except for money" (Boswell 3:19). While Scott personally esteemed Seward, distinctions between their tastes and practices doubtless outweighed their mutual appreciation of border minstrelsy. He hastened to conclude his task and to distance himself from connection with her verse. In an 1810 letter to Joanna Baillie, he confided his opinion of Seward's poetry, observing that most of it "is absolutely execrable" (2:315). He characterized Seward's letters as gossipy and sentimental.

In the early twentieth century, Margaret Ball noted Scott's apparent hypocrisy with regard to Seward. Although he "was not double-faced," he "wrote such an introduction" to her writings "as hardly prepares the reader for the remark he made to Miss Baillie" (84–85). Ball qualified her observation by describing the critical remarks in his edition's biographical memoir as "sedulously kind" but "carefully guarded, and throughout . . . the editor implies that the woman was more admirable than the poetry" (85). Ball's assessment understates Scott's insidious tone. He implies a pejorative view even in his description of Seward's infant precocity. In his preface, he recalls Seward's claim that she could recite passages from Milton's "Allegro" when she was only three years old:

> It were absurd to suppose that she could comprehend this poem . . . but our future taste does not always depend upon the progress of our understanding. The mechanism, the harmony of verse, the emotions which, though vague and indescribable, it awakes in children of a lively imagination and a delicate ear, contribute, in many instances, to imbue the infant mind with a love of poetry, even before they can tell for what they love it. (Seward, *Poetical Works* 1:v)

Seward obviously intended her remark to intimate a native aptitude for verse, if not to predict her future genius. Scott implies that infatuation with mechanical rhythms and harmonious sounds, which naturally comprised her toddler experience of verse, probably continued to dominate the mature Seward's expectations of poetry. The appeal of "vague and indescribable" emotions to lively and sensitive children is perhaps not a general observation so much as a suggestion that Seward, who often described herself as an enthusiast, developed into a poet whose verse, according to her detractors, likewise fails to convey specific or genuine feeling.

Scott confirms these implications later in his preface, in a discussion of Seward's poetic style and tastes:

> Miss Seward was in practice trained and attached to that school of picturesque and florid description, of lofty metaphor and bold personification, of a diction which inversion and the use of compound epithets rendered as remote as possible from the tone of ordinary language, which was introduced, or at least rendered fashionable, by Darwin. . . . Yet her taste . . . readily admitted the claims of Pope, Collins, Gray, Mason, and of all those bards who have condescended to add the graces of style and expression to poetical thought and imagery. But she particularly demanded beauty, elegance, or splendour of language; and was unwilling to allow that sublimity or truth of conception could atone for poverty, rudeness, or even simplicity, of expression. To Spenser, and the poets of his school, she lent an unwilling ear; and what will, perhaps, best explain my meaning, she greatly preferred the flowing numbers and expanded descriptions of Pope's Iliad to Cowper's translation, which approaches nearer to the simple dignity of Homer. (1:xxv–xxvi)

Scott proposes Erasmus Darwin as the Satan to Seward's poetic Eve: since Darwin mentored the adolescent poet, he must have corrupted her style. While Darwin no doubt influenced Seward, especially by motivating her to refine the already-refined style of Pope, there is no reason to believe he was completely responsible for Seward's style. Seward studied all the English poets admired during her lifetime. Thomson, Akenside, Young, MacPherson, and others contributed to her stylistic ideals. Like her models, Seward believed that serious poetry merited a distinctive, usually an elevated, language. By the time Scott edited her posthumous works, however, Seward's models had become passé. As a late eighteenth-century poet who died when a succeeding and often hostile era was defining itself, Seward unwittingly chose a detractor rather than a champion for her first biographer.

Scott's remark about Seward's dislike of Spenser—a dislike she explained frankly in her letters—reveals their respective generational estimates as much as it damns her taste. Spenser had entered the British canon while Seward was a girl. In *Making the English Canon*, Jonathan Brody Kramnick argues that Spenser's vogue was the product of scholars eager to establish a professional role for themselves as explicators of Britain's esoteric, "ancient" culture (137–89). Independently confirming Kramnick's analysis, Seward indeed seems to have considered Spenser to be a deliberately inaccessible writer in comparison with her beloved Shakespeare (although, as we will see, she defended the poetic principles of Milton, another difficult poet canonized at this time). Yet Spenser had been securely established as a precursor of the literary gothicism enjoying its reign when Scott began his career. Seward's continuing preference for the intricacies of Pope, now deemed too refined, rather than the "simple dignity" of Spenser and of Cowper's Homer, marked her as an old-fashioned writer and critic. Scott, meanwhile, championed the discovery and publication of vernacular Scottish ballads, another consequence of the taste for the ancient and "primitive." Seward was reluctant to allow that such verse, with its "poverty, rudeness, or even simplicity, of expression," could attain sublimity or manifest a noble conception. She advocated regularized versions of old ballads, purged of most archaisms and dialect. Although he published one of her ballads in a collection of ballad imitations, it's no wonder the fashionable Scott found most of her poetry second rate. Seward represented a literary era now as seemingly "ancient" as that of the incomprehensible Elizabethan she deplored.

Scott's comments on Seward's poetry follow from the premise that it is now simply outmoded. Of her elegies on Captain Cook and Major André, he notes that "it would be too much to claim for these productions, the warm interest which they excited while the melancholy events which they celebrated were glowing in the general recollection." He admits nevertheless that "when the advantage which they derived from their being suited to 'the form and pressure of the time' has passed away, they convey a high impression of the original powers of their author" (1:xii). But appreciation for Seward's most acclaimed poems now requires interpretive reclamation. To understand her elegies for national figures, we must reconstruct the historic contexts that inspired them. To appreciate her occasional verse, we must recall the importance of such verse to genteel eighteenth-century ladies and gentlemen; as Mellor has reminded us, ladies were expected "to create and sustain community" by composing poems commemorating events and friendships (*Romanticism* 11).[6]

A clearer evaluation of certain other of Seward's poems means shaking free of dependence on criteria that gentlemen only could fulfill, eliminating women poets from consideration before their writings are even read. Backscheider describes such critical practices as denying women agency (24), and Scott was certainly unwilling to grant that Seward had a career with its expectations of "experimentation, progress, and incremental mastery" (Backscheider 24). Scott admires Seward's *Collection of Original Sonnets*, for example, but dismisses her *Translations from Horace*, "which, being rather paraphrases than translations, can hardly be expected to gratify those whose early admiration has been turned to the original" (1:xix–xx). This assessment firmly denies Seward the role of national poet to which she aspired and instead relegates her to the position of an unlearned gentlewoman-poet, best at composing brief lyrics and out of her depth when attempting imitations of the classics. The latter are the purview of educated gentlemen, who need not bother with her amateur specimens. Scott concludes his cursory critical remarks by observing that the verses Seward published after the sonnets were "unequal to those of her earlier muse" (1:xxi). Since he had apologized for or given qualified praise to all but Seward's sonnets, Ball's comment that Scott's preface gave no hint that he found her verse "execrable" misrepresents his remarks.

Seward's poetry's lack of appeal to her first biographer is understandable given their different ages, professional status, and genders. Indeed, the fact she was a woman makes Scott's praise of Seward's character and personality, generous as it is, fairly predictable. Of her compliance with her parents' wishes that she exchange poetry writing for needlework as a young girl, he notes, "When it is considered that her attachment to literary pursuits bordered even upon the romantic, the merit of sacrificing them readily to the inclination of her parents, deserves our praise" (1:viii). There is no criticism of the Sewards for nearly smothering their daughter's writing career at its outset. Scott praises Seward's charity, her kindness toward younger writers, her partiality toward friends' compositions. He comments frequently on her strong feelings, expressed in both the personal and professional aspects of her life. Scott hints obliquely at the self-control that enabled Seward to avoid the outright scandal of a liaison with the married man she was in love with, John Saville, but never explicitly defines their relationship. The image of Seward that lingers is one of a poetic "priestess of Apollo," complete with "tiara and glittering zone" (1:xxvii), or of a literary queen, distinguished by strong enthusiasms and exquisite beauty (1:xxii). Unfortunately, she was a queen whose "taste for the picturesque" deprived her poetry of excellence (1:xxvii). Scott concludes his brief biography by noting that literature has lost in Seward one of its best advocates. "To the numerous friends of Miss Seward, these volumes will form an acceptable present; for, besides their poetical merit, they form a pleasing picture of her senti-

ments, her feelings, and her affections. The general reception they may meet
with is more dubious, since collections of occasional and detached poems have
rarely been honoured with a large share of public favour" (1:xxxix). Seward's collected works are best considered as a three-volume keepsake album for friends of
the deceased. Scott may have predicted accurately the neglect of Seward's *Poetical Works*, but his resigned comment describing "the faithful discharge of [his]
task" (xxxix) hardly invited readers or critics to anticipate taking much pleasure
from the collection.

Unfortunately, Scott's condescending attitude toward a writer for whom he
professed respect and admiration during her lifetime has proven not merely prophetic but durably influential. The propensity to dismiss Seward's verse that
began with Scott gained currency as succeeding editors and biographers followed
his lead. Like Scott in his letter to Baillie, even critics ostensibly committed to
reviving interest in Seward indulged in irony at her expense, as if embarrassed by
their subject. Because few have attempted book-length studies of Seward, those
few books have not only become relied-on sources but have seemingly replaced
efforts to read and evaluate Seward's writings themselves. The first such book,
appearing nearly a century after Scott's posthumous edition of her works, was
E. V. Lucas's *A Swan and Her Friends* (1907). Professedly idiosyncratic, Lucas's
study of Seward and her Lichfield circle approaches the poet as a figure of perplexing charisma. Why should Seward command a modern writer's attention?
Because "nothing could be less out of place in the present day than Anna Seward's
pontifical confidence, her floridity and her sentimentalism," and "[to] expose
these characteristics . . . ought not to be unentertaining" (2). Lucas defines Seward
as a humorless bluestocking in that unfortunate period before Jane Austen revived
feminine humor. She wrote poetry before its Romantic rebirth, and her critical
"opinions were almost always wrong" (4).

Margaret Ashmun's *The Singing Swan* (1931) succeeded Lucas's "impression-
istic" study but not with the goal of correcting his impressions (xiii). Although
hers was the only full-length biography of Seward until Teresa Barnard's 2009
study appeared, it is prefaced by a note from Frederick Pottle explaining that its
"chief charm" is Ashmun's descriptions of Seward's contemporaries (x). As for
the literary merits of Seward's circle, they are few, as far as Pottle is concerned. He
dismisses Darwin, Day, Edgeworth, Hayley, and Seward herself: "As writers they
are all either a little mad or more than a little ridiculous" (ix). But while he confesses that he would not have found Seward worthy of a biography before reading
Ashmun's manuscript, Pottle admits he now believes her personality, if not her
writing, merits such distinction. After this unpromising foreword, Ashmun main-

tains the ironic tone inaugurated by Lucas. Seward's first published poem, for example, a commendation of Lady Miller's Batheaston salon, is described as "somewhat incoherent" (72). "Severe as may be our critical judgment of the result" of Batheaston's inspiration, "we may," Ashmun adds, "at least congratulate [Seward] on having found an outlet for her emotions" (73). Ashmun is only mildly dismissive of the elegies for Cook and André, which she considers Seward's best verse: "The high-flown and overwrought style which ruins most of her work was not so deadly in these monodies as elsewhere" (88). Regarding Seward's other work, Ashmun is generally scathing. Of Seward's popular novel composed as a series of poetic epistles, she remarks that "the age is as much to blame as the author for an artificial, far-fetched piece of bathos like *Louisa*" (125). Ashmun cautions that we should not begrudge Seward the praises showered on her translations of Horace, "though they seem to be somewhat richer than she deserved" (146). Of a poem Seward published celebrating the glories of Llangollen Vale, Ashmun admits that "certain stanzas have a liveliness, a dash, and a technical finish which entitle them to a degree of commendation; though the poem as a whole is artificial, forced, and uninspired" (213). In reviewing the many events and relationships in Seward's life, however, Ashmun makes every effort to be fair. She produces contemporary testimony corroborating Seward's insistence on Samuel Johnson's rudeness, particularly respecting other writers' merits (121–23). She discusses Seward's devotion to the married John Saville with both sense and sympathy (178–87). Ashmun also supplies a great deal of information that would surely have been lost without her assiduous research. But her criticism begins with the premise that Seward was a mediocre writer inexplicably valued by her contemporaries, and she never deviates from that premise to consider what readers might justly have admired in Seward's publications.

Hesketh Pearson's one-volume *The Swan of Lichfield* (1936) offered those intrigued by Ashmun's account an opportunity to peruse Seward's correspondence without immersing themselves in the entire collection. Pearson unfortunately prefaces his book by declaring that Seward's "flowery sentences" nauseated nineteenth-century readers while "to us they are simply funny, as they were to her contemporaries" (9). Seward, he contends, was "a blue-stocking, a highbrow, . . . and she has suffered the invariable fate of such," so that "their only hope of survival is to be restored as 'period pieces'" (9). Although Ashmun advises caution when approaching Seward's letters on the grounds that "the emotional nature of the poetess gave her a lofty contempt for mere accuracy" (xiii), Pearson takes the view that Seward sincerely expressed her feelings and opinions without regard for those of her correspondents and that she was adamant about maintaining what she believed to be

facts unless presented with incontrovertible evidence to the contrary. These statements are quite true: they usefully modify Ashmun's observation. Pearson recommends Seward's letters as both a window into her time and the record of "not only
an honest but a good woman" (11). James Clifford's 1941 article advising caution
when seeking biographical facts in Seward's edited correspondence both complicates Pearson's assumption of Seward's honesty and further diminishes the value of
both Ashmun's and Pearson's work, so heavily reliant on that source. But Pearson's
preface often reverberates in succeeding criticism, and unfortunately what echoes
is not his commendation of Seward's personality but his insistence that her writing style is the florid affectation of a highbrow, a bluestocking, a figure of fun.

Among the few scholarly efforts focused on Seward in the wake of Lucas's,
Ashmun's, and Pearson's volumes is Samuel H. Monk's article, "Anna Seward and
the Romantic Poets: A Study in Taste" (1939). Monk's purpose was pejorative. To
the question he raises at the outset, whether Seward's "opinions articulate the
blunted, limited, and perhaps perverted poetic sensibility of her times" (119), the
answer is a resounding "Yes." Poor Seward is not to be held responsible for her
views, since they were merely those she picked up from her environment as her
Aeolian harp caught its harmonies from a breeze. But she epitomized, in Monk's
view, "the age of gush" (122), an entire generation's perverse adherence to "criteria
which robbed poetry of all distinction, and put it within reach of the Hayleys, the
Whalleys, and the Sewards" (126). Monk values Romantic poetry because it satis-
fies his primary critical demands for "plastic language" and "imaginative synthe-
sis" (126). He scorns Seward's preference for content over form and thought over
imagination—although Seward would have noted her careful choices of form
and her devotion to poems that excited her fancy. Monk, however, had no interest
in eighteenth-century ideas about genre. Her critical acumen disparaged, her
writing style deemed ridiculous, Seward was thus banished from serious consideration by the very scholars who had troubled to examine her life and writings in
the first place. Having lived in what has been termed "the trough of the wave"
between Augustan and Romantic verse, Seward might in any case have been ignored for many decades.[7]

Seward's sparse reappearances were usually as background to studies of other
figures. In his 1970 biography of Sir Walter Scott, Edgar Johnson refers to Seward
as "a bluestocking of the most ultramarine dye, equally ready to admire fashionable mediocrity and reject unfamiliar merit" (1:271), a description that confirms his
lack of familiarity with Seward, who was often among the first to hail new talent—
such as Scott himself—or to criticize work she deemed unworthy even when
published by her favorite acquaintances. He also refers to her as a "highbrow,"

which suggests the influence of Lucas and of Pearson, although he cites only Ashmun as the source for his characterization (1:272). Such descriptions simply indicate that Johnson was too busy researching Scott to become knowledgeable about his early patron.

Even when poets of her generation began to receive renewed critical attention, Seward was left out of most studies. Her career unfolded in the years covered in A. D. Harvey's *English Poetry in a Changing Society, 1780–1825* (1980), but he omits all reference to Seward. He mostly confines himself to discussing poets who vanished after impressing their contemporaries, but it still would have made sense to mention Seward given her practice of, and fondness for, several of the poetic modes he examines. Even when her critical leadership was prominent, he de-clines the opportunity for mention. He remarks, for example, that "during the 1780s a popular, though rather pointless, topic of controversy was whether Pope or Dryden was the greater poet" (150). That debate had culminated in a long-running epistolary battle in the *Gentleman's Magazine* throughout which Seward defended Pope's reputation against several antagonists.[8] The controversy was not pointless, because by defining what they considered the strengths of both poets (Dryden's vigor and lack of polish, Pope's exquisite harmony and refined style) contemporaries were deciding which qualities they prized in modern poems. Harvey might have found such evidence useful, and by dismissing it he also lost the chance to include Seward even among "the third-raters" of his book (170).

Over the past twenty-five years, however, Seward has been included once again in chapters and studies devoted to late eighteenth-century poets, especially women poets.[9] She appears in various dictionaries and anthologies, although at times the information about her seems to have been hastily gathered.[10] Scott, Lucas, Ashmun, and Pearson are still consulted for background information. When these sources are echoed, a patronizing or ironic tone often emerges, as in Greer's comment about Seward's "great drift of indifferent verse." Greer's sources include Scott, Pearson, Todd, and Ruth Hesselgrave's portrait of Lady Miller and her Batheaston assemblies, contemporary with Ashmun's biography and equally face-tious in its treatment. Greer's general intention is sympathetic, but her remarks tend to affirm the sentiment that Seward ought to be consigned to oblivion. She defines Seward as the victim of male oppression, stressing her shyness and docil-ity, a characterization the mature poet herself would have disputed. The emphasis of Brewer's sensitive chapter is similarly on the cultural forces that caused Seward and her work to disappear soon after her death. Such an account again resembles the plot of a whodunit by identifying Seward as a victim before concentrating on the perpetrators of her failure and consequent disappearance.

But other recent studies suggest positive contexts for renewed study of Seward's writings. Histories of sensibility, for example, chart the trajectory of its vogue, creating an opportunity for placing Seward, avowedly passionate, in relation to the culture of sentiment.[11] Since Walter Scott concluded that her poems rarely contained "natural effusions of real passion" (*Poetical Works*, 1:xxvii), we must assume that by the time he was writing his preface in 1810 a revolution in taste had already obscured what Seward's original readers considered the "vigour of sentiment" (Urban 379). As Thomas J. McCarthy observes in *Relationships of Sympathy*, the late century's larger, more democratized readership "shifted the focus in the reading of lyric poetry away from the universal, the commonly held values, to the individual, the particular, and the idiosyncratic" (148). Readers' preferred emphasis on "the inner life of feeling" (McCarthy 198) supported the vogue for Charlotte Smith's sonnets, and so Seward's "Miltonic" occasional sonnets appeared less compelling, despite their technical perfection. Another pertinent body of scholarship concerns eighteenth-century Britons' growing sense of themselves as a nation and their consequent patriotism.[12] Although Seward wrote many occasional pieces and sonnets that were deemed "feminine" by contemporaries, her proudest accomplishments were public funeral odes on the deaths of national heroes. Her reputation was established by the monodies on James Cook and John André. On the other hand, Seward deplored William Pitt the Younger's policies, which, in her opinion, had dragged England into fruitless wars against her American colonies and France. Seward's complicated relation to the evolving concept of patriotism also locates her more accurately amid Romantic-era women writers, whose opinions of Britain's late-century politics, both domestic and international, have received attention.[13] Seward's letters to Helen Maria Williams, for example, trace her growing disillusionment with the French Revolution and are often read as evidence of her political conservatism. But her subsequent disgust with British warfare against the French complicates such a simple conclusion, expanding our conception of the nuanced political positions held by women all along the political spectrum.

It is disappointing that Seward has not figured more prominently in books about sensibility or patriotism. More surprising, however, is her exclusion from most feminist studies except for passing references. Seward's writings should have benefited from the great wave of feminist scholarship that has transformed literary studies in recent decades, but several reasons for her near-omission are apparent. One is Seward's membership in groups that did not attract late twentieth-century scholars. A clergyman's daughter, and a woman of independent means who preferred Lichfield to the capital city she facetiously called "Babylon," Seward has no place in recent studies of laborer-poets, oppressed aristocrats, and professionals struggling to earn their livelihoods in London.[14] Unlike Leapor and Yearsley, whose meager records inspired masterful efforts to reconstruct their lives, Seward was thought to have enjoyed the benefit of Scott's and Ashmun's biographies. As we have seen, that benefit was only apparent: Scott's and Ashmun's refusal to take seriously Seward's writings left her with an apparently well-documented life and negligible literary reputation, which has undoubtedly contributed to Seward's neglect even when her inclusion would seem logical in a particular study. Seward's social rank and retired life have perhaps made her career seem less serious than that of, for example, Charlotte Smith, who struggled against deadlines in order to support her family. Seward is too easily caricatured as a "lady poetess" or dilettante rather than seen as an ambitious poet worthy of serious study. Analyses of the progressive identification of writing as a masculine profession, such as Linda Zionkowski's in *Men's Work*, invite speculation about the consequent demise of esteem for poetry written by gentlemen and ladies, formerly poetry's custodians. Brewer identifies this trajectory as responsible for modern neglect of Seward and her literary acquaintances such as William Hayley and T. S. Whalley. The socioeconomic and cultural history that created this revolution cannot be ignored, but literary scholars can do better than ignore or mock those who maintained their amateur status amid the changes.

A welcome development is resurgent interest in the bluestockings, the group of genteel women who influenced London's intellectual and social life through two generations. In their recent anthology, *Reconsidering the Bluestockings*, Nicole Pohl and Betty A. Schellenberg expanded the term to include those provincial women such as Seward whose homes, like those of the original London "Blues," were the cultural centers of local society (5). Pohl's and Schellenberg's volume features Janice Blathwayt's extensive bibliography, which cites manuscript collections of Seward's letters that clarify her personality, relationships, and writings, and the degree to which she manipulated these in her edited, posthumous correspondence. The volume also includes an article by Susan Staves that examines the relationship between Church of England clergy and the bluestockings, and one by Gary Kelly that addresses Clara Reeve's status as a provincial bluestocking. Both Staves and Kelly mention Seward but neither discusses her at length, opening two more avenues for research. Seward, a clergyman's daughter, numbered many clergymen among her friends and often professed her faith in the Church of England. Yet she departed from the views of powerful church officials in her political opinions and pushed the boundaries of decorum by persisting in her relationship with John Saville. Seward's complicated relationship with the clergy in Lichfield and beyond invites analysis. Likewise, Seward's resemblance to the London bluestockings requires study. She has been identified as a member of a younger, extended group of bluestockings that influenced cultural life throughout Britain.[15] Seward inherited her role in Lichfield's cultural life from her parents, who entertained all local residents and visitors distinguished in arts and letters. Following their example, she presided in her drawing room until late in life, often holding dramatic readings or concerts in addition to hosting visits. A study of Seward's role in promoting culture in Lichfield would enlarge our perspective on her activities, which to date has been confined to the personal consequences of her social events and relationships. Gary Kelly has supplied a valuable tool with his six-volume collection, *Bluestocking Feminism* (1999), featuring writings by women formerly accessible chiefly in rare book rooms and online databases. Jennifer Kelly's edition of Seward's writings for that collection provides a concise introduction to Seward's life (albeit drawn chiefly from Ashmun's biography), some discussion of the context in which she wrote, and a representative collection of her verse and prose from the Scott and Constable editions.[16]

Seward is taken quite seriously in such important studies as Paula Backscheider's 2005 *Eighteenth-Century Women Poets and Their Poetry* and Susan Staves's 2006 *A Literary History of Women's Writing in Britain, 1660–1789*. While I do not completely agree with either of these distinguished scholars in their assessments (Backscheider views Seward primarily through the lens of same-sex desire, and Staves prefers Smith's sonnets to Seward's), both consider Seward a major poet of her era. Paula Feldman's anthology of *British Women Poets of the Romantic Era* includes a dozen of Seward's sonnets, and Backscheider and Catherine Ingrassia's anthology of eighteenth-century women poets includes a selection of Seward's verse. Both anthologies enable teachers of eighteenth-century and Romantic-era poets to include Seward in their courses. Articles and book chapters on various aspects of Seward's interests—environmental, musical, scientific—are beginning to proliferate, although most concentrate understandably on her knowledge and attitudes rather than on her poetic techniques. Examples of such studies are Sylvia Lorraine Bowerbank's chapter on Seward's environmental beliefs in her book on *Women and Ecologies of Early Modern England*, Gillen D'Arcy Wood's article on Seward as exemplar of her era's sociable music culture, and Teresa Barnard's article on Seward and science.[17] Barnard's 2009 critical biography, *Anna Seward: A Constructed Life*, is the most important contribution so far to Seward studies. Barnard corrects our understanding of this complicated woman, whose preservation and editing of her correspondence for posthumous publication refined the persona that has descended to us as the poet's if indeed it did not outright create it. Barnard's research answers some of the questions that have perplexed students of Seward, enabling writers like myself to reconstruct her motives and career more accurately than has been possible to date. Also welcome to readers who, like me, are intrigued by Seward's relationship to contemporary poetic kinds and techniques are books such as Jennifer Keith's *Poetry and the Feminine from Behn to Cowper*. Keith features sensitive readings of seven poems, examining Seward's paradoxical fascination with the sublime: a concept she associated with masculinity but explored in a number of anguished sonnets.

John Guillory's insights in *Cultural Capital* offer some clues about why a poet who so exquisitely encapsulates the poetry of the long eighteenth century is no longer included in most discussions of the subject. According to Guillory, it was during Wordsworth's career that a standardized English language appropriate for prose was adopted as the proper language of poetry (131). He points out how Wordsworth repudiated Gray's "elaborate" poetic diction 124) in order to distinguish his own verse from that of earlier writers. Guillory deems Wordsworth's effort self-contradictory (128), but Wordsworth's apparent success in stigmatizing poetic diction, the style that had previously distinguished poetry as a higher genre than prose, effectively condemned poets such as Seward. Because she had so publicly defended the practice of a style appropriated to poetry, Seward was especially vulnerable in the new literary climate even though, in poems like "Lichfield, an Elegy," her old-fashioned diction and style could yield beautiful, moving verse. Other factors besides her diction worked toward exclusion, however. Wordsworth himself emulated Miltonic diction. Shelley's style, rarely simple, strives to convey his philosophy. John Keats was ridiculed for his elaborate diction. All three were admitted into the canon. Seward's diction and complex musicality, as well as her reliance on heroic couplets and devices such as personification all worked against her recognition, along with her sensibility, gender, social position, and even her latecomer status among eighteenth-century poets.

Guillory remarks elsewhere in *Cultural Capital* that when academics seek to expand the canon, they almost always mean by including more writers of a different race, class, or gender than are currently represented in it (9). Seward fits very uneasily amid the women who have recently been included on account of her privileged status and conservative Anglicanism. Her mastery of a style deemed obsolete by poets emerging at the end of her life ensured her posthumous oblivion. But, as Guillory also observes, the creation and dissemination of a literary canon has always been the province of academic institutions. We are revising the canon of eighteenth-century British poetry, for example, to reflect a more complex understanding of how literary trends rose, persisted, overlapped, and declined.

Such a canon accounts for, and can be enriched by, Seward's challenges to our cultural assumptions. Guillory's focus in *Cultural Capital* is elsewhere: he believes our internal canonical debates miss the larger challenge facing our profession, the increasing marginality of literary studies themselves. From that perspective, reinstating Anna Seward as an important late eighteenth-century poet will hardly make history, although the near disappearance of an important poet will certainly have been exacerbated by the marginalization of literary studies. But to the extent that Seward's reclamation restores an enigmatic chapter in the saga of poetry's development throughout the century, it might remake literary history, which is ample reason for undertaking it. Since current scholarship has produced the foundation for more accurate evaluation, and even for appreciation, we will commence with Seward's perplexed relationship to contemporary professionalism, including her debut with that maligned institution, Lady Miller's Batheaston assemblies.

CHAPTER TWO

"Fancy's Shrine"

Lady Miller's Batheaston Poetical Assemblies

A nna Seward participated in a local poetic coterie and circulated poems in manuscript, but she did not publish in print until 1780, a transitional time for poetry, publishing, and the professionalization of writing (Barnard, *Anna Seward* 110, 122). In this chapter, I examine the poems Seward chose to publish in her collected works (1809) from among those she presented to her first, semi-public audience, the guests at Lady Anna Miller's Batheaston salons. These poems, although neglected when not maligned by later critics, demonstrate that Seward entered the public marketplace as a polished poet, ready to please her anticipated readers. They position her as a poet skilled in the century's principles and techniques, ready to brave contemporary professional criticism. Seward's decision to compete in Lady Miller's poetry contests before seeing her work into print, besides illustrating the nature and values of her poetry, invites us to ponder her relationship to the rapidly evolving profession of writing. I offer several explanations for Seward's choice to begin her career in Batheaston rather than in London. Seward's career can be seen as a next-generation version of Alexander Pope's, which, as Margaret Ezell has reminded us, was typical of a poet's trajectory in the early eighteenth century in that his poems circulated both in manuscript and print (*Social Authorship*, 60–83). As Ezell also observes, provincial writers were slow to adopt print publication, often preferring manuscript publication not because they were less skilled but because they were wary of the commercial context or were interested in an interactive readership, among other reasons (121). Seward opted to share her early verse in manuscript as well as to perform them at Batheaston, contexts that informed her poems' structures, content, and sounds. Once she was ready to commit her poems to print publication, she could reasonably hope that she might achieve national recognition, a topic I take up in the next chapter, owing to the wide circulation of books and periodicals.[1] Seward's career illuminates the distinction between amateurism and professionalism in an era when the latter did not necessarily connote a certain financial condition, gender, or social position.[2] Finally, my readings of Seward's Batheaston poems show how their models, structures, and sound effects challenge the twenty-first-century reader while demonstrating the national concerns of provincial literary spheres, such as that at Batheaston, and Seward's professional perspective as she used patronage for nonfinancial motives.

Whether viewed as an "amateur" or a "professional," Seward cherished an exalted notion of the poet and consequently held fellow writers to exacting standards.[3] In doing so, she participated in a national trend: as Mary Poovey observes in *Genres of the Credit Economy*, the late eighteenth century witnessed efforts to discriminate between "Literature" and other forms of writing (285–335). Poovey concentrates on William Wordsworth's campaign in the following century to convince the public that poetry had an aesthetic value discernible only to elite readers. Paradoxically, however, as Poovey notes, Wordsworth's literary reputation depended on the wide sales of inexpensive editions of his poetry (290–98). But Seward's generation was already entangled in such questions as whether the best poetry required critical elucidation and whether a broad audience indicated lack of merit or the reverse. Ezell cites the vogue for "series" of publications said to constitute the "classics" but often reflecting the mere availability of certain texts as a phenomenon that has persuaded too many succeeding critics to accept eighteenth-century publishers' decisions regarding the British "canon" (*Social Authorship* 136–39). The very identity of the poet was in question: should such a writer be "professional," regularly producing income-yielding volumes, or a leisured gentleman or lady, writing only to satisfy the muses with no thought of payment? In this chapter, I observe the growing split between "professional" and "amateur" writing characteristic of Seward's lifetime. I also note the confusion evident in later critical responses to Seward's poems, produced for an eighteenth-century readership prior to the decisive changes Poovey documents but subject to post-Romantic definitions of literary value and poetic identity. By retrieving the context in which Seward made professional decisions, I am responding to Paula Backscheider's call, in *Eighteenth-Century Women Poets and Their Poetry*, for scholars to pay serious attention to women's careers. As Backscheider notes, Seward's is a prime example of a career that integrated serious writing with social and domestic responsibilities while "demonstrating more sustained dedication than we find in the lives of many of the canonical men" (25). Backscheider states what my chapter confirms and Poovey's argument supports: Seward wrote in an environment hospitable to women poets, but later critics failed to acknowledge the shape and terms of her career (Backscheider 24–26).

_ი ი_

Seward's first biographer credited Lady Miller with initiating Seward's career. Walter Scott observed that "Miss Seward's poetical powers appear to have been dormant, or to have been only sparingly exercised, until her acquaintance with Lady Miller, whose fanciful and romantic institution at Bath Easton, was then the subject of public attention" (Seward, *Poetical Works* 1:xi). It was, he adds, "the applause of this selected circle" that "gave Miss Seward courage to commit some of her essays to the press" (1:xi). Margaret Ashmun, Seward's only twentieth-century biographer, described the Batheaston assemblies less charitably in 1931. Unfortunately, she complained, Seward was "too much of a lady, too much hampered by her sense of social values, to burst boldly forth and seek a free channel for her talents as her friend Helen Williams was to do" (72). Ashmun of course ignored Seward's circumstances, which would have made a quest like Williams's or Mary Wollstonecraft's for London employment unnecessary, if not impossible. Still, Ashmun concludes that at least Seward's "connection with the Bath-Easton group, ridiculous as they may have been, gave her a new interest in life, and fixed within her the resolve to write, in spite of all opposition" (73).

Her characterization of Lady Miller's assemblies as "ridiculous" no doubt derives in part from Johnson's comment that an eminent acquaintance who participated in her contests "was a blockhead for his pains" (Boswell 2:336–37). But another source was Ruth Hesselgrave's ironic account of the Millers and their activities, from which Ashmun drew her information. Lady Miller was doomed like Seward to a biographer who, like numerous scholars of the twentieth century's first three decades, found something intrinsically comical in the literary activities of gentlemen and ladies, especially ladies, of the eighteenth century. According to Hesselgrave, it would have been difficult indeed for Seward or anyone else to emerge with credit from the Batheaston assemblies, simply due to the nature of the hosts and their misguided effort to establish gatherings both social and literary, resembling the bluestocking salons of London, at Bath. Today, scholars such as Nicole Pohl and Betty A. Schellenberg have proposed that indeed Lady Miller's parties were provincial equivalents of the bluestockings' receptions (5). Seward certainly believed she had chosen in them a viable alternative to the capital's literary gatherings. But many others before and since have deemed

Lady Miller a distant imitator of the London hostesses and their conversation parties. A brief review of Lady Miller's life, shorn of sarcastic comments, may therefore be helpful.

John Miller was an Irish gentleman who in 1765 married Anna Riggs, the heiress of Irish estates but born and raised in England. The couple wed in Bath and soon afterward purchased Bath-Easton Villa, situated on the Avon outside the city. Expensive renovations led them to retrench by moving abroad for two years in 1770. They returned from their grand tour bearing, among other artifacts, an urn excavated at Frascati, earlier known as Tusculum, the site of Cicero's villa. Anna Miller placed the urn on a pedestal in the bow window of her drawing room, where by 1774 it inspired her invitations to fortnightly morning assemblies at which breakfast was served before the performance of a literary ritual. All the guests had been encouraged to compose poems, which were rolled up and placed in the urn. Most brought their poems with them to the assemblies, but some who could not attend sent poems nonetheless. After everyone had arrived and enjoyed conversation and refreshments, a young lady drew the poems from the urn and each was read twice, first by a random gentleman guest and then by the poem's author if present. Afterward, all the gentlemen withdrew to deliberate before awarding three myrtle wreaths and declaring one of the three poems so honored the best of that week's submissions. Mrs. Miller herself—by 1778, Lady Miller, her husband having been granted a baronetcy in Ireland—presented the wreaths and fastened them into the hair of either the poet or if the poet was male that of his spouse or choice of female guest (Hesselgrave 22–26). She then kept the poems before choosing a sufficient number for publication in a series of anthologies she titled *Poetical Amusements at a Villa near Bath*, the proceeds of which supported a poor-relief fund headed by her husband. The volumes appeared in 1775, 1776, 1777, and 1781 before Lady Miller's sudden death in June 1781 interrupted preparation of a fifth anthology (Hesselgrave 35).

Even if Hesselgrave's tone is jocular, she does emphasize the tremendous success of the Millers' assemblies among fashionable visitors to Bath. Because of the anthologies and publication of the prize poems in periodicals such as the *Gentleman's Magazine* as well as reports in the equivalents of today's gossip columns, the Batheaston assemblies became famous throughout England. While many observers expressed disdain for the upstart Millers, their pretentious salon, and the inevitable mediocrity of most poems submitted on short notice to comply with Lady Miller's requested rhymes or themes, there was never a shortage of guests crowding the villa's small but elegant rooms. An early twentieth-century French writer, Alfred Barbeau, deduced that selectivity was perhaps the chief reason for

Lady Miller's success: "For the *entrée* at Batheaston, rank, or a certain degree of fame, were almost indispensable, and in any case, an unblemished reputation. The lady of the house weeded out her visitors with extreme care, and very probably desire to be admitted to an exclusive circle contributed quite as much as the affectation of culture to establish and maintain the success of these extraordinary gatherings" (qtd. in Sutro 11–12). Stripped of irony, the accounts recall six years of levees with sufficient cachet to sustain the avid participation of most talented and well-connected visitors to Bath. Although Hesselgrave notes that such provincial success would not have translated into acceptance among the same society in London, Lady Miller, an obscure Irish baronet's wife from Shropshire, must have gloried in the sensational success of her levees among the titled and talented who came when they visited Bath. Her guests included the duchesses of Northumberland and Devonshire and writers such as Horace Walpole, Frances Burney, T. S. Whalley, Christopher Anstey, and Edward Jerningham.

Lady Miller's credentials for sponsoring a literary salon were three volumes of travel memoirs she had published after her tour in the form of letters to her mother. (Her mother was a notoriously unpolished woman worthy of a Burney novel—indeed, she was caricatured by Burney when she visited Batheaston.) Lady Miller's memoirs could make a claim to novelty, partly because they contained meticulous records of art holdings but also because of the comparative rarity of a female-authored guidebook. Unfortunately, what impressed some as the records of a woman with panache struck others as pretentious and unsophisticated.[4] Although the memoirs were a more substantial literary production than those of London hostesses Frances Boscawen or Elizabeth Vesey, they did not establish her credentials among the elite. The irresistible conclusion is that Lady Miller offended primarily by her too-obvious pursuit of literary and social success, an offense compounded by her husband's willingness to appear merely as his wife's dutiful assistant. Mrs. Delany called her "conceited" (Hesselgrave 6) and Burney "mock-important" (Hesselgrave 10). While the ton was quite willing to divert itself at her villa, it would never have embraced a woman who clearly did not know how to cloak her self-confidence or ambition in a properly feminine manner, despite the exclusivity and decorum of her assemblies.

Critical mockery of Lady Miller's assemblies might ironically have promoted Seward's attachment to Batheaston and its hostess. An exclusive drawing-room company engaged in literary pastimes would have suited Seward's decorum and her apparent preference for taking incremental steps toward print. Since Batheaston was famous before Seward made the Millers' acquaintance, it must have seemed a viable alternative to the celebrated London salons. The London bluestocking salons may seem to us a more natural environment for her debut, but their connection with fellow Lichfieldian Johnson may have discouraged Seward from seeking to participate there. Although some of the same people, such as Burney and David Garrick, appeared at both Batheaston and in the bluestockings' drawing rooms, Batheaston's morning entertainment was less formal than, for example, Elizabeth Montagu's rigid conversational semicircle. Lady Miller discouraged embarrassing or potentially offensive poems, setting a gentler tone than Seward might have imagined she would encounter in Johnsonian circles. Seward disliked Johnson's harsh criticism of other writers, publishing after his death her opinion of his "spleen and envy; potent . . . to shroud the fairest claims of rival excellence" (*Letters* 1:13). Seward may have decided not to expose her yet-unpublished verse to him or his coterie, opting instead to join a group replete with admired writers but where Johnson scorned to appear. Her attendance eventually yielded lifelong friendships with writers such as Whalley, whose *Edwy and Edilda* (1779) had won not only Seward's but the reading public's enthusiastic approval. Because the Millers' gatherings led to friendships with the Whalleys and Hayleys, Seward would have been impressed not only with the propriety of Batheaston's "fanciful and romantic institution" but also with its capacity to attract highly esteemed writers. Although not in the capital, Batheaston nevertheless hosted some authors with national reputations, a respectable audience in a domestic setting noted for encouragement.

Teresa Barnard believes that Seward entered her first Batheaston contest at the urging of Anna Rogers Stokes, a poet with whom she collaborated after their meeting in 1778 (*Anna Seward* 110). According to Barnard, the 1770s were a miserable decade for Seward owing primarily to repeated confrontations with her parents over her attachment to the married John Saville. Feuding with her parents and ostracized by many former acquaintances, Seward solaced herself by writing verse, often in collaboration with Erasmus Darwin, Francis Mundy, and Rogers Stokes, and engaging in manuscript exchanges (Barnard, *Anna Seward* 110). Barnard's account confirms that Seward's entrance into the literary marketplace via Batheaston marked her conscious passage from amateur to avowed poet. Another motive may have been to avoid not merely the literary but also the moral scrutiny of Johnson. The man who once described a close friend's wife as a whore because she had divorced her first, abusive husband and married her lover may have been a person Seward felt uncomfortable meeting in London drawing rooms, although there is no record of Johnson's ever making an unkind remark in her presence.

Seward may also have identified with Lady Miller's ambition. Seward's decision to read her verse in the drawing room of a suburban Bath villa may have been "feminine," but her literary aspirations, signaled by the national themes of the monodies she submitted to the urn, were decidedly "masculine" in their scope. While Seward's first submission to Lady Miller was a suitably light "Invocation of the Comic Muse," she also premiered some of her most ambitious poems at Batheaston. Lady Miller likewise juxtaposed feminine and masculine character-istics. Her satin gowns, diamonds, and decorum were feminine, but her bold pursuit of social cachet was not. Seward's decision to befriend Lady Miller and to take her assemblies seriously seems almost defiant in retrospect, a conscious deci-sion to associate herself with an institution that some mocked but that provided her a refined and literate if not demanding audience. Anna Miller and Anna Seward, quite different in appearance and manners, may each have sympathized with the obstacles that confronted the other in her quest for eminence. In *Borderlines*, Susan J. Wolfson studies "slips at the limits of [gender] definition" in the Ro-mantic era that correct our assumption of rigid categories, although too apparent breaches of gender decorum drew attention and ridicule (3). Wolfson describes the anxieties suffered by writers such as Maria Jane Jewsbury when she attempted to establish herself in the 1820s as a writer characterized by "manly" intelligence (79–91). Wolfson remarks that Jewsbury's culture, much like that of Mary Woll-stonecraft and Catharine Macaulay, still paid homage to the ideals of feminine softness and weakness extolled by Alexander Pope in "Of the Characters of Women" (81). Seward's and Lady Miller's mutually supportive quests were therefore coura-geous in context. Seward apparently overlooked Lady Miller's self-importance and coarse appearance, while Lady Miller embraced a guest whose dramatic read-ings drew a great deal of attention to herself and her verse (Ashmun 73–74). As if reversing Johnson's tendency to confront others and to ridicule the most popular publications, Seward participated in assemblies orchestrated to encourage and praise both the experienced and amateur. As hostess of literary and musical eve-nings at Lichfield, Seward would have recognized the difficulties of organizing such events and would therefore have admired Lady Miller's skill in founding and sustaining her unique "poetical amusements."

The mockery leveled at Batheaston also fails to account for its genuine utility as poetic sponsor. Scholarship in the past twenty years, such as Dustin Griffin's, has explored the varieties of patronage available to eighteenth-century writers, ranging from political appointment to support by wealthy mentors to subscription fees. Women had little access to the first category, but laborer-poets such as Mary Leapor and Ann Yearsley found wealthy patrons, and many women poets pub-lished by subscription. A wealthy, well-connected, mature woman such as Anna Seward had no need for the financial support crucial to women such as Leapor or Yearsley. In Erasmus Darwin she had found a reader, instructor, and champion during her adolescence. She had also begun to correspond with contemporaries like Whalley whose praise sustained her efforts. But finding a critical audience outside of her small circle in Lichfield, before exposing her works through publication in London, would have been problematic. Although Habermas's theory of the growth of a public sphere has been disputed, there is little doubt that genteel and professional men in eighteenth-century England believed themselves to be participating in the formation of national opinions when they engaged in political discussions at their clubs and coffeehouses. Taste, likewise, was fostered through critical discussions in these venues, as encouraged by Steele and Addison early in the century through their periodicals. Writers could receive not just criticism but also mutual support through clubs of like-minded individuals such as the Kit-Cats or Scriblerians. Ladies, however, were mostly confined to their tea tables, domestic rather than public spheres of influence. The bluestocking salons were devised to enable women to converse with eminent male contemporaries, ostensibly to enlarge men's sympathies but concomitantly to grant intelligent women some share in public discourse. The salons and assemblies, where books and poems were read and discussed, gave women an opportunity both to join critical conversations and to develop their personal reputations as critics and writers. Seward herself presided over a cultured drawing room at the Lichfield Bishop's Palace, but Lady Miller's venue attracted many glamorous and prominent visitors whom Seward would otherwise not have met and whose approbation made her determined to appear in print. Her victories at Batheaston showed Seward that her verse appealed to the tastemakers of elite society as well as to several widely admired writers. She also made the acquaintance of many potentially important readers and supporters, another opportunity that women's previously more confined circumstances would have rendered impossible.

Another criticism of Lady Miller's assemblies was and remains that little inspired poetry resulted from her contests. Few poets assigned a specific set of rhyme words or a topic can produce a masterpiece in two weeks or less. Hesselgrave sniffed that "the verses produced at Batheaston cannot profitably be discussed with reference . . . to their literary excellence" and that nobody, with the "possible exception" of Seward, won fame through Lady Miller's publications (53). As Marlon Ross has suggested in a discussion of Felicia Hemans, women writers were particularly disadvantaged by the prejudice against writing for contests (233). Hemans, for example, entered national contests to demonstrate her prowess, only to be dismissed for doing so by modern critics who assume no genius would ever tether her imagination to an assigned topic (233). As Ross observes, Hemans deliberately sought to prove herself and to win fame through such ventures, which were among the few ways a woman might compete with men for such recognition. He adds that many male geniuses, including William Wordsworth, wrote poems on assigned topics for patrons or as poet laureates. Ross argues for a fairer estimate of how such contests might have figured in women poets' careers. Ross's comments are pertinent not only in the case of national contests but even for such drawing-room competitions as Lady Miller's, and not only for women but even for less privileged male poets. Christopher Smart, for example, began his publishing career after winning the Seatonian poetry competition at Cambridge. In his popular although outdated biography of John Keats, Robert Gittings disparages the young poet's participation in the fifteen-minute sonnet-writing contests Leigh Hunt hosted in his parlor. "The Poetry of Earth is Never Dead" resulted from one evening's amusement (170).[5] Gittings condemns such exercises as "a dangerously domesticated attitude to adopt to poetry" (170) yet admits that Hunt's hospitality provided invaluable encouragement and instruction to Keats at that early stage of his career (137).[6] Wolfson, writing over forty years after Gittings, has described how contemporary literary critics dismissed Keats by "feminizing" his appearance and verse (243–84), efforts that evidently influenced his biographer's wish that Keats had not invited such comments by engaging in the "domestic" verse Mellor has associated with Romantic-era women (*Romanticism* 11). But domestic contests profited both the "feminized" male poet and the woman poet with "masculine" ambitions. Contests may not inspire brilliant verse, but they may inspire gifted poets to attempt publication and to brave professional criticism. For Seward and Keats, such amateur recreations pushed them toward literary careers. The gratifying response to Seward's initial Batheaston poems spurred her to compose more ambitious poems and to publish her verse. It is easy to mock contests on the assumption that all poets have adequate mentoring and ample opportunities to polish and test their skills before seeking publication. But such an assumption holds only for the privileged, usually privileged men, and ignores in any case the blurred distinction between amateur and professional writers in the eighteenth and early nineteenth centuries. For Seward as for many other poets, contests, with their opportunities to perform and receive sociable critical feedback, were a valuable part of the continuum spanning from manuscript circulation to print.

_ఌ ఛ_

None of her biographers specifies the number of poems Seward submitted to the urn, nor did the poet herself record a total. Seward included in her collected works four poems that won myrtle wreaths at Batheaston. Because she evidently arranged her volume with care, I examine them in the order she chose. Each poem reveals a facet of her skills as a poet versed in the trends of eighteenth-century verse as well as her skill in crafting a poem on an assigned topic for her projected audience. "Invocation of the Comic Muse" (*Poetical Works* 2:22–24) was Seward's first submission (Ashmun 71), in 1778, but she placed "Charity" (*Poetical Works* 2:11–14) first among her edition's Batheaston selections, possibly because of its reverential subject. Precisely the kind of poem instanced by those who despise contests (it is set in the Batheaston drawing room, reflecting its "purpose-written" origin), "Charity" nonetheless probably deserved its prize in light of the way it infuses a mundane Batheaston assembly with visionary sublimity. To the fashionable cult of sensibility the poem marries the contest's conception as a latter-day classical exercise. Seward chose an artful stanzaic structure: the ninety-two-line poem's six-line stanzas maintain an a-a-b-c-c-b rhyme scheme in which iambic octosyllabic couplets are each followed by an iambic pentameter line. The pentameter lines contribute stateliness to the brisk stanzas, as well as the drama appropriate for the apparition of a heavenly being. They also contribute variety, which as Seward often remarked, pleased the ear: Seward was well aware that her poem would be read aloud at Batheaston. Indeed, she belonged to a generation that still read poems aloud in both private and social settings, and so she took care to ensure the musicality of her verse. "Charity" begins dramatically with a rhetorical question that conjures an uncanny light streaming into the drawing room amid a Batheaston gathering. Although it is day, "with clear, yet sober beauty shine / The verdant bower, the classic shrine" (ll. 7–8), as if seen by moonlight. Could the source of this chaste light be a visiting muse, perhaps Clio? Seward describes a being of "female, but celestial grace" (l. 23) who appears too reserved and dignified, in both dress and mien, to be a "Nymph . . . of Phoebus' train" (l. 24).

Seward's apparition shortly announces herself, although her white garments and blood-stained "sacred book"—presumably the New Testament in which charity is said to take precedence over the more rigid Old Testament laws—suggest her identity well before (ll. 31–33). Charity has evidently materialized in the alcove where Lady Miller placed her vase, and now "gently o'er the shrine she bends" (l. 34) to address the "ye Fair,—ye Learn'd,—ye Gay" that constitute a typical Batheaston assembly (l. 37). Not surprisingly, she warns her audience to avoid luxury if they would pursue real happiness; goodness, even extending to martyrdom, is the path to immortal joy (ll. 43–48). Perhaps better to communicate with these devotees of a mock-Apollonian ritual, Charity designates herself "First Priestess of the Christian shrine" (l. 47), usurping the normal space of the poetry contest to convey her divine greeting. Her message —that "with tongues of

angels though ye sing, / No ear divine the tinkling sound perceives" unless motivated by charity (ll. 59–60) — is essentially that of Paul's thirteenth letter to the
Corinthians.

Charity adapts her message to the privileged group she addresses, warning that
their usual charitable activities of tending to the sick and hungry of their neigh-
borhoods, or even more extreme sacrifices such as martyrdom, will yield no blessing without divine love (ll. 61–66). Seward adds a footnote explaining the charitable function of the Batheaston society, which both argues for the appropriateness
of this imagined vision and adds a note of skepticism regarding the charitable
activities of the genteel folk typically assembled at the villa. Charity also warns her
audience to avoid suspicion, anger, pride, envy, and slander (ll. 85–87), vices committed on the grand scale by public figures but also, of more immediate concern,
by those competing for attention in domestic and social circles. Women especially,
for example, were frequently chastised for exhibiting suspicion and anger toward
their spouses, and for envying the possessions or accomplishments of others
whom they attacked through slander. When Charity explains that God sent her
to "bend the stubborn mind / To all that's patient, soft, and kind" (ll. 83–84), her
message is typical of Christian sermons but is clearly intended to resonate most
forcefully with the Batheaston guests.

Seward ends the poem on a sublime note that appropriately seeks to elevate
her audience's thoughts beyond their drawing-room setting. Charity concludes
her speech by promising that she will return at the end of time, in the literal sense
of Paul's statement that "when that which is perfect is come, then that which is
in part shall be done away. . . . And now abideth faith, hope, charity, these three;
but the greatest of these is charity" (1 Cor. 10:13). Charity declares that she will
appear again "amid the falling spheres" along with Faith and Hope, to be hailed
by God himself as first in importance. Her speech concludes dramatically with
an alexandrine; God will exalt the personified virtue "who his benign commands
did best on earth perform" (ll. 85–90). Charity then dissolves, amid the same rays
of light that earlier announced her impending visit, in a couplet that closes both
vision and poem. Seward's poem, charmingly occasional in its precise references
to the Miller's home and poetic institution, might be accused of flattery. It nevertheless approaches the theme of charity ingeniously, incorporating mystic sublimity into what might have ended up being a mundane sermon to Lady Miller's
revelers. Seward's decision to paraphrase Paul's famous letter to the Corinthians
enriches the divine visitor's speech. Seward, who later wrote several sermons for
Lichfield Cathedral services, enjoyed a clergyman's daughter's familiarity with
scripture and with pulpit rhetoric. The vision's warning is perfectly calculated for

a genteel audience of "ye Fair,—ye Learn'd,—ye Gay" who might well pay charitable visits to dependents in the afternoon before indulging in slander in the
evening. While a modern reader may not agree with the vision's condemnation
of slander as "cruel Assassin of the Human Race!" (l. 78), Seward's first audience
would have understood her emphasis and perhaps have believed that in a society
where reputation was a woman's chief asset and of crucial importance to professional gentlemen, character assassination was a cardinal sin.

"Charity" also demonstrates Seward's keen pictorial sense. Jacqueline M. Labbe
has discussed Seward's ability to create "textual images that enter through the eye,
as we read" when describing paintings, interpreting scenes in a manner that stimulates readers to participate in a kind of "sensual interaction" with the landscapes
she evokes (210–11). Although "Charity" describes a room rather than a painting,
Seward likewise conveys the uncanny light that bathes Lady Miller's parlor. Although it is morning, the room appears "as when, in calmest hour of silent night, /
In soft perspective rise the vales, / The silvered lawns, the shadowy dales, / Beneath
the full-orb'd moon's unclouded light" (ll. 9–12). Seward invites her audience to
contemplate a moonlit landscape such as Claude Lorrain might have painted and
that many rural locales, such as Batheaston itself, regularly boast. Having drawn
her readers into both the imagined landscape and the mood such a setting pro-
motes, she has prepared them for the sublime apparition of Charity that soon
descends.

In his influential *Elements of Criticism* (1762), Lord Kames had discussed the
technique of personification that Seward employs throughout the rest of the poem
(3:54–87).[7] Derided today, personification was highly regarded in the eighteenth
century; Seward would have imbibed its use as a child from her beloved Milton's
"L'allegro" and "Il penseroso." Indeed most of Lord Kames's examples of personification, both positive and critical, are taken from Shakespeare. Lord Kames
defends personification as essential when writing about abstract terms, which "are
not well adapted to poetry, because they suggest not any image to the mind"
(3:65). While Kames advises caution in its use, he refuses "to set limits to personification: taste is the only rule. A poet of superior genius hath more than others the
command of this figure; because he hath more than others the power of inflaming
the mind" (3:77). Kames urges merely that the abstract term personified should
"have some natural dignity" and that "some preparation is necessary, in order to
rouze the mind" (3:79). Seward fulfills Kames's suggestions by carefully preparing
the scene for Charity's appearance. How more effectively to convey the Golden
Rule than from the lips of an embodiment of Jesus' precept? As she did in presenting her setting, re-creating the uncertainty of the audience suddenly bathed in a

light that was neither "summer's ray" (l. 2) nor that of "cold December's noon" (l. 3), Seward reconstructs their difficulty identifying the apparition that descends above the Ciceronian vase. Is she one of the muses? A "Nymph . . . of Cupid's train" (l. 24)? She lacks the "frolic" expression and colorful robes typical of such beings, dressed instead in "snowy white . . . decent garments" and clutching a blood-stained book (ll. 30–33). Seward's readers would have responded immediately to her visual cues. Not only were they adept at reading signs and deciphering visual symbolism.[8] They also would have been familiar with popular images, such as Angelica Kauffman's, of muses and nymphs draped in colorful robes and frolicking with Cupid.[9] Seward's description told her readers what visual image not to conjure up before describing what they should envision, cleverly imposing her interpretation of Charity while following Kames's instruction to rouse their minds in preparation for the personified virtue.

Regardless of Seward's reasons for placing it first among her contest-winning poems, "Charity" rewards attentive reading. Such consideration helps us to overcome our resistance to its strangeness: Seward's delight in personification and in musical rhymes and the sociable context of her spiritual address. Seward's techniques and her sociable approach now seem archaic. But "Charity" demonstrates the mastery of contemporary poetic style and idiom with which she concluded her poetic apprenticeship at Batheaston. It also proves Seward capable of endowing even a contest poem, written in at most two weeks, with some technical intricacy and spiritual depth. Her pride in this prize poem was justified. "Monody on the Death of David Garrick, Esq.," the next Batheaston selection in her *Poetical Works* (2:15–17), written in heroic couplets, is considerably more workmanlike. Its opening at Batheaston, its formulaic review of Garrick's most famous roles, and its concluding invocation to Genius suggest hasty composition. But they also reveal what Gittings deplores in Keats as a result of Hunt's sonnet-writing contests, Seward's facility in producing a tolerable poem on short notice. The monody is worth discussing if only for its intimation of Seward's ambition in joining Garrick's many prominent poetic mourners. She was evidently determined to seize the occasion provided by the death of a renowned fellow townsman. If the personified Charity urged Seward's audience to lift their eyes heavenward, Seward lifted her own sights toward a national event in this elegy. The poem's lack of inspiration is perhaps surprising given Seward's fondness for Garrick. She often lamented Johnson's lack of regard for his former student, exclaiming to Boswell that it was "base . . . as well as unkind" of Johnson not to mention Garrick in his preface to Shakespeare. "Garrick! who had restored that transcendent author to the taste of the public, after it had recreantly and long receded from him" (*Letters*

1:63). Garrick was beloved at Batheaston, too; although Johnson disdained the assemblies, the actor visited twice in 1775 and had submitted verses both times to Lady Miller's urn (Hesselgrave 65). Garrick's death in 1779 provoked a national outpouring of funeral rhetoric, in which Lady Miller's contestants participated. Perhaps the elegiac deluge stifled Seward's creativity, or perhaps she felt compelled to write a poem in honor of her admired fellow citizen but had little time to compose her submission. She most likely placed the elegy second among her prize poems owing to Garrick's fame and her personal admiration for the actor-manager she identified — as did most of her contemporaries — with Shakespeare.

The "Monody" opens with a vignette of Sir John and Lady Miller mourning over their "damp vase" (l. 15), wet with their tears. Seward gives them the poetic noms de plume of Horatio and Laura, a practice mocked by Lucas as "a kind of law compelling poets of that day to be dissatisfied with real names" (143). Lucas ignored the fact that poets had adopted fanciful names for themselves and their addressees for centuries. The convention was especially favored by women poets and their coteries, to whom the pen names gave a modicum of privacy whether in manuscript circulation or in print; the often pastoral aliases also permitted writers a degree of idealization or fictionalization. Seward, like many women poets, continued the practice, little suspecting future jeers. In this instance, Horatio and Laura model a companionate marriage of mutually sensible partners. He gazes sorrowfully at a rainy landscape that mirrors their emotions, and she drops a myrtle wreath she had ostensibly been preparing for a competition. Like her husband's, her attention wanders toward a view that harmonizes with her sorrow: "dark cypress," used for funeral wreaths, "meets [her] earnest eye" (ll. 10, 12). Horatio and Laura appear to be Genius and Beauty personified, bending over a funeral urn. Seward again fashions a vivid image for her readers, following Kames's advice and making sparing use of personification while also acknowledging her friends' grief for their deceased acquaintance.

The central portion of Seward's forty-eight-line monody recalls Garrick's best-known roles. Although mentioning his excellence in "the light magic" of comedy (l. 16), she dwells on his triumphs as Lear, Macbeth, Hamlet, and Richard III. Seward's emphasis is on Garrick's appeal to audiences' "subject passions" (l. 31), his ability to convey the emotions of Shakespeare's tragic heroes to a degree that made his interpretations seem the inevitable outcome of the bard's intentions (l. 32). Having recollected Garrick's performances, she recalls his inimitable voice and gestures before abruptly asking "Where are they now? — Dark, in the narrow cell, / Insensate, — shrunk, — and wan, — and cold, they dwell" (ll. 39–40). Her images stress the irony of death's silence and stillness compared with the living

Garrick's famously mobile features and compelling voice. They also glance toward the lurid graveyard meditations that had been popular since midcentury. The monody's final verse paragraph returns to Horatio and Laura and bids them to continue mourning and draping the urn in cypress. "Then give his talents to your loudest fame,/And grave on your high shrines, Garrick's unrivall'd name" (ll. 47–48). The concluding alexandrine, with its stress on Garrick's name after the caesura, seems to mimic the memorial engraving Seward demands. Her request that the Millers "give his talents to your loudest fame" anticipates the very contest that produced this poem; she may refer to both the "loud fame" of multiple Batheaston tributes, to be published in Lady Miller's anthology, and the "loud fame" of certain individual Batheaston elegists, perhaps including herself. Although undeniably slight, the monody gracefully comes full circle and closes adroitly with Seward's clever evocation of her own poem.

Seward places her "Ode on the Pythagorean System" third among her Batheaston prize poems (*Poetical Works* 2:18–21).[10] If "Charity" illustrates her keen grasp of audience and occasion as well as the language of sensibility and if the Garrick monody reflects her nascent ambition, "Ode on the Pythagorean System" demonstrates her technical virtuosity. Odes were characteristically reserved for serious, usually grand subjects, and presented opportunities to devise elaborate rhyme schemes. Seward's seventy-two-line poem demonstrates that she was capable of experimenting with rhythm and rhyme, producing a musicality that appropriately reflects the ode's origins in ancient religious choral song. Rather than the irregular stanzas of Pindaric ode, Seward chose the Horatian pattern, composing six twelve-line stanzas that each follow an a-b-a-b-c-c-d-e-e-d-f-f rhyme scheme. Since Horatian odes are usually shorter than their Pindaric counterparts as well as more restrained in style, Seward's choice of structure was apt for her reflections on the Pythagorean theory. Her Anglican views on the possible transmigration of souls are predictable, but she approaches the ancient system with respect and wit. She begins by asking how any theory can presume to know the destiny of a person's spirit after death. She pronounces Pythagoras's doctrine an "inadequate" (l. 11) effort to explain how souls unworthy of eternal happiness must expiate their mortal guilt by returning to earth embodied in an appropriate animal or vegetable. In the second stanza, however, she admits that because Pythagoras's ideas do not "discard/A sacred sense . . ./Of punish'd crime, and virtue's fair reward" (ll. 14–16), they are superior to "mad Atheism" (l. 18). Pythagoras intuited the immortal nature of the human spirit but was confused about its route to hell or heaven. Nevertheless, Seward decides to entertain belief in the Pythagorean system "for an hour" (l. 32) and playfully contemplate his belief in transmigration.

She imagines all the appropriate forms such a process might take: how those guilty of revenge would return as tigers, those of gluttony as hogs, those of avarice as worms, and so forth. She asks only that her personal fate be "gentle" (l. 59), since she has no serious vices or crimes to atone for. If she must return in a lower form to make amends for her failings, however, she wishes her soul to inhabit a myrtle in Lady Miller's garden. In that case, were Lady Miller to choose her foliage for a wreath, Seward's spirit would be contented. "Scarce shall its silent destiny deplore,/Since yet I *form* the wreaths, which once with pride I *wore*" (ll. 71–72, emphasis in the original). The lines capitalize on the couplet's potential for an epigrammatic, as well as ironic, closure. Yet by referring metonymically to her identity as a poet and literally to the laurel wreaths she has won as part of Lady Miller's coterie, Seward's conclusion further intimates her serious commitment to her chosen genre.

Seward's poem is unexpectedly light-hearted for an ode, turning midway "to gayer strains" (l. 31) and ending with a witty conceit in which the poet returns as the plant woven into crowns that reward poetic achievement. Her verse is both a meditation on the strengths and flaws of Pythagoras's theory and a playful reverie about its consequences. The ode's distinctive feature is its musicality, derived from abundant internal rhyme and assonance. Both lead the ear from line to line, as when Seward asks the human spirit whether any mere system "can trace thy flight,/when thou shalt seek, freed from corporeal load,/In dim Futurity a new abode" (ll. 4–5). The negative "Ah no!" (l. 7) seems to follow inevitably from the preceding "o" sounds. Another example occurs when Seward admits the superiority of Pythagoras's ideas to atheism:

>   along their erring range,
> Of punish'd crime, and virtue's fair reward,
> They soar, though on weak wings, above the sphere
> Where broods mad Atheism o'er precepts drear;
> Or, with incessant sneer, delights to lead
> By cold Oblivion's deep and sable waves,
> His grovelling crew of sensual slaves.   (ll. 15–21)

The ideas "soar" owing to Pythagoras's intuition of divine justice, virtue's "reward," whose "ar" sound echoes and supports their flight. Atheism's "drear . . . sneer" seems onomatopoetic as it draws both its victims and its spoken sound toward the deep, Lethean waves. The sibilant effects in lines 18–21, particularly strong in line 19, borrow the technique Milton used to emphasize the snakelike sound of Satan's speech in *Paradise Lost*. Through a disparate combination of sound and visual reference, Seward nimbly incorporates both the classical Charon and the biblical Satan into her personification of atheism.

Seward cherished mellifluous sound and labored to create the musical effects of her verse. Famed for "Siddonian" readings of her own poetry as well as the poems and prose of others, she strove for sounds that both emphasized sense or meaning and created drama. In this ode, for example, she uses a caesura to suggest the victim's surprise when a hornet "rises, and darts the barbed sting" (l. 45). Seward believed strongly in the aural pleasure of variety. She sometimes uses transposition, as when late in the ode the conscious Batheaston myrtle hears "the tuneful train, the groves among,/Pour the full cadence of the dulcet song" (ll. 65–66). Transposing the last three words of line 65 concluded the line with a relatively soft emphasis, strengthening the effect of the dactyl that begins the next line and creating, through clever placement of unstressed syllables, the onomato-poetic effect of pouring. Seward thought that the ear tires of listening to lines with insufficiently varied meter and length. Her stanzas in this ode are crafted of iam-bic pentameter except for the ninth line of each, which is in octometer, and the twelfth, which is an alexandrine. As we have observed of both "Charity" and the elegy on Garrick, Seward was fond of the alexandrine's dramatic impact as a sum-mation, a sonnetlike "turn" in meaning, or even, as here, a punch line. The ode ends with a play on words, perhaps appropriate for a poem on a serious subject but intended for a morning's entertainment. As the figure of Charity remarked, Seward's audience was the fair, the learned, and the gay, and only the learned in that group would have welcomed a ponderous essay on Pythagoreanism. The ode at the same time allowed her to demonstrate virtuosity in orchestrating melodious but purposeful sound, another step in Batheaston's informal conclusion of her apprenticeship.

"Invocation of the Comic Muse" appears last among Seward's prize-winning Batheaston poems, although it was evidently the first she submitted to the vase (Ashmun 71). Perhaps the poem's slight subject caused Seward to rank it behind the others. If the poem is the slightest and least even of the Batheaston poems, it nevertheless deserves attention for its accomplished musicality. It is a charming response to Lady Miller's request that Seward enter her competition and not at all a "somewhat incoherent rhapsody" as Ashmun claimed (72). Ashmun is cor-rect, however, that Seward modeled her address to the comic muse on Milton's "L'allegro." Seward draws attention to her indebtedness by borrowing a phrase from "L'allegro," "Haste thee nymph" (l. 25), when in her second stanza she ad-dresses Thalia (l. 23). From the outset she imitates Milton's ebullient tetrameter couplets that so well convey the cheerfulness they describe. Milton had achieved his effect by skillful use of meter, and Seward likewise experiments with stress patterns to make her poem livelier. Seward refines on Milton's syllabic pattern. While the number of syllables is varied in his tetrameter lines, each of her poem's forty-eight lines has seven syllables except for the last two lines of each sixteen-line stanza. Seward used dactyls and, especially, trochees to emulate Milton's lively rhythm. "On this mirth-devoted day, / From these festal bowers away, / In your sable vestments flee, / Train of sad Melpomene!" (ll. 1–4). From the initial trochee and the dactylic "devoted" in the first line to the dactylic effect of the elided second syllable of "bowers" followed by "away" in line 2 to the subdued stress on the final syllable of "Melpomene" in line 4, Seward begins with an explosion of metric effects that chase the tragic muse from her scene. The first stanza's concluding couplet evokes tragedy's ultimate personification as Despair, dragging her miserable self through one pentameter and one alexandrine line "with the damp, wan brow, and streaming wound" of suicide (ll. 15–16).

The second stanza of the poem welcomes Thalia, muse of comedy, riding in her "pantomimic car" (l. 18). Seward describes Thalia in her guise as one of the three Graces, often portrayed "bright from [Angelica Kauffman's] unrival'd hand" in paintings widely disseminated through engravings and on decorative porcelain.[11] Seward compares Thalia to one of Kauffman's images, "Nymphs Stealing the Arrows of Cupid" that she presumes readers have seen, perhaps in one of the engravings made from the painting in 1777.[12] But even though she presumes as much, Seward still describes Thalia in vivid detail, from her blue robe (l. 21) and golden hair (l. 23) to the playful manner in which she snaps Cupid's arrow. Seward extends Kauffman's visual impression by suggesting aural dimensions such as Thalia's "varied voice" (l. 24) and laughter and the crisp "snap" of Cupid's bow as she breaks it over her knee. The stanza's more regular tetrameter moves briskly, conjuring the nymphs' quick movements as they pilfer Cupid's weapons. Seward's homage to Kauffman is not merely a description but an appreciative interpretation of the painter's lively scene.

Having paid homage to Milton and to Kauffman, Seward moves in her third stanza to compliment her hosts. She asks Thalia to exert her "all-enlivening influence" (l. 34) not only over the poems submitted to their "Delphic Vase" (l. 33) but also over the lives of the Millers themselves. She characterizes them as patrons of the arts, Sir John's taste confirmed by his choice of mate and Lady Miller's by her ability to attract so many fine poets to her villa (ll. 37–40). She begs Thalia to ensure the continued prosperity of their literary enterprise (ll. 43–44) as well as their continuing health and happiness by gilding their lives with "beams of bliss" (l. 48). The address confirms that Seward considered Lady Miller her patron not

because she received financial reward from her but because she provided Seward
with an appreciative audience and a select venue in which to present her work.
Despite her wish for Thalia's inspiration, however, the poem declines somewhat
from the technical fireworks of the first stanza to its rather staid conclusion.
Seward had met Lady Miller before writing the poem but had not yet visited
Batheaston and was therefore unable to include the details of setting and ritual
that enrich other Batheaston poems. The final stanza cannot convey either the
deep familiarity of her first stanza's emulation of Milton or the visual appeal of
her salute to Kauffman in the second. The poem therefore ends on a rather flat
note—but not before demonstrating Seward's grasp of Milton's comic techniques
as well as her ability to interpret visual imagery for her readers. Even if "Invocation of the Comic Muse" is less consistent than the previous Batheaston poems,
Seward was justified in presenting this clutch of winning poems to posterity as
equivalent to the masterpiece by which a craftsman proves his skill, concluding
her years as an apprentice poet by competing at the Millers' salon. From the sublime and tragic to the witty and comic, and in an array of genres and stanzaic
forms, Seward's Batheaston poems display abilities far beyond the amateur. She
had mastered eighteenth-century poetic kinds and techniques. Her status as a
poet, however, has been defined until recently not by her ability but by what succeeding generations perceived as her identity, that of an amateur gentlewoman
residing in a provincial town. My next chapter elaborates Seward's identity as a
professional writer seeking national renown, concluding with her elegiac tribute
to Lady Miller, whose support of Seward stretches our definitions of patronage.

CHAPTER THREE

The Profession of Poetry

In *Men's Work*, Linda Zionkowski outlines the process through which, over the course of the eighteenth century, writing gradually became defined as manly work (210). In many ways, of course, the gendering of "professional" as masculine and "amateur" as feminine was a fictional creation. For example, women were perhaps less likely than men to write, teach, or perform musically for payment, but numbers of them did so. For poets, as Zionkowski demonstrates in *Men's Work*, the process was particularly torturous. Samuel Johnson's pronouncement that "no man but a blockhead ever wrote, except for money" (Boswell 3:19) seems deliberately forgetful of the fact that a generation before, even so renowned a poet as Alexander Pope posed as a gentleman amateur rather than lose caste by defining himself as a professional writer. Johnson's remark may have been facetious, an example of his fondness for witty retorts. But much like the concept of sensibility, amateurism devolved from positive to negative as it was gendered feminine.[1] Amateurism, initially associated with privileged gentlemen, became the term for performances by gentlemen and ladies who were not only sheltered from salutary competition in the marketplace but who presumably could not have prospered in such a critical environment. As Zionkowski shows, women were caught in a double bind by this shift. Traditionally assessed in terms of their personal rather than their literary qualifications, women poets were praised most when their writings could be excused as the products of leisure time and their publications as exceptions to otherwise retired lives. When leisure and retirement were no longer viewed as concomitant with poetic excellence and criteria such as steady labor, sustained output, and commercial appeal came to be exalted instead, women poets suffered more than men owing to conventions as to what counted as acceptable feminine behavior, which made conformity with the new norms problematic.[2]

Other factors besides the new esteem for professionalism contributed to women's effacement. In *The Contours of Masculine Desire*, Marlon Ross tracks the gradual re-creation of poetry toward the century's end as the province of lone, superior men's minds rather than the product of gifted and social men and women. Typical among earlier poets, John Dryden had prided himself on his close relationship with members of Charles II's court. He spoke in his poems as representative of the Stuarts; his satires upheld their policies and preferences as norms breached by Charles's opponents. Dryden's support for the Stuart family extended so far that he converted to Catholicism upon James II's ascension to the throne, an act of loyalty that shortly cost him his laureateship and most of his income when James abdicated and William and Mary succeeded him. In the next generation, Alexander Pope spoke as a representative first of Queen Anne's supporters and, later, of the opposition formed to dislodge Robert Walpole, prime minister under George I and II, from power. Both Dryden and Pope would have been astonished by the conception of poets as necessarily distanced from contemporary social and political life. Their highly traditional view of the poet as spokesperson for the views of a ruling class or of the opposition was compatible with women's emergence into the poetic marketplace. Women could not be disdained for expressing their loyalty to the royal family or its opponents, especially when their poems also supported Christian virtues. They had certainly done so, in print, since the Protestant Revolution, a trend encouraged by the circumstances surrounding the Civil War, Interregnum, and Restoration. Women, embedded in family and social networks, might speak comfortably within and for these circles. Moreover, their works could achieve large readerships by circulating in manuscript or could yield needed income through subscription campaigns among women's networks.[3] When circumstances changed and such publication methods lost prestige and when the poet's presumed point of view shifted to that of a solitary observer of the natural scene or a dissenter from social conventions, women necessarily lost ground. If the archetypal poet was now William Wordsworth poised over an abyss amidst the Welsh peaks, Lord Byron musing before Roman ruins, or Charlotte Smith gazing over a cliff during a midnight storm, then the typical lady, hardly ever expected to venture forth without a servant or companion, had no hope of approaching, let alone fulfilling, that ideal.

Anna Seward, although esteemed by contemporaries as among the most prominent female poets of the late eighteenth century, witnessed completion of the trajectory from positive, masculine to pejoratively viewed, feminine amateur.

John Brewer contests the latter view of amateurism in his magisterial *The Plea-sures of the Imagination*. He devotes a chapter to Anna Seward as the ultimate representative of a culture of letters, centered in the provinces rather than in London, which fostered liberal ideals of excellence, as well as of participation, in literature. Brewer's admiring and sympathetic analysis pits Seward as the pro-vincial Whig amateur against Johnson as the urban Tory professional, a doomed contest for literary influence but one that Seward fought in an unrelenting cam-paign of poems, letters, and critical articles. Brewer's persuasive study apparently leaves few avenues for development regarding Seward's career and subsequent disappearance from literary history and therefore inadvertently consigns her to oblivion. One area, however, that he remarks little on and that I discuss here is the gendered nature of critical remarks about Seward's career. Brewer omits this dimension because he focuses on Seward's provincial and Whig affiliations that were opposed to the urban and Tory associations of so much "professional" writ-ing. But he could easily have added the term "feminine" to those of Whig and amateur, because subsequent writings about Seward so frequently dismiss her as a bluestocking or poetaster. Gendering the discussion of amateurism elucidates contemporary observations, including Seward's, of her career. By complicating the notion of amateurism, which helps to reconstruct the perspective of Seward and many contemporaries, we can more accurately assess her writings. In par-ticular, ideas about feminine amateurism influenced public estimates of Seward's first semi-public venue, Lady Miller's poetic assemblies at Batheaston. After com-plicating but at the same time clarifying, I hope, Seward's place in the contempo-rary professional-amateur continuum, I conclude this chapter with a reading of Seward's appreciative elegy *To the Memory of Lady Miller*. Seward and Lady Miller's relationship provides an unusual example of the multiple forms patron-age took throughout the eighteenth century, including—as in Seward's case—influence and encouragement instead of the financial assistance that often but did not always constitute patron-client bonds until the client was able to establish an "independent" professional career.[4]

A number of studies reveal that amateurism and professionalism were still fluid concepts in the late eighteenth century. The Romantic era's emphasis on the poet as a lone creator made even more problems for women, however, than the call for adherence to decorous publication methods and social conventions. As Mar-garet Ezell has demonstrated in *Social Authorship and the Advent of Print*, many gentlemen and ladies throughout the century preferred to share the act of author-ship and to exchange their collaborative verse in manuscript rather than to print as sole authors. Teresa Barnard has explained that Seward herself participated in at least one manuscript circle of this kind (*Anna Seward* 110). In *Family Authorship and Romantic Print Culture*, Michelle Levy has examined how the demise of manuscript publication was hastened by the new paradigm of solitary creativity (3). Levy's focus is on family authorship rather than on the friendly circles in which Seward participated, but her conclusions are pertinent. She follows families such as the Wordsworths, Coleridges, and Shelleys, demonstrating how in each case, as he established his fame, the male writer worked to cloak his former participation in the group enterprise. Levy deprecates the resulting loss of acknowledgment for many women whose contributions to their male relations' publications were obscured or denied. She admits nevertheless the appeal of "the authorial persona" (9). Eventually, "it won Wordsworth a dedicated following, while for Byron it was immediately successful. There is also reason to think that some female authors, anxious to establish their own reputations, were drawn to it as well" (9). Seward was one such author; she obscured the contributions of her manuscript circle to her first publication and resented Erasmus Darwin's efforts to take partial credit for its composition. Seward thus anticipated the Romanticists' vogue, although it would certainly be incorrect to state that Seward "laundered" her collaborative poems at Batheaston as one would obscure the origins of money in a Swiss bank. But her Batheaston performances were a definitive step away from coterie writing and toward a culture in which individual writers claimed their productions. Seward's decision to distinguish herself as an "individual genius" (Levy 2) belies Brewer's mournful description of her determination to champion provincial amateurism even while poets of that description were becoming obsolescent. The deceptively stark and gendered distinctions between Seward's career and that of Samuel Johnson, her Lichfield-born nemesis, show how difficult it is to make generalizations about a privileged and ambitious woman born in the mid-eighteenth century and seeking poetic fame on the cusp of the Romantic era.

   If Samuel Johnson's career suggests the archetypal journey of an eighteenth-century professional man of letters, Seward's just as certainly epitomizes that of the genteel woman of letters. Johnson's march to London accompanied by David Garrick became the stuff of legend. His years of hack writing for Edward Cave's *Gentleman's Magazine*, his lone compilation of the *Dictionary*, his subsequent fame and the pension that ended years of poverty, all radiate "masculine" attributes such as endurance, solitariness, learnedness, and magisterial self-confidence. Scholars have often disputed the facts behind the Johnsonian myth as it appeared to contemporaries, especially after publication of Boswell's biography. But the journey to London followed by unrelenting, anonymous toil before emergence as Britain's literary colossus came to be seen as the very trajectory of a professional

writer's life. And although a number of women writers, from Aphra Behn to Charlotte Lennox, also traveled to London where they established careers, their labors
were never rewarded with the kind of success or reputation that finally distinguished Johnson's. Since women rarely possessed the learning or belonged to
the literary clubs that established such reputations, to mention only two barriers,
the masculine character of Johnson's professional career is not surprising. Even
young Johnson's initial venture would have been difficult if not impossible for an
unprotected young woman, especially one who regarded herself as a lady. Such
female travels had a questionable reputation, associated with characters like Moll
Hackabout in Hogarth's *The Harlot's Progress*, who after her arrival in London
quickly falls prey to a procuress. The picaresque journey of an impoverished
young writer to London was an essentially masculine story, despite the instances
of women whose desperation or ambition led them to attempt the same route.

Seward's entry into the publishing world followed an altogether different path,
a path as "feminine" as Johnson's was apparently masculine. Seward, discouraged
from writing in late adolescence by parents who feared its impact on her mar-
riageability, was dejected by 1778 after her sister's and mother's deaths and the
departure of foster sister Honora Sneyd following her marriage. Her chosen suitors having been rejected by her father and she having rejected his choices in turn,
Seward had evidently decided against marriage and to persist instead in her close
friendship with John Saville. As hostess of her father's literary circle at the Bishop's
Palace and member of a supportive group of local poets in Lichfield, the thirty-
six-year-old Seward had neither need nor incentive to pursue a London-based
career. Instead, she accepted an invitation from Lady Miller to submit a poem for
one of her poetry contests. Seward's poem won first prize and led to several appearances at the Millers' assemblies, subsequent contest entries, and eventual publications in Lady Miller's Batheaston anthologies and national periodicals such as
the *Gentleman's Magazine*. Once an established writer, Seward maintained her
national literary reputation by publishing in various genres (poetry, criticism, biography) while remaining in Lichfield for her whole life.

The contrast between Seward's and Johnson's careers could not be more striking. While Johnson traveled to London, and specifically to the heart of "Grub
Street," Seward traveled away from the capital, to the spa town of Bath. While
Johnson engaged with Cave to produce a stream of works ranging from a translation of Father Paulo Sarpi's *History of the Council of Trent* to ghost-written tran-
scripts of Parliamentary debates, Seward entered a light-hearted contest, apparently to gauge her poetry's appeal amid a like-minded group of gentlemen and
ladies. Johnson endured the rough-and-tumble world of professional journalism,

competing for public attention but specializing in work that capitalized on his knowledge of languages and broad range of interests. Seward likewise destined her writings for a national audience but submitted her writings to "the Mag" because it was her selected publishing venue, not for the pay. Unlike Johnson, Seward shared the popular predilection for poems of sensibility. While Johnson's articles were usually anonymous because that was the norm for staff writers, Seward's were often anonymous by her choice for purposes of decorum. Johnson was mentored by Cave and established friendships with fellow hack writers such as Richard Savage. Seward was encouraged by Lady Miller and befriended other genteel writers, such as T. S. Whalley and William Hayley, whom she met at the Millers' Batheaston salon. At each point, the early careers of Johnson and Seward read like opposing, masculine and feminine, versions of the literary life. There were women writers, of course, whose careers resembled Johnson's. Charlotte Smith toiled throughout her adult life to support her family without ever achieving financial stability, let alone a government pension. Mary Wollstonecraft attempted careers as a governess and as a schoolteacher before joining Joseph Johnson's stable of paid writers. But while Smith and Wollstonecraft opted to compete in a largely masculine arena, Seward maintained her distance, to the detriment of her reputation today.

Johnson and Seward actually had many opinions and qualities in common, as Brewer observes. Both enjoyed "talking for victory" (although presumably Seward's less brutal diatribes were mostly epistolary), and both extolled the superiority of British literature. But the contrasting schemata of their initial forays into the world of letters seemingly define "typical" masculine and feminine careers, if such a division were possible. One career begins with a search for employment at fairly low wages; the other features submission to a select private jury in quest of peer applause. Both require willingness to undertake assigned topics, but while the male covers public-interest stories, the female composes flattering lyrics on themes such as the comic muse. One career demands exposure to a range of people and experiences; the other shelter among select acquaintances. The masculine writer submits to harsh critical scrutiny and emerges triumphant because he has even more stringent personal standards; the feminine writer attempts to control public exposure through anonymous, provincial, and/or subscription publication and conforms to popular taste. One is "professional"—he has competence and earns a livelihood, while the other is "amateur"—she has less-practiced skills and an avocational status.

In describing these contrasts, I have used terms such as "myth" and "scheme." One reason I have already mentioned is that the careers of neither Johnson nor

Seward can be so neatly categorized. Another is, as I have noted, that there were numerous women professional writers and even more male amateurs. But the feminization of amateurism, with its attendant loss of status, does not refer literally to amateur writers' gender but to the feminine qualities associated with a kind of writer who represents "the Other" to the "masculine" professional writer. To understand how Seward became a prime example of the amateur writer, we should first examine contemporary references to Lady Miller and her assemblies and then review Seward's elegy for Lady Miller. By championing Lady Miller, Seward consciously allied herself with her culture's definition of the feminine. Yet despite attempts to split writers into "amateur" and "professional" categories, writing and publishing were still fluid enough to warrant a more complicated understanding of these activities in respect to individual careers. Although Seward lived in Lichfield and did not depend on the profits of her publications, she most likely did not understand herself to be an "amateur" in the sense of an unpracticed or less skillful writer. As someone who aspired to national prominence, she would no doubt have rejected the pejorative connotations that were becoming associated with amateur status even in her lifetime. Unless we recover and attend to the older sense of amateurism and refuse to devalue women's amateurism simply because it is "feminine," we will have difficulty recovering a true estimate of Seward's writings.

Seward's early twentieth-century biographers were certain that her gifts would have been better served by exposure to the competitive environment of London. As E. V. Lucas remarked, "Everything conspired to increase Miss Seward's self-esteem and importance; for the three things that might have corrected it were all lacking to her: poverty, London life, and marriage. When a vain single woman is in a position to fortify herself in the provinces behind ramparts of admirers she is in a dangerous way. Miss Seward early fell a victim and never recovered" (321). Whether poverty and marriage would have enhanced Seward's literary productions is debatable, as the careers of Charlotte Lennox and Charlotte Smith will suggest. Virginia Woolf decisively refuted that notion in *A Room of One's Own* not long after Lucas endorsed it. Women of straitened means were burdened then as men were not by daily familial cares. Poor laboring women usually returned home in the evening to a range of household chores, and even genteel women found it difficult to withdraw for the purpose of writing. The assumption that marriage, poverty, and London would have improved Seward's character and stimulated her genius seems once again based on a "masculine" archetype, such as that of Johnson's struggle to support his wife by moving to London, thereby embarking on one of the capital's fabled literary careers while maintaining her in genteel, if modest, premises. Anna Seward was in fact privileged to command a private room in the Bishop's Palace where she read and wrote, although she conscientiously kept family accounts, hosted visitors, produced decorative needlework, and generally earned her opportunities for private correspondence and composition. She managed her father's care until his death in 1790, after which she presided as head of the household.[5] In short, the assumption that life in Lichfield brought Seward constant adulation, thereby diminishing the potential quality of her writing, is absurd despite the collective agreement on this point by her early chroniclers. In fact, for many years she endured her parents' injunctions against writing and, as she noted to correspondents, in her maturity she spent a great deal of time running her household, which hindered her writing more, presumably, than did the volleys of praise she received from friends.

Seward, however, persisted in writing throughout her youth, and eventually, when marriage no longer seemed probable, her father evidently relaxed his objection. At this juncture, in 1778, she complied with Lady Miller's invitation to participate in a Batheaston contest, the first exposure of her poetry to an audience other than her family, close friends, and mentors. Why choose such a venue rather than seek immediately the wider readership of London? Even the avowedly timid Frances Burney, albeit through an elaborate subterfuge to conceal her identity, submitted *Evelina* to a publisher and entered the literary marketplace. Seward, like Burney, had been writing secretively for years, and like the novelist required courage to seek an audience beyond her immediate circle. But Burney's circumstances were different. As the daughter of a musicologist scrambling to maintain a genteel household, Burney had less social capital to lose by appearing in public, although she found the process agonizing. Residing in London, she had readier access to its publishers than Seward did. The novel, too, was a relatively new genre, one that women had participated in ever since its origin in the seventeenth-century French romance. Except in exceptional cases like Samuel Richardson's, the novel had not historically circulated in manuscript, was not perused like poetry by restricted groups of readers. Instead, the novel was among the preeminent products of print culture, designed not for connoisseurs but for mass readership.

Although Barbara Benedict has reminded us that poetry became just another mass-produced commodity in the eighteenth century, as likely to be cranked out by hacks as composed by leisured gentlefolk, Margaret Ezell has cautioned that some writers preferred manuscript circulation to such commodification (Benedict 63–82; Ezell, *Social Authorship* 121). While to us the situation appears questionable—why indulge in parlor games instead of seeking professional publication from the outset?—Seward's context appeared differently to herself. Unlike the novel, for which no learning was required and which had as yet a comparatively low status among genres, poetry still claimed its high generic status, requiring at its best great technical skill and, preferably, a classical education. In other words, poetry maintained its "masculine" affiliation despite the fact that numbers of women had published their verse. A female poet still understood herself to be practicing a masculine art. As a gentlewoman whose father was the canon residentiary of Lichfield Cathedral, Seward might have chosen to make her debut at Lady Miller's villa partly because her contests were merely a step beyond manuscript circulation within a polite circle and thus compatible with the traditional method sanctioned for publication of gentlewomen's verse. A second reason is that by limiting her initial audience, she tested her social reception after many Lichfield associates had rebuffed her on account of her attachment to Saville. Another reason is that Seward did not desire association with "mass-produced" poetic hack work but with the kind of verse admired by gentlemen and ladies, who, like the visitors her father welcomed to his parlor at the Bishop's Palace, esteemed literature and intellectual exchange. Such was the company she expected to meet at Lady Miller's famously selective parties.

Although Seward did not write to earn her living, as did Samuel Johnson for many years, neither did other prolific eighteenth-century writers such as Jonathan Swift and Ann Radcliffe. Swift resembled many writers in deriving his income from his profession outside literature, while Radcliffe earned enormous sums for her novels but was independent because her spouse was a prosperous journalist. Early in the century, Alexander Pope had earned a small fortune for his Homeric translations through a combination of poetic genius, patronage, and canny business dealings. He then spent the rest of his career celebrating his financial independence and mocking those who wrote for their daily bread. Like many exceptional people, he did not recognize the degree to which his achievement was unusual. Throughout the century a growing number of writers, from Daniel Defoe to Mary Wollstonecraft, wrote for booksellers and managed to support themselves, although few duplicated Pope's feat of acquiring independent wealth through their writings. More often, writers like Charlotte Lennox and Charlotte Smith wrote indefatigably but achieved only meager incomes in relation to the needs of their families. Few poets could be considered "professional" in the sense of earning a genteel living solely through the proceeds of their poems. Some parlayed literary success into other enterprises: James Beattie launched his political career in the wake of *Ossian*, and Ann Yearsley evidently "used the proceeds from her later writings" to establish a circulating library in Bristol.[6] It is therefore inaccurate to assume that Seward was an amateur or a poetaster simply because she volunteered her critical contributions to the *Gentleman's Magazine* and was not dependent on her poems' sales. Thomas Gray, William Mason, William Cowper, Joseph and Thomas Wharton, and William Lisle Bowles were among those with similar publication profiles.[7]

Seward no doubt considered herself "professional" not in our sense of earning a living through the practice of writing but in the sense that she was an accomplished, nationally recognized writer. Her poetry was widely read, each publication going through several editions in both Britain and America.[8] It was also deemed worthy of close attention by all the principal reviewers, who often lavished her writings with praise. Seward regarded herself as an experienced practicing poet, an identity frequently on display in her correspondence with various protégés. Throughout the active years of her career, she delighted in advising and promoting young poets. She was exhilarated, for example, in 1788 when, at fifteen, the "young bards" Henry Cary and Thomas Lister began writing and publishing in Lichfield. Seward entertained the young men, encouraged them despite familial objections to their absorption in poetry, and "puffed" them among influential friends such as William Hayley and George Hardinge. She worked to convert the young poets to her opinions, as when Cary evidently complained about Mason's strictures on Johnson's *The Lives of the Poets*: "I hope and trust, my dear Cary, that the time will come when witty sarcasm, and splendid periods will no longer have power to dazzle your judgment against the claims of your predecessors, and to make you fancy that none have a right to speak as freely of Johnson, as he spoke of others, who were even greater in point of genius than himself" (*Letters* 2:145). More often than impressing her opinions on young writers, she offered specific advice about matters such as diction, as when she advised Cary that "[Robert] Burns is honoured by your having adopted his word 'chittering;' yet I know not if it is well to apply the epithet generally to so sweet a songster [as the red-bird]" (*Letters* 2:159).

Seward also advised several young women regarding their careers. She was especially fond of Helen Maria Williams, coaching her as she had Cary in matters of style. For Williams's poem on the slave trade, published in 1789, Seward had much praise, but added that "perhaps I could wish this poem of yours had been written in the ten-feet couplet. . . . I think that of eight feet requires the frequent intermixture of the line of seven syllables . . . to give spirit and variety to the measure" (*Letters* 2:248). In 1793, Seward complied with the request of Reverend Richard Sykes for advice to his protégée Miss Cayley with minute directions about prosody, instructing the young woman, for example, "that frequently to begin a line, and frequently to close one with a verb-active, gives impressive strength to versification" (*Letters* 3:322–23). She graciously closed her advice by urging Miss Cayley to learn by imitating "the best models, not with servile minuteness, but with generous emulation and critical attention," adding "these are the habits with which I cultivated my own little poetic stock" (*Letters* 3:324). Seward's letters to beginning poets exude generosity, as she was attentive and willing to share her carefully developed principles. They also demonstrate the confidence of a poet who, despite her professed modesty, considered herself a master of her craft. She took women writers as seriously as men, assuming that a Miss Cayley might develop into a fine poet as plausibly as might Henry Cary or Thomas Lister.

Seward's confidence also materializes in exchanges with peers. She argued confidently for her opinions, as when she began a letter to Dr. Gregory in 1787 with "And now, Sir, our day of combat is come.—You deny Sterne originality—and say no classic ear can endure his style. These assertions more than surprise—they astonish me" (*Letters* 1:375). Seward proceeded to battle Gregory's prejudice with conviction and spirit. Even revered contemporaries such as Hayley, whom she has been accused of flattering, received detailed analyses of each publication that mingled acerbic criticism with enthusiastic praise. When Hayley published a poem commemorating the hundredth anniversary of the Glorious Revolution, for example, Seward commended his effort but also shared cavils both technical ("'science-pointed steel' does not instantly present the image of a gun being fired") and philosophical ("forgive me for owning that I could have wished the two lines, which bring the humanity of William into competition with the mercy of God, had been omitted") (*Letters* 2:191). Seward's exchanges with peers never exhibit the kind of "feminine" modesty that shied from maintaining a conviction or that deferred to men simply because they were supposedly more intelligent by virtue of their sex. She did, in fact, confess to errors of fact or opinion when her correspondent presented undeniable evidence to the contrary. But her capitulations were based on reason, not feminine deference. Her bracing epistolary exchanges amply demonstrate that Seward considered herself a peer among peers; she no doubt thought of herself as one among the "rich . . . galaxy of poetic stars" that had graced Britain "within the last half century" that she describes in defending the poets of her time against the charge of "weakened nature" and "exhausted art" (*Letters* 1:186).

Although Seward did not need to bargain with publishers regarding the profits from her works, she was attentive to the publication process. She published in Lichfield not to prevent their wide circulation (on the contrary, she eagerly awaited the London reviews of each work) but so she could more easily communicate with her publisher. She assiduously corrected her own proofs in the belief that neither the typesetters nor even professional proofreaders would do justice to her poems. Although she contemplated leaving her sonnets and Horatian paraphrases in manuscript, she finally printed them because, as she explained to Sarah Ponsonby, "they would not so well have escaped from press-errors beneath the eye of a posthumous editor" (*Letters* 5:230). Seward placed a high value on her writings. At the time of her death, she was engaged in negotiations with Archibald Constable regarding a complete edition of her works. When Constable, aware of changing poetic fashion, offered to print a two-volume edition of her poems for a payment of £130, she resisted his plan. She wished him to purchase either the copyright to all her poems for 600 guineas or the copyright to all her verse and prose, except her letters, for £1,000 (Ashmun 257–60). Constable refused her offer, and their negotiations ended with her death. But Seward's efforts were certainly not those of a retiring lady amateur, wistfully contemplating posthumous honors. Her correspondence with Constable, as with her literary acquaintances, reveals Seward's pride in her career and her strong desire to receive the profit due to her as the author of popular and critically acclaimed works. While Seward may have commenced as what Brewer called an "amateur versifier" (573), her journey to Batheaston led her beyond merely amateur status to a career in the national literary arena. Just as she mingled "masculine" and "feminine" qualities in her writings and personality, so too Seward blurred the categories of amateur and professional in the manner familiar to her generation.

Lady Miller's sudden death created a challenge for Seward. The event demanded a tribute from the now-famous elegist, but it also required great tact. Seward's *To the Memory of Lady Miller* (1782) blends masculine and feminine characteristics in her typical manner while acknowledging her mentor's crucial influence. Seward's tribute appropriately commemorates the patron at whose salon she evidently first read her *Elegy on Captain Cook* (1780) and *Monody on Major André* (1781). Batheaston's approval sanctioned her publication of these poems which established her national fame. Their debuts at Lady Miller's villa made a memorial tribute seem especially appropriate after the her unexpected death. Seward was aware that such an elegy would be perceived as unusual. Women were no strangers to the art of funeral panegyric, a traditional path to recognition and reward, which for many was its chief purpose. Since women were conventionally associated with domestic and occasional poems, deaths as well as births were familiar topics of their verse. Many women had commemorated the deaths of husbands and children as well as of noble patrons, celebrated writers, and others whose demise presented a decorous opportunity for publication.[9] To the

acceptably feminine task of lamenting the dead was added the supposedly masculine privilege of serving as representative public mourner, a role women might
fulfill by, for example, claiming to be the king's figurative children or spouses
under a regime in which the ruler represented his people's father or husband.
Women likewise invoked literal family or patron-client relationships in mourning
prominent figures, excusing their boldness by pleading exceptional sentiment.

   Therefore, it was not the fact that the elegy would be authored by a woman
that made Seward's decision to elegize Lady Miller unusual. Rather, Seward believed that "the marked inferiority of subject" of such a poem, succeeding her two
elegies on figures whose deaths had caused a national sensation, might seem anticlimactic. She was, moreover, keenly aware of the ridicule that had circulated
regarding Lady Miller's coterie. As she explained to Whalley, those who denigrated Lady Miller while she lived could not be expected to desist after her death,
and such detraction "never fails to descend upon those who dare defend the
claims of the deceased" (Hesselgrave 70–71). In other words, Seward's recently
established reputation might be tarnished were she to follow her elegies on two
heroes with a similar poem about her mentor, likewise a celebrity but as often the
object of ridicule as of acclaim. Publishing a tribute that acknowledged her personal esteem and gratitude required some courage because it might endanger by
association her own career. That Seward set aside her misgivings and published
her elegy demonstrates her loyalty, integrity, courage and self-confidence. She composed the 282-line elegy in 6-line stanzas, each with an a-b-a-b-c-c rhyme scheme,
a less monumental scheme than the Cook and André poems, which were both
composed in lengthy verse paragraphs of heroic couplets. While Cook's death
had given her the opportunity to create such unforgettable images as that of a
Tahitian queen mutilating herself before the explorer's *morai* (ceremonial altar)
and André's had inspired stirring rhetoric such as her accusation against General
Washington, Lady Miller's comparatively uneventful life offered little scope for
such colorful writing. Seward had to avoid, moreover, making any claims for Lady
Miller that might be perceived as exaggerated or that could create grounds for
humor.

   The resulting poem is appropriately subdued in tone and style, describing
Lady Miller's achievement in as unadorned a manner as the genre permitted
while making a claim for her distinctive worthiness. Although mocked by her
only twentieth-century biographer as "not much in the way of literature" (Ashmun 91), *To the Memory of Lady Miller* (*Poetical Works* 2:150–64) is actually a tour
de force, explaining Seward's indebtedness to a woman whose love of literary and
charitable activities provided a domestic balance to the international scientific and

martial exploits represented by men like Cooke and André. Seward begins her poem by acknowledging that elegiac tributes are usually reserved for warriors. But where does that practice leave women? Identifying herself, or rather her muse, in conventionally feminine terms as the poet who wove André's poetic shroud and embellished Cook's pyre (ll. 13–18), she implores the muses' help once more to assist in mourning "Laura," whose love of poetry and support of poets deserves their tribute. By identifying Lady Miller with her labors on behalf of poetry, Seward suggests the appropriateness of an elegy inspired by the very deities who most often preside over tributes to great or heroic men. As a kind of muse herself, Lady Miller, whose "heart . . . glow'd with all [the muses'] fires" (l. 23), is perhaps a more fitting subject for their mourning song than are warriors.

Seward describes Lady Miller's assemblies in refined but accurate terms. The Millers had attempted to re-create their home as a classical Roman villa, and Lady Miller was known to have decorated her ancient urn with ribboned swags of laurel. It is therefore no exaggeration when the poet reminds the muses that Lady Miller had often been seen "in her classic bowers, /Weav[ing] the rich myrtle round the early rose" to "grace . . . the festive hours" (ll. 25–28). Surely, Seward pleads, awakening the literary aspirations of elite youth is a feat deserving lyric praise. She characterizes the assemblies as "chaste revel[s]" (l. 40), an appropriate description of the Millers' light breakfasts. She compares their poetry readings to the morning devotions paid by ancients to Apollo, again an appropriate analogy given the ritualistic nature of the competition and the early hours at which the assemblies took place. Seward's portrait of Lady Miller captures many visitors' reports of her role in the contests:

> [B]ending o'er her vase, fair Laura seem'd
>   The smiling Priestess of the sacred Nine,
> As her green wreath she wove, to grace the Bard,
>   Whose sweet superior song might claim the wish'd reward.   (ll. 45–48)

The elegy's classical imagery, suggested by Lady Miller's association with the muses and by the Millers' emulation of life in an ancient villa, is less an example of contemporary poetic diction than an elegant compliment to a woman who would have appreciated the recognition.

Seward celebrates Lady Miller's poetic ambitions as well as her efforts to create a decorous ambience at her assemblies. She describes the Millers' well-known discouragement of inappropriate verse, no matter how clever, as their attempt "from sterling wit to clear each base alloy" (l. 65). Seward praises Lady Miller's high-mindedness, which enabled her to disdain "Pride's cold frown, and Fashion's

pointed leer;/... Envy's serpent lie, and Folly's apish sneer" (ll. 71–72). Seward
alludes to the known fact that each year drew more established writers to the
Millers' home, a retort to the London journalists' mockery. She situates herself
among those writers as a novice enticed to compete by Lady Miller's gracious
invitation. The Millers' encouragement is thus pointedly contrasted with the
fruitless jeers of their detractors, for their sponsorship of Seward conducted her
through "thy gentle ordeal's lambent flame" (l. 85) toward pursuit of national
recognition (ll. 85–90). Seward's ensuing list of poets associated with Batheaston
has since provoked critical mirth. "In these verses we see Miss Seward in a very
characteristic attitude," remarked Lucas, "for never throughout her life could she
resist a bad poet" (Lucas 145). But Seward's list—while as opaque to us as, for
example, the rolls of Charles II's opponents and supporters in Dryden's *Absalom
and Achitophel*—represents some of the decade's most esteemed poets. Edward
Jerningham, T. S. Whalley, Christopher Anstey, and William Hayley (who evidently never visited but sent poems at his wife's request) were considerable names,
although the succeeding generation all but obliterated them from literary history.
When the poem was published Seward might well have celebrated her friend by
boasting their association with her poetic institution. And of course her preceding
self-description as a successful aspirant to the Batheaston prize reminds readers
that Seward won her honors in gatherings that included such writers amid other
merely well-born guests.

   Having established Lady Miller's credentials as literary patron, Seward devotes
eight stanzas at the heart of the elegy to her charitable activities. The Millers
sponsored a fund for the paupers of Bath, supported partly by the proceeds from
Lady Miller's annual collections of prize-winning Batheaston poems. Seward describes Lady Miller's activities in lines that Lucas singles out for mockery (145) but
that are no more than a deserved compliment:

> When Fashion o'er her threw the shining vest,
>   When Pleasure round her trill'd the Syren song,
> The sighs of Pity swell'd her polish'd breast,
>   The tones of Mercy warbl'd from her tongue;
> She bade the fires of classic lore pervade
>   With charity's kind warmth, misfortune's barren shade.   (ll. 175–80)

Lady Miller could have chosen to concentrate solely on her successful and popular assemblies, building social connections and promoting young poets to the
exclusion of other activities. Since she demonstrably longed for social eminence,
such a preoccupation would have been almost predictable. Instead, she and her

husband took the lead in reviving an older charitable institution to which she dedicated the profits of each year's *Poetical Amusements* (Hesselgrave 35–36). While well-to-do ladies were expected to engage in charitable activities, Seward observes that the very parties that aggrandized Lady Miller contributed to her benefactions; she did not separate her charitable and social activities. Seward invokes Queen Philippa, Edward III's wife, as Lady Miller's prototype: when Edward threatened to murder all the captive burghers of Calais after a successful siege in 1347, Philippa intervened and saved their lives with her plea for mercy. "'Twas then thy virtues, loveliest queen, outshone/Thy Edward's victor-plume, waving o'er Gallia's throne!" (ll. 203–4). Seward compares Lady Miller's preference for charitable activity over pursuit of literary fame to Philippa's compassionate gesture (ll. 205–10).

At first, the comparison seems merely awkward. Sir John Miller was no Edward III; far from ambitious, he seems to have contentedly played host at his spirited wife's gatherings. The Millers' grand tour, undertaken to recover their finances during renovations to their villa, was hardly comparable to an invasion of France. And no matter how considerable the sums involved, raising money for the poor does not equal begging for the lives of captured enemies. But Seward does not apparently so much intend her readers to draw a parallel between Queen Philippa and Lady Miller as to see that the queen exemplified the priorities that Lady Miller tried to emulate in placing the demands of charity above "the shining vest" of fame or "the Syren song" of pleasure. Since Philippa apparently left the security of their strongholds more than once, accompanying Edward on campaigns in Scotland as well as in France and urging his compassion in both, she represents the principle of charitable exertion that Lady Miller imitated rather than the Batheaston lady's counterpart. By extending her role of society hostess into the domain of charity, Lady Miller imitated Philippa's practice of extending her role as queen consort by becoming an intercessor on behalf of the victims of her husband's conquests. Philippa also reiterates Seward's initial point that feminine activities are sometimes as worthy, or even more worthy, of elegiac praise than are the exploits of warriors and heroes. Seward's apparently odd choice of analogy thus serves as a unifying motif for her poem's theme.

Seward concludes her elegy with eleven stanzas devoted to praise of Lady Miller in her roles of daughter, wife, and mother. Even here Lady Miller's sociable nature is cause for praise. Just as she blended the social with the charitable, so Lady Miller blended her roles of parent and spouse with that of society hostess. Since society women were frequently accused of forsaking their domestic duties for activities such as shopping, flirting, gambling, and hostessing, Lady Miller's ability to perform as admirable parent as well as hostess and literary patron deserved special attention. Instead of characterizing her as distracted or competitive, Seward emphasizes Lady Miller's ebullience, a quality frequently observed in reports on her assemblies. Her personality irradiated her family's life:

> Where neither gloomy Care, nor noisy Strife,
>   Dark Spleen or haggard Jealousy were found;
> For Chearfulness and Love, with potent sway,
>   The Lares of thy hearth, chas'd ev'ry Fiend away.   (ll. 231–34)

Instead of inculcating the pleasures of dissipation or flirtation, Lady Miller's parties were infused with the "sweet domestic [comfort]" of her home. Her children learned the potency of "Chearfulness and Love" in securing happiness through their mother's good-natured example. Seward's description of Lady Miller's virtues recalls Pope's praise of Martha Blount's serene good humor in his "Epistle to a Lady," but in contrast to Martha Blount, Lady Miller exemplified those qualities without also maintaining the retirement and reserve that Pope celebrated as ideal feminine qualities. Instead, Lady Miller's hospitality beguiled her aging mother (ll. 249–52) and taught her children to distinguish true happiness from "dissipation's giddy circle" (l. 241). Seward leaves her readers with the image of Sir John, his children, and elderly Mrs. Riggs visiting Lady Miller's tomb, where they will "bend o'er the holy earth, and consecrate her urn!" (l. 282). The image is conventional, but it is also beautifully appropriate, recalling the image at the beginning of the poem of the living Lady Miller "bending o'er her vase," the "smiling Priestess" presiding over her poetry competitions (ll. 45–46). To "consecrate her urn" is therefore not only to honor Lady Miller's remains as if classically interred but also to honor her achievement at Batheaston. Lady Miller is worth remembering as an exemplary wife, mother, daughter, and philanthropist, but her championship of poetry at Batheaston, symbolized by its famous Roman urn, is her chief claim to the muses', and therefore to the public's, memorial honor.

The concluding stanza of Seward's elegy gracefully echoes the epitaph she composed for Lady Miller's monument in Bath Abbey. There, she wittily if conventionally urged the marble panel itself to "amidst the wrecks of time / Uninjured bear thy Miller's spotless name" (ll. 1–2; Hesselgrave 13). Seward lists her friend's virtues, first among them "truth and genius," followed by "love and pity," then "liberal charity and faith" (ll. 9–10; Hesselgrave 14). These are the same qualities Seward extols in her elegy, although in the poem she reverses their order so that the poem culminates in a focus on charity and concludes with a salute to Lady Miller's domestic love. Seward leaves no doubt, however, that the subject of her elegy should be remembered as a patron of the arts, a mentor who emphasized encouragement over criticism and thereby nurtured Seward's career among those of other aspiring poets. She makes no exaggerated claims regarding Lady Miller's gifts or accomplishments, and the poem's sole historic allusion describes a model for privileged women's charitable activities. By taking most of her imagery from the classical culture beloved by Lady Miller and using it to recall Lady Miller both living and deceased, Seward creates an organic pattern that unobtrusively brings her poem full circle at its conclusion. Both the queenly reference and the classical image of Lady Miller as Apollo's priestess emphasize her femininity, but they also speak to her worthiness as the subject of a tribute usually reserved for masculine exploits. Seward's mingling of classical and gothic, social and domestic, and masculine and feminine categories in her elegy captures the flux of poetic models, professional boundaries, and gender roles characteristic of late eighteenth-century British culture.

Lady Miller's death deprived Seward of a champion but not before Seward had established a national reputation based at first on her Batheaston triumphs. The women, both of whom nursed "masculine" ambition that tested but never flouted "feminine" propriety, were mutual benefactors. Lady Miller might have boasted her discovery of Seward, whose Batheaston debut led directly to prominence. Seward, however, emerged only after testing her poems before a select audience composed of both estimable writers and genteel tastemakers. A modern writer might admire Seward's strategy, which created a prepublication market among some of England's most sophisticated and fashionable consumers. She is habitually described as "amateur" because she chose, in midlife, to compete in Lady Miller's drawing room contests before venturing into print, even though if she lived today, we would admire the cleverness with which she pursued the professional goals of publication and critical acclaim. Thereafter, Seward limited her print appearances until the end of her life when she arranged her poems, some never published before, into a collected edition. She may therefore have agreed to call herself an amateur, a title that preserved her status as a wealthy gentlewoman. But Seward was not amateur in her skill, and certainly not in her ambition. Seward would have claimed amateur status in the older sense that denoted a genteel writer's privileged access to the learning and leisure required for genuine literary achievement, in contrast to the paid writer's drudgery. She would have repudiated the notion that amateurism necessarily entailed self-indulgence or the uncritical approval of a restricted circle. Batheaston did not function for Seward as the kind of place where a spoiled child might show off her uncertain skills among admiring friends. Rather, it provided a select testing ground where she might assess her poetry's impression on a sophisticated audience. Her poems competed against a wide range of verse, from awkward riddles to hasty but accomplished submissions. She won a number of prizes owing to the artistic virtuosity and cleverness she brought even to these poems limited in finish by their two-week deadlines and in scope by their assigned topics. Within these restrictions, she was able to display real ingenuity as well as mature skill. Seward's poems, like all the Batheaston poems, have been mocked for their invariable compliments to the Millers. But because most poets have written complimentary verse for patrons or addressed to family, friends, or heroes, such mockery is not to be taken as the verdict on Batheaston's or any other occasional verse. Seward's Batheaston poems were not only accomplished. They also launched her toward a career that she would have recognized as "amateur" because she was never required to publish as well as "professional" in our modern sense because she possesses virtuosity and pursued a national readership and critical admiration. Batheaston served Seward as the threshold between manuscript and print culture; it poised her characteristically— and successfully—between the patterns of her earlier eighteenth-century youth and late-century maturity.

CHAPTER FOUR

British Patriot

Just as Anna Seward's approach to publication via Batheaston challenges our twenty-first-century notions of Romantic-era amateurism, professionalism, and careers, so too knowledge of eighteenth-century poetics challenges aesthetic standards that some have used to categorize her as a mediocre poet, as a careful reading proves her to have been quite accomplished by her century's criteria. In this chapter, I show how Seward's work usefully complicates some of our current ideas about late eighteenth-century women's domestic identities as well as their political roles and opinions, specifically, the idea that women poets preferred to adopt a domestic identity when addressing the nation. Seward's patriotic elegies, the foundation of her contemporary fame, represented interventions during an ongoing political crisis. These influential poems performed a cathartic function of venting strong public emotions during Britain's tragic war against her North American colonies. Crucially, Seward used what later generations would devalue as sentimentalism to shape Britain's heroes and in turn to shape British readers' conception of heroism. These and other patriotic poems cast Seward as British muse, spokeswoman for national anguish, pride, and resolve. The speaker in her poems does not conform to the role of domestic muse recently proposed as the niche women poets created for themselves when addressing national issues.[1] Instead, as elegiac speaker, Seward apparently satisfied the century's demand for a voice genuinely sorrowful yet able to model for readers the appropriate sensations with which to respond to noteworthy deaths.[2]

Walter Scott rather ambiguously states that Batheaston approval of her poems "gave Miss Seward courage to commit some of her essays to the press; and the public received with great favour the elegiac commemorations of André and of Cook" (Seward, *Poetical Works*, 1:xi). Did the elegy on Cook, at least, as Teresa Barnard speculates, originate in a collaborative circle of Lichfield-area poets? As Barnard remarks, such a genesis would account for Erasmus Darwin's claim to have coauthored the poem, although by publishing the work under her name, Seward was claiming the chief part of its composition (*Anna Seward*, 122–23).[3] Scott's remark leaves room for conjecture regarding the poems' composition, which Seward herself obfuscated after their publication. Her reluctance to specify the Cook elegy's collaborative origin anticipates the practice, as I've noted, of Romantic-era authors who obscured their publications' genesis in familial projects, as observed by Michelle Levy (2). Certainly Seward could not have composed poems that are as polished and as long as the finished elegies in just the two weeks that Lady Miller allotted to contestants to write their poems. At any rate, both are attributed to Batheaston by Seward's biographers, further evidence of that institution's stimulus to her creativity and self-confidence.[4] Although occasional in nature, and thus among the genres deemed appropriate for women poets, both poems also belong to the tradition of published elegies on the deaths of great national figures, a tradition in which women had long participated for a host of reasons, such as to honor a friendship or to secure patronage.[5] Whether undertaken for the sake of personal respect or the hope of reward, such poems claimed to represent collective sentiment and therefore invited public notice. In publishing her timely celebrations of two beloved figures, Seward was announcing her personal ambition to command the attention of not merely her Lichfield circle or the Batheaston guests but of the nation. If the poems Seward produced at Batheaston stand as examples of her poetic apprenticeship, her Cook and André poems are the masterpieces confirming her mature skills. They also satisfied her wish for a national rather than a regional or provincial reputation. By emerging in spectacular fashion through these poems—the elegy for Cook went through five editions by 1784—Seward demonstrated her command of current poetic expectations. Perhaps more significantly, she participated in what Linda Colley has described as the century's national struggle to define what it meant to be a Briton, and not just an English, Welsh, or Scottish man or woman.[6]

⸺⟡⟡⸺

In January 1780, when the news reached London of Cook's death the previous February, Britain was enmeshed in an apparently losing battle to retain her empire's chief possession, the American colonies. The conflict, as Colley notes, caused massive consternation among Britons accustomed to believing that the British adherence to Protestantism made their colonial enterprises superior to those of the French and Spanish(142–43). The prospect of losing a war against territory principally occupied by white British Protestants forced many Britons to reconsider the grounds of their patriotism. Colley describes the next several decades as an overwhelmingly successful effort by everyone from the monarch to the laboring classes to reconstruct Britain's claim to global eminence. But as the American War approached its nadir, most Britons would have welcomed reassurance that their navy did indeed rule the waves thanks to qualities manifest in Cook: patriotism, diligence, curiosity, and above all, concern for humanity. As Suvir Kaul has argued, Britons throughout the century cherished an "'idea' of 'Great Britain'; of British greatness demonstrated not in dominance of Europe but across the globe; of a self-legitimating British greatness that exported enlightenment in exchange for the surplus of territories they controlled as traders or colonists" (269–70). While Kaul focuses on the anxieties manifest even in poems celebrating Britain's empire, Dustin Griffin has more recently demonstrated the leading role poets assumed throughout the century in disseminating the concept of patriotism, whether as loyal opponents to government policies or as thoroughgoing proponents of British greatness. Griffin argues that while much twentieth-century criticism posited the gradual withdrawal of poets from public discourse, a wealth of poems rebuts the myth of "'public' Augustan poetry and a 'private' poetry of late century" (293). Griffin warns critics that they ignore these poems at the risk of forming a less than "comprehensive, balanced, and historically accurate" image of eighteenth-century poetry. Seward's elegies, as well as her other poems about national figures and affairs, are certainly part of the poetic heritage that Griffin believes has been ignored. Ignoring them has not only distorted the record of eighteenth-century poetry; it has distorted our impression of Seward and her role as enunciator, and even shaper, of public opinion.

In a sensitive chapter of *Small Change*, Harriet Guest argues that Seward's elegies on Cook and André accomplish precisely the union of public and private utterance, a distinctive resolution of the dichotomy that Griffin explores. Guest suggests that Seward based her poems' authority on her personal identity as a retired gentlewoman who not only wrote poems and conducted a wide correspondence but did so "in conjunction with her diligence in private duties," leading her to "claim a peculiarly feminine social distinction that approximates to the professional ambition" of a gentleman (257). Seward, in Guest's view, believed her superior fulfillment of a domestic regimen justified self-comparison with an industrious professional man. Such an assumption would have reflected wide-spread contemporary belief, as chronicled by G. J. Barker-Benfield in *The Culture of Sensibility*, that refined ladies had an important role to play in reforming the coarser, usually masculine-identified, aspects of their culture.[7] The private lady paradoxically had a public mission based precisely on her retired status. Building on suggestions like Anne K. Mellor's that Romantic-era women writers primarily emphasized the private over the public realm (*Romanticism* 9–10), Guest argues that the "Britain" who mourns Cook in Seward's elegy is identified not with Britannia, the personified nation, but with his obscure widow: "The Elegy claims to express national but private sentiment" (259).

While I disagree with Guest about Seward's grounds for claiming poetic authority— Seward appealed to her superior literary skill as demonstrated at Batheaston rather than to a feminine social distinction—her reading is astute in several respects. Guest observes, for example, that Seward repeatedly disavowed the pursuit of literary fame on the grounds that she had household duties to attend to as well as the care of her debilitated father. Guest notes that Seward's stated domestic priorities apparently "license[d] the production of a huge correspondence, and a very considerable body of poetry, and an active involvement in a fairly intensive social life" (256). The fact that Seward selected and edited her correspondence before bequeathing it to Archibald Constable shows she was aware that readers would regard her filial devotion, so often mentioned in the letters, and superintendence of the Bishop's Palace, in which she took such pride, as integral to her future stature. Barnard has revealed that Seward's many references to nursing her father were exaggerated; in fact, servants cared for the ailing canon (*Anna Seward* 37–38). Guest also astutely observes that Seward's persona, both striking and unimpeachable, seems to have engaged public attention almost as much as, if not more than, her poems themselves. She cites critical as well as poetic tributes that decree Seward herself the British muse, "as though [Cook's and André's] status as national heroes accrued to her reputation" (253). Guest quotes Ashmun's remark that "the *Monody on Major André* reaped the reward of timeliness," a statement no less true of the Cook elegy, elaborating that the poem reassured "provincial liberal whigs" that there was a sort of " patriotic or national feeling . . . they might salvage from the war" (254). Guest concludes that Seward's reassurance capitalized on sentimental constructions of her heroes, as mourned in domestic privacy by their survivors and, by extension, in all British homes. This task was best enjoined by a retired domestic muse such as Seward herself.

Guest's reading surely defines much of these poems' appeal for their original readers. My reading of the poem differs somewhat from Guest's, but since a complicated poem will bear repeated analyses, mine contributes another per-spective on Seward's strategy in creating what contemporaries deemed a tour de force. My divergence from Guest's interpretation begins with the observation that while Seward indeed took pains to present herself to both intimates and the pub-lic as an exemplary lady, she based neither her poetic authority nor her poetic persona on domestic retirement. If that were so, the *Ladies Monthly Museum* article that Guest cites, sketching Seward after the publication of her sonnets in 1799, would not have lamented her decision to write poetry rather than marry and raise a family (255). Readers distinguished between Seward as accomplished writer and Seward as mistress of the Bishop's Palace. Seward herself seems to have believed not that her domestic activities authorized her to write poetry, any more than a gentleman's professional activities authorized him to write poetry, but that ladies, like gentlemen, had certain duties that were to be fulfilled before they could indulge in literary composition. Attending to those duties might, as Seward often observed, hamper both men and women in their creative efforts, but both must adhere to the established priorities of their separate spheres. As writers, how-ever, men and women shared the same standards, just as they shared the same genres and occasions for writing. The male or female writer spoke with the degree of authority established by his or her degree of virtuosity. Thus, Seward might hail T. S. Whalley for his sentimental gothic poem *Edwy and Edilda*, which seems to us quite "feminine" in its emotional emphasis, and also champion Helen Maria Williams for undertaking *Peru*, an epic (that chief and most "masculine" genre). While Guest is justified in calling attention to Seward's "female patriotism" (254), a description supported by Colley's observation of contemporary women's quest for a viable patriotic role (238–50), she seems to me to overstate the degree to which Seward intends her voice to "speak for the nation . . . because it is private" (267). This distinction is subtle but relevant to both Seward's characterization of the muses in the *Elegy on Captain Cook* and her final address to Cook's widow.

Cook's death, after his two previous voyages had yielded so much knowledge and conferred so much prestige on the British navy, must have come as a heavy blow to a public already demoralized by the American War's downward spiral. In her recent fine study of how Cook and his companions struggled to comprehend South Pacific cultures, Guest describes how Seward's elegy reflects her disillu-sionment with Britain's selfish colonial policies, to which Cook's practices seemed an antidote (*Empire* 145). Seward indeed consoled the nation with a poem mani-festly drawn from Cook's published records of his voyages (Seward notes her many paraphrases of his accounts) yet worthy of sentimental fiction. Reading the elegy, one is tempted to ask whether the poem was made for Cook or whether Cook—

including his adventures and his downfall—was made for the poem. The answer explains the elegy's tremendous popularity. Seward carefully tailored her brief version of Cook's expeditions so that the captain and his mission perfectly fulfilled both the most traditional rationale for British naval exploration and lived up to ideals of sentimental heroism current at the time. If, ten years before, Benjamin West's painting *The Death of General Wolfe* had "started a vogue for paintings of members of the British officer class defying the world, or directing it, or dying in battle at the moment of victory" (Colley 179), Seward offered the public a literary complement to such paintings in her depiction of Cook. Like West, she accomplished this feat by making an inspired selection of reported details that she then mixed with the poetic equivalents of West's visual stagecraft. Over two hundred years later, West's cleverness in selecting and posing certain figures around Wolfe must be rehearsed for viewers who are no longer aware of the scene's degree of fictionality and who are in any case too removed in time from the event to respond emotionally to its depiction. The *Elegy on Captain Cook* (*Poetical Works* 2:33–46) likewise benefits from some knowledge of the explorer and his voyages, if only to illuminate Seward's creativity in epitomizing ideas about heroism that prevailed at the time.

In many respects, Captain James Cook perfectly fulfilled the eighteenth-century conception (in fact, any era's conception) of heroism. As J. C. Beaglehole, Cook's chief modern editor and biographer, observes, Cook was for his time a remarkably humane master to his men (adherence to the customary punishment of flogging notwithstanding) as well as a humane visitor to the Pacific islands (706–7). Although his crew spent much of their discretionary time in the islands pursuing native women, Cook gave no thought to any woman but his wife Elizabeth (713). Cook was absorbed by navigation and geography and fascinated by botany and astronomy. He was a remarkably modern anthropologist who recorded such practices such as cannibalism but did not attempt to change those practices (358–59). In other words, he shared the enlightened pursuits of such groups as the Lunar Society and the Royal Society, the latter of which he was elected to in 1775 following his second voyage (450–51). He was quite passionate about his work (710). But in other respects Cook was an unpromising hero of sensibility. Beaglehole admits that Cook "was not . . . romantic, dramatic . . . imaginative. . . . He was the genius of the matter of fact" (698). Cook was eminently professional, competent, rational, and obedient to his superiors (698). Seward was manifestly transforming Cook's acknowledged concern for his sailors into the tears of sensibility when she described his imagined response to the breakup of a polar ice floe:

Appal'd he hears!—but checks the rising sigh,
And turns on his firm band a glist'ning eye.—
Not for himself the sighs unbidden break,
Amid the terrors of the icy wreck;
Not for himself starts the impassion'd tear,
Congealing as it falls.   (ll. 91–96)

Cook, as he emerges in his personal journals, was less likely to weep or sigh in such an emergency than to deal practically with the situation in a way that posed the least risk to his ship and crew. But a suppressed sigh and congealed tear, evanescent and thus irrefutable in any case, were eminently plausible to readers who assumed a connection between deep concern and physiological response.

Similarly, Seward conjures an imaginary lure for Cook in her description of London before his departure. She asks why the famed captain would leave the capital, "where Beauty moves with fascinating grace" (l. 25). As Beaglehole drily remarks, after describing the debut of Omai, a Tahitian youth who accompanied Cook to England and was promptly taken up by social leaders including the Duchess of Devonshire, who gave him a handkerchief, "Cook's own social life shone with less refulgence. He seems to have been indifferent to duchesses' handkerchiefs. He had, after all, a wife and family, and the few pieces of evidence that exist indicate that he was not indifferent to them" (449). London as Seward evokes it, with its ice cream, hot-house flowers, and opera performances (ll. 17–24), was in fact not likely to have deterred Cook. By all accounts, what stirred Cook into pursuing a third voyage while still exhausted from his second was hope of discovering the fabled northwest passage (and failing that, a northeast passage) that would open a swift trade route to Asia. Seward would have been well aware of this mission, reported in such accessible sources as Cook's obituary in her favorite *Gentleman's Magazine* ("Historical Chronicle" 44–45).[8] But while acknowledging the mercantile basis that inevitably motivated eighteenth-century voyages of discovery, Seward repeats the classic British defense of such exploration, familiar from poems and essays by Dryden, Addison, Pope, and Thomson, among scores of examples.[9] British exploration and the trade that comes with it are superior to those of any previous empire because they are motivated by humane purposes of mutual exchange. Seward establishes Cook as the culmination of this tradition.

At the poem's outset, Seward conjures the muses to explain Cook's motivation for undertaking his dangerous third voyage (ll. 15–17). In the first published edition of the poem, the answer is "Humanity!" (l. 35), but Seward subsequently replaced that word with "Benevolence." Perhaps she felt that the general sensitivity implied by her first choice did not convey the active charity suggested by her second, a posture more attractive to reform-minded contemporaries. Popular fiction, for example, abounded in heroes and heroines praised for generosity and compassion (Barker-Benfield 226). In his classic study of sentimental fiction, R. F. Brissenden identified benevolence as the sentiment that, for eighteenth-century thinkers, chiefly motivated human beings: "A person who cannot, or does not, wish to act benevolently, was thought to be less than human" (32). By defining Cook in terms of benevolence, Seward took to its sublime extreme a principle already associated with the explorer. Cook was well known for his charitable behavior toward native peoples; his *Gentleman's Magazine* obituary emphasizes "that he never knowingly injured, but always studied to benefit the savages whom he visited" (45). Having revealed Cook's motive, Seward expatiates on the compassion that drove him to seek out the "shiv'ring natives of the frozen zone" as well as "the swart Indian" (ll. 36–37) in order to "plant the rich seeds of [Benevolence's] exhaustless store" (l. 40).[10] Seward devotes thirty lines to praise of what Pope would have called Cook's ruling passion; in reality just one among numerous striking qualities of a complicated man but brilliantly selected by Seward as the focus of her portrait. Benevolent activity both defines her portrait of Cook and conflates him with the virtue Britons most liked to believe characterized their maritime activities.

Shortly after Seward published her Cook elegy, Hugh Blair defined the "moral, or sentimental sublime." In representations of magnanimous or heroic behavior, Blair explained, we recognize the sentimental sublime "wherever, in some critical and high situation, we behold a man uncommonly intrepid, and resting upon himself; superior to passion and to fear; animated by some great principle to the contempt of popular opinion, of selfish interest, of dangers, or of death" (215). Seward conveys the moral sublimity of Cook and his voyages not only by describing him as animated by benevolence but also through stylistic devices associated with epic. The epic poet conventionally sought the muses' assistance to reveal details beyond living memory or, in Milton's case, human knowledge. Seward's request in this case was justified, because her poem was published four months before the survivors of Cook's expedition arrived home to confirm the details of their experiences (Williams 334). She built her narrative around the facts reported in Captain Clerke's letter announcing Cook's death and from details in Cook's published journal of his second voyage, and she re-created his murder by extrapolating from both. The device of consulting the muses also permitted Seward to announce Cook's motive—or his fictional motive—otherwise inscrutable to all but intimates. Since, as we have observed, this motive was both plausible to ascribe to Cook and eminently desired in contemporary explorers, Seward's muse-born vision places the captain among epic peers. Benevolent Cook is the eighteenth-century counterpart of wily Odysseus and pious Aeneas.

Seward further establishes Cook's sublimity by emphasizing the voyages' extreme climatic range and by introducing personifications that impart a visionary quality to her descriptions. Benevolence, for example, is not only Cook's attribute but also a "Nymph divine!" (l. 59) directing his ship through perilous seas. A goddess presides over the South Pole, invisibly guiding Cook's ship through the ice much as Achilles and his ancient counterparts were assisted by their divine parents (ll. 75–76, 83–84). In New Zealand, the goddesses Flora and Fauna reveal species of plants and animals hitherto unknown to Europeans (ll. 174–90). Besides employing personifications that function like the classical deities, Seward frequently compares Cook's exotic adventures to those found in ancient myth and epic and even in the Bible that would have been more familiar to literate Britons. Cook's introduction of European plants and animals to New Zealand resembles Poseidon's gift to Athens of the horse (ll. 129–34). The naturalist's fascination with the exotic plants and animals along New Zealand's rocky coast, from which Cook prudently but regretfully steered away, is compared with Odysseus's resistance to the Sirens (ll. 195–200). Tahiti is "the smiling Eden of the southern wave" (l. 211), complete with bowers and hovering cupids (ll. 202–4). The composers of ancient epic invoked analogies with familiar domestic or agricultural scenes in such extended comparisons in order to give their mostly rural audiences some conception of warfare or prolonged voyages. In Seward's poem, ironically, ancient tales of divine intervention function to convey Cook's uncanny wisdom in preserving his ships to an audience classically and biblically literate but unlikely to comprehend the dangers confronting contemporary sailors on the far side of the globe. The metaphors further associate Cook with the pattern of epic heroism, as the modern hero is surrounded, at least in imagination, by deities and he replicates experiences known only through ancient sources. Seward assists the illusion of Cook's epic persona by inserting frequent notes, drawing attention to the fact that many details and phrases are those of Cook himself in describing his adventures. Cook's accounts of gigantic polar icebergs, South Pacific cannibals, vast coral shoals, tropical storms, and such unfamiliar animals as kangaroos must have seemed almost as magical to contemporaries as Odysseus's adventures did to ancient listeners. Seward's notes assimilate Cook into myth by interweaving his verifiable experiences with her hardly more fantastic allusions.

A classical allusion also helps Seward to explain Cook's nearly inexplicable demise. Having described him, guided by Benevolence, charming the Tahitian natives with lessons in European knowledge and morality (ll. 206–10), Seward must abruptly record his murder and dismemberment by a Hawaiian mob (ll. 215–20). If Benevolence directed his movements thus far, why could she not protect Cook from harm in this instance? If other cannibalistic natives had welcomed, provisioned, and even seemingly worshipped Cook, how could this sole ungrateful island fail to recognize his goodness? Seward, and all contemporary readers of Cook's journals, knew that in fact most islands Cook visited were dangerous, volatile places. Cook had repeatedly risked his life by venturing unarmed into native villages and had proved an able diplomat negotiating between his sex- and profit-driven crews and their theft- and violence-prone hosts. Even today, his biographers have difficulty reconstructing the last tumultuous minutes of Cook's life, but enough was known to provide Seward with the details of an assault with clubs and spears and the mutilation of Cook's body before enough fragments were collected to permit a burial at sea (ll. 669–72, 674–76). Seward briefly narrates a horrific scene in which "darts of death" pierce the hero before "on his limbs the lust of hunger feeds!" (ll. 218, 220); neither she nor many other Europeans would have understood the significance to these peoples of consuming parts of their conquered enemies. Where was Benevolence at this juncture? Seward asks only why the Tahitians could not "save / That angel-goodness, which had blessed thy plain?" (ll. 212–13). Unfortunately, Cook died on "a far distant, and remorseless shore" (l. 215) peopled with "human fiends" (l. 216) on whom his "angel-goodness" was wasted. She explains the tragedy by recourse to the myth of Orpheus. Like Cook, the divinely inspired musician had brought "Fair Arts and Virtues" to Thrace (l. 222). But although savage beasts were calmed by his lyre, a human crowd of "inebriate maniacs" tore him limb from limb (ll. 227–30). While far from accounting for his demise, the analogy consoles by explaining that Cook was not the first civilization-bearer torn apart by an uncomprehending mob. The metaphor was neither accurate nor fair: Cook probably died in retaliation for the kidnapping of a native chief, during an altercation worsened by his personal participation (Beaglehole 670–71). The Hawaiians then dealt ritualistically with his corpse. But the Orpheus analogy confirmed Cook's mythical, even semidivine, status. It provided a classical, European framework for an action few western Europeans could grasp, figured in a role Seward would have especially admired, the archetypal poet. It completed the amalgamation of modern sentimental and ancient mythic heroism that Seward had pursued throughout her elegy.

The Orpheus myth also resonates with intimations of Christ's sacrifice, important to the elegy's conclusion, which presents two contrasting images. In the first, Seward implores Omai to adorn a *morai* (a ritual altar that Seward mistakenly describes as a funeral altar) for Cook (ll. 231–36). She then commands Oberea, whom Cook believed was the Tahitian queen, to perform the Polynesian women's self-mutilating funeral ritual described in Cook's journals. Seward imagines the once-lovely queen stabbing herself with shark's teeth:

> Now stain'd with gore, the raven tresses flow,
> In ruthless negligence of maddening woe;
> Loud she laments!—and long the Nymph shall stray
> With wild unequal steps round Cook's Morai!   (ll. 243–46)

This wholly imagined scene (in fact, Oberea had died before Cook's last visit to Tahiti [Beaglehole 549]) represents the supposed response of friendly but "uncultur'd" (l. 207) islanders to the news of a great chief's death. Oberea's hair is no longer strewn with roses, symbols of what Cook and his companions had taken to be the Tahitians' untrammeled eroticism. Instead, her tresses flow with gore, a savage and equally passionate token of Oberea's devotion to the great explorer. Seward contrasts this vivid ceremony with the lonely vigil of Cook's wife, watching on a storm-swept British cliff for his ship's return. This scene is, of course, likewise fictional, since Cook's voyage had been cut short by his death and the news forwarded in advance of the survivors' return. But against the hysterical dance of Oberea, Seward poises the silent grief of his widow, whom she now commands to retire:

> Go, wretched Mourner!—Weep thy griefs to rest!
> Yet, though through life is lost each fond delight,
> Though set thy earthly sun in dreary night,
> Oh! raise thy thoughts to yonder starry plain,
> And own thy sorrow selfish, weak, and vain;
> Since, while Britannia, to his virtues just,
> Twines the bright wreath, and rears th' immortal bust.   (ll. 262–68)

Mrs. Cook's consolation is to be the knowledge that her celebrated husband has been assumed into heaven by Benevolence ("The ATTENDANT POWER, that bade his sails expand" [l. 271]), where angels will "choir him, while he waits for THEE" (l. 276). Oberea may wail fruitlessly, in savage despair, at Cook's *morai*, but Mrs. Cook should forgo any display and instead retreat and wait patiently for heavenly reunion with her husband. As Guest observes, Seward enjoins private mourning on Mrs. Cook, and possibly by extension on the nation. But her rather harsh exhortation ("Go, wretched Mourner!—weep thy griefs to rest!") and comfortless

assurance that the widow's life is henceforth shorn of delight hardly seems calculated to recommend the private sphere.

Instead, Seward's poem adheres to the doctrine of separate spheres by assigning Mrs. Cook a role as the domestic, feminine counterpart of her adventurous
husband. Captain Cook braved ice floes, tornados, and "human fiends" to bring
"future herds and harvests" (l. 122) as well as "Wisdom's lore" (l. 208) to primitive
natives; her equally arduous but far less glamorous task will be to endure a living
martyrdom. She must mourn her "immortal" husband throughout the rest of a
"wretched" life. She must become the chief attendant at a kind of spiritual *morai*
composed of the wreaths, busts, and tributes dedicated by "Britannia." Only by
enduring such a widowhood, Seward implies, will Mrs. Cook become worthy of
joining her husband in the poem's final tableau, a scene resembling Catholic
paintings of Christ greeting the Virgin upon her assumption into heaven: "Where
soars, on Joy's white plume, his spirit free, / And angels choir him, while he waits
for THEE" (ll. 275–76). Oberea's gory tribute is dramatic but ineffectual because
ultimately self-reflexive, while Mrs. Cook will abjure "selfish, weak, and vain"
sorrow in recognition of her husband's altruistic deeds. The Christ-like aspect of
Cook's Orphean demise, the sacrifice that merited his assumption into heaven in
the arms of Benevolence, will be matched by her patient endurance of a "dreary"
life. Seward's conclusion thus blends colonial and European, classical and Christian, masculine and feminine ideologies in the apotheosis of Captain and Mrs.
Cook as British Protestant heroes.

If Mrs. Cook is not merely an "everywoman" in her retired lot but instead the
chief mourner assigned a difficult and martyrlike task, what role has Seward assigned herself in this elegy? Her contemporaries certainly recognized her guise
when they hailed her as "the genius of Britain" and "Our British Muse," among
other epithets they invoked that are cited by Guest in her description of their critical accolades (252–53). For Seward wrote not in the persona of retired gentlewoman
but as the epic singer, privy like Homer, Virgil, and Milton to events known only
to the Muses. She begins her poem with a classical invocation (ll. 7–14), demanding a funerary tribute by "the Nine" (l. 1) who formerly celebrated Cook's triumphs. "Say first," she commands, "What Power inspir'd his dauntless Breast"
(l. 15), a form of the conventional request through which epic poets establish from
the outset the motivation, such as anger or pride, for their poem's action. An epic
poet assumes the visionary ability to discern such forces, invisible sometimes even
to their protagonists. The muses also grant the epic poet the power to describe
events that occurred far away or in the distant past. In practice, of course, poets

constructed their narratives from materials such as oral traditions, as did Homer, for example, or from written sources such as the Bible, as Milton did. In *Elegy on Captain Cook*, Seward's choice of benevolence functioned like wrath in the *Iliad*, providing the explanation not only for Cook's disparate adventures that she had read about in his published journals and his martyrlike death but also for his reception in heaven, which she of course invented. The epic poet's was a privileged role. It was not a public role in the sense of active participation; the epic singer was usually by definition far removed from the heroes and actions she or he celebrated. On the other hand, neither was the epic poet's a strictly private role. Early poets, of course, sang their poems for audiences, and later poets circulated or published their poems. But beyond the public role that came with performance, the epic poet also assumed the voice of one privy to obscure, often sacred, knowledge, and was charged with conveying that knowledge to a broader, usually a national, audience. *Elegy on Captain Cook* is not an epic poem, but Seward's epic devices seem calculated to endow it with authority beyond that of a retired and previously unpublished gentlewoman. Her choice to adopt the role of epic singer, conveying the essence of Cook's greatness to a national audience, suggests Seward's awareness of the public importance of such a poem. That sense of having performed a public duty explains the lingering resentment she still felt when she complained to Josiah Wedgwood in 1788 that she had been overlooked when memorial medals of Cook had been distributed to those instrumental in his commemoration (Guest, *Small Change* 257). Guest finds Seward's response paradoxical in view of her professed attachment to retirement. I find it perfectly explicable in view of her conception of the dignified, public, and national role of poet.

Seward's seamless (to contemporary readers) amalgamation of traditions and of factual journals with mythical legends captivated readers hungry for such vindication. Her elegy would elate British youth, thought the Sheffield poet Susanna Pearson, and "young Genius rouse, or kindle daring thought."[11] Unlike the poems Suvir Kaul has examined, Seward's incorporates classical allusions but not to intimate the British Empire's eventual doom. Instead, she alludes to past models in order to establish hers as a superior modern and Christian hero, a man of benevolent sentiment whose actions merit heaven. The portrait was so appealing that critics as demanding as Samuel Johnson and even Cook's friends applauded the elegy. Today, with so much more knowledge about Cook and his voyages than would have been available to contemporary Britons, we find some aspects of the poem preposterous, including the notion of Cook as a man of sentiment. But a public trained to believe in sensibility as an invariable component of goodness would have found it more difficult to accept a portrait of their hero without that quality. Seward's achievement, we have seen, was to gratify the reading public by half-inventing her modern epic hero. Her next elegy was to be more controversial. Although John André himself was easily construed for her enthusiastic public as a hero of sensibility, certain details of Seward's portrait disobliged his relatives and those of Honora Sneyd Edgeworth. But their anger over Seward's narrative confirms that in both the Cook and André poems she exercised creative artfulness to an extent that has not often been appreciated, or even discerned, by recent scholars.

If Seward's *Elegy on Captain Cook* appeared on the scene at a low point in the prospects of the American War, her *Monody on Major André* (*Poetical Works* 2:68–88) was published at an even more dismal—or, for her, propitious—moment. By April 1781, the war's conclusion was still two years off, but Britons were approaching the era described by Colley when "instead of being sated with conquests, alarmed at their own presumptuous grandeur as they had been after 1763," they "could now unite in feeling hard done by" (144). News in October 1780 of a young officer's ignominious death by hanging filled the public with resentment as well as distress. Seward seized the opportunity to capitalize on her fame as Cook's elegist as well as on her personal acquaintance with André. The poem seems saturated with anger, not only at his fate but also at American conduct throughout the war. At 456 lines, the monody sacrifices the elegy's dramatic compression. The elegy had summarized three world-changing voyages in 276 lines. André's career paled in significance beside that of Cook, but Seward recognized his value as a symbol of the war's fruitless waste of youthful potential. While the speaker of the Cook elegy remains an anonymous epic-like poet, Seward boldly identifies herself as the speaker, justifying this poem's designation as a monody. She inveighs passionately against the loss of youthful love to prudential marriage, against war, against American treachery, and most pointedly against General Washington. Her animus resonated with the public; *Monody on Major André* caused a sensation (Ashmun 86). Her indignation at the fate of André accorded perfectly with the national mood: a large monument was erected to him in Westminster Abbey, and his bones were finally interred there in 1821.[12]

As in the Cook elegy, Seward mingles the classical and sentimental in her monody on André. The poem's dramatic opening anticipates Blake's personifications, as she elicits patriotic indignation: "Loud howls the storm! The vex'd Atlantic roars! / Thy genius, Britain, wanders on its shores!" (ll. 1–2). While Britain tears the "victor-garland" from his own brow (l. 8), Valour pushes his bride, Mercy, from his chariot, mounting Vengeance beside him in her stead (ll. 13–20). The significance of this confusing but sublime scene becomes clear when Valour brandishes

André's "bloody" death warrant in one hand while pointing across the ocean toward André's "ignominious grave" with the other (ll. 21, 24). Seward now enters
the poem among Valour's "awful train" (l. 27). Having sung the praises of Cook,
a stranger, she feels compelled to honor this "Belov'd companion" of her youth
(l. 41). Since their last meeting probably occurred soon after André joined the
army in 1771 (Lucas 72), it is unsurprising that Seward first devotes over one hundred lines of verse to their early friendship and particularly to his courtship of her
foster sister Honora Sneyd. These lines demonstrate the sincerity of Seward's
grief, which, as Esther Schor has observed, complicated public reception of elegies in the age of sentiment (50). Although André probably joined the military
because he disliked his job in a counting house rather than because he had fallen
into despair over his rejected marriage proposal to Honora, Seward draws on her
memories of his infatuation and constructs André as the pattern of hopelessly
devoted love. Although she was obviously aware that André had joined the army
two years before Honora's marriage, for example, Seward specifies that he purchased his commission upon hearing "tidings of Honora's marriage" (l. 115n):
"Honora lost! I woo a sterner bride, / The armed Bellona calls me to her side"
(ll. 141–42). Like Cook in Seward's elegy, André tears himself away from "Volup-
tuous London!" (ll. 123) and departs "to win bright glory from my country's foes"
(l. 121). Of course, Seward also knew that André's regiment departed for America
in 1774, long after Honora's wedding had taken place, so she probably conflated
his enlistment and departure to compact her narrative and heighten her poem's
drama. She astutely recognized André's resemblance to a hero of sentimental fiction and molded his biography to fit that model.

    In re-creating André, Seward was doing no more than she had done for Cook.
But since the former poem concentrated more on Cook's adventures and discov-
eries than on the captain's assumed personality, her resulting characterization
was uncontroversial. In fact, we have seen, the public and even his friends were
pleased with her construction of Cook as a hero of sentiment. Because the most
striking event in André's life had also been its conclusion, Seward concentrated
on developing his image as a victim worth national mourning. Unlike Cook, he
left few published records to draw on. But Seward had saved some letters from his
youthful courtship of Honora that demonstrated his refinement, charm, and wit.
Seward published these letters to support her portrait and built her description
around the brief episode of their romance. André, she attests, was no mere son
of an émigré who disappointed his family's mercantile ambitions by joining the
army. While Cook had exemplified achievement, André was distinguished for
his character. He was a youth endowed with "each generous virtue and each taste

refined" (46), a capable poet, musician, and portraitist (ll. 49–56). His miniatures of Honora (ll. 57–60) figure in the poem as tokens of fidelity, both the poet's as she now recalls both young lovers and André's when, later in the poem, he risks his life to preserve the tiny image of his lost love (ll. 259–84). Seward imagines André as an Apelles charmed by the object of his "fatal art" (l. 65), vowing never to part with "th' enchanting portrait" (l. 71). Seward imagines André's life had he succeeded in marrying Honora, their long lives adorned with friendship, hospitality, "science, and soft affection's blended rays" (l. 89). Unfortunately, Honora predeceased André (ll. 95–100); Seward implies that both would still be alive had not "Prudence, in her cold and thrifty care, / Frown'd on the maid, and bade the youth despair" (ll. 105–6). These lines understandably provoked Honora's surviving husband, Richard Edgeworth, and her family, who were well aware that consumption and not thwarted love had killed Honora after eight apparently happy years of marriage. Seward specifies that Honora's attachment had dissipated following the lovers' enforced separation ("the fair-one's sighs / Disperse like April-storms" [ll. 109–10]). But the suggestion remains, if only because Seward wished to fortify André's credentials as the faithful lover. While his beloved's sighs disperse, he first consecrates his youth to regaining her (ll. 111–14), then volunteers upon learning of her wedding (ll. 115–19).

Seward's inspiration was to recognize how easily she might transform John André into a recognizable and desirable icon, the man of feeling. As Barker-Benfield has demonstrated, heroes of sensibility dominated eighteenth-century fiction. Both men and women writers honored women's desire to reform men from indifference to their tastes and needs into responsive mates. The reform movement, Barker-Benfield observes, coincided with mercantile efforts to provide the accoutrements of refined households (213), and both phenomena encouraged the market for sentimental fiction and poetry (247). Literary heroes were usually distinguished by piety and, as in Seward's portrait of Cook, benevolence. They shared with heroines the traits of good manners, polite refinement, and preference for the domestic comforts of companionate marriage (247–48). But the hero's chief virtue was his concern for the feelings of women and his respectful behavior toward them (249). Barker-Benfield concludes his description of the hero of sensibility by noting that although men and women's gendered traits drew closer in such portraits, the male was still "free to enter or leave 'the world' with . . . ease" in contrast to their counterparts, the sentimental heroines (250). Thus heroes in novels by Charlotte Lennox, Charlotte Smith, Ann Radcliffe, and many others withdraw from the heroine's (usually the main) plot in order to make their fortunes, seek assistance, or simply attend to business. Nevertheless, these men are often portrayed as more slight and boyish looking than their brutish antagonists or even predecessor-heroes, although authors are careful to specify their manliness (340–41).

A voracious reader, Seward drew from all these characteristics when recreating André for her monody. He is a "dear, lovely Youth" with "snowy breast, red lip, and shining hair" (ll. 35, 330), whose artistic propensities manifest refined taste. His feelings are so exquisite that he excels his beloved in constancy. Seward assures us that companionate marriage and a comfortable home would have suited André far better than the military, but as only a man could do, he plunges into battle in the effort to forget his grief. Finally, she emphasizes his patriotism, although fueled by despair: "But while my country's foes, with impious hand,/Hurl o'er the blasted plains the livid brand/Of dire sedition, Oh! let Heav'n ordain,/ While ANDRÉ lives, he may not live in vain!" (ll. 155–58). In case any questions arose about his decision to leave his mercantile position or about how his mother, three sisters, and young brother would be economically supported, Seward creates a parting speech in which André recommends his mother's care to his siblings—each described as a sentimental paragon—and assures his mother that only pursuit of glory can assuage his broken heart.

Seward had little information about André's activities and less knowledge about warfare to draw on in describing his six-year career overseas. She predictably turned to her only sources of military insight, Homer's *Iliad* and Virgil's *Aeneid*. This would not have seemed to contemporaries the disabling handicap it would be today. We have noted the fashion initiated by Benjamin West for heroic portraits of British officers. So pervasive was this "new cult of élite heroism," notes Colley, that it "also shaped individual conduct. Some men even became so caught up and entranced by it that the reality of their lives, and even more of their deaths, became inextricably mixed with the highly coloured images of heroism available in Plutarch and Homer, or in the art of West, or Copley, or Devis" (182). On the American side, Phillis Wheatley published poems such as "On the Capture of General Lee" describing the revolutionists in the manner of Pope's Homer. Seward's ignorance therefore mattered little to a public accustomed to such images. She describes an action in which André was taken hostage not long after his arrival in North America. In reality, André was among a British detachment occupying a Canadian fort besieged by Americans and captured because the British ran out of food and ammunition after what he described in a letter as "pitiful cannonadings and bombardings for seven weeks" (Hatch 50). Seward instead stages the scene as one of Homeric warfare in which Bellona herself incites "opposing legions," "Carnage hurls her flaming bolts afar,/And Desolation groans" (237,

39–40). André predictably fights like a new Achilles, "foremost in all the horrors of the day" (l. 243). When captured, he is stripped of a uniform reminiscent of Homeric armor; the victors "seize the spoils of war with bloody hands" and "snatch the dark plumage from his awful crest" (ll. 348–49). Caring nothing for his "useless spear" (l. 255), he resolves to preserve Honora's miniature at all costs and hastily conceals it in his mouth. "That darling treasure safe," he resigns himself to the life of a hostage (l. 281). André's biographer denies Seward's account, explaining that in fact the Americans allowed the British to reclaim all of their possessions and even permitted the officers to keep their swords. He also refutes Seward's claim that André described in a letter his concealment of Honora's miniature (l. 268n).

Seward herself admitted the fictional nature of this scene in a footnote to the first edition of the monody (l. 244n). But only his family seems to have objected to her inaccuracy.[13] Most readers, familiar with the stirring portraits described by Colley and steeped in the values promoted by sentimental fiction, welcomed her description. One can easily imagine Orlando, for instance, the young hero of Charlotte Smith's *The Old Manor House* (1793) who fights in the American War, clinging to a miniature of his Monimia. Seward summarizes André's rapid ascent to the confidence of Sir Henry Clinton, commander of the British forces, resulting in his engagement to meet and parley with General Benedict Arnold. She compares his fatal mission to the nocturnal reconnaissance of Virgil's Nisus and Euryalus, noble youths who also died while undertaking a dangerous exploit. The episode gives Seward the opportunity to mock the Americans, whose "generals fly," "sick of the mischiefs artful Gallia pours,/In friendly semblance on thy ravag'd shores" (ll. 341–44). Like many Britons, Seward found it incomprehensible that the Americans, bound to Britain by birth and culture as much as by colonial status, would turn for assistance to France, Britain's chief national enemy. As Colley observes of public opinion, the alliance disgusted even those Britons formerly sympathetic to America (141–43), a reaction Seward describes in an impassioned forty-four-line address to the enemy. Although distressed when "haughty Britain in a luckless hour" decided to impose its will on the American colonies (l. 355), Seward is now even more disappointed by America's recourse to France. "Infatuate land! From that detested day/Distracted councils, and the thirst of sway,/Rapacious avarice, superstition vile, and all the Frenchman dictates in his guile/Disgrace your Congress!" (ll. 375–79). How else can one account for the failure of Truth and Mercy to secure at least an honorable death for André? Seward's poem culminates in an outburst of rhetoric directed to Washington himself.

As a gentlewoman, Seward was ignorant of wartime military protocol. As a patriotic Briton, she responded only to the fact that an officer had been hanged by his adversaries like a felon rather than shot as his rank demanded. As André's friend, she personally grieved for the insult. She was especially incensed because André himself had requested an honorable death of Washington and had been denied even this favor. Seward was not aware that hanging was the established punishment for André's offense, administered even less ceremoniously to Nathan Hale by the British not quite five years before (Hatch 68–69). Such a form of execution is considered a powerful deterrent and has been practiced throughout history. It has likewise been consistently protested by those condemned, by fictional characters such as the conspirators in Otway's *Venice Preserv'd* and by real war criminals such as the Nazi generals at Nuremberg. For Washington to have granted André's plea would have been an apparent admission of American injustice and was therefore impossible. Years after the war, Washington himself sent an assistant to Miss Seward to explain that fact. But as she noted in later editions of the poem, although she absolved the general of responsibility for André's execution, she never forgave his refusal to spare André from hanging (Kelly 70nl, 412). She never removed the accusatory passage. Another reason she may have left it in was her pride in the sheer power of her oratory: "Oh WASHINGTON! I thought thee great and good,/Nor knew thy Nero-thirst of guiltless blood!" (ll. 387–88). Declaiming against the pitiless foe who refused even "the cold mercy of the warrior-sword" to his captive (l. 398), Seward returns to her poem's opening scenario and her role in Valor's train. She promises that "the day shall come/Of deep repentance for this barb'rous doom!" (ll. 403–4). Fueled by resentment of their comrade's fate, British troops will fight with renewed vigor, "And when thy heart appall'd, and vanquish'd pride/Shall vainly ask the mercy they deny'd,/With horror shalt thou meet the fate thou gave,/Nor pity gild the darkness of thy grave!" (ll. 413–16).[14] Harsh words indeed addressed to the man who would be celebrated throughout Europe as the new Cincinnatus and in America as the "father of his country." But Seward addressed not Washington, in truth, but a demoralized public roused by her oratory. Most lines of her end-stopped couplets rise to a climax rather than rest at a caesura, reinforcing their power, as when she predicts that André's fate will "each falchion sharpen that the Britons wield,/And lead their fiercest lion to the field!" (ll. 407–8). Those lines' repeated "n" and "l" sounds increase her emphasis, an effect repeated throughout the poem. As a dramatic reader, Seward took care to ensure the musical power of her verse, and these lines are among her finest. No embassy from Washington could ever, in all likelihood, have led to their excision.

Although Valor waved André's death warrant at the poem's commencement, Seward urges the troops forward at its conclusion. She dwells on the image of André's dishonored corpse, unceremoniously buried in a Tappan field, and complains that Washington's behavior was worse than Achilles' toward Hector: at least the Greek returned his victim's body to Priam (ll. 419–26). Finally, she introduces biblical imagery and claims that André's "dust, like Abel's blood, shall rise,/ And call for vengeance from the angry skies!" (ll. 433–34). Meanwhile, in place of a "christian requiem," wildflowers will grace André's grave, and "Imperial Honour . . ./With solemn strains shall lull thy deep repose" (ll. 444–45). Seward's conclusion notes the British army's official mourning for André, a historic fact, and begs that some abler poet undertake his elegy, a modest gesture that her poem's reception proved unnecessary.

At the time, Seward's mixture of sentiment, classical allusion, and dramatic harangue appeared seamless to most British readers. As with Cook's elegy, they appreciated a portrait both plausible and gratifying. André had indeed seemed, to many people who met him, remarkably like a fictional hero, the androgynous man of feeling. When his regiment was stationed in Germany from 1771–73, he met a poet who afterward described him as a distinguished "man of almost womanlike modesty and gentleness" (Hatch 30). In America, he had become the protégé of the British commander. Even one of Washington's relatives remarked that "possessed of a fine person and an excellent understanding, he had united the polish of a court, and the refinements given by education, to the heroism of a soldier" (Smith 169). André, like the officers Colley describes who conformed themselves to heroic prototypes, died after blindfolding himself and calling on those present to witness "that he died like a brave man!" (Smith 167), a detail that Seward would certainly have incorporated into her poem had she known of it. André had seen himself, and contemporaries had seen him, very much as Seward describes. Her poem comprehended for Britons, in one young officer, the image of British military leadership, indeed of masculine heroism combined with the "feminine" feeling that justified his cause, they needed to believe would prevail despite America's league with France. As Hugh Blair noted in 1783, heroism, by "filling the mind with admiration, and elevating it above itself," constituted the "sentimental sublime" (Goring 215). If nothing else, Seward's poem encouraged Britons to look beyond themselves and toward the national predicament. *Monody on Major André* is therefore an important document of the period. Seward's rhetoric, moreover, still resonates despite its lack of practical consequence (a failure no greater, after all, than that of, for example, Pope's poems urging the fall of Walpole). As Griffin observes of other poets, her objective was "to speak to and for the nation at [a time] of crisis" (6). In the poem, it is neither the Genius of Britain nor Valor who speaks, but Anna Seward. And she did not speak largely as a poet of domestic retreat but rather spoke decisively as a patriot at the center of the national stage in these spectacular elegies.

Guest is, however, correct to link Seward's emergence with "the feminization of politics in the 1770s and 1780s" (*Small Change*, 271). In both the Cook and André poems, Seward participated in a phenomenon Colley also describes, the efforts of contemporary women to define a role for themselves as loyal British subjects. I also agree with Guest that Seward would never have identified herself with the "radical utopianism of city whigs like Catherine Macaulay" (Guest 265), although it seems to me that Seward's moderate Whig positions were probably shared by many urban as well as provincial Whigs. But Colley's recognition that "[to pose] as the pure-minded [Woman] of Britain was, in practice, a way of insisting on the right to public spirit" (281) means that Seward was not merely engaging in private patriotism expressed through domestic gestures or through membership in charitable or political organizations. Such a belief in the right to speak publicly justified publishing an eloquent denunciation of the national enemy in verse that rhetorically cries out to and even threatens their commander in chief, "Remorseless WASHINGTON!" (l. 403). Indeed, her poem succeeded in rattling the American general, who by sending an emissary to vindicate his behavior acknowledged Seward as British muse. Although Seward's poems are not as unusual as, say, Catharine Macaulay Graham's learned history of Britain or as the Duchess of Devonshire's electioneering on behalf of her party's candidates, they are on a continuum with their efforts, all of which represent women's attempts to express their political opinions and participate in national life. Unlike Macaulay Graham or the duchess, Seward managed to escape the opprobrium sometimes heaped on women who trespassed too far into the masculine territory of political expression. Both Claudia Johnson (14) and Julie Ellison (20–21) have described how sentiment was originally considered a masculine trait, and both have described how male affectation of sensibility forced women into corresponding postures such as, in Johnson's opinion, stoicism. Such a dynamic may have been at work when Cook's elegist demanded self-control of Mrs. Cook. But Seward's elegiac performances seem not to have been criticized as usurpations of a masculine prerogative. By hailing her as a British muse, critics identified Seward with the goddess of inspiration, a title she had assumed for herself in the André monody. While in her Cook elegy, Seward had called on "the Nine" for help (l. 1), in the monody, Seward identifies herself as "the Muse" who joins "the awful train" attending Britain's genius (ll. 15, 16). Seward also names herself "Julia," the playful name she had adopted in her letters to André. By twice gendering herself, once as the muse and once as Julia, Seward seems to have created a decisively feminine yet authoritative persona, at once mortal (Julia) and immortal (the muse), for her representative national mourner.[15]

Seward's poems merit notice, too, as records of one patriotic British woman's response to the wars successively waged in her lifetime. Seward's opinion of the American War resembled that of many liberal Britons both before and after André's hanging precipitated a jingoistic outburst. Less than a year before the André monody, she had published with the Cook elegy an eighty-two-line *Ode to the Sun* lamenting that the previous year's unusually temperate weather had accompanied the agonies of war:

> On a rock that braves the flood,
> [Britain's] genius sits, and pours the tear,
> Mindless of thy rosy year;
> Since War's terrific brood
> Bid in chains his Commerce languish,
> Fright his shrines with groans of anguish.   (ll. 67–72)

Only the metaphorical sunshine of Peace, dispelling "the wintry clouds of War" (l. 76), can release Britain from the threat to her merchant fleets and the destruction of her crews and troops. Seward's ode confirms the close association in Britons' minds between maritime commercial activity and national greatness. Her poem indeed focuses more on the war's disruption of trade than on its danger to human beings. Briton is imagined deploring "his wasted wealth, his bleeding joys" until he can "unbind fair Commerce" and bask once more in the sunshine of mercantile dominance (ll. 78, 80). While "bleeding joys" logically refers to the casualties that British churches resonate "with groans of anguish" for, the phrase's proximity to "wasted wealth" seems also to function as a reference to thwarted trade, the bearer of "joys" to British consumers. It is possible to conclude that until her friend André was killed, Seward's chief objection to the (in her view, unjustified) war was its threat to British prosperity. By publishing the poem in tandem with her *Elegy on Captain Cook*, Seward made no scruple of sharing her opinion with the reading public.

"Verses Inviting Mrs. C—— to Tea on a Public Fast Day, during the American War," an astringent fifty-seven-line poem in hudibrastic couplets, confirms Seward's sour view of British aggression even after André was hanged. Seward's note to the closing line confirms that the poem was composed in spring 1781, when the notorious murder trial of Captain John Donellan was engrossing public interest. Seward's invitation is perhaps fictitious, because the fast day she commemorates took place on February 21, over a month before the March 30 trial and April 2 execution of Donellan. Or she may have appended to an earlier draft the rather flippant reference to Donellan's choice of poison, which occurs in an anomalously brief concluding verse paragraph. Throughout the poem, however, Seward's irreverent tone underscores her less than pious attitude toward the fast:

> Wisely ordained to please the Lord,
> And force him whet our edgeless sword,
> Till, shipping o'er the Atlantic rill,
> We cut provincial throats at will. (ll. 5–8)

Seward's choice of the word "provincial" reveals that, like many Britons, she regarded the American colonists almost as fellow Britons because of their ethnic and cultural relationship. She invites her friend to an appropriately meager repast, but her poem concludes by imagining the "patriotic" response to her intended beverage:

> Have we forgot that dread libation
> Which cost the life of half the nation?
> When Boston, with indignant thought,
> Saw poison in the perfum'd draught,
> And caus'd her troubled bay to be
> But one vast bowl of bitter Tea. (ll. 35–40)

The Tea Party rivals Atreus's banquet, at which he avenged his brother Thyestes's affair with his wife by serving him a dish containing Thyestes's 's sons (ll. 45–46), by inspiring the war that has spilled "Brothers!—Children's!—Parents' blood" (l. 44). The allusion might be read at least two ways; either the Americans are like Atreus, whose vengeance far exceeded its cause, or they are like Thyestes, who betrayed his brother. Britain is either persisting in warfare rather than negotiating or suffering for its mistreatment of the American colonies. Neither interpretation is flattering to either side. The "Patriot" concludes by dissuading her from preparing a drink that has proved to be "hapless Britain's laurel-water" (l. 52), alluding to the poison Donellan used to kill his brother-in-law, Theodosius Boughton.

The references to Thyestes and to Donellan confirm that, to Seward, the American conflict was a kind of civil war in which members of a family were fighting one another. The dark humor of her poem accentuates the unnaturalness of the war: both the poem's tone and the war itself are indecorous, inappropriate. Seward's poem also mocks, if subtly, the notion that private observances such as fasting and refraining from cards can appreciably affect the war's outcome. Since, as both Colley and Guest have argued, contemporary women sought a viable role for themselves as citizens by joining patriotic associations, making clothes for soldiers, and signing loyal petitions, Seward's poem seems to remark the futility of such civilian gestures. How can a day of abstinence possibly influence the war? And since, in her view, Britain's cause is unjust, should it? Should citizens abet the cause with their prayers, or even by refraining from tea? Seward's poem cloaks serious questions, and serious objections, in the jaunty meter often reserved for light-hearted mockery. Following satirists such as Samuel Butler and Jonathan Swift, who had used tetrameter couplets to devastating effect, Seward wrote a poem that might have been labeled seditious if it had been published during the French Revolution or the Napoleonic wars. She did not publish the poem. She probably recognized that its indecorum would have risked the loss of public approbation following the Cook elegy and her André monody, whose publication coincided with the events alluded to in this poem but was no doubt more acceptable to current British taste.

Seward's *Ode on General Eliott's Return from Gibraltar, in 1787 (Poetical Works* 2:374–80) forms a coda to her American War–era poems. The poem is linked to the others because it commemorates Sir George Eliott's greatest achievement, his successful defense of Gibraltar during a 1779–83 siege by the French and Spanish. Their navies had sought to take advantage of Britain's overextended forces while also fighting her across the Atlantic as America's allies. Eliott then remained to superintend reconstruction of the fort's defenses before returning home in 1787. Seward's poem, a classical encomiastic tribute, celebrates not only Eliott's victory but also his dedication in staying behind to reinforce the British post rather than capitalize on his fame by returning to London as soon as the siege was lifted. But the poem is tied even more directly to an earlier poem. As she wrote a Miss Scott shortly before its publication, the ode was inspired by "individual gratitude, uniting with patriot admiration" (*Letters* 1:299). General Eliott had befriended one of her distant relatives, a Lieutenant Seward, at Gibraltar after learning his relation to the author of the *Monody on Major André*. "It is sufficient, Mr. Seward, that you bear her name, and a fair reputation, to entitle you to the notice of every soldier, who has it in his power to serve and oblige a military brother," declared the great commander (*Letters* 1:299). When Eliott finally approached Britain, Seward roused herself to compose and publish her 128-line ode, declaring that his "private virtues, the bravery of his defense of that garrison, which threw such a lustre on the termination of a war, unjust, ill-managed, and every way inglorious" entitled him to such honors (*Letters* 1:297). That last phrase demonstrates that despite her resentment of the Americans following André's execution, she remained steadfast in considering the war itself a colossal British error.

Her *Ode on General Eliott's Return*, however, is a chastened but proud reflection on Britain's military tradition and on the latest hero to embellish its records. Neither pindaric nor irregular, the ode is composed of sixteen iambic eight-line stanzas, alternating between a scheme of four pentameter lines followed by two tetrameter lines and concluded with a pentameter and an alexandrine line, and a pattern of two tetrameter lines followed by two pentameter, then two more tetrameter, then one more pentameter and an alexandrine line. Seward plays with syllabic length, using some catalectic lines to achieve compression, as when she declares that Britain should honor its heroes: "palms unfading round their urn / Let their favour'd country strew!" (ll. 73–74). She also experiments with contractions and elided syllables to achieve the opposite effect, describing, for example, Eliott's deeds as "the acknowledg'd bulwarks of her falling power" (l. 108). Only the elision of the first two and final two syllables maintains, in that instance, the pentameter pattern. Through such effects Seward incorporates both her cherished variety and something of Cowley's irregularity into her ode. But the rhyme scheme of each stanza is a-b-a-b-c-c-d-d, giving the poem a subtle but reassuring stability, perhaps like the modest but invincible man she celebrates.

The opening stanzas of the ode confirm Colley's deduction that loss of the American War inflicted a deep psychological wound on Britons. Seward reiterates the lingering sense of failure; Eliott's triumph "shone on the darkness of [Britain's] long defeat," and his return in peacetime invites rejoicing, "as loss had ne'er chastis'd, oppression ne'er been thine" (ll. 4, 8). The latter line refers both to the French and Spanish siege and to Britain's unjust treatment of her colonies that led to the war. Seward reminds Britain of the siege that occurred when "to blast thy gloomy pride, avenging fate / Unequal war's disastrous terrors spread," when France and Spain joined the American cause (ll. 11–12). The assault on Gibraltar would have crippled British dominance of the sea-lanes had not Eliott trained his cannons on the French and Spanish ships (ll. 25–32). Seward describes vividly the horror of assailants trapped on their burning ships after Eliott's bombardment as a British convoy approached. "Alike they hear the British lion roar / In the o'erwhelming flood, and raging fire! / Groaning they plunge! — in wild despair, / With raiment scorch'd, and blazing hair!" (ll. 35–38). As they struggled in a sea "purpled by the gore, / illumin'd by the flames" (l. 40), however, Sir Roger Curtis, whose ships had arrived to support Eliott, rescued many of the wounded belligerents. Seward hails Curtis as an angel of mercy who embodied her favorite heroic mixture of bravery and sentiment, or, as she expresses it, "the undaunted soul, the generous melting heart" (l. 56). Curtis's magnanimity in plucking his enemies from the burning sea redeemed Britain after her recent acts of oppression: "O Britain! — O my country! Then 'twas thine / T' emerge from ev'ry cloud that veil'd thy light!" (ll. 49–50).

Seward then recalls three of the century's greatest military heroes and their deeds. Her citation of the Duke of Marlborough's victories in the War of Spanish Succession "in Freedom's cause" forgets the actual cause or objective of the war and instead alludes to the traditional ideological rationale for battling the French (l. 59). Gibraltar, the guardian of British sea-lanes and thus of British trade, had been among the great prizes won through that war. She next celebrates Prince William's conclusive victory at Culloden, ending Bonnie Prince Charlie's 1745 invasion, as the turning point "when gaunt rebellion grimly cower'd" (l. 62). She goes on to recall Wolfe's death after winning Quebec in a narrative tableau derived from Wolfe's famous painting. She describes Wolfe beholding the triumphant British flag: he "lifts the pale eye, a gleam of transport fires, / And smiling on his wounds, [he] triumphantly expires!" (ll. 71–72). Seward recapitulates the century of warfare that established Britain's empire and her worldwide political influence after the British defeated the French abroad and French-subsidized Jacobites at home. But in her poem's climax, she hails Eliott as superior to his great predecessors. While they established British power and influence, Eliott restored Britain's reputation, stained, in the aftermath of the Seven Years War, through "rash attempts, irresolute and vain" (l. 80) — a poetic restatement of her assessment of the American War, in the letter to Miss Scott, as "unjust, ill-managed, and every way inglorious." She compares his achievement to a beautiful evening following an unexpectedly stormy spring day (ll. 91–98). Like the ensuing morning when spring returns, British commerce will resume following its wartime hiatus, and the arts will flourish as the nation prospers. Eliott, who by preserving Britain's maritime freedom has made possible this renaissance, thus becomes another of Seward's heroes of sensibility. Superior to heroes such as "the Butcher of Culloden," he resembles instead a gallant fictional hero, restoring the reputation and thereby the future prospects of a misguided but now vindicated heroine, Britannia.

Seward devotes her four concluding stanzas to praise of Eliott's modesty in remaining at his post instead of "[rushing] to meet [his] country's paeans warm" (l. 98). Her conclusion might seem anticlimactic, but it mirrors her hero's reticence. A man of "unassuming greatness" (l. 114), he will slip quietly into port after completing his mission. She concludes with a blessing on Eliott and a prophecy that the prosperous future the hero will see is not merely his own or his family's but Britain's: "Generous, brave, and free,/Wide o'er the world, as in her laurel'd prime," she will "dart the commanding glance,/and lift the brow sublime!" (ll. 126–28). Seward, like many contemporaries, envisioned Britain's ascendancy following the Seven Years War as both a halcyon period—"her laurel'd prime"— and a failed test of her ability to rule justly an immense territory. Through the American War, "avenging fate" had blasted her "gloomy pride" (l. 11). But also like many Britons (Colley 144–45), Seward expressed a renewed if chastened patriotism as she contemplated the postwar future. Britain at its best, in her opinion, adopts a pose of "unassuming greatness" like Eliott's rather than of "gloomy pride." If she maintains that perspective, the propensity to rescue drowning enemies rather than overextend her rule, Britain will regain her power and influence. Seward once again speaks as a prophet, a public poet, calling on the public to greet their "unassuming" hero: "And can it be, that the elapse of time/The sacred sense of gratitude consumes?/No, Britain, no!" (ll. 115–17). Seward may represent the domestic tributes hailing Eliott, but she steps forward to elicit those tributes. Hers is again the public posture of national poet, the eloquent voice of the nation. Her final image of Britannia, familiar not only from song and verse but from dozens of paintings and prints, depicts the personified nation in a characteristic pose. No doubt poised on the Atlantic cliffs (much like the corresponding but tragic image of the Genius of Britain in *Monody on Major André*), Britannia surveys her empire, "[darting] the commanding glance, and [lifting] the brow sublime!" (l. 125). Perhaps not coincidentally, Britannia's pose is also that frequently seen in paintings of a muse, as in Reynold's portraits of Sarah Siddons or, more to the point, as in Romney's portrait of Anna Seward herself (1782).

The denouement of the *Ode on General Eliott*, reconstructed by Seward in a letter to the relative Eliott had befriended (*Letters* 1:322–24), was quoted by Lucas (81–83) and narrated by Ashmun (154–55), both of whom were amused by her pride in the visit the general paid to Lichfield to thank her for the poem. Ashmun characteristically mocks Seward's poetic pretensions, observing snidely that "of the General's intended visit the poetess had sufficient notice to have all her publications 'elegantly bound,' as the choicest gift she could offer" (155). She also sports with Seward's big-fish-in-a-small-pond gratification: "Truly, she must have felt her heart swell at such a tribute on her own ground and among her own companions, some of whom had seemed at times to entertain but a small appreciation of her worth!" (155). Ashmun's condescension is cruel, but she may have deemed unfeminine Seward's delight in the general's conspicuous distinction, "one of the most flattering . . . of [her] life" (*Letters* 1:322). Seward had conveyed news of the impending visit to Lichfield's civic leaders, who assumed an overnight stay and prepared a "general illumination through our little city. . . . The words Elliot, Gibraltar, Victory, enwreathed with flowers, were to have shone in phosphorous upon the walls of our town-hall, and over the arms of our city" (*Letters* 1:322). To her dismay, the general proved as unassuming in life as she had portrayed him in her poem. He avoided the civic tribute and spent only part of a day in Lichfield, visiting Seward at the Bishop's Palace where she presented him with her bound works. She was immensely gratified, however, when, after taking his leave, the great man "would not suffer his aid-de-camp to carry the book to the inn, but held it in his own hand, as he walked through our streets" (*Letters* 1:324). Perhaps Ashmun considered the gesture comparable to Seward herself parading through the streets with the general. In any event, the anecdote contradicts the argument that Seward espoused a purely private or domestic role as muse. In fact, she was justifiably proud that her poem drew the general to Lichfield, that his principal engagement there was to visit her, and that he very publicly transported her poems through the city. Unlike in the case of her Cook elegy, when she had not received the medal struck for his celebrants, Seward had been singled out on this occasion for public thanks. The event fulfilled her ambition to be recognized not as a retired lady but as a British muse, speaking for, and to, her country.

CHAPTER FIVE

Wartime Correspondent

The French Wars and Late-Century Patriotism

The *Ode on General Eliott* was the last of Seward's panegyrical odes. The following decade witnessed a torrent of patriotic verse as Britain waged war first with revolutionary, then with Napoleonic, France. As Simon Bainbridge has observed, war became the central theme of British poetry, as poets seized their opportunity to portray and interpret the wars for domestic readers (2–5). But not for Seward. Having assumed the role of British muse in poems specifically related to the American War and, in the elegy on Cook, Britain's superior claim to world domination, Seward did not perpetuate her fame by swelling that torrent. For nearly a decade, her poetic voice was conspicuously muted except for a few verses in scattered periodical contributions. When she finally resumed major publication, it was to celebrate the glories of rural Wales (*Llangollen Vale, with Other Poems*, [1796]) and to rival Charlotte Smith's popular sonnets (*Original Sonnets on Various Subjects; and Odes Paraphrased From Horace* [1799]). Seward's reticence at this juncture surely contributed to her subsequent critical disappearance. As Bainbridge argues, the wars endowed poetry with a rationale and impetus that reinstated its public importance. Poets male and female, for and against the conflict, competed to mold public opinion by describing battles horrific, sublime, or both. Seward's protégé Walter Scott finally emerged, in the early nineteenth century, as the preeminent bard of war (120). But even before Scott's dominance, not only the role but the nature of poet and poetry had changed amid the wars' circumstances (35). Bainbridge describes the turn from a "feminized" sentimental poetry to a "masculine" poetry that did not shrink from scenes of carnage whether the poet was a manly bard or a "martial maiden" (35). By not capitalizing on her association with national patriotic verse and instead concentrating on occasional and lyric verse, Seward apparently defied both the fin de siècle's supreme verse opportunities and its crucial changes in poetic taste.

In this chapter, I explore the reasons Seward withdrew, during most of the 1790s, from her outspoken role of national muse and did not join the chorus of men and women poets who shared her hatred of Britain's interference in French affairs. Seward's opinions were more complicated than has been recognized, but only private correspondents would have known the extent to which she excoriated William Pitt the Younger and railed against his policies. I conclude, in part, that Seward may have feared not only her own influence were she to publish anti-ministerial verse at a juncture when civil war seemed possible but also the possible legal retaliation against such verse when prosecution for sedition hushed many potential dissidents. Numerous historicist studies have debated the precise nature of, for example, Wordsworth's allusions to French revolutionary events and British responses to them in "Tintern Abbey."[1] While disputing whether history is integral to or transcended by the poem, all agree that Wordsworth's reticence betrays anxiety about revealing his political sympathies. The Wye Valley tour memorialized in "Tintern Abbey," after all, preceded a trip to Germany, itself most likely a "draft dodge" (Levinson 21). While Seward never faced persecution, let alone conscription, as a gentlewoman she had a more fragile reputation to guard than did Wordsworth or any of the younger women writers we now recognize as "Romantic." She had, moreover, established her reputation as both sentimental muse and "martial maiden" in poems supporting international British exploits. To recoil in print from patriotic advocacy was therefore problematic for several reasons that deserve unpacking.

Strong evidence suggests that Seward held herself back from publishing verse relative to the late-century French wars not because she was indifferent to the national emergency but because she hesitated to publicly express her personal and quite complex position except on the occasions when it dovetailed with ministerial policy. Seward's printed correspondence preserves an engrossing record of her opinions from the outbreak of the French Revolution in 1789 through the British invasion of Denmark in 1807. The letters witness her concurrence in British euphoria as the revolution began as well as in national repugnance for its ensuing bloodbaths. Seward's growing concern for the protection of Britain's social hierarchy and for private property was typical; her worry that Britain's identification with the Anglican Church was jeopardized seems appropriate for the daughter of an Anglican clergyman. The conservative aspects of her response are all, in fact, somewhat predictable, just as Anna Laetitia Barbauld's published rebuke of

Edmund Burke was the logical outcome of her association with his Dissenting opponents. When Seward did speak publicly, as in a letter that appeared in the *Gentleman's Magazine*, it was to make a passionate plea to expatriate Helen Maria Williams to return from France before the revolution's "carnage" engulfed her (*Letters* 3:202–9). That letter alone has led most current scholars to place Seward firmly among conservatives regarding the war.[2] But Seward's conservatism did not lead her to approve of British war as a means of preserving her cherished status quo. Instead, she soon turned adamantly against the war and remained so despite some small alterations in her opinions of individuals and events. In her correspondence, she created a personal and prophetic narrative that remained consistent throughout the revolutionary and Napoleonic campaigns. The apparent contradiction between her staunch anti-Jacobinism and her simultaneous, equally passionate antiwar sentiment would have been difficult to reconcile in print, given that any public criticism might be construed as sedition. It would have become even more difficult as the wars dragged on.

Seward certainly had opportunities to resume her role of military elegist. Writing to Mrs. Jackson in 1794, she related an invitation to compose an elegy for a Lieutenant Colonel Buller, which she had declined on the grounds that the Cook and André poems had exhausted her stock of original images for such poems. Besides, she continued in a bitter joke, "Were I to attempt compliance with requests of this sort, my muse must e'en turn undertaker; and I had better put up a board over my door, 'poetic shrouds to be let, and ideas for military funerals furnished in the cheapest and readiest manner.' This dreadful war would give me business in plenty" (*Letters* 4:35). Behind the grim humor was Seward's genuine outrage at the numbers of slaughtered soldiers—British casualty rates were perhaps higher in these wars than they were during World War I (Bainbridge 6)—and civilians. She repeatedly exclaimed against the endless deployments of troops, "their lives sacrificed in vain attempts . . . to destroy, with bombs and shells, a few French houses and their guiltless inhabitants" (*Letters* 6:344). Seward thus refused to join the women poets who, whether for or against Britain's campaigns against France, agreed in expressing horror at the number of casualties.[3] Eliza Tuite's "Song, in the Year 1794," for example, rallied popular support for George III's policies while acknowledging that Britannia "fondly mourns her warriors slain" (Backscheider and Ingrassia 448–49). But unlike after André's execution, Seward did not react in print, averse to rallying the nation toward ever-greater casualties and evidently despairing of her ability to intervene on behalf of peace. Only in 1804, when she decisively answered the critics of Darwin's poem celebrating the fall of the Bastille, did Seward make public her antiwar view, and then she did so as an apologist for a work published in 1791 (*Memoirs* 161–62).

Perhaps Seward feared to commit herself again in print during a conflict that had already forced adjustments of her published opinion. At the onset of the French Revolution, in August 1789, she hailed the Gallic "exertions" in a sonnet published in the *Gentleman's Magazine*.[4] Her poem's conceit is that the French "lilies" (l. 6) were dipped in the "living waters" (l. 4) of freedom during the recent American War, inspiring the current rebellion. She joins British "exultation" (l. 7) as the French shed their shackles: "Few of Britannia's free-born sons forbear / To bless thy Cause" (ll. 9–10). The sonnet accurately reflects contemporary public opinion. Accustomed to jingoistic stereotypes of the French as "slaves" compared with "free" Britons, the British assumed the revolution would rapidly lead to a French society much like their own. Seward's sonnet concludes with that explicit wish:

> —France, we bid thee share
> The blessings twining with our civic wreaths,
> While Victory's trophies, permanent as fair,
> Crown the bright Sword that Liberty unsheaths.   (ll. 11–14)

In retrospect, Seward need not have suppressed this poem in her later sonnet collection and posthumous edition. Like, for example, certain early twenty-first-century Americans and Britons who assumed that revolutions in Afghanistan and Iraq would lead inevitably to the establishment of Western-style democracies, Seward and her compatriots believed sincerely in the superiority of their political system and concluded that, given an opportunity, the French would necessarily emulate Britain's constitution. Seward admits but obscures the necessity of revolutionary bloodshed. America was the site of "Freedom's sacred fountains . . . / . . . though with crimson stains" (ll. 1–2), and "British veins / swell"—the very veins whose wounds recently stained American battlefields—at the news of French rebellion (l. 6). Like William Blake, Wordsworth, and a host of other poets, Seward acknowledged the brutality of the goddess Liberty's unsheathed sword. But also like most contemporaries, she imagined that the bloodshed was a temporary phenomenon, the price of permanent freedom and stability like their own.

When Edmund Burke published his *Reflections on the Revolution in France* (1790), Seward first devoured extracts of his pamphlet in the newspapers, then ordered and perused the whole. Her immediate reaction was negative. As she explained to T. S. Whalley, Burke's "Quixotism about the Queen of France . . . did not please me at all. Unbiassed as I profess myself as to my reason, Mr. Burke will find it difficult to convince me, that the oppressive and barbarous monarchy of France ought to have subsisted" (*Letters* 3:46–47). Although her opinion of Burke's main argument fluctuated with events over the ensuing years, Seward never condoned his extravagant defense of the Bourbons. As an Englishwoman, she remained offended by his rhetorical flights on behalf of an absolute monarchy long after his argument seemed prophetic. In June 1791, she lamented the capture of Louis XVI and Marie-Antoinette in their attempted escape but insisted on the positive tendency of France's "experiment . . . to render mankind more independent of each other, more virtuous, and consequently more happy. . . . Time has already . . . given the lie to [Burke's] gloomy prognostics of anarchy and ruin" (*Letters* 3:80). She happily anticipated a future when "crowns and nick-names, red ribbons and blue, will soon cease to excite the reverence of multitudes; but be cast aside over the earth" (*Letters* 3:88). Like many other Britons, Seward reversed these sentiments after Louis was deposed, anarchy seemed imminent, and Prussia and Austria invaded France. Louis now appeared "truly great beneath the barbarous tyranny he suffers" and his captors "fierce banditti" (*Letters* 3:201). Instead of praising individual liberty, Seward now extolled the "chain of subordination, which binds the various orders of national society" and blamed Thomas Paine's "absurd and mischievous system of equality" for the crisis. She repented her sonnet of 1789 (*Letters* 3:203, 205–6). She now declared her convictions that "people of property" are "the only real patriots" and that national politics must be joined with national religion. Prime Minister William Pitt's efforts to extend political rights to Dissenters must consequently cease lest chaos ensue (*Letters* 3 216–17).

Like most Britons, too, Seward initially supported Pitt's declaration of war against France in 1793. To a friend who still approved of the French rebellion, she extolled Lichfield's "orthodoxy and . . . loyalty," describing herself as an old-fashioned Whig, proud of the Glorious Revolution's heritage of balanced government (*Letters* 3:300–302). By autumn of that year, she was condemning the "impious and awless [*sic*] guilt" of a nation that executed its "hapless Queen" upon an absurd charge of incest (*Letters* 3:335). France had become a "nation of Macbeths! A nation that licences the plunder of property, that makes massacre its pastime, and atheism its fate" (*Letters* 3:339–40). In spring 1794, she rejoiced at the beginning of the Reign of Terror, for now "the poisoned chalice" was "returning to the lips of the demons who administered it" (*Letters* 3:358). All of these sentiments were consonant with the changing flow of British public opinion, if more eloquently phrased. Seward even championed the suspension of the Habeas Corpus

Act in summer 1794 as a temporary measure to foil seditious plots (*Letters* 3:368). But by late July, she had become disgusted with the war effort, which she deemed "absolutely hopeless." It was not for Britain to punish French "villainy"; that privilege was reserved for Providence. To persist in the war was to emulate "the Crusades, which spilt rivers of Christian blood in vain, warring against infidelity." Worse, the conscriptions and taxes needed to supply the war would encourage internal sedition, leading to the same fate as befell France (*Letters* 3:377–79).

Throughout the rest of her published correspondence, Seward remained disgusted both with the French and with British war efforts. Fearful of appearing to support the Jacobins, however, she refused to publish her grievances with the ministry. When the radical publisher Joseph Johnson, aware of her antiwar position, asked her to write a poem supporting reinstatement of the Habeas Corpus Act, she refused. "I durst not run the slightest risk of strengthening the apprehensions of the public concerning an evil which appears to me entirely imaginary, viz. that the government of this country is likely to become despotic" (*Letters* 4:3). Seward's fear of increasing public alarm arose from her even greater fear of a British rebellion by poor people oppressed by forced military service and the effects of war taxes. This guiding fear led to her changed opinion about political rights for non-Anglicans when Pitt reneged on his promise to extend civil rights to Irish Catholics in return for their loyalty after they thwarted an incipient French-supported Irish rebellion in 1798. Seward was outraged by his failure to pursue a measure that would have appeased the oppressed Catholics and united them with the English against their common enemy (*Letters* 5:107). Seward also changed her mind about the Habeas Corpus Act. When, by 1800, Pitt pronounced his confidence in national loyalty but refused to restore "this national column," Seward complained bitterly that the British government had become a "despotic power": "They prevent their state prisoners from being brought to trial! They make them languish whole years in imprisonment!" (*Letters* 5:282). Such injustices invited the kind of uprising that had engulfed France. But while Seward's opinions of individual measures changed, her attitude toward the war remained essentially the same. The continental campaigns were an ill-judged effort to supplant providential justice, a waste of blood and treasure that would finally incite a French-style rebellion at home when the government was too depleted to confront the grievances of its war-weary poor.

Seward herself, recalling her original enthusiasm for the revolution in a letter to Edmund Wigley, reflected that at least "I am not too proud to confess myself mistaken" when events proved her opinions wrong (*Letters* 4:280). Her correspondence indicates that she devoured newspapers, pamphlets, and books about the war, modeling how a relatively free press enabled the literate of both genders to form and express opinions and thereby influence others within their circles. Her publications might suggest Seward was indifferent to the war, but she was in fact intrigued by it. Of politics, she confessed to Colonel Dowdeswell in November 1797 that "in a period so momentous, their attraction, to thinking minds of both sexes, is resistless" (*Letters* 5:20). She boasted to T. S. Whalley that her opinions were formed by "a strictly dispassionate attention to the arguments for and against the war . . . collected from a ministerial paper, the Evening Mail—the only one I read, for I do not wish to see the errors of ministry on the exaggerating page of their avowed and indiscriminate foes." She supplemented those views by reading, "with equal eye," the polemical books of Burke, Williams, Boothby, Macintosh, Erskine, and Gifford. Although certain that the war was disastrous, Seward was nevertheless as "disposed to censure the opposition as the ministry, when any thing falls from their lips or pens, which tends to produce tumult and revolt" (*Letters* 5:134–35). Seward's fear of a British revolution, supplemented by fear of being thought seditious (her letter to Johnson of 1794 seems composed with an eye toward suspicious ministers, should they intercept Johnson's correspondence), deprived Britain of a thoughtful, sometimes witty, always passionate commentator. It is useless, however, to lament that Seward did not pursue a journalism career like Helen Williams or Mary Wollstonecraft did. It is remarkable enough that she permitted dissemination of these robust letters after her death.

Seward's letters reveal the complex spectrum of British responses to the wars, usually described more simply in terms of radical and conservative, pro- and anti-Jacobin. Although she consistently described herself as a loyal Briton, she just as consistently declared her disapproval, mounting to near hatred, of Pitt. Before Britain even declared war against France, Seward shared with David Samwell in May 1791 her hope "that Mr. Pitt's brain will not become incurably diseased by the manie militaire" (*Letters* 3:59). When the war did not come to an end after its ostensible purpose, the restoration of Louis XVI, was rendered moot by his execution, Seward deplored the "shallow, reasonless" ministerial "oratory, which is so perpetually shifting its ground, to defend this now totally unmotivated war" (*Letters* 4:34). Pitt's failure to define Britain's purpose in warring against France remained a theme of her correspondence, as did his lack of what a twenty-first-century citizen might call an exit strategy. When Edmund Burke wrote another pamphlet in an "attempt to re-frenzy the nation," she derided his logic:

> Mr. Burke presents no clue for extrication. He would have us continue the wasteful war, yet justly ridicules the absurdity of planting guns and cannons

against system;—and he calls this a necessary war, that struggles with a pernicious system, which he says must be subdued, or England is annihilated as an
empire; while, in another place, he tells us the same system is laid too deep in
the corruption of human nature for the hope that it will ever be renounced.
(*Letters* 4:275–76)

Americans and Britons who lamented their governments' failure to define the
purpose of the Iraq invasion in 2003, who questioned the practicability of Presi-
dent George W. Bush's and Prime Minister Tony Blair's commitment to a global
war against terrorism, might have found the ancestor of their critiques in Seward's.
In another instance of prescient rhetorical dissection, Seward described her fury
after reading accounts of Pitt's parliamentary oratory in 1800. She resented his
contradictory argument that continued war with France was necessary for national security even though, in other speeches designed to rally national support,
he represented France as militarily, economically, and politically vitiated (*Letters*
5:280). Such analyses were the startlingly modern response of a literate and concerned citizen who believed she had a stake in national affairs. Seward's letters
suggest that widespread literacy, prosperity, and access to information had not
only created a public sphere but equipped it to challenge government decisions
on a broader scale than ever before possible.

While Linda Colley has demonstrated women's unprecedented efforts to support the revolutionary and Napoleonic wars, Seward's letters illustrate her caveat
that the majority of women probably disapproved of them (260–62, 254). Yet unlike Colley's examples of the subscriptions women raised to support the wars,
Seward's diatribes remained private, perhaps because, as a gentlewoman, she had
no platform from which to declare her views except at the expense of her reputation and, perhaps, her freedom. Both Guest (*Small Change* 224–25) and Bainbridge (153–54) have described the critical assault on Barbauld for disagreeing in
print with Burke's *Reflections* and objecting to the subsequent wars. Again like
modern citizens, Barbauld and Seward were supplied by the press with ample
information on which to base their opinions, then pressured by the government
and by the same press to support the wars or appear disloyal. Constrained by
gender and status, Seward risked being attacked as unfeminine, even seditious,
were she to publish her opinions. Since she frequently acknowledged her fear of
professional literary criticism, admitting the devastating effect of negative reviews,
it makes sense that Seward was reluctant to publicize her political opposition. On
the other hand, the size of her correspondence and the number of her addressees
guaranteed that Seward's views were read by a broad if select readership, one of

the century's noteworthy instances of manuscript circulation substituting for print publication among genteel readers.

Seward's letters complicate Colley's thesis that patriotism, manifested in support for a series of wars culminating in the revolutionary and Napoleonic campaigns, played a leading role in "the invention of a British nation" (367). Seward herself found such an explanation illogical. Writing to Thomas Park in 1797, she castigated the ministry for boasting that the war itself had prevented a British revolution. If the war had, she asked, what would be the consequence of peace? (*Letters* 4:372). Nevertheless, her consuming interest in the war, as well as the sweeping geographical nature of her concerns (for example, during invasion crises, she invariably wrote to the Llangollen ladies to commiserate with them over their fears for relatives and property in Ireland), supports Colley's arguments that the wars encouraged a sense of national identity and that women considered themselves to have as much at stake in the wars as did men. Seward's letters also complicate Bainbridge's terse description of her as a conservative writer (83). Seward's mind was too capacious, her reasoning powers too keen, to merit such a simple epithet. In February 1792, for example, she responded favorably to Mary Wollstonecraft's *Vindication of the Rights of Woman*, deciding the author was "oftener right than wrong" in her analysis of female education (*Letters* 3:117). Later that year, she confessed to Helen Williams that she had misgivings about Williams's decision to reside in Paris during the current crisis but applauded her friend's "moderate" political stance (*Letters* 3:146–48). She repeatedly praised Britain's political system but was far from chauvinistic about its current operation. "The impotent rage and improbable schemes of our late ministry," she noted in 1806, "assisted and goaded" Napoleon "to the attainment of empire" (*Letters* 6:251). She detected the fallacy behind Britain's defense of the Bourbon monarchy: Bonaparte could not be called a usurper, because the Glorious Revolution had denied the concept of divine-right monarchy. "Let us not have one law for ourselves and another for our enemies! Liberal policy spurns the groveling partiality" (*Letters* 6:353). Seward considered her dismay the result of old-fashioned Whig principles. Such a philosophy made it impossible for her to espouse the kind of simplistic "my country, right or wrong" reactions associated with conservative patriotism today.

Yet when, in 1796, Robert Southey published his remarkable antiwar epic *Joan of Arc*, Seward was moved to respond in print with a keen rebuke. Published in the *European Magazine* in August 1797, Seward's "Philippic on a Modern Epic" (*Poetical Works* 3:67–69) denounced Southey for abusing his "sun-born Genius" (l. 3) by portraying Henry V as a Nero concerned only with aggrandizing himself.

Seward drew on historical accounts to absolve Henry of indifference to his soldiers' fate (on the contrary, he led his troops into battle, his helmet conspicuously
adorned with white feathers [ll. 9–12]). She also defended the Battle of Agincourt
as a legitimate pursuit of rights ceded Britain by the French after the Battle of
Cressy (ll. 12–16). Southey's misrepresentation of heroic kings Edward and Henry
amounted to "parricide," especially infuriating from the pen of such a young poet
("O! unnatural boy!" [l. 23]). Seward points to Britain's abiding reputation for
fairness and generosity in the conduct of wars (ll. 31–34). Southey must be "dark
of heart" to libel his country by instead depicting cruel kings and nobles. Since
his descriptions are patently false, his laments are "crocodile's" tears (ll. 37–38),
thinly disguised Jacobin propaganda. Seward concludes by bidding Southey to
acknowledge his real purpose: "And o'er the murder of the royal victims,/And
o'er the Christian faith's apostacy,/Witness'd in France, cry, "Vive la Liberte!"
(ll. 39–41). Southey may as well dip his hands in the blood of French victims,
"and throwing thy red cap aloft in air,/Laugh with the fierce hyena!" (ll. 44–45).
Southey's distorted version of history resembles a hyena's chilling, inhuman, and
ultimately meaningless laughter.

    Since the original philippics were Demosthenes' public excoriations of King
Philip of Macedon, Seward's title announces her resumption of a national and
public role. Yet her resolve to denounce in print not George and Pitt, whose policies she detested, but a young poet whose antiwar opinion she shared, demands
an explanation. Seward's refusal to publish her antiministerial views was, we have
seen, predictable, but why attack Southey? Seward evidently wrote her response
soon after reading *Joan of Arc* in December 1796. Either her philippic echoes
phrases from her letters describing the new epic or the letters borrow phrases from
her already-drafted attack (*Letters* 4:290, 295–98). The letters also suggest Seward's
complicated rationale for the publication. Upon first reading Southey's poem,
Seward ecstatically shared her opinion that "this is the age of miracles. A great
one has lately arisen in the poetical world—the most extraordinary that ever appeared, as to juvenile powers, except that of the ill-starred Chatterton:—Southey's
Joan of Arc, an epic poem of strength and beauty, by a youth of twenty." Her praise,
however, was severely tempered because Southey not only misrepresents Henry V
but "defames the English character in general, stigmatizes our constitution, and
deifies the Moloch spirit of that of the French" (*Letters* 4:290). Succeeding letters to Sarah Ponsonby elaborate her concern. Southey's poem appeared during
a series of invasion crises that made his celebration of the French people seem
dangerous, given his immense powers: "O Southey! Is this a period in which to
exalt the French character, with parricide impulse, to depreciate that of England?"

(*Letters* 4:295). "He cannot think the system of our ministers more execrable than I think it," she remarked, but in her view, he should not have "calumniated" the national character and constitution at that juncture (*Letters* 4:328).

Seward's philippic, then, was inspired as much by thrilled recognition of a brilliant young talent as by her fear that his powerful epic might demoralize her compatriots when threatened invasion required their courage and pride. With the French at their doorstep, British readers should not be imbibing revolutionary philosophy: "I am too ardent in the common poetic cause, not to wish the highest poetic celebrity to a work of such exalted genius as Joan of Arc; but I would not have its intellectual splendours dazzle the British heart into adoption of its very pernicious principles" (*Letters* 4:370). Seward initially submitted her poem to the *Morning Chronicle* for publication in spring 1797 (*Letters* 4:328), but when peace talks began, she withdrew it until late summer, "unwilling, beneath the pending pacific negotiation, in which I trust our hot-brained government is at last sincere, to say anything with my pen, which might feed the general hatred of this country towards its too-successful foes" (*Letters* 4:369). Confident as always in her own powers and public appeal, Seward hesitated lest her competing portrait of the French as murderers and atheists impede the longed-for peace process. Her poem's appearance in August's *European Magazine* thus represented Seward's impulse, as an older poet still celebrated for her patriotic verse, both to acknowledge the emergence of a new talent and to caution the public against what she believed, at that historic moment, to be his work's dangerous implications. Bainbridge has argued that Seward's emphasis on Southey's age "suggests that it is Southey's youth and lack of manliness that are responsible for his political beliefs" (86). Her letters suggest that Seward indeed wished to rebuke a poet who she thought immature to curb his potentially disastrous genius. She published her poem as the antidote to his "deadliest aconite," as a healing medicine that could only be derived from her powerful "laurel wreaths" (ll. 27–28).

Seward later became not only Southey's friend but an enthusiastic mentor. Her conversion, so to speak, occurred after he published *Madoc* and his second volume of miscellaneous poems in 1806–7. Seward wrote rapturously to her friends regarding each volume; Southey became aware of her praise and initiated a correspondence. Perhaps their friendship led Seward to reread *Joan of Arc* from the perspective of intervening events. In 1807, she appended a note to her philippic retracting, and essentially apologizing for, her criticism. "Cooler reflection, and a long experience of the mischiefs resulting from the sanguinary system which this government has unwarned pursued through the last 14 years, have justified this Poet's representation of Henry the Fifth's conduct in invading France," she explained. Southey's condemnation of "monarchical ambition and rapacity . . . proceeded from benevolence to the Human race, and from a spirit of justice too firm to be warped by the vanity of national enthusiasm." Seward's note appeared in her posthumous edition, which contrary to her expectation guaranteed the poem's oblivion (*Poetical Works* 3:69). The note witnesses her capacity to change her mind when circumstances revealed fresh perspectives, as she had done with regard to the initial French rebellion and English declaration of war, the suspension of habeas corpus, the refusal to extend political rights to non-Anglicans, and other wartime issues. But because she confided her political strictures in letters, Seward appears in the midst of the war poets only to chasten a young man whose views, paradoxically, resembled hers. Hesitant to intervene partly because she recognized the power of verse, especially her own, Seward thought she had seized an opportunity to rally her countrymen when *Joan of Arc* might have demoralized them. Events proved her denunciation wrong, she confessed, but her philippic lingers, an indicator not of her nuanced position but of her response to one poem at one dangerous juncture of the wars.

Seward wrote three other war-related poems, all but one obscure if for different reasons. In October 1798, the *European Magazine* published her "Additional Stanzas to 'Rule Britannia,' in Celebration of Nelson's Victory" (*Poetical Works* 3:115–18).[5] The poem begins by quoting the second and fourth stanzas of James Thomson's anthem before adding seven more, commemorating victories by Howe, Jervis, Duncan, and Nelson. Her conclusion invites all participants in those battles to join the chorus when they "return, the charter'd song to pour, / When *Nelson* and the *Nile* are nam'd" (ll. 51–52). Seward's reference to her song as "charter'd" suggests that it was commissioned, and indeed she boasts in a note in the posthumous edition of her works that the "stanzas were . . . sung at a music meeting at Birmingham" honoring Nelson's triumph (*Poetical Works* 3:117). Seward's agreement to step forward once more as the British muse reflects her genuine relief after a chain of victories that devastated the French navy, easing fears at the time of an invasion. A year later, Seward was again complaining to correspondents about the seemingly endless war (see, for example, *Letters* 5:248–50). But Nelson's victory brought momentary relief and made Seward feel sufficient optimism to fulfill the civic request for a victory anthem. Her decision to appropriate Thomson's ode might suggest that her antiwar sentiments obstructed any strong creative effort. In any case, a stringent deadline probably demanded hasty composition. But the choice of frame, including quotation of the earlier poem, also reflected Seward's awareness that Thomson's ode epitomized for contemporaries, as Suvir Kaul observes, "English poetry on public themes" (1). While Kaul regards Thomson's ode skeptically because it overlooks the actual or virtual slavery of many British subjects, Seward's appeal to it reflects popular British belief in themselves as "free" compared with their French adversaries. In the wake of an invasion scare, Nelson's and his colleagues' victories seemed to rescue Britons from the prospect of slavery to the French and their dictatorial Napoleonic government. Seward borrowed the now-classic anthem as an actress might assume a "Britannia" costume for a pageant, secure in her identity as British muse rousing her compatriots' morale. Workmanlike rather than inspired, the Nelson poem shows Seward acquiescing in her national, patriotic role during an episode when circumstances evoked her participation.

In 1799, on the other hand, Seward's volume of sonnets and Horatian odes concluded with "To the Roman People, on Their Renewing the Civil Wars" (178–79). In this ode, rendered as a thirty-line, heroic couplet poem, Horace declares his horror that Romans have not been satisfied by centuries of warfare against others. "Is not our scorn of safety, health, and ease, / Shewn by devasted [sic] climes, and blood-stained seas?" (ll. 5–6). He fears that Rome is now destined to destroy herself in "expiation" (l. 30) for their aggression. Civil war is now inevitable, "when foes no more her might resistless feel, / But Roman bosoms bleed by Roman steel" (ll. 17–18). The poem had not been among those published in the *Gentleman's Magazine* between 1786 and 1787, suggesting it was composed later. In fact, the ode echoes fears Seward expressed throughout the 1790s that by pursuing continental war, Britain had guaranteed herself the same doom. Conscription and heavy taxes would inevitably spur the British poor to revolt in emulation of their French counterparts. Seward's intention is unmistakable, but she virtually buried it at the end of her book. Reviewers concentrated on her sonnets' artistry or on her temerity, as a woman unschooled in Latin, in paraphrasing Horace.[6] No correspondents selected this ode for comment. The ode is the closest Seward came to prophesying the war's outcome, to conveying her horror over the seemingly endless, pointless bloodshed. No one seems to have noticed, perhaps because her point was made so obliquely, through Horace, and its ostensible subject was an ancient civil war. France, not Britain, might have been mistaken for her analogy, so soon after the revolution. Seward might even have been relieved that her political insinuation remained unobserved, but to readers of her correspondence it is manifest.

Seward never published her final war poem, although it best represents her attitude toward what Goya called "the Disasters of War." Several of her letters mention captured French generals quartered in Lichfield (French officers were often quartered before being escorted to prison in Liverpool). Seward was among the few local citizens to extend them hospitality. In June 1806, one such officer called to pay his respects before returning home after a three-year detention (*Letters* 6:272–73). M. De Brosses then wrote from Liverpool before embarkation to thank her for paraphrasing a poem, "The Sorrows of Absence," his wife had written during his exile. Seward admitted adding many details to the poem, particularly mention of his children as she had seen them portrayed in a small painting Madame De Brosses had sent her husband as a Christmas present. She was "flattered" by De Brosses's delight in the poem but worried because he reported giving numerous, doubtless flawed, copies to admiring friends (*Letters* 6:294–95). Seward's "Elegy, Written as from a French Lady, Whose Husband Had Been Three Years Prisoner of War at Lichfield," was printed posthumously in her collected works (*Poetical Works* 3:375–79) and has recently been reprinted in Paula Backscheider's and Catherine Ingrassia's anthology *British Women Poets of the Long Eighteenth Century* (455–57). The eighty-four line monologue is written in a-b-a-b, iambic pentameter, stanzas. The pattern is a type of heroic stanza, a choice that underlines the speaker's simple dignity.[7] The speaker could be any matron anywhere whose husband has been detained; the French lady mourns her "wasted youth," regrets the passing days, and believes her husband is as mournful as she. She must imagine his sorrow, because he has not been permitted to write, even to explain why he is imprisoned. "Ah! Why are bonds for him who knows not crime?" she implores. "Fierce War ordains them! / Fiend of human kind!" (ll. 44–45). Her anguished cry no doubt resembles those of anyone in her situation, but it also echoes many of Seward's letters denouncing the war.

Seward worried that the many extant transcriptions of her poem inevitably contained serious flaws. Such concerns often spurred eighteenth-century writers into print. In this case, although she was proud of the poem (she replied to more praise of it, by another French prisoner, in November 1806 [*Letters* 6:320]), she refrained from sending it to a London journal. She may simply have reached the point in her life at which she no longer coveted, or had the energy to pursue, publication. Perhaps she felt that since the poem was the expanded paraphrase of verses she had not translated, it might attract the kind of criticism leveled at her Horatian odes. Perhaps she worried that having condemned the French as godless murderers in her philippic, she would appear inconsistent and insincere. Perhaps she feared the poem would be perceived as pro-Jacobin in its sympathetic portrait of a lonely, fearful French wife. Seward's poem indeed conveys the touching vulnerability of the wife, who maintains her home as if her husband had never left:

All things around me seem to expect him here;
My Husband's favourite robe enfolds me still;
Here have I rang'd the books he lov'd,—and there
Placed the selected chair he us'd to fill.   (ll. 57–60)

The books, the chair, and especially the detail of the husband's old robe, comforting his wife by "enfolding" her as he used to do, suggest that the war, while little understood by noncombatants, has destroyed families rather than aggrandize nations. At last Seward had written a poem that elevated the domestic over the national, the "private, sentimental, and impassioned" (Guest *Small Change* 267) over the stern demands of patriotism. The "Elegy, Written as from a French Lady" is spoken by a victim of British military prowess rather than by the poet as British muse. It is therefore anomalous, but it adds to Seward's scant record of wartime verse the expression of her deeply felt conviction about the war's inhumanity and, ultimately, its futility. Taken together, Seward's war poems offer the barest glimpse of her complicated political responses. Seward's correspondence, in its passion, richness, and scope, is the distinguished successor to her national patriotic poems, even though she confined her epistolary reflections to a select group of trusted friends.

Seward's war poems and letters invite speculation about the complex relation of women to the public sphere in what we now call the early Romantic era. Anne K. Mellor has been among the chief scholars disputing the paradigm that assigned men and women to "separate spheres." In *Mothers of the Nation*, she points to women's numerous publications on social and political issues as well as their leadership in political and philanthropic movements and argues that "if women participated fully in the discursive public sphere and in the formation of public opinion in Britain by the late eighteenth century, then the assumption that there existed a clear distinction in historical practice between a realm of public, exclusively male activities and a realm of private, exclusively female activities in this period is also erroneous" (7). Her chapter on women's political poetry acknowledges the achievements of "poetesses" like Felicia Hemans who identified themselves with "femininity," but Mellor champions women who wrote powerful verse advocating causes like abolition and women's rights: the ancestors of modern feminists. Charlotte Smith's "The Emigrants" (1793), which invites sympathy for those French who have fled their homes during the Reign of Terror, exemplifies the woman poet's abhorrence of patriarchal abuse and her advocacy of an "ethic of care" (73–74). Mellor's point transforms our conception of the late eighteenth century. If there were, objectively speaking, no separate spheres, then why did not

Seward pursue her public career as British muse throughout the 1790s? Why did she not publish her "Elegy, Written as from A French Lady" as Smith published her poem on a similar topic? France declared war on Britain in early 1793, so Smith's plea on behalf of French refugees was courageous at the time. Seward's retreat from poetry on national affairs seems pusillanimous in comparison.

Part of the answer lies in the fact that although there may have been no literal separate spheres, there were assuredly ideological separate spheres to which men and women, and especially gentlemen and ladies, were encouraged to adhere. If Seward had not understood this to be so, she would not have described herself in letters as her father's nurse instead of, as she really was, his business manager (Barnard 72–73). Most importantly, she would have defied propriety more openly in conducting her relationship with John Saville. Instead, she behaved with such great discretion that until Teresa Barnard's recent biography, many scholars did not suspect the length and depth of their commitment. Yet, as Barnard observes, Seward's chaste liaison brought on her the consciousness that at any time she could be accused of sexual impropriety, at a time when such a charge would also have damaged her pretension to speak as the British muse (89, 93). Indeed, Seward's attachment invited unwanted attention from men such as James Boswell, who assumed that she was open to sexual propositions (Barnard 135–39). Seward's relationship was literally self-limiting; in unpublished letters, she revealed it as the principal reason she stayed in Lichfield after her parents' deaths (Barnard 21). The revelation makes "Lichfield, an Elegy" even more of a creative tour-de-force: contrary to her declaration there that memories of Honora kept her from moving to London, a living beloved was the motivation she did not dare proclaim. In the case of her patriotic poems, the socially precarious relationship with Saville would have compounded her reasons to avoid print, should she have wished to express her disillusionment despite public pressure to support official government policies. As in the case of her amateurism/professionalism and her posture as national muse, Seward's wartime correspondence usefully complicates what we know about women writers in the early Romantic period. As a gentlewoman and an ambitious writer, protecting an unconventional romance as well as a national literary reputation, she falls between the poles represented by Mellor's "poetesses," on one hand, and her admirably outspoken political poets, on the other. Thorough consideration of Seward's position increases our understanding of women poets' obstacles and their triumphs in the 1790s, as well as the challenges faced by all poets throughout that tumultuous decade.

In light of her correspondence, Seward's verse deserves the kind of historicist reading that has found contemporary political references in other apparently unrelated poems like "Tintern Abbey." One of Seward's best-known poems, "Llan-gollen Vale" (*Poetical Works* 3:70–80), was written in 1795 after her first visit to that Welsh terrain, which culminated in her meeting with Sarah Ponsonby and Lady Eleanor Butler, the famed "Llangollen ladies" whose invitations were much cov-eted. In a letter to a Miss Wingfield on August 14, Seward described the valley's history, which she soon transformed into a poem (*Letters* 4:89–93; on Septem-ber 7, she minutely described to her cousin, the Rev. Henry White, her visit to the Llangollen ladies at their exquisite neo-Tudor home [*Letters* 4:98–109]). Most criticism of this episode and the ensuing poem, from its publication until now, has concentrated on Seward's description of the fascinating ladies. The letters and poem have recently come to be regarded as part of a Sapphic tradition, enthusi-astic celebrations of a well-known same-sex partnership by a poet identified as lesbian. Barnard, having clarified Seward's sexual identity (Saville was actually her traveling companion, although the published letters do not mention his pres-ence), instances "Llangollen Vale" as an example of Seward's antiquarian interests (127). The poem indeed resembles eighteenth-century models such as Thomas Warton's "Ode Written at Vale-Royal Abbey in Cheshire" (1777), a reflection on evocative medieval ruins, and also recalls Thomas Gray's earlier "The Bard" (1757), with its stirring description of a thirteenth-century Welsh bard defying Edward I from Snowdon's heights.

But in the context of her letters, Seward's concentration on the bloody history of the valley before celebrating the women who have redeemed its barbarous past assumes new significance. In June 1795, for example, she had written to her friend Dorothy Sykes expressing her horror at the sadistic treatment of Louis XVI's or-phans. She described the plight of the Dauphin and his sister in heart-rending terms before inveighing against their "inhuman" guards: "That such inhuman and impious wretches are not permitted to be crushed, rendered a warning to other nations, and an awful example of the chastizement of an outraged Deity, seems incomprehensible; but God, in his own time, will punish these blasphemous and cruel republicans" (*Letters* 4:74). Of her own country's government she had little better to say. "Persisting in a war originally just, but now become hopeless, we seem to forget that there is a God to punish the wicked without our waste of blood and treasure in a desperate cause" (*Letters* 4:74–75). Seward's comments seem a perfect illustration of Mellor's argument, in *Romanticism and Gender*, that women writers embraced a political model based on "domestic affections" in place of the twisted patriarchal paradigm that was wreaking havoc in Europe (66). Seward in-stances the perverse treatment of "sweet innocent children" (*Letters* 4:74) as proof of the French republicans' failure to establish an acceptable government but re-

frains from wishing them "crushed" (presumably by the British and their allies).
The misguided British government, too, she consigns to divine punishment. In
retreating from the fantasy of wishing to see either government blasted by divine
retribution, Seward joins other women writers who, as Mellor observes, replaced
the extreme revolutionary ideal with one of gradual, organic development (65) —
or at least with punishment meted out "in [God's] own time" rather than according to violent human impulses. From this perspective, Seward's initial, seventy-
eight-line narrative of the Llangollen valley's medieval history, over half the poem,
mirrors in her account of English-Welsh warfare the recent and equally fruitless
war of British against French. She represents Owen Glendower, for example, as
a Welsh hero, but describes his birth amid a visitation of the plague. Even Glendower's victory over Henry IV, inaugurating a period of peace in which bardic
song flourishes, is described as pyrrhic: Wales's "Thermopylae" (l. 60), won by
"slaughtered heaps" of soldiers (l. 57). After Glendower's revolt, the bard Hoel
won "deathless fame" singing of his "ill-starred love" for a local lady. Seward's
tribute to Hoel is followed by her lengthy description of Ponsonby and Butler and
their peaceful domicile, a place where they "to letter'd ease devote" themselves,
and a place that is "Friendship's blest repose" (l. 96).

Seward describes the music created by the ladies' Aeolian lute, then asks what
human could duplicate such ravishing sound. "The proud sex as soon, with virtue
calm, / Might win from this bright pair pure Friendship's spotless palm" (ll. 105–6).
Having stated her doubt that any man could merit that privilege, she concludes
her poem by comparing the area's former domination by Valle Crucis Abbey,
scene of bleak rituals and enforced vows, with the ideal life of the Llangollen
ladies. She ends by wishing them long lives and after death a mutual tomb commemorating their friendship, which, she implies, has redeemed this valley from
its history of superstition, warfare, and fruitless courtly love. The poem might well
illustrate Mellor's theory regarding women's Romanticism, with its emphases on
women's superior reason and on friendship as the basis of a domestic partnership
that is, in turn, the ideal model for government, far preferable to the abusive patriarchal system of the time (*Romanticism and Gender* 38). Seward's descriptions
of Owen Glendower's revolt, of Hoel's songs, and of Valle Crucis no doubt appealed to readers intrigued by Britain's Celtic past, but each also speaks to her
own culture, with its bloodthirsty revolutionary battles and counterbattles and
institutionalized repression, tragedies seemingly unaffected by the eloquent verse
of contemporary poets. Likewise, readers wishing for a glimpse of the Llangollen
ladies' elite milieu would have been gratified by Seward's description of their
"gothic" abode, but the ladies' blissful existence seems to have struck her because

it was precisely the enlightened reverse of Llangollen's brutal past. We can conclude that Seward was circumspect indeed if her implication regarding a superior,
nonhierarchical, feminine domestic realm, opposed to the bloodthirsty, patriarchal political system she deplored, escaped notice as particularly appropriate given
recent events. But after reading her wartime correspondence, we can appreciate
both the social challenges that dissuaded her from writing more forcefully against
the French wars and the subtlety with which, even writing within eighteenth-
century poetic conventions, she occasionally insinuated her convictions.

CHAPTER SIX

Seward and Sensibility

Louisa, a Poetical Novel, in Four Epistles

In 1784, two years after publishing her elegy to Lady Miller, Seward published her most popular work. *Louisa, a Poetical Novel, in Four Epistles* went through five editions between its first appearance and 1792, not including an additional fifth edition published in Philadelphia in 1789. The story was calculated to attract and instruct an audience accustomed to admiring keen sensibility, and so in this chapter, I look at it in relation to the cult of sensibility and assess its place amid a body of literature exploring the consequences of sentiment. We have already witnessed Seward's ability to re-create Captain Cook and Major André as models of heroic sentiment. Instead of intervening in national politics, however, Seward explores domestic politics in the tangled familial plot of her novel. She also suggests the relative values of sensibility and the economic concerns driving British social relations, including marriage. She does so while revising the work of four predecessors, each of whom might be considered a chosen mentor or literary father: Pope, Rousseau, Milton and Prior. Seward chiefly reworks Pope's *Eloisa to Abelard*(1714) and Rousseau's *Julie; ou, La nouvelle Heloïse* (1761), which appeared in an English translation as *Eloisa* shortly after its publication in French, to create a heroine who is not consumed by passion like either of those heroines but is rather a modern British woman of sense as well as sensibility. Her compression of a lengthy prose novel into a relatively brief quartet of poems assists her effort to contain the destructive passions motivating many heroes and heroines of sensibility. Conversely, by stretching Pope's couplet verses to novel length, she develops a plot that dissipates much of the explosive passion that consumes Eloisa, revising the concept of sensibility from a positive, feminine perspective. This chapter concentrates on the first of *Louisa's* four epistles, in which Seward blends a poem (*Eloisa*) and a novel (*Julie*), a combination that demands scrutiny. *Louisa* expands our perception of the novel's late-century development even though Seward's experiment did not inspire emulation.

Louisa attracted wide notice and critical attention both laudatory and depreca-tory. The novel's—or more properly, novella's—reception resembled in minia-ture that of the "blockbuster" that inspired Seward, Jean Jacques Rousseau's *Julie*. In the case of *Louisa*, however, we have almost lost the keys that once enabled readers to engage the poem with rapture. Simultaneously, we have lost in the poem a valuable gloss on or literary key to mid-eighteenth century values and tensions as well as a link in the history of the novel. That key is sensibility. To a reader unprepared to accept sensibility as the guiding principle of Seward's tale, *Louisa* will appear to be little more than "description, with interpolations of apos-trophe and other forms of maundering which appeal but slightly to the reader of today" (Ashmun 125). As usual, biographer Margaret Ashmun proved unwilling to reconstruct the context of Seward's work, even for her best-known publica-tion. Seventy-five years ago, sensibility had evidently been consigned to oblivion, gravely if not fatally obscuring many eighteenth-century artistic productions. Thankfully, the past twenty years have restored sensibility to prominence as the century's dominant theory of human behavior. Once dismissed, following the lead of Romantic-era writers who disowned it, sensibility has again been recog-nized as a pervasive influence, motivating social movements, including philan-thropy and companionate marriage, as well as personal behaviors, such as refined manners and sympathy for the oppressed and suffering members of society.

G. J. Barker-Benfield has located the emergence of sensibility as cultural para-digm in the writings of George Cheyne, whose publications during the 1720s and 1730s popularized the theoretical connection between the nervous system and moral responses to experience, building on the theories of Newton and Locke (6–15). Barker-Benfield consequently agrees with George S. Rousseau and others that sensibility, the belief that the nervous system conveys perceptions to the brain or soul, which reacts according to a person's degree of refinement, captured popu-lar awareness in the 1740s (6) after Samuel Richardson based the psychology of *Clarissa's* characters on Cheyne's theories (16–17). In *Cato's Tears*, Julie Ellison disputes Barker-Benfield's time line, discovering in such Restoration tragedies as *Venice Preserv'd* the positive depiction of masculine sentiment, portrayed as the personal and domestic antidote to callous political maneuvers. But whether El-lison's or Barker-Benfield's chronology is preferred, there is little dispute that by the mid-eighteenth century, sensibility reigned as the chief factor understood to motivate human behavior. Some human beings were privileged by refined nervous systems to respond more quickly and sensitively to environmental stimuli, and these beings were understood to be superior to other more obtuse people, whose hardened nerves made them more or less oblivious to much of what they encountered. Literary heroes and heroines, such as Clarissa and Parson Yorick, tended to emerge, like Louisa, from the former class.

Before examining *Louisa* from the perspective of sensibility, we should recall that sensibility was a gendered construction. Sensibility's gendered identity has, however, been disputed since John Mullan's influential *Sentiment and Sensibility* traced its first manifestations as a trait of men privileged and refined enough to weep over the plight of those less fortunate to its eventual condemnation as the weakness of debilitated women.[1] Barker-Benfield argues that despite George Cheyne's definitive autobiographical writings, sensibility was usually associated with the feminine, which explains its connections with refinement, consumerism, companionate marriage, and other trends that made social life less brutal and more comfortable for women throughout the century. Claudia Johnson, in turn, has questioned both Mullan's and Barker-Benfield's accounts. She argues forcefully in *Equivocal Beings* that sensibility was always gendered masculine and that its consequences functioned not to empower women but to put them in their (domestic) place. Moreover, while men's displays of feeling were usually regarded as the effusions of refined beings, women's sensibility was stigmatized as debility or at best as inferior to men's (14). Women were thus, according to Johnson, reduced either to exhibiting a lower order of misguided sensibility or to eschewing sensibility and assuming behaviors once associated with men, hence becoming "equivocal beings" (12). Johnson traces this dichotomy through the writings of Wollstonecraft, Radcliffe, Burney, and Austen, but her argument suggests that one would do well to exercise caution in assessing Seward's apparent endorsement of sensibility in *Louisa*.

Sensibility, then, as a theory regarding the motivation behind human behavior, emerged gradually during the seventeenth and early eighteenth centuries but burst into full public consciousness in the 1740s, remaining a convincing motivator in fictional characterizations into the nineteenth century despite a growing number of pejorative portraits and critical complaints. Published in 1784, *Louisa* fell within sensibility's reign but after its heyday, as its positive connotations were beginning to wear off. In her preface, however, Seward claimed to have written the first 156 lines of the poem when she was nineteen, which would place *Louisa* closer to the meridian of sensibility's positive cultural value ([ii]). If indeed Seward began the poetic novel in 1761, the midcentury date helps explain why she chose, aside from wishing to revise Pope, heroic couplets for the tale over the blank verse she would probably have used for a long poem in the 1780s. It also helps clarify the origins of the poem in Seward's effort to address and correct what she considered the less salutary manifestations of misguided sensibility, such as those portrayed in Pope's and Rousseau's books, as well as in Matthew Prior's "Henry and Emma" (1709). I return several times to Seward's account of her poem's late-adolescent inception, but her preface to the poem complicates Johnson's argument that feminine sensibility was always associated with debility by positing Louisa as the ideal mean between the extremes of "voluptuousness" and "too conceding softness" illustrated by Pope's Eloisa and Prior's Emma, respectively. Seward's decision to represent her heroine as occupying this middle position suggests that while there were manifest dangers associated with sensibility, contemporaries might envision ways its expression exalted rather than degraded young women.

One final aspect of *Louisa* I want to address as a preliminary is the question of why Seward wrote a verse novel. In an age when prose fictions were evolving to become the dominant form of written entertainment, why did Seward diverge from her most immediate model? *La nouvelle Heloïse* was remarkable, to contemporaries, as Rousseau's only novel; why did Seward, whose letters and other nonfiction writings demonstrate her facility in prose, decide against attempting a medium that might have guaranteed a wider, or more lasting, audience for her book? In a superb recent study, G. Gabrielle Starr describes how lyric poetry was absorbed into the early novel. Starr discusses the preference of poets like Pope for the poetic epistle over the lyric as a vehicle for passionate expression (47), although both lyric and epistle forms were often incorporated into early novels. Starr agrees with William Dowling that earlier eighteenth-century writers approved of the epistle partly because it assumed an audience, a community with shared values, rather than vaunted a solipsistic consciousness (Starr 82). Dowling in fact views *Eloisa to Abelard* and all heroides as exceptions, intimations of women's isolated circumstances rather than of masculine community (28). But while Starr observes the frequent recourse to epistolary and/or poetic expression in early novels, and Dowling describes the eventual ascendancy of *Eloisa to Abelard* as a reflection of the "mysterious depths in the consciousness of the beholder" (168), neither addresses the possibility of an heroic epistle absorbing a novel, rather than the other way around, or driving a fictional plot rather than invariably remaining the token of solipsism. Seward's appears to have been a unique attempt, understandable in that her chosen medium for artistic expression was verse rather than prose. *Louisa* is the product of an era when the novel form was still in flux, and readers might have been drawn by the sheer novelty of two fused genres, not to mention by the pleasure they continued to derive from poetry. Starr is adamant about the need for greater flexibility in considering the flux of materials out of which the novel emerged. Seward's verse novel—which I refer to as both poem and novel in the course of this chapter—grew from her decision to answer Rousseau while also refining his model, Pope, an experiment worth mention in histories of the novel. At the same time, Seward claims the assumption of community for the heroic epistle: because Louisa sends her despairing letter not to her inaccessible lover but to a sympathetic female friend, her plight is ameliorated.

As she often did in her career, Seward chose to bend an Odyssean bow, or rather, three bows, in adapting Pope's, Prior's, and Rousseau's texts. Pope's fictional letter from the lovelorn nun to her former lover remained popular throughout the century, confirming the poet as an early proponent of sensibility rather than, as he was later viewed, an exemplar of the "age of reason." Seward, who metaphorically quarreled with her predecessor as often as she emulated him, invited comparison with his heroine, with Eloisa's setting, and with her responses to personal crisis. Seward wished to refine what she perceived as indelicate in Eloisa, whose "impassion'd fondness" (*Louisa* preface [i]) had led her to abandon her reputation and, worse, jeopardize her soul. Eloisa, then, illustrated the kind of depraved, sensual response that Claudia Johnson believes characterized the century's view of women's sensibility. On the other hand, Prior's Emma represented an equally debased alternative. In that heroine's credulous belief in her fiancé's tale of his (fictional) disgrace, and her instantaneous offer to accompany him into exile, Seward detected a mindless response that maintained personal integrity but equally abdicated self-respect in favor of affection. Both heroines exemplified the dangers posed by innocence, the bane of heroines from Clarissa to Evelina and beyond. Against those dangers Seward posited the value of self-respect, which enables her heroine—as isolated and abandoned as Eloisa, as unsuspecting as Emma, and as ardent as both—to resist her impulse to commit suicide and to moderate her outrage while justly condemning Eugenio for his desertion. While young women are peculiarly vulnerable to betrayal owing to their enforced innocence, Seward suggests that dignity is possible under all circumstances and is indeed sometimes necessary for survival. Her position, while arguable, revises Johnson's contention that sensibility was always condemned in women; at least by Seward in the 1780s, self-possession was deemed not only compatible with but indispensable to sensibility in young ladies. Seward acknowledges Pope's and Prior's heroines of sensibility but assimilates their characteristics into her new, positive model of feminine sensibility.

Surely it was this revision of beloved images into a modern, correct, and fashionable vision of feminine sensibility that enchanted early readers. As Jean Marsden has shown in *The Re-Imagined Text*, mid-eighteenth century readers and audiences manifested their reverence for Shakespeare not by consuming his plays in as pristine a form as possible but by embracing adaptations by David Garrick and others (75–102). Marsden observes that Garrick's adaptations, mostly performed and published in the 1750s, mark the boundary after which increasing reverence for Shakespeare rendered interference with his texts a profanation. But Seward conceived her novel at a time when adaptation was still very much an accepted tribute. By creating a character incorporating the passion and sensitivity of Eloisa and Emma but omitting Eloisa's recklessness and Emma's dogged, not to say spaniel-like, devotion, Seward re-presented for contemporaries two well-known but unrefined heroines. Archetypes of sensibility but in many ways archaic, Eloisa and Emma needed adaptation in order to reinstate Pope's and Prior's forceful portrayals of feminine devotion as viable patterns of sensibility. Seward's gesture, then, revisioned as well as revised Pope and Prior for her readers, validating the heroic nature of exceptional passion while intimating that powerful emotion can be controlled by morality and self-respect. As Seward explained in her preface, Louisa's "sensibilities . . . know no bounds, except those which the dignity of conscious Worth, and a strong sense of Religion prescribe" ([i]). Her project was both daring, in its wish to improve the work of two acknowledged giants, and a palpable act of devotion.

I briefly recount *Louisa*'s plot because the verse novel long ago lost its readership and indeed has rarely been discussed even by scholars of sensibility. In its first epistle, Louisa, the eponymous heroine, confides to her absent friend Emma that her brother Lorenzo, visiting for the summer after finishing Oxford, brought home his best friend, Eugenio, son of a wealthy mercantile family. Louisa and Eugenio fell in love and, with Lorenzo's blessing, became engaged. At the end of the summer, the three part; Lorenzo heads off for the grand tour and Eugenio goes home for a visit with his family before establishing himself in the family business in advance of his marriage. Louisa, deeply smitten, pines for Eugenio for several months before, to her horror, reading in the newspaper of his marriage to a wealthy heiress. She perceives herself to be dying of grief and fears that her brother might challenge Eugenio to a duel when he learns her fiancé's perfidy. In the next letter, Eugenio writes in turn to Emma explaining his mysterious desertion. He betrayed Louisa because his father, on the verge of bankruptcy, begged him to save his family by marrying the hugely dowered and audaciously flirtatious Emira. Eugenio's action resulted from the tragic necessity of choosing between

two evils: he believed that Louisa might recover from her grief, especially if outraged by his supposed callousness, but his family would certainly be destroyed by
financial ruin. Louisa responds to Emma's news in the third epistle by resolving
to live, knowing that Eugenio is not a base traitor but in fact made an honorable
decision that she must commend despite its consequences. The novel's final epistle, from Louisa to Emma, relates the outcome of Eugenio's marriage. Ernesto,
Eugenio's father, appears in Louisa's bower and whisks her away in his coach to
Emira's deathbed. En route, he describes the misery caused by Eugenio's marriage of convenience. Knowing herself his second choice, Emira deserted Eugenio for a life of debauchery, rejecting even their infant daughter as the product
of a loveless union. Unfortunately, her scandalous carousings exposed her to a
fatal illness. Emira's last wish is for Louisa's forgiveness and her promise to raise
Emira's and Eugenio's child. When Louisa arrives, Emira confesses that not only
was she aware of Eugenio's love for Louisa when she courted him but also that
she did so because his love for another piqued her competitive pride. Louisa
consents to raise her child and forgives Emira. Louisa concludes by inviting
Emma to join her and Eugenio, since Emira's death has ensured their impending marriage.

   Contemporaries responded warmly to a novel that sanctioned a nearly fatal
degree of emotional response if buttressed by conventional principles and a firm
sense of personal worth. By the time Seward published *Louisa*, numerous sentimental fictions had already appeared cautioning men and women against excessive passion while simultaneously devoting many pages to the re-creation of feelings. Oliver Goldsmith's *The Vicar of Wakefield* (1763), Laurence Sterne's *A
Sentimental Journey* (1768), and Henry MacKenzie's *The Man of Feeling* (1771)
are but the most famous among novels that privilege the relation of emotional
responses to experience over the description of incidents. Seward was perhaps
being disingenuous when she declared in her preface that *Louisa* had "little
chance to be popular. . . . An Imagination that glows, while the Heart is frozen,
has a propensity to fancy every thing prosaic which is not imagery, and will probably yawn over the reasoning of these Lovers, and sicken over their tenderness"
([ii]). A generation that had sobbed throughout Clarissa's account of her demise
and that would shortly devour the English translation of Goethe's *Sorrows of
Werther* (1786) was unlikely to disdain the combination of evocative scenery and
baffled passion that characterize *Louisa*. Since *Werther*'s anonymous translator
would demur in similar terms that "those who expect a Novel will be disappointed
in this work," it is more likely that Seward's disclaimer made a claim for her novel,
identifying *Louisa* as part of a popular subset, the novel of sensibility (v). At the

time, her achievement must have delighted readers who recognized familiar if old-fashioned poetic heroines refined into a model for fashionable young ladies.

What supplied the immediate impetus to Seward to compose *Louisa* seems to have been the publication in 1761 of *Eloisa*, the English translation of Rousseau's *La nouvelle Heloïse*. Seward would have known "Julie" as "Eloisa" because Rousseau's anonymous translator changed her name to prevent confusion (1:v–vi; I try to avoid confusion by referring to Rousseau's heroine as "Julie"). While in her introduction to Seward's poems for the *Bluestocking Feminism* series, Jennifer Kelly cites "transcending passion of the kind found in Rousseau" as the model for Louisa's characterization, Seward's correspondence suggests she was more concerned to correct than to replicate Rousseau's version of "high-minded passion" (xviii). Among the poems she bequeathed to Walter Scott, Seward included some early fictional letters to a correspondent she calls "Emma" that witness her youthful critical powers. The letters suggest that Seward herself was the model for Louisa, who likewise addresses an Emma in her fictional epistles.[2] The Emma of the letters, however, was the recipient of Seward's strictures on Rousseau, whose novel she was reading when Seward composed the first of her extant replies. "You talked of reading the New Eloisa," she added in a terse postscript; "throw it aside, I beseech you" (*Poetical Works* 1:xlvii). Her next letter explains that she objects to *Eloisa*'s "softening tendency," by which she apparently means the glorification of romantic passion to a degree that might provide a salutary example to the "vain and selfish hearts" of society ladies but endangers most young women whose tender hearts are already too susceptible (*Poetical Works* 1:xlviii). Seward's analysis reveals that Emira was designed to supplement *Eloisa* by presenting young ladies in "high life" with an image of "love, in its most enthusiastic excess" with "no hazard to principle and to happiness so desperate as pride; boundless dissipation and unprincipled extravagance being in their train" (*Poetical Works* 1:xlix). Emira illustrates Seward's psychology of desperate pride; she resorts to "habits of sensuality" that "once established" make the heart go "cold and impenetrable amidst the indelicate indulgence of the senses" and cause it to lose "all power of sympathizing truly and equally" (*Poetical Works* 1:l).

But while Emira is constructed as a warning to those whose passions are frozen by pride, Louisa and Eugenio counter Rousseau's Julie and St. Preux as acceptably didactic models of passion. Julie's marriage to Wolmar becomes Eugenio's marriage to Emira, for example, so that Louisa fulfills the era's preferred ideal of chaste feminine attachment: it is given only once, even if lifelong celibacy should be the consequence. Louisa's passion, while as deep as Julie's, is not reckless. While St. Preux suffers "the horrid temptation . . . to plunge into [the lake's] waters with a mistress, irrecoverably lost to his hopes" (*Poetical Works* 1:lxv), Louisa momentarily contemplates suicide but immediately heeds the cautions of a guardian angel to desist. Eugenio's inconstancy is merely apparent; he pledges his platonic devotion to his beloved despite a marriage engineered by his father and bride. On the other hand, he assiduously fulfills his marriage vows, siring a child and forswearing all contact with Louisa. While St. Preux contemplates desperate measures, Eugenio responds to his wife's adultery with the sober reflection that his coldness was partly responsible for her delinquency. Although Seward delighted in Rousseau's emotive and descriptive powers, she feared his examples of "transcending passion," and *Louisa* may have been inspired by her desire to create comparable but less dangerous models of sensibility: English models as opposed to Rousseau's continental figures. Seward's wish to clarify what in Rousseau appeared "labyrinths of sophistry" in which "the distinctions of right and wrong are blended and lost" may have been pedantic, but her audacity produced a novel with wide appeal (*Poetical Works* 1:lxiii).

Seward's impulse, at nineteen, to revise *La nouvelle Heloïse* was indeed audacious. Rousseau's novel had recently captivated readers throughout Europe.[3] The first English translation appeared only two months after the book's French publication; there were to be ten English editions in addition to seventy-two editions in French by 1800 (McDowell 2). The 156 lines Seward first drafted indicate some of her general responses, positive and negative, to *La nouvelle Heloïse* in addition to revising the plot and characterizations in specific ways. Rousseau's plot recreates that of the medieval Abelard and Heloïse in plausible modern terms. St. Preux is not a middle-aged cleric but the youthful son of bourgeois parents. Engaged by her mother to tutor Julie d'Étange, a young noblewoman, he falls in love and gradually musters the courage to communicate his passion by letter. Julie admits her corresponding devotion but the consummation of their affair is delayed by the omnipresence of her mother and St. Preux's other pupil, her cousin Claire. Eventually, however, the lovers embark on a clandestine romance that is constantly endangered by the possibility of detection and the vengeance that would follow of Julie's father, Baron d'Étange, who is determined that his daughter (and sole surviving child) will marry only a fellow aristocrat. Aided by Claire, however, the lovers prolong their affair for several years despite intermittent separations, until their secret is compromised and they must part before Julie's reputation is destroyed. Julie reluctantly consents to St. Preux's virtual exile to England under the patronage of the lovers' confidant, Lord Bomston, and to marriage with Monsieur Wolmar, her father's chosen suitor. Wolmar proves a generous husband despite knowledge of Julie's previous attachment; he eventually befriends St. Preux, who

resumes his now-chaste dedication to Julie before her untimely death after rescuing her son from the icy waters of Lake Geneva.

No summary so brief could encapsulate Rousseau's novel, which includes
numerous philosophical digressions and detailed descriptions of the lovers' emotions as well as the responses of all their acquaintances. Despite the unauthorized
and clandestine nature of their attachment, however, Julie and St. Preux are admired by all but her father for their intense devotion to one another. Rousseau, as
Judith McDowell has observed, introduced a fresh conception of virtue as adherence to one's deepest impulses (16). He granted unprecedented importance to the
passions and consequently to those heroes of sensibility who remain true to their
passions despite all obstacles. Hugh Blair would include such characters in his
description of the sentimental sublime in 1783: "On some occasions, where virtue
either has no place, or is but imperfectly displayed, yet if extraordinary vigour and
force of mind be discovered, we are not insensible to a degree of grandeur in the
character" (215). Julie and St. Preux are extolled by their circle not because they
eventually bow to social necessity. They are admired for the depth and intensity
of their attachment even though it led to transgression followed by mutual self-
sacrifice. Julie's death conforms to contemporary fictional demands that a fallen
heroine had to die to atone for her crime. To this extent, Rousseau himself was
willing to satisfy conventional expectations. But unlike the heroines of early "she
tragedies" or even Clarissa, Julie dies surrounded by loving and admiring family
members who regard her as exemplary rather than as a reformed sinner. What
would the nineteen-year-old daughter of an Anglican clergyman have made of
Rousseau's emphasis on the passions? Of his suggestion that emotional attachment can achieve a level of sublimity and is thus admirable on its own terms apart
from social, or even conventional moral, considerations? The opening lines of
Louisa convey Seward's intention to craft an alternative British version of Rousseau's plot, one based on British precedents but that remained mindful of her
great predecessor across the channel.

Julie and St. Preux are paradoxically doomed by the very passion that exalts
them. Love leads them to rationalize their affair and into numerous situations that
endanger both themselves and their principal confidants. Claire, for example,
is peacefully resigned to marrying her parents' chosen suitor. But once apprised
of her cousin's liaison, she devotes herself to managing the lovers' trysts, even re-
cruiting her fiancé to assist their affair. Seward evidently found Claire's role as
go-between distasteful; Julie's cousin should not have sanctioned, let alone facili-
tated, her illicit relationship. Rousseau's young people enjoy a level of autonomy

Seward evidently found unrealistic given the social structure that eventually prevents the lovers' marriage. The first change Seward made to his plot was to separate Louisa from her confidante, Emma, who is thus reduced to a more limited role. Emma has been in India for four years while her family attends to their business. Her exile places *Louisa's* action firmly in the modern British world of mercantile imperialism rather than in the enclosed world of Rousseau's Swiss lovers. By insisting on the recognizably British, commercial context of her love plot, Seward suggests that a *New Heloïse* for her compatriots needs a setting quite different from that of the remote shores of Lake Geneva. She also suggests that young women possess little autonomy, let alone the ability, to carry on lengthy clandestine love affairs. Modern Britain seems to control its citizens by enforcing distances between them. But Louisa's distance from Emma is also metaphorical. Alone on her brother's estate, Louisa has nobody in whom to confide when her lover breaks his engagement. Louisa has no support in her dilemma, possibly mirroring Seward's recognition of women's emotional isolation. If young women were neither instructed about nor expected to entertain strong feelings, how should they respond when plighted lovers died or decamped? How were they to conduct themselves in such situations, let alone when drawn toward an affair such as Rousseau describes?

Seward revised Pope's and Rousseau's heroines and their situations. Louisa is not a middle-aged nun lamenting her wasted youth and misplaced vows, as in Pope's epistle. She is not described as noble or beautiful like Rousseau's Julie is; in fact, we know little about her social station or appearance. Instead of a tyrannical uncle or father, Louisa appears to have only her beloved brother, whom she describes as "the youthful master of this quiet vale" (1:80). Unlike her predecessors, who succumbed to their lovers' forbidden advances, Louisa's courtship by Eugenio is approved by her brother, who introduces the couple. After Eugenio's admiring friendship evolves into professed love, Louisa accepts his proposal, and Lorenzo's "smiles fraternal hail'd our mutual vows" (1:328). Seward's description insists that romantic intensity can accompany even such mundane circumstances as a family-sanctioned courtship. She proposes that great passion can coexist with propriety, a concept that Rousseau's novel seems to deny (Claire and Julie frankly admit their lack of passion for their husbands). Eugenio is, moreover, a perfectly appropriate suitor, Lorenzo's university friend from a wealthy mercantile family. Theirs is to be a love match between a young woman from a landowning family, although without a large dowry, and a young man whose fortune is assured. Although Louisa is fortunate to secure her handsome, affectionate lover without the large portion his family might have demanded, Seward emphasizes the conventional nature of Louisa's circumstances before launching into her sorrowful plot.

Although Seward seems from the first to have intended a poem that would recall Rousseau's readers from their daydreams about impossible, secret love affairs, she clearly admired his ability to convey emotional states through vivid descriptions of setting. In her preface, Seward notes as models Pope's evocation of Eloisa's passions through her scenic descriptions and Rousseau's of St. Preux's through his description of the landscape of Meillerie as it appeared to him when one winter, he was lamenting his separation from Julie and when years later, he escorts her there with her husband's permission on a summer afternoon. Rousseau's description evocatively projects the seasonal features of a sublime terrain onto his hero's states of mind; St. Preux's passion resembles the Alpine scenery both in its winter harshness and summer fertility, depending on his mood. Seward both emulates her predecessors' techniques and refines them. Louisa is almost entirely defined by her setting, the "bower" in which she sits awaiting Lorenzo's visit while singing and accompanying herself on a lute. Unlike Pope's Eloisa, who thinks of herself as imprisoned and consequently describes herself trapped in a chapel, a cell, or a crypt, and unlike Julie, who evades supervision in her parents' and relatives' homes among other places, Louisa is found outdoors. She never alludes to a house, and we never hear of parents, guardians, maids or anyone who might control her behavior. The bower is evidently her favorite spot: Seward places her there like Eve or like a classical heroine within a single setting: a small, enclosed space at the base of a cliff that terminates her brother's garden.

Seward's immediate response to *La nouvelle Heloïse*, as we have seen, was to revise Pope's *Eloisa to Abelard*, an English version of the history that inspired Rousseau. Her poem cleverly evoked both her English and French models while correcting them according to her own notions of propriety and realism. If she indeed completed the novel upon rediscovering her draft in 1782, as her preface claims, the 156-line fragment she found provided the characters and plot for a story both laden with sensibility and more plausible to the broad swath of middle-rank British fiction readers. Louisa, as she describes herself, is both at liberty and self-constrained by deference to her brother and attachment to her bower. Her circumstances might have appealed to readers who would have envied her autonomy while recognizing in Louisa's near-stasis the bounded nature of most British ladies' lives. Seward, however, had several reasons for identifying Louisa with a single setting. Distilling Rousseau's sprawling novel into a poetic novel of fewer than one hundred pages required numerous reductions in scale. Charac-

ters, incidents, descriptions—all had to be compressed into four epistles of between four hundred and five hundred lines each. Seward chose to exploit her
favorite scenes from Pope and Rousseau by maintaining her focus on Louisa
within her bower. As Paul Goring has observed, novels of sensibility invite scrutiny of characters in given situations by tending toward the highly theatrical in
their descriptions (153). By observing heroes' and heroines' physical responses as
well as overhearing, as it were, their thoughts, readers learned to emulate the
reactions of sensibility. Seward had clearly studied the techniques of masters such
as Richardson; like his Pamela and Clarissa, Louisa is not merely an overheard
consciousness, writing to the moment, but a visible participant in the drama of
her courtship and desertion.

Seward composed her description of Louisa's bower with glances toward both
her predecessors. Pope's Eloisa complains from the outset that her convent's "relentless walls" enclose "rugged rocks" and "grots and caverns shagged with horrid
thorn" (ll. 19–20). Eloisa specifies that the convent's appearance reflects her personal melancholy, which "saddens all the scene, / Shades ev'ry flow'r, and darkens
ev'ry green, / Deepens the murmur of the falling floods, / And breathes a browner
horror on the woods" (ll. 165, 167–70). Early in *Eloisa*, St. Preux evokes a similar
scene to convey his misery. Exiled in the mountains above Julie's home, he confesses to her that

> the horrors of [my location] are increased by the gloomy succession of ideas
> ever present to my imagination . . . . It is dark; it is dreadful, then it suits the
> habit of my soul; and a more pleasant prospect of nature, would reflect little
> comfort on the dreary view within me. A ridge of barren rocks surrounds the
> coast, and my dwelling is still made more dismal by the uncomfortable face of
> winter. And yet, [Julie], I am sensible enough that if I were once forced to
> abandon you, I should stand in need of no other abode, no other season. (1:73)

Both Eloisa and St. Preux manifest the exquisite sensitivity to their surroundings
that marks the heroes and heroines of sensibility. Both find in such natural phenomena as seasonal weather reflections of their own states of mind. They observe
landscape features that resemble their personal misery: Eloisa's environment is
rugged, horrid, and sad, while St. Preux's is gloomy, dreadful, dreary, and barren.
Their perceived connection with the natural world demonstrates their sensibility,
their spontaneous, nervous reactions to environments that affect, even as they
reflect and deepen, already pensive moods.

One particular episode in Rousseau's novel inspired Seward's creation of Louisa's setting. After he and Julie have been separated for years, St. Preux takes her

for a summer outing to Meillerie, site of his former distress. In this season, his "solitary seat formed a wild and desert nook, but full of those sorts of beauties, which are only agreeable to susceptible minds, and appear horrible to others" (3:162). Although surrounded by glaciers and dark forests, the spot no longer seems desolate but instead reminds St. Preux of sufferings now past. The clearing to which he leads Julie suggests the small metaphorical space that is permitted to their emotional bond:

> In the midst of these noble and superb objects, the little spot where we were, displayed all the charms of an agreeable and rural retreat; small floods of water filtered through the rocks, and flowed along the verdure in chrystal streams. Some wild fruit trees leaned their heads over ours; the cool and moist earth was covered with grass and flowers. Comparing this agreeable retreat with the objects which surrounded us, one would have thought that this desert spot was designed as an asylum for two lovers, who alone had escaped the general wreck of nature. (3:163)

St. Preux attempts to convey the misery he formerly experienced in this spot, but, unfortunately, Julie insists they withdraw from a place so charged with their youthful passion. Both lovers understand that the refuge is illusory; its edenic fruit trees and crystal streams are literally hemmed in by forbidding crevasses and crags. They must withdraw to preserve not only their memories of past love but their precariously achieved adult respectability. To underline the scene's sense of a paradise lost, St. Preux concludes his account with a description of his subsequent despair and temptation to plunge with Julie into Lake Geneva as they are rowed from Meillerie. He recovers, however, and regards his and Julie's refusal to succumb either to renewed passion or to despair as a triumph of virtue (3:166–67).

Writing to her imaginary friend in 1763, Seward praised this letter as one of three in the novel she thought "not . . . excelled by any thing I have read" (*Poetical Works* 1:lxiv). "'St Preaux' [sic] solemn apostrophe to Eloisa [sic] is striking past expression," she exclaimed. "How we tremble for them both" (*Poetical Works* 1:lxiv). She particularly admired the concluding scene, with its "mutual and final conflicts, in the boat, of a passion with so much difficulty vanquished!" (*Poetical Works* 1:lxv). When, twenty-one years later, she returned to her novel, Seward capitalized on Louisa's initial setting, recognizing its potential for the kind of emotional reflection imagined by Eloisa and St. Preux. We first see Louisa in medias res, writing to Emma in the aftermath of her desertion by Eugenio. The bower where she sits to write little resembles the scene of summer courtship. It is now

late autumn, and the glade offers but a "thin shelter" (1:38). Louisa's description
recalls features of both Eloisa's and St. Preux's environments:

> Unequal steps, and rising sighs, disclose
> The thorny pressure of tyrannic woes;
> And where th' incumbent Rock, with awful face,
> Bends o'er the fountain, gurgling from its base,
> And marks the limit of the silent Dell,
> Sadly I sit my bosom'd griefs to tell.   (1:35–40)

While Eloisa beheld "grots and caverns shagg'd with rugged thorn," Louisa's heart
is wracked with "thorny pressure." Like both Eloisa and St. Preux, she seeks a
desolate spot congenial to her sorrows. As in Pope's and Rousseau's works, an
ominous cliff looms over Seward's setting, closing off the dell much like Louisa's
prospects, terminated by misfortune. Louisa later specifies that she first encountered Eugenio "on this shady bank" (1:85). At that time, the cliff with its spring
offered cool protection from the summer heat. The spot, which Louisa explains
is the end of a small valley within the estate's grounds, is her chosen refuge. As
such, its features are suggestive as well as emblematic. The enclosed site recalls
the Eden described by Seward's beloved Milton in *Paradise Lost*; unlike Milton's
garden, however, the bower witnesses not just Louisa's temptation but also her
triumph. Louisa's bower also resembles the retreat of another of Seward's favorite
poets, the lovelorn Petrarch, whom she knew had retired "to a romantic valley"
where the Sorgue river terminates in a "fountain . . . overshadowed by . . . summits"
(*Poetical Works* 1:liv). Louisa has chosen a liminal point at the garden's boundary
as her retreat. Its enclosed nature connotes Louisa's maidenliness as well as her
retiring personality; she is on the verge of adulthood yet lingers within the shelter
of her brother's garden. Suggestively, when her brother appears, he "gaily bounded
down the glade" (1:105), literally crashing into her bower with an enthusiastic
embrace. Thus backed into a corner, so to speak, Louisa first meets the young
man who has followed Lorenzo into her sanctuary and who will subsequently
deprive her of her peace of mind as well as the happy associations of her beloved
retreat.

Seward thus supplies Louisa with the equivalent of Pope's Paraclete and Rousseau's Meillerie, a space where natural seasonal changes seem uncannily to reflect and exacerbate her changing moods. Like theirs, it is a theatrical space as
well. As Goring suggests regarding similar contemporary novels, the bower is designed as a stage on which Louisa performs her sensibility (144). Working within a
small compass, Seward sets most of her novel's action on a single stage, complete

with looming rock and bubbling spring for scenery. Although the rock might be construed as a sort of phallic threat towering over Louisa's virginal enclosure, it also functions simply as a backdrop against which we observe her changing responses from unmediated joy at her brother's return, to hopeful but chastened attraction to Eugenio, to exultant joy over requited love, to despair after her betrayal. In each case, the attendant woods provide both insight into Louisa's consciousness, confirming her natural sensitivity, and appropriate changes of scenery. Readers observing her reactions might learn, to apply Goring's argument to Seward's novel, from the exemplary Louisa how to conduct themselves in similar trials. Goring's insight into the didactic function of such theatricalized fiction suggests the seriousness of Seward's objection to *Julie's* "softening tendency": as a reader who fully appreciated Rousseau's artful staging of climactic scenes, she worried about his novel's effect on readers accustomed to emulating the physical responses of admired characters. Louisa is both a swooning exemplar of sensibility and a proper maiden who models resistance to despair, the depths of which are intimated by the bleak surroundings, echoes of faded bliss, that she both frequents and laments.

Louisa's almost symbiotic relationship with the natural world demonstrates Seward's attention to literature of sensibility. Louisa exemplifies the keen nervous responses typical of contemporary heroines. Visual impressions mutate into tortured feelings almost as rapidly as they meet her eyes when she surveys her wintry bower: "O ye known objects!—how ye strike my heart!/And vain regrets, with keener force, impart!" (1:47–48). Exceptionally attuned to natural objects, Louisa recalls welcoming her "blooming" brother on the summer afternoon of his fateful return (1:81), and her first impression of Eugenio is not of a distinctively human body but of a form "tall as the Pine, amidst inferior Trees,/With all the bending Ozier's pliant ease" (1:112–13). Eugenio's hair even forms a "shade" for his brow like the leaves of a tree (1:114). Sensitive to natural beauty, Louisa reacts immediately to this particularly impressive "tree." Eugenio, equally impressed, blushes and conveys his admiration with his eyes; Louisa instantly reads in Eugenio's face the effect of her personal beauty, deciphering "each flattering meaning": "Sweet, serious, tender, those blue eyes impart/A thousand dear sensations to the heart" (1:117–19). As the courtship progresses, Louisa proves adept at discerning the warmer feelings revealed by Eugenio's physiology but not by the polite expressions that "Friendship dictates." While his verbal skills falter, Eugenio speaks eloquently enough with "disorder'd praise,/Scarce half express'd; the musing ardent gaze;/The varying cheek; the frequent smother'd sigh" (1:154–56). Seward claimed to emulate Pope's *Eloisa to Abelard* by leaving the lovers' éclaircissement to her readers' imagination. But the scene in which Eugenio declares his passion is consistent with the rest of their courtship. Like their first meeting, the occasion reflects its setting in the familiar bower, but at sunset of a summer day. Louisa recalls how "calm on the gilded grass the fountain lay" (1:187) as "the setting Orb emblaz'd the West;/and sunk with splendor" (1:199–200). As soon as Eugenio confides his love, "a calm more sunny o'er my bosom spread!" (1:189), and although she tries to dissemble for modesty's sake, "from these eyes the sun-bright gladness beam'd,/And all the triumph of my bosom stream'd!" (1:204–5). Not merely reflecting the sunset ambience, Louisa seems transfigured, as if she has become the sun that gilds her bower. Through such descriptions, Seward implies Louisa's almost uncanny reflexivity. Unfortunately, Louisa's sensibility will prove nearly fatal when it exacerbates her sorrow after Eugenio's apparent desertion.

Seward endows her chief characters with a gift that suggested, to contemporaries, the double-edged potential of sensibility for joy and sorrow. Like many heroes and heroines of sensibility, Eugenio and Louisa are especially moved by music, which, as Barker-Benfield observes, had become a metaphor for the transmission of nervous impulses through the sensitive frame (21–23). Eugenio hears Louisa's "voice, that floated on the waving wind" before he sees her, as she sings verses from *Il penseroso*, set to music by Handel, and accompanies herself on a lute (1:86). While Louisa comments only on the "presaging" import of the song relative to her own plight, Eugenio is evidently melted by her melancholy tune in true sensible fashion. For her part, Louisa at first registers not Eugenio's words but the extremely musical quality of his voice:

> And when he speaks—not Music's thrilling pow'r,
> No, not the vocal Mistress of the bow'r,
> When slow she warbles from the blossom'd spray,
> In liquid blandishment, her evening lay,
> Such soft insinuating sweetness knows,
> As from that voice in melting accents flows!   (1:122–27)

In retrospect, as a jilted maid, Louisa represents the dangerous power of music to "thrill" or stir the nerves to an instant response. Music "insinuates" itself into the heart that consequently "melts" before the conscious mind can guard against its power. Louisa defends her credulity as a "primal grace of youth" (1:142), but she is obviously vulnerable not only as a sheltered, inexperienced girl but as a person affected by each sense experience. Seward perhaps designed Lorenzo's presence as a rational if sympathetic chaperone for two such flammable lovers. Louisa and Eugenio face none of the external obstacles of their predecessors, but Seward was determined not to portray lovers who fall victim to their own appetites. These lovers are achingly aware of their senses, but they will maintain their grasp on propriety at all costs.

Just as Henry Fielding supplied Joseph Andrews and Fanny Goodwill with Parson Adams to guide them home, so Seward, recognizing the importance of responsible mentors for even the most decorous young lovers, supplies Louisa and Eugenio with Lorenzo. Unfortunately, Lorenzo embarks at the end of summer on the grand tour, an event that often, as in this tale, lasted for several years. Propriety is observed, however, and Eugenio leaves the same day for his parents' estate in Wales. But when, five months later, Louisa learns that Eugenio has jilted her for another bride, she must face alone one of the great moral problems haunting the age of sensibility: the possibility that a person might simulate delicate responses and tender sentiments in order to harm the innocent. Both Henry and Sarah Fielding had explored the general danger of hypocrisy for the sincere, open-hearted individual, in novels such as *Joseph Andrews* and *David Simple*, respectively. But the most important novelists had pondered the danger specifically posed by hypocritical men to innocent young women (Barker-Benfield 331–41). From Richardson's Clarissa to Austen's Marianne in *Sense and Sensibility*, writers apportioned various degrees of blame among their seductive heroes and innocent, susceptible heroines. While Louisa is in no danger of seduction, she exemplifies the kind of instant response to the attractive (and apparently good) that frequently deludes heroines in the fiction of the time. Louisa's first letter returns often to the question, "False could I think that vow, whose starting tear/Sprung, the warm witness of a faith sincere?" (1:258–59). Seward intended her plot's contemporary details to ensure that young readers both identified with and learned from Louisa's and Eugenio's behavior. She not only narrates a conventional courtship but creates a modern setting for Louisa's trials in keeping with contemporary realistic fiction. Louisa exchanges letters with confidence using the postal delivery system; Eugenio intends to join his family's mercantile firm before his impending marriage; Louisa reads a daily newspaper, where to her horror she learns about Eugenio's marriage in a society column. But despite these mundane details, Louisa finds Eugenio's desertion uncanny, evil. She struggles to comprehend his marriage to a wealthy belle and can only conclude he was motivated by an ambition and covetousness that were not apparent during their courtship.

Her struggle to comprehend brings Louisa to the brink of suicide. Her strong feelings, previously reliable guides to her reason, now seem baffled and uncontrolled. Louisa considers summoning her brother to defend her honor but recoils at the prospect of either duelist's death. She remembers when Eugenio seemed angelic and blames her own naiveté for her failure to perceive his treacherous nature: "For if Credulity her warmth impart,/With veils of light she screens the selfish Heart" (1:20). Eugenio, once a thriving tree, now reminds Louisa of a deserted church, its aisles haunted by ghosts at midnight. The image suggests to Louisa her own death, and she contemplates ending her misery through suicide. A guardian angel seems to intervene, however, promising that grief over Eugenio's marriage will prove Louisa's "sure, tho' lingering passport to the tomb"; criminal effort on her part will not be required to bring about her death (1:438). Louisa concludes by alerting Emma to her anticipated death and announcing her relief and joy at this resolution.

Throughout the narration of her mental conflict, Louisa's phrases strongly recall both Eloisa's and St. Preux's struggles. Abelard, "bound and bleeding" (l. 100), becomes the specter of Eugenio "pale, and bleeding on the plain" (1:248). Eloisa imagines herself "propt on some tomb," while "in each low wind methinks a Spirit calls,/And more than Echoes talk along the walls" (ll. 304–6). She then hears the spectral voice that beckons her toward the scene that will resolve her conflict when Abelard witnesses her exemplary death. Eloisa concludes by wishing for Abelard a glorious entry into heaven, where "Saints [will] embrace thee with a love like mine" (l. 342). Louisa borrows Eloisa's evocation of the crypt for her characterization of Eugenio as a darkened church where "Thro' the dim Ailes [sic] pale Spectres seem to fleet,/And hollow groans the whispering Walls repeat" (1:399–400). This vision leads to the climax of her struggle, her contemplation of suicide, which is brought to an end like Eloisa's conflict by a guardian spirit's intervention. Like Eloisa, Louisa invites a witness to observe her peaceful demise; unlike Eloisa, she denies Eugenio her final thoughts and promises Emma she will wait "to welcome thee to HAPPIER SPHERES!" (1:462). Seward no doubt borrowed the incident of contemplated suicide from St. Preux's account of his despair and recovery in the boat after his visit with Julie to Meillerie. But Seward refined both her models. Louisa intends to divest herself of thoughts about Eugenio before she dies; only the similarly chaste friend who has never betrayed her will be worthy of her heavenly embrace. And unlike Rousseau, Seward does not presume Louisa alone capable of conquering her suicidal thoughts. St. Preux describes his recovery in terms typical of sensibility: "A gentler sentiment little by little wound its way into my soul; tenderness overcame despair. I began to shed copious tears, and this state, compared to the one I had emerged from, was not without some pleasures. I wept hard and long and was comforted" (3:167). St. Preux describes a process nearly free of reason or volition. His emotions carry him along, from deadly passion to tender, even pleasurable, sentiment. Rousseau, like his hero, endorsed the primacy of the passions. *La nouvelle Heloïse* suggests confidence in the passions' ability, at least in the best individuals, to direct human behavior. *Louisa* embraces a more conventional philosophy. While the passions of innocent and good-hearted people such as Louisa are usually sufficient guides to correct behavior, in extreme situations, humans must rely on divine support. This solution seems a timorous response to the problem of hypocrisy—in essence, Seward is admitting that innocent people will often be victimized because they follow their generous impulses and claiming that God will help them bear the consequences—but it is not very different from the conclusions of contemporaries such as the Fieldings and Goldsmith. Seward's didacticism and her emphasis on Louisa's moral growth, typical in realistic fiction of the time, separates this verse novel from other sentimental fiction that, as Ann Jessie Van Sant has observed, subordinate plot and character development to the effort of moving the reader's sensibility (118–19). Despite Seward's emphasis on the spectatorial as conveyed by Louisa's stagelike bower and the description of Emira's deathbed penitence, she is not interested only in showing scenes that evoke empathy but also in showing Louisa's growth to maturity.

The lines Seward drafted at nineteen acted as a blueprint for the rest of the first letter. In the tradition of the Ovidian epistle, Seward commences her plot after the heroine's initial infatuation and desertion. From Louisa's foreboding salutation, readers know that "for her . . . Sorrow shrouds/Hope's crystal mirror with impervious clouds" (1:15–16). When she retrieved the manuscript twenty-one years later, Seward followed clues latent in the fragment to create the story of Louisa's courtship and betrayal.

Seward not only drew extensively from both Pope and Rousseau for the content of her verse novel but also on Pope's form. His style lurks behind many of Seward's beautifully crafted lines: his preference for onomatopoeia, for example, influenced such descriptions as Louisa's evocation of Emma, wandering "where broad Bananas stretch their grateful shade" (1:6), in which the lengthy "w" and "n" sounds, distinct concluding consonants, and evenly weighted syllables stretch the line to emulate the trees' protection. Louisa describes herself for Emma as walking toward the bower: "Unequal steps, and rising sighs, disclose/The thorny pressure of tyrannic woes" (1:335–36). The couplet's first line, with its double caesurae framing rising vowel sounds before the final, low-pitched syllable of "disclose," beautifully suggests Louisa's faltering breath. The second line imitates, in its harsh consonantal blends, the metaphorical thorns lacerating her consciousness. Such couplets are frequent throughout the first epistle, evidence of Seward's technical agility in speeding and slowing lines and in crafting lines that echo sense in sound. *Louisa* is manifestly intended for reading aloud, another reason it has completely faded, since its effects were designed for an archaic purpose. Seward's intricate couplets reveal her intention not only to revise but to pay homage to her chief stylistic model.

Seward uses couplets to speed and slow her lines for specific purposes. When the poem opens, for example, Louisa asks Emma to "bend o'er the West thy longing eyes, and chide / The tardy breeze that fans the unfreighted tide" (1:7–8). This bit of exposition, imagining Emma's disappointment over Louisa's failure to correspond, moves as quickly as a prose statement. More quickly, in fact: Seward's use of enjambment, of long vowels, and of "s" and "z" sounds speeds the line, as does the intended elision of "the unfreighted" at the couplet's close. For dramatic pronouncements , however, Seward reverts to her usual pattern of end-stopped couplets, as when Louisa says hopefully at the end of the first verse paragraph, "And oh! I fondly tell my anxious heart, / The dearest truth experience can impart, / That yet, to quench this sympathy of soul, / Time, and a world of waters, vainly roll" (1:23–26). Louisa's exclamation interrupts the first line, and her anxiety is communicated when she interjects the second, as if to reassure herself that her faith in Emma's enduring love is justified. Both the third and fourth lines have double caesuras, which convey Louisa's faltering confidence by further slowing her pace. The double "w" sounds of "world of waters" stretches the phrase to resemble the Atlantic that separates the friends. Louisa abounds in such effects, which Seward uses both to control the novel's pace and to convey her characters' psychological states. In developing the heroic couplet's potential for characterization beyond that of Pope's dramatic monologue, Seward may not have revived its popularity, but her use of verse both to unfold plot and elaborate states of consciousness forms a bridge between verse like Pope's and later developments in the Romantic period. *Louisa* illustrates the tensions that render Seward a transitional poet. Her emulation of Pope's couplets and allusions to *Eloisa to Abelard* look back, but her choice of his passionate epistle looks forward to poets like William Blake, who admired Pope as the inspired bard of *Eloisa* and the "Elegy to the Memory of an Unfortunate Lady." Her attraction to Rousseau, balanced by her need to revise him, was also both typical of contemporary readers and prophetic of writers like Mary Wollstonecraft, whose oeuvre is haunted by her reactions, by turns admiring and disdainful, to the Swiss writer. Seward's refinement of these predecessors was dynamic. While their principles chiefly guided her writing, her responses place her in dialogue not just with Pope and Rousseau but also with successors who ultimately parted more decisively with their early- and mid-eighteenth century models.

CHAPTER SEVEN

Louisa and the Late Eighteenth-Century Family Romance

When Seward revisited *Louisa* in 1784 after having set the project aside for some years, she had to develop the remainder of it without the aid of the map that Rousseau and Pope had provided to her as she wrote the first epistle. In this chapter, I analyze Seward's variation on the sentimental fiction of the 1780s and 1790s. In her recent literary history, Susan Staves suggests that self-abnegation was a requisite for female heroism in eighteenth-century women's literature (*Literary History* 332), but I find Seward disinclined to such a view. *Louisa* seems to me to be contending with Rousseau's emphasis on sensibility, somewhat in the manner of her younger contemporary Mary Wollstonecraft, who both admired and despised Rousseau and whose *Wrongs of Woman* (1798), her final novel, portrays a woman adapting to life in a madhouse under the influence of Rousseauian sensibility.[1] Seward's Louisa struggles with depression and the impulse to commit suicide when she believes herself deserted by her lover. Unlike some other heroines of sentimental novels, however, she persuades herself to accept her circumstances and live. In the end, unlike the eponymous heroine of Mary Hays's *The Memoirs of Emma Courtney* (1796), who also considers suicide when her beloved marries another woman and then recovers but who marries another, only to suffer her husband's maniacal jealousy, Louisa's restraint is rewarded when Eugenio becomes free to marry her. My reading of *Louisa* considers the gendered implications of this plot. Finally, I examine how Seward's relationship with her own father, the Reverend Thomas Seward, may have powerfully if obliquely influenced her verse novel. *Louisa* emerges as a dense record of Seward's fraught, even defiant, attitudes toward the patriarchs, real and imagined, in her life. If Seward made an effort to control her career by orchestrating her first publications, *Louisa* implies the degree to which she chafed under the domination of her father and her chosen literary precursors. Seward's verse novel opens a window into her wish to control social and emotional aspects of her life, resulting in her positive revision of a sentimental plot.

In the classical Ovidian epistle, the heroine has typically been seduced by her lover, and although he is culpable, she too has transgressed and her fate is therefore somewhat deserved. Seward's twist on this plot is that not only is Louisa innocent but Eugenio is finally exculpated, and unlike works in the Ovidian genre, whose conclusions were uniformly tragic, the novel ends with the lovers' joyful reunion. Early in *Eloisa*, St. Preux explains to Julie that although he is her teacher, they are not much like their gothic counterparts. St. Preux is not a salaried employee of Baron d'Étange as Abelard is of Eloisa's uncle. He is close to Julie's age, their attraction is mutual, and neither is under binding obligations that might prevent their union (1:67). Of course, St. Preux's nonnoble pedigree proves an insurmountable obstacle, entangling the lovers in years of subterfuges and trials. Rousseau intended to update the famous medieval lovers' story along with their predicament: six hundred years later, the accident of birth proved as fatal to St. Preux's courtship as Abelard's priestly-employee status did for his. But while suggesting the injustice of rigid class barriers between exceptional people, Rousseau bowed to convention in the unequal punishments he meted out to his lovers. Julie and St. Preux are cruelly separated, and both suffer smallpox. St. Preux endures years of exile, sailing around the world with Admiral Anson. Julie, married to a kind and large-minded gentleman, devotes herself to two children and a beautiful garden before she is disturbed by St. Preux's return. Although she surmounts her temptation to resume their affair, she dies not long afterward, a victim seemingly as much of the conventional insistence that fallen, even if redeemed, heroines die as of her rash effort to save her drowning son.

Seward, as we have seen, reworked all her models to accommodate her personal ideal of chaste sensibility. She devotes her second and longest epistle to Eugenio's exoneration and the third and briefest to Louisa's response after reading Eugenio's self-exculpation. Louisa immediately resolves to live, if only to "expiate by a Mind/Bow'd to its fate, and cheerfully resign'd,/The dangerous rashness, which my peace had thrown/On human chance, and errors not my own" (3:167–70). Seward wished to emphasize the danger of unbridled sensibility even to a young person thwarted by "chance, and errors not my own." Louisa apparently condemns herself to life as a punishment for the "frail excess of Love" that nearly led to suicide when, knowing herself innocent, she "coldly view'd that Heaven

[Eugenio] could'st not share" (3:34, 40). In light of the epistle's paucity of incident except for Louisa's self-accusing response, it seems clear that Seward intended this chiefly as a didactic episode. Unlike Julie, Louisa will live after her recognition of frailty. Unlike Eloisa, she has been primarily a victim. But her near despair sufficiently warrants a deep sense of guilt and prepares for a denouement in which both lovers have been chastened before entering a union that might have seemed too easily won had their marriage taken place as planned.

To underscore Louisa's suffering and redemption, Seward includes a sixty-one line interpolated tale in the third epistle, nearly one-quarter the length of the entire letter. To explain her sense of renewed joy in life once assured of Eugenio's innocence, Louisa instances her friend Clairmont, a mercantile adventurer whose bride was swept overboard during a storm en route to South America. Despite his survival, his life had been miserable for years until he received the news that "Clarissa lives! — on coasts unknown / Wreck'd, like himself, unfriended and alone, / By destiny severe, an hapless slave" (3:123–25). Now, Clairmont has been revived by the mere knowledge that she lives and his hope of somehow recovering her. Most interpolated tales in eighteenth-century novels served as both an entertaining digression and a pointed analogue to the protagonist's experience, and Clairmont's story is no exception. Clairmont too has innocently suffered the loss of his beloved. He has been healed by learning of Clarissa's physical survival, much as Louisa rejoices upon learning that Eugenio's morality remains wholly intact. Seward might also have intended to offer a masculine version of Louisa's plight as a way of extending her story's appeal, since Clairmont and his bride have had exotic adventures denied to Louisa in her dell. But another suggestion lies within the episode's details. Clairmont was torn from his bride, somewhat as Louisa was torn from her fiancé, by circumstances beyond his control (in this, he also resembles Eugenio). He now knows not only that Clarissa lives but that "Fate may aid the ardent strife, / And to his arms restore his long-lost Wife!" (3:129–30). In that hope, Clairmont's "agony subsides almost to peace" (3:132), concludes Louisa, "So I — but to Eugenio swift impart / How full the pardon of Louisa's heart!" (3:133–34). The couplet is revealing. Louisa ostensibly means that she will live consoled by the mere fact of Eugenio's continuing, innocent existence. (She exhorts him, through Emma, to behave as nobly, as a husband and father, as he has acted as a son [3:155–58]). But the couplets preceding her message to Eugenio describe Clairmont's hope that although Clarissa is "by destiny severe, an hapless Slave," fate might intervene and reunite them (3:125). "So I," adds Louisa, before interrupting herself to convey the urgent message of pardon. Louisa's "So I" refers to Clairmont's general circumstances, but it also refers to his recent hope that, although he and Clarissa are currently "wreck'd . . . unfriended and alone," they might eventually be rejoined. Eugenio is metaphorically "enslaved," condemned to a loveless marriage "by destiny severe." But might he not one day become free? There can be no "ardent strife" on his behalf; Louisa has to accept his marriage, much as Seward had to accept John Saville's marriage. But surely, buried in Louisa's self-interrupted analogy, as it likely was in Seward's heart, is the barely conscious wish that someday she and Eugenio might fulfill their vows. That wish is stifled as soon as it is suggested, but it prepares us for the conclusion in which fate reunites the separated lovers. It also humanizes Louisa, whose self-condemnation is martyrlike in its severity. She still cherishes her original feelings, although in repressed form.

The longest and most incident-fraught letters of Louisa are the second and fourth, which narrate Eugenio's trials. Caroline Franklin, Louisa's most recent editor, correctly asserts that its plot is "typical of the age of sensibility in that it pits the importance of the feelings against the power of 'attractive Commerce'" (x). That power has separated Emma from Louisa, Louisa from Eugenio, and Clarissa from Clairmont. Many novels, such as Clarissa and David Simple, denounced familial greed and might have supplied hints for Seward's plot. But since such plots and themes were ubiquitous, their power to move contemporaries depended on the skill with which they were deployed. Eugenio's pursuit by a headstrong heiress, his reluctant marriage to save his family from ruin, and his consequent misery—none of these developments would have surprised Seward's first readers. Spoiled heiresses, conflicts between parents and children over marriage choices, and the unhappiness of marriages contracted for fiscal reasons were all standard topoi. Seward's handling of these conventional topics, however, warrants close attention in several respects, because of her skillful orchestration and also because of the insights they provide into her personal opinions of romantic and familial relationships.

Seward might have found numerous visual and literary clues for the characterization and demise of Eugenio's wife, Emira. "Emira" is first of all an anagram for "Marie" or "Mary," another fanciful version of an English name that, in keeping with the romance tradition that informed many early novels, elevated Seward's tale about plain Laurence, Eugene, Mary, and Ernest into a glamorous fiction. The mostly Italianate names also suggest the real-life practice of slightly veiling names in newspapers' society columns. Emira is both the ubiquitous spoiled heiress and the embodiment of the mercantile forces threatening such exemplars of pure sensibility as Louisa and Eugenio. Her name suggests the title of a Muslim ruler and thus hints at her domineering personality as well as the source of her fabulous wealth in the same commerce that has torn other loved ones apart in the novel. The Eastern-sounding name also connotes the corrupt sexuality associated with Turks, which stands opposed to Louisa's passionate but chaste sensibility. As Louisa models British sensibility, guided by religion and social decorum, Emira represents the self-indulgent passion Seward would have thought "Eastern" or— as in Rousseau's characters—European.

As he recalls in the second epistle, Eugenio meets Emira while out riding. He is reflecting on the beautiful moonlit evening, when he is torn from his reverie by a woman's shrieks: she has been pulled from her horse by three armed assailants. After killing one of the criminals (the other two run away), Eugenio leads their victim toward his father's home. Only when they emerge from the woods into the moonlight does he perceive with surprise her splendid garments and the "gorgeous trappings" of her horse (2:167). The clothes serve the narrative function of enabling Eugenio to assure Emma that he was not enchanted by Emira—the fact that he was distracted by Emira's garments proves that he was not paying attention to Emira's face. But readers might discern from her fashionable, oriental-style clothing, such as the embroidered belt "clasp'd by a Gem, the boast of Orient Mines" (2:173), that Emira personifies the wealth her family has evidently gained from Eastern trade. No doubt, like most aristocrats (Emira boasts about her "lineal Blood, allied / To Rank, and Pow'r" [2:270–71), Emira's family has invested in commercial ventures to support and extend their landed property. Eugenio's family soon recognizes in their guest the topic of popular gossip owing to her beauty and fabulous marriage portion; unfortunately, Emira has been characterized as "insolent" and "vain" (2:211). Her flirtation with Eugenio resembles, to him, the attempted seduction of Telemachus by Calypso, a story familiar to Seward's readers through the popular, didactic prose epic by Fénelon.[2] Like Telemachus, who pines instead for Eucharis, Eugenio prefers the charms of a more retiring nymph. The comparison to Calypso emphasizes Emira's dangerous power, her obsessively persistent will, her personality's "foreignness" as opposed to the virtues of sensibility. The association of Emira's privileged status with mercantilism aligns Louisa, genteel but not wealthy, with spiritual and aesthetic values that Seward admires. The characterizations imply both a critical view of national policies and an early example of what Mary Poovey describes in Genres of the Credit Economy as the gradual disconnection of the literary from the economic or monetary. While Seward was one of many novelists who, as Miranda J. Burgess describes it, "represented commerce as a diffuse force that penetrated into and destabilized the safest corners of private life," her resolution of the problem was somewhat different from that of writers like Frances Sheridan and Frances Burney who believed they were witnessing "the overthrow of British institutions by individual desire" (87)

Emira is also associated with the fashionably exotic pastime of the masquerade. Terry Castle has written the definitive study of British preoccupation with this Italianate entertainment; suffice to say, fictional masquerade balls were associated with sexual corruption, social contamination, and foreign decadence of all kinds. As in *Louisa*, they also usually provoke the climax or turning point of a plot (Castle 117–18). English audiences and readers were evidently fascinated by the socially disruptive possibilities inherent in events at which all participants are disguised. Accordingly, in drama and fiction, wives and heiresses are either carried off or narrowly rescued at masked balls; seducers and female rakes either fool their victims or are foiled. Masquerade plots rang multiple changes on the theme of social order tragically breached or comically restored. Seward might have recalled a visual representation of such an episode from Hogarth's *Marriage à la Mode*, when the countess dies after a rendezvous with her lawyer, Silvertongue, at a masquerade. Hogarth's plot satisfied contemporary expectation because his dissipated but previously faithful young heroine slips over the boundary separating virtue from vice after deciding to attend this palpable occasion of sin. Seward could have found no more an economical device to convey Emira's self-destruction, nor one more familiar. In the novel's fourth and final epistle, Ernesto narrates for Louisa the disastrous course of his son's marriage. Emira recognized from the outset of her marriage that Eugenio still pined for Louisa. Her pride wounded, Emira turned first to frivolous and then to licentious pastimes rather than fulfill her roles of wife and mother. Seward does not clarify, but Emira manifestly intends to wound Eugenio as much as amuse herself through such dangerous activities as "Play, ruinously high, and dark Intrigue" (4:103). Eugenio attempted to reason with her but recognized her escapades as efforts to assuage marital disappointment. Ernesto recalls one particular scene that in its poignancy may have suggested to Elizabeth Inchbald the scene between Dorriforth and Miss Milner before the latter defiantly attends a masked ball in *A Simple Story* (1791).

Ernesto is haunted by memories of an evening when Emira was "hastening to the midnight Mask" (4:134). She is "consummate from her toilette's anxious task," anxious perhaps because she is thinking about an impending tryst or simply because she is vain. Significantly, she has not been part of the group in her drawing room, where Ernesto cuddles her baby daughter while Eugenio broods. Instead, she has come only to take leave of her family. Eugenio sighs with exasperation when he surveys her costume and recognizes that Emira has disguised herself not as an emir, but as the member of a seraglio, complete with feathered, bejeweled turban, loose belt, and clinging, translucent sleeves (4:141–48). Eugenio tries to warn Emira about the dangers of masquerades. He adjures her, if not as an injured husband, as an interested friend, to beware the possibility of "ambush" lurking at such balls (4:166) He asks her how her pride will endure the gleeful destruction of her reputation by rivals happy to witness her likely fall. When Emira turns away from him, Eugenio makes a last, desperate effort to dissuade her. He places their baby in Emira's arms and begs her to think of their daughter before continuing on her destructive path. Emira pauses, involuntarily shedding tears on her daughter's head. But she soon remembers her anger and returns the baby to Ernesto, declaring, "Go little Wretch!—of tender mutual flames/Thou wert not born!—then why should I embrace./And live for thee, whose birth is my disgrace?" (4:300–302). By stifling her positive, maternal sensibility, Emira has sealed her fate. She chooses instead a venue famous for duplicity, for concealed identities and feigned motives. Emira has resorted to sensual habits, hardening her heart, to quote Seward in a 1762 letter to her imaginary friend, whereas Louisa chastely endures (*Poetical Works* 1:l).

Although Emira's fall does not immediately follow, she eventually (and predictably) succumbs to a tryst after "the loose revel of [a] wanton mask" (4:342), much like Hogarth's countess. In choosing masquerade over motherhood, Emira has deliberately chosen the path to self-destruction. Her anguished words to her daughter suggest that beneath Emira's pride lurks genuine, if self-willed, heartbreak. If to bear children in an economically driven marriage signifies "disgrace," then Emira has learned what Louisa and Eugenio already understand, that such a marriage resembles, for the wife, a kind of prostitution. This argument, too, was a commonplace in eighteenth-century arguments against forced marriages. But Emira takes the analogy seriously, using it as the rationale for her outrageous behavior. She throws herself away on a "haughty Lord, licentious, false, and vain," who loves an opera dancer and sleeps with Emira merely "to support his consequence" (4:351, 359). Their affair becomes public knowledge after he boasts of the liaison. Eugenio forbears to separate from or divorce the woman for whose shame he feels somewhat responsible, although he moves to a different bed. Emira, however, completes her ruin by contracting a contagious disease while carousing among "the light Throngs, that croud the garish Mart" (4:391). If by "Mart" Seward meant not a generalized commercial locale but a marketplace, Emira is appropriately infected while shopping, another association of mercantilism with general corruption. The poem concludes after Emira begs Louisa, through Ernesto, to attend her deathbed and pardon her for severing Eugenio from Louisa. Assured that Louisa will raise her child, Emira dies, leaving Eugenio and Louisa to resume their interrupted betrothal, now "more sweet, for generous Pity's min-gled sighs; sweet above all, from the exulting pride/Of self-approving Virtue, strongly tried" (4:528–30).

Seward beautifully orchestrates the conclusion to pull together several strands of her narrative. The transfer of Emira's child to Louisa completes the character-ization of Emira as foil of Louisa. Throughout epistles 2 and 4, Emira is developed as Louisa's antithesis. Emira is proud, artful, and given to display, while Louisa is modest, artlessly responsive, and retiring. Louisa must be loved for her intrinsic qualities, given her "want of gold" (2:81), while Emira is married only for her op-portune wealth. While Louisa remains rooted in her bower, almost like one of the plants around her beloved spring, Emira engages in a mad round of activities. Seward emphasizes Louisa's despair when she has become convinced that Eu-genio does not love her. Her psychological struggle is resolved through moral reflection and confidence in divine support. Once reassured of Eugenio's good-ness, she resigns herself to live patiently, consoled by awareness that Eugenio, too, likewise endures despite forces beyond his control. Emira, on the other hand, indulges her despair when she realizes that Eugenio will never love her, despite his gratitude to her for forestalling his family's bankruptcy. She does not try to win his friendship or even reflect on her rash behavior; rather she exacerbates her pain by courting disgrace. Seward's portrait of Emira is not unsympathetic. Not only does she seem, like Louisa, to have no parents but she also seems to have no brother, sister, or guardian who might have provided direction. (Literary head-strong heiresses have inattentive or ineffectual parents and guardians and there-fore are often left to their own devices.) Louisa enjoys the dignity arising from "the peace of Innocence, the pride of Truth" (1:446), but Emira makes a spectacle of self-degradation after she fails to secure Eugenio's love along with his marriage vow. Emira's choosing the masquerade over her infant would have horrified con-temporaries, who idealized maternal love. On the other hand, her exclamation conveys genuine anguish. She "bought" her husband from his desperate father, and their baby resulted from the consummation not of love but of a financial ar-rangement. She now despises Eugenio and Ernesto, but above all, she hates her-self. Unfortunately, her self-loathing leads to the virtual self-immolation that comes with a tawdry affair. Seward could rely on contemporaries to draw the parallel between Louisa, who chastised herself for the "frail excess of Love" that led to the "sad extremes" of sickness and despair (3:34–35), and Emira, who deliberately turned away from reflection and persisted in extreme behavior. Seward leaves no doubt that Emira represents the twisted alternative to Louisa's wholesomeness, but she grants Emira a degree of self-consciousness that, while far from excusing

her willful self-destruction, suggests she too is the victim of a culture that encourages women to consider themselves commodities in marriage. Louisa, as we have
repeatedly noted, is connected with the natural world and with religious and aesthetic values, as if to underscore sensibility's distance from commodification.

Although Seward found most of her plot elements—the spoiled heiress, the
sacrificial marriage, the climactic masked ball, the deathbed confession—scattered
among contemporary paintings, plays, poems, and novels, Emira demonstrates
Seward's ability to infuse these stock characters and situations with sensibility.
Seward's chief male characters, particularly Eugenio's father, Ernesto, are likewise elaborations of familiar types, but they are developed with genuine originality. Ernesto in particular reveals Seward's ambivalence about one of the major
cultural shifts of her generation, the transfer of familial allegiance from blood kin
to relations by marriage as outlined by Ruth Perry in *Novel Relations*. In her illuminating study, Perry detects, in much later eighteenth-century fiction, traces
of the anguish caused as economic and social changes gradually wrought corresponding changes in family structure. Fiscal considerations led parents to make
decisions about their children's marriages that threatened women's status as never
before. Traditionally, Perry explains, women could claim a certain equality with
their brothers as children of the same father, bearers of the same familial blood.
As genteel families struggled to retain their status in the developing economy,
however, daughters could now seem drains on their fathers' fortunes and their
brothers' future inheritances owing to escalating dowries (Perry 13–20). While British parents could not, like Italian parents, forcibly lock supernumerary daughters
in convents to reduce the cost of their support, many daughters evidently lan-
guished at home or in the low-paying occupations available to ladies, victims of a
system in which they were now inconveniences rather than intrinsically valuable
family members.[3] Perry finds evidence of the trauma caused by this shift throughout British popular literature, particularly in novels, where plots featuring daughters who find long-lost fathers or who are protected by loving brothers represent
the wish-fulfillment fantasies of women writers or of sympathetic male writers such
as Richardson.

Louisa contains many of the characters and plot configurations Perry finds
typical of late-century fiction. Louisa has no parents, but she has a strong bond
with her brother. As Perry observes, "A loving brother was better than a father because closer to the heroine's own interests and more of a friend" (151). Lorenzo,
fulfilling his role as ideal brother, brings his best friend to meet Louisa, no doubt
hoping for just the outcome that results from his introduction. Lorenzo's intervention is presumably crucial because, since Louisa has no large dowry and has

not been paraded in London as an eligible match, the young men's friendship brings about her opportunity for marriage. Lorenzo leaves for the grand tour, confident that his sister will soon be welcomed by a loving husband to a new home. Eugenio is to be a kind of replacement brother, as well as a husband, for Louisa. Perry cites the number of fictional heroes, such as Lord Orville in *Evelina* and Henry Tilney in *Northanger Abbey*, who serve as kindly "brothers" as well as suitors to heroines. Eugenio, although destined to join his father's business, resembles Louisa in his sensitivity to natural beauty and in finding his personal emotions reflected in the landscape. As he rides toward his family's estate in epistle 2, for example, Eugenio discovers that the familiar landmarks "assum'd new grace, and wore a softer mein, / From the blest thought, that soon the nuptial Hour / Would lead Louisa to my native bower!" (2:60–62). However, Eugenio shortly proves to be the era's "ideal" young man in his role as son as well. Eugenio faces a tragic double bind when his father begs him to marry Emira. Perry emphasizes that for fictional heroes and heroines, consanguineal bonds trump conjugal interests in any given situation. Eugenio is forced to choose between Louisa and the imminent destruction of his family. Ernesto describes in heart-wrenching terms Eugenio's frail mother and delicate sisters, even the innocent investors whose fortunes will be ruined along with his. He asks whether Eugenio is prepared to ask Louisa to join him in a life of poverty. To the reasonable objection that hard work would in time restore the family's wealth, Ernesto responds that his wife would meanwhile surely die, and in any case, his faithless business partner will have irreparably damaged his reputation unless their debts are somehow paid.[4] Faced with these unanswerable arguments, Eugenio makes the painful but noble decision to assist his family at the expense of his betrothed. As Perry remarks about an Austen novel, "Taking care of one's blood relatives . . . was coming to be seen as the heart and soul of proper feeling" (142). Even the heart-broken Louisa cannot help but "approve, absolve, [and] admire" Eugenio's sacrifice when she reads the explanation he sends to Emma (3:67). Eugenio decides against communication with Louisa not because he is thoughtless but because he knows that if he explained the circumstances, Louisa would approve of his decision to marry Emira and consequently resign herself to "fruitless Constancy, and fond regret" (2:542). If she believes instead that he deserted her for an heiress, he reasons, her "high-soul'd Scorn" will "[subdue her] rooted Love" (2:553). Only after his death is Emma to confide the circumstances of his apparent betrayal.

If Seward constructs, in Eugenio, a hero of sensibility, torn between individual preference and family needs but choosing "warm Duty" over "bleeding Love" (2:517), his father, Ernesto, likewise resembles his fictional counterparts. Like David

Simple, or Mr. Wilson in *Joseph Andrews*, he has retreated from active involvement in urban affairs. Richer than either Simple or Wilson, he occupies a rural estate in Wales with considerable property but evidently a relatively modest home (Emira refers to his villa as a "sylvan Cell" [2: 221]). Unfortunately, like Simple, or like Parson Primrose in *The Vicar of Wakefield*, Ernesto's very innocence and retirement nearly ruin him. His partner, Belmor, has given poor advice or misled him, and the failure of their current venture is about to bankrupt everyone involved. But as the head of his family, he rallies to save his wife, daughters, son, and fellow investors from imminent ruin. Ernesto must ask his son not to marry the woman who would supply "a Daughter's tenderness, an Angel's care" (2:88), but to save his own daughters, Eugenio's sisters, from poverty. Ernesto embodies paternal sensibility to such a degree that when she sees his "venerable Form" approach (3:209), Louisa responds instinctively, with "cordial confidence," to the "rays of love, and angel-pity" beaming from his "look benign" (4:9–11). The orphaned Louisa shares with Ernesto a version of the father-daughter recognition scene familiar in other fictions. Who, she asks, is this stranger who "gazest on me with paternal love?" (4:16). Ernesto begs her forgiveness, which she immediately grants, falling to her knees as her tears wet his hands. "Oh! What a Wretch were I, should I upbraid,/Because th' exalted Youth, whose heart I won,/Deserves the blessing, to be born thy Son!" (4:36–38). Seward implies that Ernesto recognizes Louisa as his metaphorical daughter and literal daughter-in-law, bringing her plot to near completion by restoring her to the family she coveted but nearly lost. From this perspective, *Louisa*'s conclusion anticipates that of *Mansfield Park*, in which Fanny Price proves worthier to be Sir Thomas Bertram's daughter than either Maria or Julia. Both Louisa and Eugenio have proved they can subordinate their sensibility to higher principles. Eugenio cannot be blamed for attempting to satisfy his personal desire at the expense of his family; instead, Louisa will be absorbed into the family. Ernesto is thus absolved of any guilt for delaying their marriage, because his despairing request set the lovers a trial that has refined them.

Near the end of the poem, Louisa develops a biblical simile to describe her relief at the outcome of her suffering. She recollects Abraham's joy when an angel interrupts his imminent sacrifice of Isaac:

> Thus, on Moriah's consecrated height,
> Flow'd the obedient Patriarch's fond delight,
> When o'er the filial breast, his faith to seal,
> On high had gleam'd the sacrificing Steel;

Thus flow'd, when at the Voice, divinely mild,
His raptur'd hands unbound his only Child!   (4:533–38)

Seward deliberately leaves the simile's referents vague, because the comparison applies to all three witnesses of Emira's death. Louisa has observed the unbinding of her lover's marital chains. Eugenio, who believed himself to be sacrificing Louisa's happiness to serve his family, now sees his victim released from her suffering. Ernesto, the family patriarch, believed he had sacrificed his son's potential marital happiness and now weeps for joy because of Eugenio's unanticipated freedom. However the simile is construed, it identifies Louisa and Eugenio as well as Ernesto with the role of patriarch. The patriarch's perspective is the perspective from which to view the poem's events; to share that viewpoint is to understand the narrative correctly. But certain details of the poem contradict such a reading of it and complicate Seward's relation to the conventional kinship plot.

Louisa enjoys the close relationship with her brother that is typical, as Perry observes, in many fictional plots. But Lorenzo, having arranged his sister's betrothal, leaves for the grand tour. When Louisa is desolate, she has no brother to console her, let alone defend her honor. Lorenzo is not mentioned after the first epistle; at the poem's conclusion, he has evidently been gone for nearly four years, leaving Louisa to fend for herself. Eugenio, likewise, fails to offer crucial support to the innocent woman he must desert in order to fulfill his duty as a son and brother. Although he explains his motive to Emma, and Louisa accepts his reasoning, his plan fails to prevent Louisa's prolonged suffering. In fact, Louisa is only informed of Eugenio's intention when Emma senses this knowledge might prevent her grief-stricken death. This scenario derives from Seward's third model, Prior's "Henry and Emma," in which a young man tests his beloved's fidelity by inventing a tale of his disgrace. After she declares she will follow him into exile, he reveals the truth. Seward found undignified Emma's continuing attachment to a self-professed criminal, and so she replaced Henry's false story with a true test of Louisa's strength of character. On the other hand, "Henry and Emma" ends with the revelation that the trial has been illusory; Emira's timely death, which reunites the chastened lovers, follows Prior's framework. Although Seward refined Prior's plot, then, Louisa still had to suffer under false pretenses, such as Eugenio's decision not to inform her, even though he might easily have communicated his predicament. Louisa properly recoils when she believes he deserted her for a wealthy bride and forgives him only when, several years later, she learns the truth. Meanwhile, despite Louisa's admiration and her eagerly renewed devotion after Emira's death, careful readers must ask why Eugenio failed to realize that knowledge of his circumstances, rather than ignorance, would have assisted his fiancée. The structural necessity, imposed by Prior's plot, for Louisa to face a fictional test before there can be a happy conclusion, requires Eugenio to share Henry's impulse toward deception.

Ernesto most strikingly departs from the model patriarch beloved in the fiction of the time. Louisa, we have seen, reveres Ernesto for his efforts on behalf of his family. She drops to her knees at his approach in a gesture resembling the recognition scenes between fathers and daughters in many novels, including Oliver Goldsmith's *The Vicar of Wakefield* (1766), Henry MacKenzie's *The Man of Feeling* (1771), and Frances Burney's *Evelina* (1778). Ernesto is rewarded after his family's trials with his son's happiness and a new "daughter." Seward apparently endorses popular yearning for consanguineal fidelity, signaled by Eugenio's sacrifice followed by Louisa's seamless absorption into Ernesto's family. Again, however, Seward undermines this familiar plot. Even if the novel's first readers ignored the fact that Ernesto requires Eugenio to overturn an established betrothal—a far more serious breach in the eighteenth century than it would be today—they must have been dismayed by the frankly mercenary nature of the marriage he proposes:

> We know that Fortune on Emira pours
> Her golden treasures in unstinted showers.—
> Eugenio! she stands ready to replace
> Thy Father's comforts on a lasting base!   (2:402–5)

Ernesto's plea on behalf of his wife and daughters is made in the guise of just the sort of capital-building matches that kinship proponents usually abhorred because they advanced the family's wealth and status at the expense of individual members' security and happiness. Seward has mixed the terms so that her family patriarch espouses precisely the sort of alliance such characters ought to despise. Trapped in his own double bind, Ernesto succumbs to Emira's offer. Ideally, he would have dissuaded the frantic heiress and not accepted her bribery. Ernesto is forced to choose the lesser of two evils; even Louisa absolves him of culpability under the circumstances. But those circumstances have caused Ernesto to act in a manner that, while preserving the welfare of others, resembles the morally weak choices deplored in contemporary accounts of avaricious matches.

As if to underline Ernesto's weakness, Seward ultimately renders meaningless his sacrifice of Louisa's and Eugenio's happiness. Susan Staves has remarked on the routine occurrence "in sentimental plots [of] paragon characters who offer to make dramatic sacrifices . . . only to find that their proffered services will not be required" (*Literary History* 332). Seward's variation on this standard plot element, as we have seen, was to require genuine sacrifice from her hero and heroine, who are ultimately rewarded for it. Unlike other sentimental plots that seem constructed principally so that, as Staves observes, readers might enjoy spectacles of distress (331), *Louisa* seems designed to interrogate such scenes. While recounting Emira's dissipated career, Ernesto expresses his relief that the "vast debt" he owed to his daughter-in-law has been canceled (4:107–8). As in *The Merchant of Venice*, the ships he thought lost have returned, not only restoring but increasing his wealth. Ernesto reiterates his gratitude to Emira for rescuing him from certain ruin (4:115–18). But he laments that Eugenio has been the "youthful Victim to his Father's good" and confesses his happiness that he has been able to repay Emira's bounty, because nothing is more painful "than much to owe, where owing we despise" (4:120, 126). Nothing can ameliorate, however, the fact that as a result of Ernesto's panic-driven request, Eugenio has believed himself tied for life to a despicable woman, while Louisa feels consigned to spinsterhood. Ernesto could not have foreseen the "smiling Chance" that restored his wealth (4:113). But the fact that chance has restored his wealth, canceling the need for a finance-driven alliance, suggests on some level the ill-advised nature of such expedient marriages as well as the foolishness, if not cruelty, of parents to demand them.

Louisa, then, has suffered under both the kinship and conjugal systems of loyalty, as outlined by Perry. Her brother has been an ineffectual protector, and she nearly dies of grief after her fiancé deserts her to save his blood kin. On the other hand, Eugenio deserts her for the kind of marriage despised in most of the literature of the time as the bane of a capital-driven, individualistic society. This is the kind of marriage Emira seeks, one engineered to gratify her vanity and salvage Ernesto's fortune. Once she saves Ernesto from ruin, she has no concern for how his family's reputation might suffer as a result of her scandalous pastimes. Emira is obsessed with her own lacerated ego and would rather destroy herself than attempt the difficult effort of self-healing. Meanwhile, Louisa sits alone as a result of Emira's marital "triumph." Surveying Louisa's predicament, the reader intuits Seward's dissatisfaction with women's situation under both systems. At the novel's conclusion, Louisa and Eugenio anticipate their marriage, the fulfillment of a choice based on individual preference rather than on family considerations. On the other hand (and in true wish-fulfillment fashion), Eugenio's individual choice is best for his family, since it brings his parents an additional "Daughter's tenderness, [and] an Angel's care" (2:28). Seward, who enjoyed the protection of her father's home and the use of his fortune throughout her life, might have been expected to espouse the older fashion of kin-based loyalty. But *Louisa* seems, if tentatively, to embrace the newer idea of conjugal-based, rather than family-based, allegiance. Eugenio and Louisa's match suggests that such marriages, if not contracted for mercenary reasons, benefit not only the individuals concerned but also their families. Why might this have been so?

The figure of Ernesto, both the poem's honored patriarch and the cause of all its distress, points toward an answer. According to Seward's correspondence, when she began *Louisa*, she had yet to experience any emotional entanglements. The twenty years between the poem's beginning and completion, however, brimmed with experiences most often influenced decisively by Canon Seward. He chose as suitor for her beloved younger sister Sarah, for example, Samuel Johnson's stepson, a wealthy middle-aged merchant named Joseph Porter. According to Seward's letters, Sarah was engaged shortly after meeting Porter but died before the wedding could take place. Anna's first love, for a Major John Wright in 1764, was terminated by her father when he discovered their clandestine relationship (Barnard, *Anna Seward* 61). She subsequently engaged herself to a Captain Temple, but that affair too was ended by her father, her suitor being indigent (Barnard, *Anna Seward* 62). Ashmun comments that although Reverend Seward seems to have been "no more of a tyrant than most fathers of the period," "his willingness to see his daughter Sarah sacrificed in a loveless marriage with a moneyed man, and his refusal to give his daughter Anna where the amount of money which he had anticipated was lacking, show him conventional and mercenary, if no worse" (26). Her dismissive assessment surely does not reflect the pain experienced by Seward throughout these events. Although Seward apparently healed quickly after the Temple debacle, ensuing years brought additional disappointments. By her own account, she refused several marriage offers promoted by her father. Nobody joined with her romantic wish that her foster sister Honora Sneyd might marry the engaging but far from prosperous young John André. Eventually, Seward championed Sneyd's decision in 1773 to marry Richard Lovell Edgeworth despite the initial disapprobation of both Honora's father and Reverend Seward, who later performed the wedding ceremony (Barnard, *Anna Seward* 80–81). Unfortunately, Honora's frail health deteriorated at Edgeworth's Irish estate, and Seward blamed Edgeworth for his wife's demise. A final, but perhaps chief, example concerns Seward's relationship with John Saville, the married but separated vicar choral whom she loved for many years. The year before Honora married Edgeworth, in 1772, Seward almost lost Saville to her father's anger when he was warned of the impropriety of their relationship (Barnard, *Anna Seward* 69–71). Saville suffered the "altered eye of hard unkindness" from him, and bled under the sense of it. No prospect of worldly disadvantage—and I was threatened with the highest— could induce me to renounce the blessing of a tried and faithful friend; but by ill-advised and mistaken authority, most of its sweetest comforts were merci- lessly lopt away. (Whalley 1:344)

Saville was banished not only from Seward's private sitting room, an upstairs par- lor where he had spent many happy hours visiting with the Seward sisters, Hon- ora, André, and other intimate friends, but from the Bishop's Palace for most of the 1770s (Barnard, *Anna Seward* 71). Although Seward refused to alter her own feelings and frankly claimed her devotion to Saville for the rest of her life, her father's less high-minded response to local gossip must have rankled.

Seward ensured her father's care throughout his long, slow physical and men- tal decline and sincerely mourned his death. But even though she loved him, she may have expressed in the figure of Ernesto her resentment of the paternal au- thority that had robbed her when young of at least two potential suitors, failed to introduce any other satisfactory suitors, and nearly disinherited her over her at- tachment to Saville. Her father had failed to engineer Sarah's marriage to the unattractive but rich Porter only because Sarah died, but he successfully discour- aged André before finally advocating Honora's marriage to the wealthy Edgeworth. *Louisa* comments obliquely on all these situations. Louisa herself is young and, although her brother owns property, she does not command a huge dowry. We first meet her as a writer, composing the tale of her woes for Emma, much as the youthful Seward confided in an Emma. Like Seward, too, Louisa is characterized by her passion for music and landscape and by her voluntary confinement—one to a cathedral enclosure, the other to her bower. Filial devotion pushes Eugenio to abandon Louisa for Emira, who, while young and beautiful, is identified with the wealth that evidently attracted Reverend Seward when considering mates for his daughters and for his ward Honora. Emira has physical allure but she is mor- ally unattractive. Ernesto is of course the central figure behind Eugenio's maneu- ver. Seward's dedication to Saville despite the fact that he was married may lie behind Louisa's decision to live single; she believes with Eugenio that their souls will be united after death (2:582, 3.14). In this regard, Louisa's trust in fate and the short shrift given to any mourning after Emira's (convenient) death might likewise veil the wish-fulfillment aspect of Louisa's and Eugenio's unexpected reunion. Barnard, too, has observed the fantasy involved when the virginal Louisa inherits Eugenio's child (*Anna Seward* 14); Seward's letters demonstrate her quasi-maternal care for Saville's daughter Elizabeth. From another perspective, the feminized Eugenio, who flees the bed of his debauched, masculinized wife, resembles in his plight not only Saville but also daughters forced into marriages engineered to gratify their fathers, the destiny Seward evidently thought she escaped only by repudiating marriage.

Seward does not explicitly blame Ernesto for any of the novel's unhappiness, although he blames himself for the anguish he has caused his son and Louisa (4:17–22). Eugenio never reproaches his father, and Louisa herself greets Ernesto with "deepest reverence" (4:28). There is no reason to assume that Seward was publicly accusing her own father of causing his children's misery: Louisa, conspicuously, does not have a father. But the hero's and heroine's protestations notwithstanding, the plot points toward Ernesto as the chief cause of grief. His misplaced trust in a deceptive business partner, his panic-stricken request, his willingness to sacrifice a child to maintain his family's refined way of life make Ernesto ultimately responsible for all *Louisa*'s woes, no matter how strenuously the other characters deny his guilt. In involuntarily bowing to him in what we have noted as a variant of the classic father-daughter recognition scene (4:27–28), Louisa not only acknowledges Ernesto as Eugenio's father but as her own—and, indirectly, as the parent whose indisputable but misguided authority wrought all the complications that have marred her life.

Seward's relationship to the typical later eighteenth-century novels of sensibility is therefore complicated. Her plot overtly adheres to such novels' preference for kinship loyalty over individual conjugal alliances: Ernesto is treated sympathetically, Eugenio's choice is lauded as exemplary, and Louisa praises both father and son before entering their family as another "daughter." But Louisa finally occupies a liminal position in relation to the novel's kinship structures. Throughout the narrative, she literally occupies a space outside her home, near the estate's boundary, suspended between her brother's absentee guardianship and Eugenio's uncompleted marriage vow. Both she and Eugenio admit that their passion was too great and merited chastisement; in other words, Eugenio's choosing his mate without speaking to his family was rash, and so they deserved to be punished. After a period of intense suffering, however, their individual choice is finally blessed and acknowledged to surpass Eugenio's father's choice. Louisa is at last within bounds, as it were, with Ernesto's granddaughter in her arms for safekeeping, but she is nevertheless an outsider whose personal happiness with Eugenio has been endorsed. Seward's personal history is probably responsible for this conclusion. Conservative in most ways, she would never have publicly defied her father's wishes or disgraced her family, and thus she maintained the family solidarity under a patriarch that distinguished kinship orientation. As a single woman, she benefited from the old-fashioned belief that daughters were valuable family members, to be cherished and provided for rather than marginalized. But she must have resented the degree to which her own feelings and those of her sister were ignored by Reverend Seward. His control over her romantic attachments and marital prospects had led to her spinsterhood and almost stifled her relationship with Saville. Although Seward enjoyed great privileges throughout her life as Canon Seward's daughter, chatelaine of the Bishop's Palace in Lichfield, she was denied marriage by her father's insistence when young and then by Saville's inability to divorce.[5] *Louisa* represents a fantasy in which the father's sanctioned but brutal marital arrangement is undone so that the lovers can fulfill, with his blessing, their personal wish to marry. Louisa eats the bitter herbs of exile but has her wedding cake, too. *Louisa* at first appears to fulfill the nostalgic demands of the kinship-oriented plot, typical in novels of sensibility. But on closer inspection, Seward reveals her ambivalence toward the romance of family, and tentatively endorses the individually fulfilling conjugal bond she was denied in her own life.

Louisa finally represents Seward's attempt to answer the kinds of questions posed about sensibility by skeptical contemporaries as well as by Claudia Johnson and Susan Staves. If masculine identification with feelings left women with no options besides an extreme, debilitating capacity for emotion or the abandonment of all pretension to emotional response, Seward poses those alternatives as an edifying spectacle for her heroine. Emira is the classic "unsexed" female or, rather, the classic female libertine. Stifling all sympathetic impulses, she lives only to satisfy her appetites. Impervious to threats that usually constrained women's behavior, she ignores social ostracism and takes advantage of Eugenio's hesitation to sue for divorce. When she finally succumbs to a contagious disease, Emira's fate is symbolically apt; women who "exposed" themselves courted self-destruction. Eugenio more intriguingly represents the debilitated extreme of sensibility. As Staves remarks in *Eighteenth-Century British Women Writers*, exemplary fictional heroines often found themselves interrogating their propriety in acceding to loveless marriages in order to obey their parents or in contemplating the morally correct response to spousal adultery (344, 349). Such heroines usually resolved to wait patiently for a reform ultimately won by silent tears if not by uncomplaining endurance. Eugenio, much like these heroines, nurses his baby daughter and hesitates to lecture his wife until motherhood urges her reformation. Like the heroines whom Staves describes, Eugenio must suffer for contracting a loveless marriage even though filial piety required his sacrifice. Even his hesitation to confront, let alone discipline, Emira more closely resembles the behavior of an abused wife than that of an eighteenth-century husband.

Situated outside these extremes, Louisa develops a moderated response to her woes. While Staves finds that the midcentury bluestockings preferred the life of reason to that of sensibility and moreover suspected that "sentimentalism too often entailed moral incoherence" (358), Seward envisioned a heroine whose sensibility is refined by the self-respect and moral principles that Emira lacks. Because we learn from Louisa herself about her battle with despair, while we hear of Eugenio's endurance through Ernesto's narrative, her psychological struggle appears more dynamic than his. Louisa emerges as a figure of exemplary because disciplined sensibility. As Emira recognizes, Louisa will be a superior mother to her child, raising the infant for "Eugenio's sake!—who gave her birth" (4:497), as if Eugenio were the mother and Emira the baby's libertine father. Louisa appears at Emira's deathbed long after conquering her own suicidal impulse. She is the ideal spectator of Emira's miserable death, a death she earned as an offender against "Truth—and Love!" (4:508). Having offended neither, Louisa will finally become Eugenio's wife. In *Equivocal Beings*, Johnson questions whether even Mary Wollstonecraft, who struggled to reconcile sensibility with female dignity, could imagine a heterosexual marriage that satisfied a "sturdy, purposive, mutu-ally respecting, and rationally loving couple"; *The Wrongs of Woman* envisions such a marriage only between females (69). In *Louisa*, Seward offers an alterna-tive for women unhappy with contemporary marital configurations. The heroine, not the hero, appears to release the suffering spouse and restore a happy marriage. Louisa, moreover, assumes attributes of the husband when she agrees to raise the child of another parent "who gave her birth." Louisa, in other words, takes back the admirable sensibility along with the capability and effectuality that Johnson believes had been usurped by male proponents of sentiment. When Ernesto im-plores her forgiveness, she even triumphs morally over the novel's patriarch, al-though she believes his error was justified and reverently seeks his blessing.

Louisa is more than a private wish-fulfillment fantasy. Seward's verse novel replaces the patriarchal tales of Eloisa's and Julie's suffering with an updated, feminine "translation," a version in which the heroine's exquisite feelings are privileged instead of punished and in which she is granted some agency after com-pleting her emotional trials. Louisa flees her bower in response to Ernesto's plea, not like Eve in the wake of transgression but like an angel of mercy emanating from heaven. Her gesture of absolving Eugenio and Ernesto makes possible a final tableau that she invites Emma to view as paradise restored. She and Eugenio will resemble the redeemed Adam and Eve, "as thro' the Vale of Life [they] stray" in a starlit, spring environment (4:551). But in this version, Eugenio and his father have sinned more than Louisa, who was guilty of nothing but too heedless a love for her fiancé. Like novels from *Pamela* to *Pride and Prejudice*, *Louisa* imagines a conclusion that was almost impossible for most women as it certainly was for Seward herself. But by rewriting Pope's and Rousseau's fictions of feminine sensibility and subtly challenging her father's authority, Seward acknowledged women's superior capacity for feeling while claiming sensibility's potential for moral growth and emotional maturity. Her poetical novel deserves recognition among those of other late-century writers, including not only Wollstonecraft and Hays but also Charlotte Smith, Eliza Fenwick, Frances Sheridan, Elizabeth Inchbald, and other women who explored the paradoxical gift of sensibility.

CHAPTER EIGHT

Milton's Champion

S eward's intervention in the developing novel genre is generally forgotten today, but her contribution to a particular lyric poetic form is widely acknowledged. Two hundred years after their publications captivated the British reading public, Charlotte Smith's *Elegiac Sonnets* (1784–1811) and Seward's *Original Sonnets on Various Subjects* (1799) are generally regarded as landmarks in the late eighteenth-century sonnet revival.[1] But while both poets are usually mentioned in discussions of this phenomenon, Smith has recently been honored as the chief influence on her Romantic successors and probably the better poet of the two. Smith's influence is unquestionable, but the latter claim is arguable. Because we view both poets in the aftermath of the Romantic triumph, we tend to adopt a teleological view of literary history that values poets according to how closely they approximate or anticipate the Romantics. Smith's self-referential emphasis, persistent melancholia, and vaunted uniqueness echo throughout Coleridge's and Wordsworth's poems and down through Byron's. Seward, measured against Smith's proto-Romantic qualities, is judged the lesser poet. But by measuring Seward against Smith, we ignore Seward's adherence to well-established principles and her development of the aesthetics of sensibility. At times, her sonnets argue critical opinions or contemplate moral insights drawn from her correspondence, but every sonnet, regardless of theme, illustrates Seward's preference for poetry that connects the self to others and to the surrounding world rather than for poetry that emphasizes, as Smith does, the individual's isolation. Seward conducted her campaign against Smith in the guise of Milton's champion, defending his sonnets' form and occasional topics as the models for her own. By studying Seward's defense of the Miltonic or "legitimate" sonnet, we can recover the ways her favored sonnet form supported and advanced her beliefs about the function of poetry and the role of the poet, and come to see why she thought Smith's rival approach involved stakes so high that her sonnets must be vehemently condemned.

In *Eighteenth-Century Women Poets and Their Poetry*, Paula Backscheider has made a strong case for Smith's preeminence. Responding to critics, including Seward, who have accused Smith of literary infractions ranging from monotony to plagiarism, Backscheider explains that Smith constructed the most challenging form of sonnet sequence, the chain, in which tones, images, and other repetitions create variations on a single theme (328). To Seward, Smith's sonnets are "everlasting lamentables" (*Letters* 2:287). By contrast, Backscheider praises Smith for composing a suite of poems on "the great mood of the poetry of her century" (326). Petrarch, Shakespeare, Spenser, and other predecessors had written similar cycles on the topic of love; Smith, Backscheider shrewdly perceives, applied the same organization and techniques to melancholy. She also argues that Smith's copious echoes of other poets should never have been described as plagiarism. Although Seward was not alone in deeming Smith's sonnets "hackneyed scraps" (*Letters* 2:287), their intertextuality performs numerous functions, such as distinguishing the speaker from Smith herself and incorporating the moods and themes of predecessors into her poems (Backscheider 335–38).

Backscheider's argument echoes those of other recent commentators who have explored Smith's artfulness and the sources of her appeal to contemporaries.[2] Susan Staves's opinion that Smith's *Elegiac Sonnets* was "the most important volume of women's poems of this period" (i.e., the later century) now seems nearly indisputable (*Literary History* 396). The widespread appeal of a volume that went through nine editions in Smith's lifetime, combined with her sonnets' rich texture, leads inexorably to the question: why did Seward find these poems so objectionable? It is difficult to find a recent critical discussion of *Elegiac Sonnets* that does not quote Seward's opinion of them as "everlasting lamentables" and "hackneyed scraps of dismality."[3] Why did Seward—an avid student of English poetry (she once explained her self-confidence as the result of "having made the grace, harmony, and elegance of the English language [her] long and particular study" [*Letters* 2:140])—fail to recognize Smith's claims to excellence? Backscheider concludes with several other critics that Seward's response was chiefly that of a competitor and notes that Elizabeth Robinson also adopted a combative tone when introducing her own sonnets (340–41). But Seward's dismissive attitude seems extreme, even if she was defending her title as "Britannia's Muse." If Smith's sonnets were so execrable, why did Seward hammer away at them in letter after letter, damning them to her correspondents (especially those who admired Smith's verse) while admitting that she had read only the first of many successively expanding editions? In this chapter, I consider the reasons behind Seward's dislike of Smith's sonnets and outline her competing vision of sonnet excellence. I argue that Seward contributed to the sonnet renaissance a unique version descended from Milton's model but refined according to principles, such as the appropriate tone and topics for sonnets, she claimed to derive from his. I also consider the consequences of Seward's refusal to acknowledge Smith's poems as viable models. Because Seward's ideas and inspirations are now less accessible than Smith's, her volume has not received a comparable degree of attention. I hope to restore the social and aesthetic stakes of her sonnet interventions. In chapter 9, I sketch some fruitful approaches to her one hundred occasional sonnets after reviewing her beliefs and methods, concluding with close readings of a handful of representative and compelling sonnets. Having explored Seward's sonnet legacy, I turn in my tenth chapter to the sonnets that have attracted modern critical attention, her mysteriously passionate responses to the loss of her friendship with Honora Sneyd.

Seward's reiterated objections to Smith's sonnets, especially as preserved in her posthumously published correspondence, may have resulted from what James Clifford has uncovered as a pattern of expansion as she revised her letters for publication. As Clifford observes, Seward tended to revisit earlier comments and make lengthy additions, either to bring them into line with her mature sentiments or to clarify passages she found obscure (118–19). While her original letters are now scattered or lost, Clifford's article provides a salutary warning against assuming Seward's published letters faithfully reflect her opinions at the time she wrote them (and offers an additional useful caveat about her sloppiness in dating the revised copies). One supposition, then, is that Seward's opinions were first more tactfully expressed or were not developed in such detail until, in her last decade, she altered many earlier letters to elaborate her objections. By 1788, Seward had, however, publicly expressed her adamant belief that the only true or "legitimate" sonnets were those patterned on Petrarch's and Milton's. She augmented Henry Cary's slim volume of sonnets with two prefatory sonnets lauding his poetic promise (Cary 5–6), the first of which praises Cary for adhering to the "strict energic measures" of the Petrarchan sonnet instead of daring to "lawless assume" the name of sonnet for a lesser form (ll. 12, 5). In a letter to William Hayley, Seward confessed that her sonnet was intended to combat Smith's assertion, in the preface to her

first edition, "that the legitimate sonnet is not suited to the genius of our language" (*Letters* 2:222–23). Even if Seward revised her earliest reactions to Smith,
therefore, it seems likely that she simply amplified her well-known opinion.

Smith was not the only poet whose verse attracted Seward's passionate criticism. Gillen Wood has recently interrogated the vehemence of Seward's "Remonstrance," a poetic rebuke of William Cowper's disapproval, mentioned in *The
Task*, of the grandiose Handel Commemoration in 1784. Wood wisely refrains
from dismissing Seward as ill tempered or injudicious because of her fervent response to a "rather mild objection" not to Handel's music but to the composer's
near deification by throngs assembled in Westminster Abbey to hear his choral
compositions. Instead, Wood perceives the outlines of a larger dispute in Cowper's
and Seward's disparate opinions. In Cowper, Wood argues, Seward recognized
the beginnings of a movement away from the notion of art as communal and sociable and toward the Romantic conception of art as the product of solitary observers usually critical of their surroundings. In Wood's view, Seward was astute
in perceiving that Cowper's seemingly innocuous refusal to join in the universal
adulation of her beloved Handel indicated rejection, in essence, of her beliefs
about the purpose of art and the role of the artist. Handel had become a figure in
Britain's pantheon, not unlike Shakespeare and Milton, and his oratorios, in particular, were acclaimed by national consensus as part of the fabric of British culture. Poets maintained a central role by guiding public taste toward appreciation
of their cultural heritage. To Seward, dissenters from Handelomania encouraged
a factional approach to culture and, ultimately, to national identity. Cherishing
her personal reputation as British muse and shunning the—in her view—vicious
critics sponsored by London review journals, Seward would certainly have found
Cowper's remarks critically heretical and even unpatriotic. Sensing the threat to
her beliefs about culture—indeed, to her worldview—she responded brutally to
lines that now seem unexceptionable.

I agree with Wood's thesis about Seward's conception of art's function and the
role of the artist, although his argument presents a number of difficulties. Seward,
for example, assiduously avoided London (although with Teresa Barnard we may
suspect her motives), which, like Cowper, she also called Babel.[4] While despising
professional literary critics, she occasionally published harsh reviews in the *Gentleman's Magazine* and other periodicals. Her cult of sociability and preference
for a literary consensus was therefore not as pure as Wood conceives or even as
Seward herself might have claimed. Wood's general argument, however, like his
response to the conundrum of Seward's overreaction, is admirable. He correctly
refuses to dismiss "Remonstrance," perceiving instead that it reveals Seward's dis-

tress at a time when her values were being undermined not just by Cowper but by increasing numbers of critics, writers, and readers. Wood's argument, and especially his approach, provides guidance for any writer seeking to reassess Seward, as he avoids the simplistic conclusions typical of much previous Seward criticism. Her reiterated diatribes against Smith can all too easily be mocked as the result of jealousy, critical arrogance, or misguided taste rather than as her defense of principles threatened by emergent Romantic values. It is more rewarding, however, to pursue Seward's reasons for dismissing the *Elegiac Sonnets* on the assumption that her vehemence indicates deep-seated literary-cultural antagonism rather than injured self-importance. Wood has discovered a complicated network of associations underlying Seward's remark about Cowper, including her fear that art and artists would lose status if they were no longer revered as the sustainers of their culture but were regarded instead as its maverick critics. Her fear regarding Cowper's attitude proved justifiable, although art gained a different kind of status as a result of its ascendancy. Is Seward then to be denigrated because she failed to predict the consequences of the Romantic rebellion? Because what Wood describes as her performative, sociable ideal of art lost ground to the cult of the lonely, prophetic wanderer? Because sensibility transformed and became Romanticism?

Seward might instead be viewed as among the last adherents to principles that dominated Western artistic thinking for many centuries, from the bards who declaimed epics in the royal courts to the bluestockings who hosted chamber music and poetry readings in their parlors. Backscheider refers to her as "one of the last neoclassicists" for "maintaining the English ability to master and then *improve* a respected form" (343). Seward would also have insisted on the limits after which improvement became desecration, a conservative position that was under attack in many guises during the radical conclusion of the century. In *Relationships of Sympathy*, Thomas J. McCarthy has explained that "for Romantic readers, the emphasis on feeling in language led to their tendency to approach the written word as speech . . . . As a result they presumed that the feelings, experiences, and events in a work of literature were those of the author himself" (40). McCarthy argues that literary emphasis on "the inner life of feeling" predominated after 1800, "rather than social attitudes or opinions" (148). If McCarthy is correct, Seward and like-minded peers were fighting a losing battle in upholding a sonnet ideal that emphasized technical virtuosity and encouraged topics such as social commentary. While it would consequently be impossible to reinstate Seward's theories, there is more to be gained from reconstructing her positions than from dismissing them. In view of our current fascination with the roots of Romanticism, it is not surprising that Seward is sometimes overlooked. She resisted the onset of Romanticism even as she helped popularize some of its characteristic forms, such as the ode and the sonnet, and some of its themes, such as the insistence on the relationship between the human consciousness and the landscape, not to mention its reverence for Shakespeare, Milton, and the English poets. Wood locates some crucial distinctions between Seward's and the Romantics' point of view. Might we glean from Seward's reaction against Smith some further insights into the Romantics' break with their predecessors, however closely the latter anticipated the former? Might we even glean renewed appreciation of Seward's sonnets when we understand what was at stake in their composition?

Despite being doctored evidence, Seward's correspondence is a faithful guide to her theories about the sonnet. In fact, since she revised her letters in the decade following publication of her sonnet collection, they probably constitute her final, posthumous campaign on behalf of her sonnet principles. From her many statements, it is clear that Seward did not view herself solely as Smith's adversary. Alert to the sonnet revival that Paula Feldman, Daniel Robinson, and others claim was taking place at the time, she demanded a leading role not only in promoting that movement but in guiding public judgment about what constituted sonnet excellence. As Feldman, Robinson, Backscheider, and others observe, Seward and Smith were but two of a number of poets publishing their sonnets, each aware of his or her peers and eager to claim preeminence. Seward seems to have viewed Smith as the head of a party disputing the sanctity of a particular form, the so-called legitimate sonnet. By using that term, Seward announced her intention to enter a lively public debate over what might properly be considered a sonnet and which techniques produced admirable sonnets. Reviewed in isolation, Seward's remarks appear repetitive, pompous, even shrewish. But considered in the context of public discussion, it becomes clear that she adopts contemporary terminology to argue a recognized position. As Backscheider notes, Mary Robinson similarly glanced at Smith in the introduction to her sonnet sequence *Sappho and Phaon* (1796), complaining like Seward about poets who take liberties with the form's conventions (341). Sandro Jung has described the sonnets of Susanna Pearson, a working-class Sheffield poet, as Petrarchan both in form and in their departure from Smith's hopelessness. By the time Seward distinguished her sonnets from "those minute Elegies of twelve alternate rhymes, closing with a couplet, which assume the name of sonnet" (*Original Sonnets* iii), her covert reference to Smith must have been palpable, but she was also participating in a well-known controversy in which Smith represented the opposing side. Like a politician campaigning for office, Seward "stayed on point" throughout her epistolary and published remarks.[5] As we survey the main points of her discourse, we must ponder the cultural stakes for which she thought herself fighting by defending the correct form of a relatively late poetic form that, until recently, had been considered minor.

Seward unfailingly invoked Milton as the model for succeeding authors of English sonnets. Milton had patterned his sonnets on those of Petrarch, imitating his characteristic structure and rhyme scheme. In her preface, Seward quotes an article in the *Gentleman's Magazine* (1786) by her cousin Henry White, whose opinions are suspiciously nearly identical to her own. (White sometimes published articles in the *Gentleman's Magazine* that it seems Seward suggested or even composed but for various reasons did not wish to publish under her own name.) White explains that the sonnet "partakes of the nature of Blank Verse, by the lines running into each other at proper intervals" (*Original Sonnets* iv). White added that although the rhymes of the octet cannot be varied, those of the sestet might. The concluding couplet was optional. Perhaps Seward was recalling White's article when, in 1789, she suggested to Mary Knowles that the sonnet is "the intermediate style of poetry, between rhyme and blank verse; and the undulating and varied pauses of the latter, give to the true sonnet an air of graceful freedom, beyond that of all other measures—though . . . it is in reality the most difficult" (*Letters* 2:226). White pronounced Milton's sonnets "the great models of perfection" (*Original Sonnets* iv), and Seward likewise confessed to Knowles that she was "enamoured of the legitimate Miltonic sonnet" (*Letters* 2:226). Seward and Robinson were two among many poets who named Milton as their exemplar. Curiously, the deference accorded Milton ignored the sonnet achievements of Surrey, Sidney, Shakespeare, Spenser, and others who composed significant sequences with rhyme schemes more compatible with the English language because of the concluding octave's additional pair of rhymes. How had Milton's sonnets superseded his predecessors' to the degree that theirs were considered bastard efforts, unworthy of what Seward calls "our National Poetry" (*Original Sonnets* v)?

The answer to this question parallels the disagreement between Seward and Cowper that Wood found so revealing. As Jonathan Kramnick has demonstrated, Milton was a relative newcomer to the British pantheon in Seward's lifetime.[6] Kramnick argues that Spenser and Milton were elevated in the mid-eighteenth century not because, like Shakespeare, they were believed to be universally appealing but because they required the guidance of trained scholars and professional critics (42–43, 103–4). Thus, their recognition supported not only British national identity but its entire print culture and all who labored to create it. Seward and her generation would have grown up believing both in Milton's excellence and in his difficulty, beliefs that in turn granted elite status to those capable of explicating his texts and techniques. Seward often extolled Shakespeare as England's greatest dramatic poet, but she ignored his other poetry. Assuming, like most contemporaries, that Shakespeare was poorly educated, she would not have regarded as authoritative his choice to adopt a less rigorous rhyme scheme for his sonnets. On the other hand, like Dryden's championship of Ben Jonson above all continental playwrights in *An Essay on Dramatic Poesy*, Seward's choice posed Milton as the heir of Petrarch and, indeed, centuries of Italian sonneteers. While Dryden loved Shakespeare, he recognized that contemporary French dramatists could only be challenged by a writer following classical precedents. Likewise, Milton's reputation guaranteed at least respect for his choice of poetic forms, even from notoriously stringent critics. Seward instances Boileau in a letter to T. S. Whalley in 1789, complaining that "national jealousy, and the prudery of French taste in poetry, too often made [him] unjust to the excellencies of Milton's compositions for us to believe he meant to exalt that author, when he declared the constituent excellence of the sonnet to be grave and simple energy" (*Letters* 2:303). But, she concluded tartly, that quality is "carried to its last perfection in a few of Milton's." In an era of constant warfare against the French, the British were especially determined to uphold their national arts against those of their competitor. It no doubt gave Seward great pleasure to recognize that Milton had excelled in precisely the quality Boileau pronounced definitive while writing not in the more lenient English rhyme pattern but in the Italian scheme. Writing within a year of the centenary of the Glorious Revolution, and as Britain anxiously monitored events in France, Seward joined those compatriots who extolled Milton not only as a champion of English liberty but also as their literary champion against continental challengers. Surely their choice of Milton's style had an array of cultural inducements besides its literary pedigree.

The prestige accorded difficulty was important, however, especially to the many women who participated in the sonnet revival. Like Mary Robinson, who lamented that "every romantic scribbler" (9) thought sonnets easy to compose, Seward often remarked on the form's difficulty. Backscheider observes that although Smith chose the "easier" Shakespearian rhyme scheme, she elected to create a complex chain of sonnets rather than discrete examples. Backscheider believes that women, conscious that their work was often trivialized by critics, consequently believed "the honor of their sex was at stake" as they worked to reinstate the sonnet (343). Competitive aggression thus partly led Seward to overlook Smith's purpose in echoing sentiments among her sonnets and to describe them instead as "everlasting lamentables." What appears to us simple professional jealousy was part of a complex exercise in which women contended for prominence against other women, each anxious to claim for her poems the greatest degree of difficulty and to disparage those of her peers. "Where there is tolerable vigour of intellect," Seward boasted to Mary Knowles, "difficulty rather stimulates than discourages." Confessing "more propensity to poetic efforts, than leisure to employ them," she added that nevertheless "we may sooner write forty lines, in any other measure, than fourteen in that of the true sonnet—but I can easier write fourteen on that arduous model, than an hundred on the easier ones" (*Letters* 2:226). The sonnet, then, suited both Seward's lack of time for composition and her genius, since, unlike other poets, she found it easier to write in the most "arduous" pattern than in any of "the easier ones." She thus used the sonnet, like Apollo, who "invented the strict, the rigorous sonnet as a test of skill," to set herself apart from all those "who assumed the name of poet, on the slight pretense of tagging flimsy rhymes" (*Letters* 2:162).

Even scholars sympathetic to women poets might be tempted to dismiss Seward's vendetta against the *Elegiac Sonnets* as mere jealousy or as an example of the phenomenon in which one woman wins approval from men (in this case, male critics) and is determined to prevent other women from sharing or usurping her rewards. Her harsh comments are believed to confirm suspicions that women always behave invidiously toward one another. Only when read against the background of women's participation in the sonnet revival, as Backscheider ably describes it, can Seward's role not as a spoiler but as one among many women contesting for glory be appreciated (338–51). Since Seward was already acclaimed as one of Britain's reigning poets, perhaps its chief woman poet, her adamant tone is more rather than less understandable. But because her point of view ultimately lost its cultural capital, her campaign is often described as if it were ridiculous or, at best, perceived as mystifying. When we remember that numbers of women were advancing their cases, in print, for variations of the "legitimate" or Shakespearian sonnet, Seward appears as she viewed herself: as an established poet with a leading role to play in the ongoing debate. She believed in her importance not because she was delusional but because public opinion had confirmed her eminence. When she chose to side with those promoting the legitimate sonnet, she was campaigning for the form apparently sanctioned by both patriotism and tradition.

Seward's pronouncements bear comparison with Pope's *Dunciad*. It is easy today to look back to the cultural glories of the Georgian era and laugh at Pope's expressions of despair. The introduction of Italian opera, the institution of the grand tour, the explosion of print: neither these nor any of the phenomena Pope deplores brought down the curtain on Western civilization as they do at the conclusion of Pope's masterpiece. We understand, however, what Pope believed was at stake and refrain from laughing at his very public combat against modern culture. Seward and her fellow legitimate-sonnet advocates similarly thought British literature was being cheapened by the proliferation of a "facile form of verse" (*Letters* 2:164). They sought to defend the honor of a tradition that most Britons considered a source of national pride throughout the late-century years of war and empire building. As in Pope's era, the curtain did not fall on the sonnet or on literature as a result of Smith's innovations. Instead, a burst of energy impelled British writers to initiate the literary movement that still influences our creativity. But Seward's rearguard action on behalf of tradition is no more risible than were Pope's diatribes against Daniel Defoe, Eliza Haywood, Colley Cibber, and other "dunces" whose writings we have learned to appreciate despite his condemnation.

Seward, moreover, proselytized on behalf of the Miltonic sonnet with the zeal of the converted. In a letter to Whalley dated April 10, 1789, she regrets their divergent "ideas of sonnet-excellence" but adds that she does not "despair of [his] conversion." Continuing her spiritual analogy, she explains that Whalley has "a soul superior to that false shame, which annexes the idea of disgrace to changed opinions, even when their change results from the force of excellence, emerging from the mists of our accidental neglect, or hasty prejudices." She is confident that Whalley would agree with her if only, like her, he were receptive to the arguments of those with superior knowledge. She proceeds to describe her own epiphany, the result of conversations with "Mr. [Brooke] Boothby, his friend Mr. [Edward] Tighe, Mr. [Court] Dewes, and Mr. [George] Hardinge," all "warm admirers of the best of Milton's sonnets[,] . . . good judges of English poetry, and masters of the Italian language. Mr. Boothby and Mr. Tighe first opened my eyes . . . and I soon became of their opinion, that [the Miltonic sonnet] formed a beautiful and distinct order of composition in our language; that dignity and energetic plainness were its most indispensable characteristics." She admits that before that exchange, she believed sonnets were characteristically lighthearted. Boothby and Tighe, however, "began my conversion" by arguing that Petrarch's sonnets were far from happy. They argued that although the word "sonnet" seemed to call for a light composition, "great writers have a just claim to have their compositions considered as models in every style in which they have excelled; that . . . [Milton's] sonnets have annexed an expectation of strength and majesty to that title, which though sorrow or affectionate contemplation may soften down, the sonnet must not part with in exchange for any of the lighter graces" (*Letters* 2:256–57).

Seward's narrative deserves unpacking. It may well be fictitious, if a letter dated October 27, 1786, to George Hardinge is authentic. There, she expresses her surprise at Hardinge's belief "that Milton's sonnets have a singular flow of numbers, and that their author thought smoothness an essential perfection in that order of verse" (*Letters* 1:201). In a January 29, 1789, letter, she told Hayley that "the best of Milton's [sonnets], I have always thought, formed the model for sonnet-writing" (*Letters* 2:216). It is not improbable that Seward boasted to Hayley of opinions that had not "always" been her own but had been derived from others. But it is odd that Hardinge, supposedly one of those who presided over her "conversion," would later have claimed to hold an opinion more appropriate to Seward's original supposition of the sonnet's lightness and gaiety. The episode may have been invented to give Seward's belief the weight of several literary authorities (which might also be why she chose to publish her opinions on sonnets under White's name, if that was the case.) On the other hand, regarding Seward's sonnet principles as the result of one or, probably, more discussions, in which she was persuaded to defer to her friends' opinion, helps explain several aspects of her seeming vendetta against Smith. For one example, as Laura Runge has observed, critical language throughout the long eighteenth century was gendered. Runge instances Dryden and Scott among critics who habitually used terms such as "hard," "severe," and "dignified" to describe a writer's "manly" excellence, as opposed to the "soft," "tender," and "graceful" writings they deemed feminine and of secondary value (42–43, 48–50). By convincing Seward to admire Milton's sonnets for their masculine qualities, her interlocutors likewise convinced her of their prestige and their concomitant preeminence as models. Her choice of the "dignified" style and structure over the insistent pathos of Smith's sonnets was thus a bid for recognition on the grounds of what, in their culture, was deemed excellent; namely, the manly, as opposed to Smith's more "feminine" style.

Even more striking than her gendered praise of Milton's style is the conversion imagery associated with her opinion. If Seward added the conversion language when revising her account of a less stark thought process, she thereby emphasized the fact the she had been persuaded that only one opinion was admissible regarding the sonnet. The scene she describes is remarkable, evoking the image of a heretic surrounded by priests determined to convince her of their belief. The antagonistic tone of her published exchanges with Hardinge makes the image of her conversion arising from his exhortations even more striking. It was to Hardinge, for example, that she had already defended the authority conferred on her by her "long and particular study" of the English language (*Letters* 2:140). Her deference to Hardinge and his friends in this case probably stemmed from her recognition of their superior educations. She stipulates their knowledge of Italian, which presumably enabled them to read Petrarch and other sonnet masters in their original language, making credible their argument about the Petrarchan sonnet's sobriety. Having taken on faith their asseveration regarding the sonnet's greatest master, Seward was prepared for their argument that Milton, of all English poets, had excelled in matching both the form and substance of his Italian model. As the final step in her conversion to the one true sonnet, Seward accepted their reasoning that because Milton had achieved greatness, his sonnets were the model for all subsequent English sonnets. Following Milton's, sonnets would be judged according to an "expectation of strength and majesty" and discounted if these qualities were less prominent than "the lighter graces." Henceforth, Seward preached this doctrine to many correspondents, in the preface of her collection, and in her sonnets themselves.

Seward's curious language of religious conversion helps explain the vehemence of her advocacy. Today, when the term "bardolatry" expresses our near deification of Shakespeare, we must pause to remember that Milton had recently been elevated to similar status by Seward's contemporaries. It is also helpful to recall that the Shakespearian sonnet was not the creation of Shakespeare but of the Earl of Surrey and others; we, however, continue to call it such because we consider Shakespeare to have excelled in that form. Adoring Shakespeare, we forget that to Seward and her generation, Shakespeare was a poorly educated but miraculously gifted dramatist, not a great poet. That a man with so little education would adopt the less rigorous sonnet form would have seemed predictable but not necessarily the best precedent for a serious poet. Milton, with his vast learning and continental cachet was the preferable model. This would have been especially true for women, who feared they would be judged unworthy if they chose the easier option. Such was the case for Charlotte Smith, whose sonnets attracted the scorn of other women poets concerned to distance themselves from such an unambitious "scribbler." By acquiescing in the belief of what she deemed the intelligentsia, Seward abandoned the confidence born of "long and particular study" for the dogma preached by her university-trained friends. Once converted, she assumed the rigidity of a zealot and shut her mind to the possibility of any other route to "sonnet-excellence." Having dismissed Smith's first volume, for example, she admitted in 1789 that she never saw any succeeding editions (*Letters* 2:224), indicating unwillingness to reconsider her opinion or think seriously about what her contemporaries found so appealing about the *Elegiac Sonnets*.

Perhaps, to continue the religious analogy, Seward refrained from examining any evidence that might counter her newfound belief that any sonnet not constructed on the Miltonic model was inferior. Her lack of fairness toward Smith is even more striking when her specific complaints are considered. Seward is best known for comments such as her admission to William Hayley that "I do not find in [Smith's] sonnets any original ideas, any vigour of thought, any striking imagery—but plagiarism, glaring and perpetual;—whole lines taken verbatim, and with no acknowledgement, from Shakespeare, Milton, Young, Pope, Gray, Collins, Mason, and Beattie" (*Letters* 2:223–24). Since Hayley was Smith's chief patron and dedicatee, Seward's dismissal of her seems particularly harsh. In the same letter, she exclaims, "When I see an author reduced to crib an whole line from Young's Night Thoughts, another whole line from Mason's Elegy on Lady Coventry, and two whole lines from Shakespeare, to make up a little poem, which contains only fourteen lines, I cannot help concluding that the imagination is barren. Yet it is even so with the eighth sonnet of Mrs. Smith's first edition" (*Letters* 2:224). Seward concludes the letter by asking Hayley not to accuse her of illiberality but to remember that poets have often diverged in their opinions. Seward and Hayley, she says, resemble Gray and Mason, who disagreed regarding both Ossian and Rousseau's *Nouvelle Helöise*. Although Seward enjoyed rigorous exchanges about contemporary publications, she seems to have excused herself from serious debate with Hayley regarding Smith. By asking him to "agree to disagree," she effectively preempted further argument. Having condemned Smith on the grounds of plagiarism, one wonders if Seward reflected at all on her judgment when, in 1800, she was aghast to discover her own "unconscious plagiarism" of Chatterton in a sonnet on winter.[7]

Writing to Thomas Park, she discusses Thomas Warton's observation of Milton's "striking resemblance" to his "poetic predecessors in English verse," much as "the opening of my twenty-seventh sonnet" resembles "a passage in Chatterton." Such "involuntary plagiarisms," she recalls, revealed the modernity of Chatterton's works: only Ossian's works seem free of such borrowings. "Every other poet, however, great, and, on the whole, original, may be perpetually traced to his conscious and unconscious sources, in the writings of his predecessors and contemporaries—Milton eternally, and Shakespeare very often" (*Letters* 5:273–74). When Smith borrowed from other poets, she committed plagiarism. When Seward borrows, it is involuntary, a transgression of which only minds stored to overflowing with literature are capable. Smith was a poetic magpie; Seward resembles Shakespeare and Milton. Milton, hampered by his tremendous stock of knowledge, borrowed "eternally," absolving his acolyte by extension from suspicion of literary theft.

Seward's gambit in excusing herself from a crime she unhesitatingly ascribed to others moved her closer toward identity with the great poets she admired. As Jane Spencer has discussed in *Literary Relations*, eighteenth-century women had particular difficulty inserting themselves into a literary lineage. Spencer describes the travails of women who wished to identify themselves as heirs of Dryden, for example, or Johnson. Many cultural factors, especially the patriarchal structure of society, made it nearly impossible to claim such literary inheritances (9–12). As the daughter of an old-fashioned man of letters who encouraged her to excel at needlework rather than writing, Seward faced literal as well as metaphorical barriers to claiming her descent from a line of writers. Milton as epic poet was not available to her as a spiritual father, but Milton the sonnet writer was. By championing the occasional sonnet in Petrarchan form, Seward found a way to insert herself into Milton's lineage without unduly violating feminine modesty. Like Burney studying Latin under Johnson's tutelage (Spencer 59), Seward became a happier version of Milton's daughters, composing Italianate sonnets under his aegis. Even her claim to share Milton's faults becomes an identifying mark linking the two poets, an apparently modest claim that nevertheless signifies their family resemblance.

Seward's tactic is suspect, but her claim of involuntary plagiarism distinguished her from contemporaries who regularly incorporated phrases by other writers into their texts. In *Strange Fits of Passion*, Adela Pinch probes the relationship between sincerity and artful expressions of emotion in late eighteenth-century writings, especially Smith's sonnets. Pinch, unlike most other recent critics, honors Seward's perspective as one legitimate response to verses that imply the expression of personal emotion but borrow the phrases of other writers to give voice to that personal feeling. Pinch interrogates the link between sensibility and literary representations of emotion. Since sensibility, or the sentimental, was gauged by the swiftness of sympathetic response to others' suffering, the witness's suffering was always one step removed from reality. In Smith's sonnets, the speaker's suffering is additionally filtered through allusions to other writers' representations of woe, such as Pope's Eloisa's declaration that only someone who has suffered for love could write her story. Pinch's argument is chiefly about whether such expressions conduced to the emergence of feminism. Observing that late-century women increasingly claimed their suffering as grounds for amelioration of their social predicament, Pinch concludes that writings such as Smith's cannot be considered protofeminist because her objective was not, apparently, intended to achieve justice for herself and her children but to attract the reading public's sympathy. In that goal, she succeeded brilliantly, making a spectacle of her suffering through nine editions during her lifetime. Pinch notes with surprise that apparently few readers responded as Seward did to the literariness of Smith's laments; that is, to their derivative quality. In Pinch's account, Seward emerges as more the Romantic than Smith, anticipating Charles Lamb's declaration that because the sonnet was a "personal poem," it should not borrow phrases from others (69).

Pinch deconstructs a phenomenon that to most contemporaries seemed natural. In their sentimental and print-oriented culture, conventions such as the presumed communion of readers over favorite literary passages failed to attract comment. Smith could assume that her public had wept over the sorrows of Satan, Eloisa, Werter, and such afflicted poets as Otway and Collins. Their memorable phrases, or their names alone, were shorthand (appropriate enough for a short poem) for heroic suffering. Through allusion, Smith imported volumes of agony into her sonnets. And, as Pinch notes, she did not merely claim identical suffering with those figures. She typically added a twist or turn that implied the superiority of her suffering to theirs. Pinch cites the famous example of Smith's quotation of Eloisa, which in Smith's first sonnet becomes more than the conventional claim that only the poet who feels deeply can adequately describe suffering. Instead, Smith's context suggests that by writing about suffering, the feeling poet increases her own agony, much like the nightingale who sings most sweetly when her breast is pierced with a thorn (62–62). Pinch's point is that Smith claimed superior suffering as the mark of "successful literary transmission"; that is, of her membership in a lineage of poets who excelled in portraits of suffering because they were miserable.

Developing Pinch's observations and mindful of Spencer's, we might observe that Smith's characteristic move was not only to claim succession but to imply superiority, as all ambitious poets must—in her case, superior suffering. A good example is the third sonnet of her collection, "To a Nightingale" (3). Earlier in the century, Anne Finch had made the nightingale's song the subject of a witty contest between bird and poet in "To the Nightingale," which ends with the poet's frustration because, try as she might, she cannot duplicate the bird's song. Finch concludes that humans often discount or mock what they cannot equal, a statement of humility in the presence of a superior gift. Smith's sonnet takes an opposing path. As Finch had done, she interrogates the bird—but not to challenge the bird's technique. Instead, she wishes to learn the "sad cause" of its "mournful melody" (ll. 3–4). Smith yearns to translate the meaning of the bird's song, the sorrow that drives her from her nest to spend her nights singing in the woods (ll. 5–8). Smith opens her sestet speculating that the bird might once have been the victim of betrayal or even of "disastrous love" (l. 12), now "releas'd in wood-lands wild to rove" (l. 10). Smith assumes, of course, the nightingale's legendary metamorphosis from human victim into most gifted among avian singers, privi-leged owing to her suffering. She concludes, however, not by identifying with the bird as a fellow sufferer whose sorrows emanate in sonnets but instead by envy-ing the bird: "Ah! songstress sad! that such my lot might be,/To sigh and sing at liberty—like thee!" (ll. 13–14). Compared with Smith, the bird is actually lucky. She is "at liberty" to sing in the woods, unlike the poet, who is burdened by her human condition and, for those readers aware of Smith's plight, by her family responsibilities and legal battles. By invoking the nightingale, whose transfor-mation occurred as a result of Philomela's rape and torture by Tereus, and then claiming superiority of woe, Smith incorporates the suggestion of sublime suf-fering into her sonnet. Agony worse than what was "rewarded" by eternity as a songbird must be great indeed. Smith also implies that as the nightingale's song, inspired by her former human suffering, is considered the most poignant, her sonnets, inspired by even greater suffering, must consequently be more affecting than the nightingale's. She does not claim as much, of course, but the reader might easily reach that conclusion. By claiming limitless woe, Smith claims peerless inspiration, the opposite of Finch's wryly modest conclusion in "To the Nightingale."

Smith, in other words, accomplished by implication a version of the claim Seward made regarding Petrarch and Milton. While Seward posed as the heir of a formal tradition distinguished by rigor and gravity, Smith presented herself as heir to a tradition of singers distinguished by melancholy. Smith's was an eclectic but recognizable pedigree that stretched from the original nightingale to Collins and included Shakespeare, Milton, and Pope in their more tender modes as well as recent poets such as Beattie and Gray. Smith emphasized her claim in the preface, explaining that "some very melancholy moments have been beguiled, by expressing in verse the sensations those moments brought" (iii). The *Elegiac Son-nets* are thus about her ineffable suffering, but they are also about why Smith is a unique and splendid poet. As Backscheider observes, Smith captured the poetic mood of her generation and presented herself as the embodiment of melancholy, even as her sonnets epitomized that privileged state of mind.

Traditionalists such as Seward and Robinson found the terms of their argu-ments and Smith's incompatible. Proponents of the legitimate sonnet argued on behalf of formal precedents. Just as Seward refused to consider that Smith might have artful purposes in incorporating so many allusions into her sonnets, Smith refused to entertain the challenge of adopting the more rigorous form (although her third edition contained several Italian sonnets). Just as Seward had accepted the argument of her more educated acquaintances regarding the sonnet, Smith claims in her preface that "I am told, and I read it as the opinion of very good judges, that the legitimate Sonnet is ill calculated for our language" (iii). Eschewing the formal debate, Smith concentrated on ringing all possible changes on her theme, captivating a public accustomed to accessing emotions via the heartfelt declamations of their favorite literary characters. Both Seward and Smith were doomed to reiterate their chosen methods with no hope of a contest in their respective forms. Having determined that what Smith wrote were not sonnets but rather "minute Elegies of twelve alternate rhymes, closing with a couplet, which assume the name of Sonnet" (*Original Sonnets* iii), Seward obscured the basis for meaningful comparison. All she could do was oppose her sonnets and her authorities to Smith's. Her preface quotes at length from her cousin Henry White's article in the *Gentleman's Magazine*, which remarked that "Mrs. Smith says she has been told that the regular Sonnet suits not the nature or genius of our language. Surely this assertion cannot be demonstrated, and therefore was not worth attention" (*Original Sonnets* v). This quasi exchange is reminiscent of those in old western films, in which the hero challenges the villain to "come out and fight like a man." Seward and Smith fought like gentlewomen, however, sheltered behind masculine mentors.

Seward's complaints were closely related. Smith's use of a bastardized form indicated, in Seward's opinion, lack of rigor exacerbated by her copious, and in the first edition, unacknowledged, borrowings. "All the lines that are not the lines of others are weak and unimpressive," she told Sophia Weston (*Letters* 1:162). As Pinch has explained, most of Seward's fellow readers were not disturbed by Smith's borrowings. They seem not only to have understood her intention but to have accorded her the melancholy primacy she sought. Seward responded to the perceived challenge with her own sonnets, many of which were published intermittently in the *Gentleman's Magazine* and other periodicals from 1785 onward. Against Smith's "pretty tuneful centos from our various poets" (*Letters* 1:163) she posed sonnets that resembled Milton's in possessing "certain hardnesses, though there is a majesty, perhaps, in that very hardness, which, besides producing an enchanting effect for the intermixture of the musical lines, seems to mark the peculiarity of the composition" (*Letters* 1:201). Seward's concession that Smith's lines were harmonious or melodious but no more, together with her insistence that the sonnet exhibit "certain hardnesses" as well as original thoughts and images, constituted her counterdefinition of the sonnet. Although Smith's supporters praised Smith's strong and "nervous" verse, Seward denied Smith's poems those masculine—and therefore positively gendered—qualities and strove to illustrate them in her own poems.

By "hardnesses," Seward probably meant expressions that are terse or taut as opposed to lines that flow harmoniously but are less direct. Unlike her Romantic successors, Seward believed that abstract terms were acceptable when they conduced to directness. "Their nervous and condensing power seems to me perfectly adapted to serious poetry," she explained to Erasmus Darwin in May 1789, instancing Johnson, whose "best prose" was "highly poetic, from his habit of using abstract expressions, which at once elevate his language, and compress his sense" (*Letters* 2:267). We have noticed Seward's insistence on varied pauses resembling those in blank verse. She disdained the turn of thought characteristic of the Shakespearian sonnet, again in deference to Milton's practice. As she insisted to Sarah Ponsonby in 1795, the "legitimate sonnet generally consists of one thought, regularly pursued to the close; . . . nothing can be less necessary, indeed more improper, than a new or detached thought for the conclusion; . . . brilliance, epigrammatic turn or point, belong not to that species of composition. . . . An harmonious and impressive close, provided it be not epigrammatic or detached, but connected with the subject, must be an advantage. Yet . . . a quiet unornamented close is not inconsistent with its excellence" (*Letters* 4:144–45). Since, following Milton's, superior sonnets reflect on occasional personal or communal events rather than ring changes on one (often fictional) state of mind, the witty turn calling attention to the writer's cleverness as much as to situational irony is rarely appropriate. Finally, Seward defended imperfect rhymes on the authority of "our best writers," especially Pope. Writing to Thomas Swift in 1785, she insisted "a poet will lose much more on the side of sense, and grace of expression, than he will gain on the side of jingle, by narrowing his scale of rhymes in the pursuit of imaginary perfection, which, when attained, cloys the very ear by its sameness" (*Letters* 1:72). Her choice of the Miltonic structure, with its demanding rhyme scheme, must have influenced her acceptance of imperfect rhyme, much as the heroic couplet's relentless demand pushed Pope to such rhymes (although not, as Seward claims in the same letter, "very lavishly").

Turning to Seward's *Original Sonnets*, we can observe how she implemented her compositional principles in contradistinction to those she perceived guiding Smith's. Sonnet 16, "Translated from Boileau" (*Original Sonnets* 18), is her succinct version of the twenty-six lines Boileau devoted to the sonnet in *The Art of Poetry*, rendered into English by William Soames and revised by Dryden, a translation with which Seward was probably familiar (2.80–98).[8] Boileau's late seventeenth-century treatise in alexandrine couplets specified that Apollo devised the sonnet

as a test to learn whether ode writers could contain their verses within strict boundaries. Apollo does not specify his rules beyond "the just Measure, and the Time,/
The easy running, and alternate Rhyme," but he decrees that a well-written sonnet will be worth more than "tedious Volumes of loose Poetry" (2.83–84, 90). Boileau adds that in the volumes of a hundred scribblers, only two or three sonnets
will be found worthy; the rest will be consigned to the pastry cook. Such is the
difficulty of "closing the Sense within the measur'd time" of this demanding form
(2.97). Seward's version is much more dramatic, reflecting her belief in the sonnet's importance. While Boileau's Apollo merely "set rules" the "Scriblers to
confound" (2.81), Seward's god is angry:

> Apollo, at his crowded altars, tir'd
>   Of Votaries, who for trite ideas thrown
>   Into loose verse, assume, in lofty tone,
>   The Poet's name, untaught, and uninspir'd,
> Indignant struck the Lyre.—Straight it acquir'd
>   New powers, and complicate. Then first was known
>   The rigorous Sonnet, to be fram'd alone
>   By duteous Bards, or by just Taste admir'd.—
> Go, energetic Sonnet, go, he cried,
>   And be the test of skill!—For rhymes that flow
>   Regardless of thy rules, their destin'd guide,
> Yet take thy name, ah! Let the boasters know
>   That with strict sway my jealous laws preside,
>   While I no wreaths on *rebel* verse bestow.

Apollo echoes Seward's remark, in her preface, dismissing "those minute Elegies
. . . which assume the name of Sonnet" (*Original Sonnets* iii). His rejection of
"trite ideas thrown/into loose verse" seems derived not from Boileau but from
Seward's opinion of Smith's "hackneyed scraps of dismality" and perhaps also
from Smith's modest admission, in the preface to her first edition, that her "sonnets, have I believe no very just claim to that title" (iii). Only poets willing to
abide by Apollo's rules will be considered worthy, and only those with exact taste
will be able to appreciate the genuine sonnet. Like Boileau, Seward does not
specify the precise rules poets are to obey, but she warns those who do not conform that they will fail to attain a laurel wreath—that is, to be considered successful poets. While not so colorful an image as Boileau's threat that poor sonnets will
be "shovel'd to the Pastry from the Press" (2.96), Seward's final lines create a more
dignified god than the French poet's "humorous" or volatile deity (2.80).

Sonnet 16 illustrates Seward's principles in the guise of Apollo's. Most striking is the array of pauses: after the first three and before the last syllables in the first line, after the third syllable in the second, after the fourth in the third and fourth, after the sixth in the fifth, and so on. Running the sense from line to line, as in blank verse, Seward concludes her first sentence in the middle of line five, where Apollo's chord breaks the line while presumably calling his votaries to attention. She thus uses the caesura to create a dramatic effect and at the same time simulates the potential of blank verse for grand statements within her tightly rhymed lines. Seward also achieves her ideal of "nervousness" or directness by using contractions. As Paul Fussell Jr. explains, eighteenth-century poets habitually used elisions to maintain five-syllable lines and to avoid what they thought were ugly vowel clusters.[9] Although strict syllabic measure was gradually giving way to the accentual standard in Seward's lifetime (Fussell 133–56), neither she nor most of her sonnet rivals strayèd far from the earlier, classically derived ideal. In sonnet 16, Seward contracts with apostrophes six words that few would pronounce as three syllables. But she also clearly intended readers to contract "Votaries" (l. 2), "powers" (l. 6), "rigorous" (l. 7), and "duteous" (l. 8). Her striking adjectival use of "complicate" instead of "complicated" in line six preserves the syllabic count while heightening the verse with a by-then nearly obsolete usage. The multiple contractions create a compactness and energy that contemporaries called "nervous." When Apollo exclaims, "Go, energetic Sonnet, go . . . / And be the test of skill!" he issues a challenge while literally sending forth this illustration of his new form.

Sonnet 16 also exemplifies Seward's ideas by developing one thought from beginning to end. Apollo's decree is not an epigram or turn but the proper conclusion of the sonnet's anecdote. As Seward reiterated, the sonnet's tone is grave and dignified, and sonnet 16 culminates in Apollo's threatening proclamation emphasizing that poets who ignore his rules are not merely poor writers and boasters but "rebels," the word italicized to emphasize the gravity of their literary crime. This sonnet's critical topic reflects Seward's "Miltonic" preference for a serious theme over an amorous or lighthearted subject. Finally, Seward instantiates the relationship between Apollo's lyre and the art of poetry through the musicality of her verse. Especially striking is her use of assonance, which frequently echoes the sonnet's end rhymes. "Trite" echoes "tir'd," "Lyre" echoes "uninspired," and "boasters" echoes "flow" and "know," while within lines, "loose," "assume," and "duteous," "straight," "complicate," and "sway" create a tissue of sounds knitting together the sonnet's octave and sestet as well as exemplifying its thematic purpose. The harmonious effect is heightened by consonance throughout, as when "verse" echoes

"Votaries" and "rhymes," "regardless" and "rules"; the final lines gain emphasis from "strict sway" and "while . . . wreaths." In her use of such effects, we see the outcome of Seward's boasted study of "the grace, harmony, and elegance of the English language" (*Letters* 2:140) as well as her conviction that the "hardnesses" characteristic of the Miltonic sonnet produce "an enchanting effect for the inter-mixture of the musical lines" (*Letters* 1:201).

Sonnet 16 is not merely a translation of Boileau but Seward's response to Apollo's challenge. By tightening and elevating Boileau's rather informal alexandrines and casting them into sonnet form, Seward demonstrates her worthiness of Apollo's wreath, much as Pope had demonstrated he was the ideal poet-critic, who may "censure freely" because he has "written well," by illustrating his definitions of poor and excellent writing in *An Essay on Criticism* (1: 240–41, ll. 15–16). One wonders what Seward might have produced if instead of following Milton's practice of writing sonnets on occasional topics, a custom also followed by Wordsworth and Keats among her better-known successors, she had allowed herself to recognize Smith's achievement in composing a sonnet cycle like those through which Shakespeare, Sidney, and Spenser confirmed their ingenuity. Sonnet 16 suggests that Seward preferred to polish her sonnets, written on a variety of thoughts and events, like lapidary gems rather than risk diffuseness by producing numerous poems on a single theme or state of being. Seward's preference for the occasional sonnet is therefore the result of taste and principle rather than invidiousness. Seward did compose a number of sonnets on a single theme, her "lost Honora," but she refrained from grouping all the related sonnets in sequence, in a deliberate rejection of the chain or cycle model. As Milton's champion, Seward not only contributed an exquisitely crafted body of sonnets to the form's ongoing revival; she also left a challenging legacy to her Romantic-era successors.

CHAPTER NINE

Corresponding Poems

S eward rejected Charlotte Smith's model of a chain, in which she rings changes
on a single mood, in favor of what she considered Milton's precedent, sonnets
written on particular occasions. In Smith's cycle, her personal state of being gives
rise to her verse; any and all occasions inspire variations on her theme. One might
speculate that Smith's drive to explore her personal ontology took precedence
over formal considerations, such as adherence to a stricter rhyme scheme. For
Seward, as we have seen, formal considerations were paramount and perhaps
influenced her preference to write about particular occasions, setting her personal experiences in social and historical contexts. Seward's correspondence apparently inspired many of her occasional sonnets. In this chapter, I explore the
way Seward shaped epistolary exchanges into sonnets reflecting not only her
inner feelings but also the moral and critical reflections occasioned by the events
chronicled in her letters. One example is sonnet 59, "To the Right Honourable
Lady Marianne Carnegie, Passing Her Winters at Ethic House on the Coast of
Scotland, with Her Father, Lord Northesk, Who Retired Thither after the Death
of his Excellent Countess, Written February 1787" (*Original Sonnets* 61). Years
before, Seward had volunteered to provide blood to Lady Marianne's mother so
that Dr. Darwin could perform a transfusion, but luckily, Lady Northesk recovered without needing the transfusion. Seward followed her life with understandable interest until learning from Lady Marianne that the former patient had
died. In a letter dated March 21, 1785, Seward replied, inquiring about the manner of her mother's death. Commenting on Lady Marianne's intention to remain
secluded with her father throughout the harsh Scottish winter, she assured the

young woman that her letter "convinces me that [you have] a mind whose tastes, pursuits, and sensibilities, preclude the irksome lassitude with which retirement is apt to inspire people at [your] sprightly time of life. Ah! Dearest Madam, may the consciousness of cheering the declining years of a beloved father gild the silent hours, when the rocks frown around you in solemn sternness, and the winds of winter are howling over the ocean!" (*Letters* 1:32).

If Seward's dates are to be trusted, she must have gone back two years later to her copy of this letter, perhaps struck by its image of a young woman choosing self-exile on the gloomy Scottish coast with her widowed father. Since by 1785 Seward herself was supervising the care of an aging father, Lady Marianne's situation must have touched her as comparable but as having more pathos owing to her correspondent's youth. The first nine lines of the resulting sonnet recapitulate her encouraging observation:

> Lady, each soft effusion of thy mind,
>> Flowing thro' thy free pen, shows thee endu'd
>> With taste so just for all of wise, and good,
>> As bids me hope thy spirit does not find,
> Young as thou art, with solitude combin'd
>> That wish of change, that irksome lassitude,
>> Which often, thro' unvaried days, obtrude
>> On Youth's rash bosom, dangerously inclin'd
> To pant for more than peace. — Rich volumes yield
>> Their soul-endowing wealth. — Beyond e'en these
>> Shall consciousness of filial duty gild
> The gloomy hours, when Winter's turbid Seas
>> Roar round the rocks; when the dark Tempest lours,
>> And mourn the Winds round Ethic's lonely towers.

Seward's sonnet changes her letter's confident assertion that Lady Marianne's epistolary style alone confirms her superior "tastes, pursuits, and sensibilities." Here, the young woman's expressions are characterized as "effusions," her thoughts flowing unimpeded and undisguised through her pen in the enthusiastic manner typical of sensibility. The very word seems to guarantee Lady Marianne's "taste . . . for all of wise, and good," since she has so artlessly confided in her mother's friend. After lifting the phrase "irksome lassitude" directly from her letter, Seward dramatizes the danger lurking in such an isolated situation. Tediousness is apt to inspire "Youth's rash bosom . . ./To pant for more than peace." In the letter, Seward says merely that Lady Marianne's style guarantees her capacity to surmount the irksomeness of retirement. In the sonnet, however, Lady Marianne's style has become a series of effusions, suggesting a sensibility that might tend in its enthusiasm toward rashness. One thinks of the overly sensible heroes and heroines Ann Jessie Van Sant has characterized as opportunities for stirring sensations in their readers (117). The image of her panting bosom, as she gasps "for more than peace," depicts a physical response to her surroundings typical in descriptions of sensibility as a double-edged sword. Lady Marianne is frank, expressive, and eager, but those very qualities make her vulnerable to dangerous inclinations. Seward does not specify precisely what change an isolated young woman might wish or even pant for, but the implication points toward emotional needs that might spill forth, like the effusions from her free pen, unless Lady Marianne disciplines herself.

Seward turns toward her sestet by recommending books for their "soul-endowing" ability. But the books are isolated at the poem's center, possibly like the young woman herself in her father's library. The only true solution is for Lady Marianne to channel her strong feelings toward her widowed father, the purpose of her wintry sojourn on the bleak coast. Only "consciousness of filial duty" will "gild / The gloomy hours, when Winter's turbid seas / Roar round the rocks." The sonnet closes with one of Seward's infrequent pairs of rhymed lines, but the lines are neither an epigram nor a couplet, however. Instead, they contain the sonnet's only striking image, that of the winter storm lashing the Scottish coast. We recognize that the storm represents the external source of Lady Marianne's temptation: it enforces the tedium of "unvaried days" spent in isolation. But the storm also represents Lady Marianne's potentially tempestuous emotions, battering the solitary young woman's peace of mind. Only clinging to her purpose, recollecting the importance of "filial duty," will shed a ray of light on the dark sea, or sustain her commitment. Seward has taken the final image in the passage quoted from her letter, a benediction as Lady Marianne undertakes her lonely sojourn in Scotland, and polished it into a metaphor for the emotional dangers latent in seclusion.

Seward's vocabulary of sensibility renders her sonnet somewhat opaque today. She capitalized on the resemblance between Lady Marianne's situation and those of heroes and heroines in many fictional plots, including her own *Louisa*. As Susan Staves reminds us, sentimental novels were populated with heroes and heroines forever sacrificing personal happiness to accommodate their parents, especially their fathers (*Literary History* 379). Such plots now hold little appeal. But we can still admire the skill with which Seward turned her friendly letter into a dramatic, if encouraging, admonition. As in sonnet 16, Seward floats her pauses for fluidity yet contracts many words to achieve complementary nervousness.

"Effusion," centered in the first line, introduces the long "u" sound that continues through four rhymed words in the octet, leading inexorably to "Youth's rash
bosom," the off-rhyme of "effusion" and "bosom" reinforcing the sonnet's focus
on late adolescent passions. "Duty" not only echoes the long "u" but stands, in
the sestet, as the antidote to unbridled effusion tested by "gloomy hours." The
dominant "u" thus knits the sonnet together while emphasizing sense as well as
sound. Seward, finally, borrows her letter's image of the good conscience gilding
the "silent hours, when the rocks frown around you." She no doubt recognized
the contradiction implied by her final evocation of howling winter winds. In the
sonnet, conscious duty gilds "the gloomy hours," shining light on Lady Marianne's dark vigil, while the winds mourn rather than howl, as if in concert with
the bereaved father and child.

Many of Seward's sonnets can be similarly identified as artful versions of ideas
first expressed in her letters. It seems barely credible that Seward would have revised early letters to resemble the sonnets. Another example is sonnet 53, "Written
in the Spring 1785 on the Death of the Poet Laureat" (*Original Sonnets* 55). In a
letter dated May 27, 1785, Seward remarked to Court Dewes, "So we have lost the
poet laureate. I always thought Mr. Whitehead's abilities too considerable for
that rhyming drudgery; and now a yet greater bard undertakes the labouring oar
of the boat which is to row our Monarch over one of the Pierian rivers" (*Letters*
1:69). In the sonnet, Seward's rather sardonic observation becomes a meditation
on the paradox of Thomas Warton's appointment. That Warton, who had achieved
fame not only as a poet but as a scholar noted for perspicuous criticism (Seward
had recently praised his edition of Milton's occasional poems), would agree to
produce annual panegyrics for the royal family seemed tragic. Her witty reference
to rowing the monarch over the Pierian river is replaced with the image of a galley
slave consuming his vitality and probably compromising his integrity:

> The knell of Whitehead tolls!—his cares are past,
>   The hapless tribute of his purchas'd lays,
>   His servile, his Egyptian tasks of praise!—
>   If not sublime his strains, Fame justly plac'd
> Their pow'r above their work.—Now, with wide gaze
> Of much indignant wonder, she surveys
>   To the life-labouring oar assiduous haste
>   A glowing bard, by every Muse embrac'd.
> O, Warton! Chosen Priest of Phoebus' choir!
>   Shall thy rapt song be venal?   (ll. 1–10)

Seward's reference to the laureate's "Egyptian tasks" implies a metaphoric version
of the life-consuming labor exacted of hapless ancient slaves. It also recalls the
lives expended in building the pyramids, those enduring tributes to now-forgotten
rulers. Will Warton's laureate productions resemble those tombs, grandiose mon-
uments built at the cost of human lives? Or, in the present case, at the cost of
Warton's principles? "What needs for *this* the golden-fringed Lyre," demands
Seward. In this sonnet, the laureateship seems a waste of honor as well as of poetic
talent. Seward even omits the reference to the Heliconian spring, source of inspiration. The laureateship represents Warton's demotion from "Priest of Phoebus'
choir," respected critic and editor, to slave of flawed human regents.

I have deliberately chosen three sonnets usually overlooked in critical discussion to show how Seward mined her letters for inspiration and how artfully these
poems demonstrate her sonnet principles. Sonnet 57, "Written the Night Preceding the Funeral of Mrs. Charles Buckridge" (*Original Sonnets* 59), was prompted
by the irony of a young acquaintance "in the first year of her marriage, and apparently in the most florid health" dying after a brief illness (*Letters* 1:247). Although
Seward claimed to have written the sonnet before the letter to Sophia Weston
dated January 15, 1787, which was written after the burial had taken place, it is
more likely that she pared down the epistolary description. She described setting
out to visit a friend on a cold, starlit night and passing the Buckridge home.

> I observed the chamber of the deceased, where both the shutters were open, to
> be extremely light, and the shadows of several people, walking about the room,
> were visible on the ceiling. As I stood contemplating the awful scene, I heard
> the knocking of hammers, that were sodering [sic] up the coffin. The lines from
> Shakespeare's description of the martial field, the night before the battle of
> Agincourt, rushed upon my recollection:
>
> > "While, from the tents,
> > The armourers, accomplishing the knights,
> > With busy hammers closing rivets up,
> > Gave dreadful note of preparation."   (*Letters* 1:249)

In the sonnet, Seward recapitulates her description of the cold winter evening
and particularly of witnessing

> in the late bridal chamber, the clear ray
>   Of numerous lights; while o'er the ceiling stray
>   Shadows of those who frequent pass beneath
>   Round the PALE DEAD.—What sounds my senses grieve!

> For now the busy hammer's stroke appals,
>> That, "in dread note of preparation" falls,
>> Closing the sable lid!—With sighs I hear
> These solemn warnings from the House of Woes;
>> Pondering how late, for young NERINA, there,
>> Joyous, the love-illumin'd Morn arose.   (ll. 5–14)

Seward retained the most striking image from her letter, the shadows of attendants hammering shut the coffin. In the letter, the noise recalls a passage in *Henry V* in which the same sound denotes final preparations before a dreaded battle. In the sonnet, Seward wisely omitted the Agincourt context, paring her quotation, which now refers only to the sound of ominous, irrevocable preparations. Seward incorporated the bridal imagery found elsewhere in the letter, which now creates a tragic sense of irony in her sonnet. The letter's anecdote, for example, refers only to "the chamber of the deceased"; in the sonnet, she observes "the late bridal chamber." The bright lights shining the night before Nerina's funeral, assisting those who shut her coffin, contrast poignantly with the final line's evocation of her awakening in the same room as a bride, when "joyous, the Love-illumin'd Morn arose." Likewise, the "Shadows" straying about the chamber are those of living undertakers, while their object, "the PALE DEAD," will rise no more until the end of time. While it is conceivable that Seward hurried home after her visit and composed this sonnet, it is likelier that she first wrote her epistolary description to Weston, then tightened and revised her recollection into this fine sonnet, part of the century's great tradition of memento mori verse.

A different example comes from another letter to Weston dated September 3, 1789. A year before, "the brilliant Sophia" had "commenced Babylonian" (*Letters* 2:108), moving to London. Ensuing letters in which Sophia shared literary gossip and news of the latest theatrical productions enticed Seward to visit. Seward repeatedly declined the invitations Sophia extended, pleading her need to attend her ailing father. Thanking Weston after Sophia's most recent invitation, she explained that "I am fixed, by my apprehensions, here, like the needle to its magnet; holding constant, though trembling residence" (*Letters* 2:321). Instead of paring an epistolary description, as in "Written the Night Preceding the Funeral of Mrs. Charles Buckridge," Seward retained only one phrase as the culmination of sonnet 78 (*Original Sonnets* 80). The letter is gracious but emphasizes only her filial duty. The sonnet is much more explicit about the allure of both Sophia and London:

> Sophia tempts me to her social walls,
>> That 'mid the vast Metropolis arise,

Where Splendor dazzles, and each Pleasure vies
    In soft allurement; and each Science calls
To philosophic Domes, harmonious Halls,
        And storied Galleries. With duteous sighs,
        Filial and kind, and with averted eyes,
        I meet the gay temptation, as it falls
From a seducing pen.—Here—here I stay,
        Fix'd by Affection's power; nor entertain
        One latent wish, that might persuade to stray
From my ag'd Nurseling, in his life's dim wane;
        But, like the needle, by the magnet's sway,
        My constant, trembling residence maintain.

As in Seward's other sonnets, we find the flowing sentences and floating pauses contrasting with elided vowels, as well as personified abstractions functioning as shorthand references to London's many cultural attractions. Sophia appears a kind of siren; like London, which offers "soft allurement," Sophia tempts with "seducing pen." While Seward merely thanked Weston before declining her invitation, the sonnet describes the city as a powerful "temptation," beckoning the poet come and participate in all the intellectual, aural, and visual stimulation characteristic of a "vast Metropolis."

Seward uses the traditional octet-sestet structure to particular advantage in sonnet 78. The octet describes a scene of considerable appeal to the homebound poet, the falling and rising register of the initial "-alls"/"ise" rhyme scheme duplicating the tug-of-war within the writer's mind as she contemplates Sophia's invitation. In the sixth line, however, Seward begins her turn of thought, as she turns her eyes from London and her heart from persuasion. Sophia has become less a hostess than a satanic figure, proffering "gay temptation" through her "seducing pen." The potential evil of desertion is emphasized by the phrase's position at the beginning of the eighth line, followed by Seward's adamant repetition of her commitment to stay "here—here." Despite all provocations, she will remain "fix'd" by her "ag'd Nurseling," resisting even a "latent wish" to depart. Her final lines almost repeat her letter's comparison of herself to the needle of a compass, now artfully opposing Sophia and London and the attractions of the octet to a greater attraction, her father and the duties entailed by "Affection's power." One wonders whether Weston read the sonnet and resented its implied equation of her gracious invitations with Satan's seduction of Eve. Perhaps Seward risked casting her sonnet in this way because, as she often complained to Weston, Weston had little discernment in poetry. Regardless, Seward saw the potential of her epistolary refusal for a beautifully crafted sonnet that incidentally casts herself, as she did for her correspondent in " To the Right Honourable Lady Marianne Carnegie," as the era's favorite sentimental heroine, the self-denying daughter. As Teresa Barnard has observed, Seward in fact traveled and participated in social engagements as often as she liked throughout her father's decline, leaving him in the care of trusted servants (*Anna Seward* 37). Seward therefore engages in artful self-representation, in sonnet 78, to a greater degree than readers at this date might suspect.

—☙ ☙—

Seward believed herself to be emulating Milton by writing occasional sonnets instead of a chain. Thomas Warton's edition, which she praised even as she deplored his acceptance of the poet laureateship, contained only twenty-three sonnets, no more than two on any single topic or to a single addressee. Seward, however, wrote several clusters of poems, some of which might constitute a chain had she not deliberately scattered them so that they would not appear in sequence. Two sonnets, sonnet 67, "On Doctor Johnson's Unjust Criticisms in His LIVES OF THE POETS," and sonnet 68, "On the Posthumous Fame of Doctor Johnson" (*Original Sonnets* 69, 70), arose from Seward's controversial efforts to discourage idolatry of "the Great Cham" after his death in 1784. Seward's conviction that Johnson behaved invidiously toward other living authors led her to engage in what was practically a one-woman offensive against his near canonization. For her pains, she has been described as naive, misguided, spiteful, and obsessive, to name just a few of the disparaging epithets leveled at her, from her lifetime until today.[1] Seward's campaign to enforce public awareness of Johnson's flaws was indeed quixotic. With hindsight, we recognize that contemporary Britons were engaged in building their pantheon. Having enshrined Shakespeare, Spenser, Milton, Dryden, and Pope, they welcomed the opportunity to honor a great scholar and critic. The national ethos was not favorable to Seward's efforts. On the other hand, Seward's persistence was neither obsessive nor unfair from certain perspectives. For example, despite his patronage of some women writers, Johnson omitted women from his *Lives of the Poets* and excoriated any woman who transgressed the bounds of strict propriety. His measured responses to contemporary writers, which seem judicious to us, probably seemed niggardly to Seward. She believed that the doctor's critical praise would have turned the balance in favor of an author and materially increased his or her prospects. As Thomas F. Bonnell has recently argued, Johnson had been engaged to write biographies for *The Works of the English Poets* precisely because of his fame and influence (135–40). Her own positive responses to certain writers, moreover, were those of an enthusiast, as when she told Whalley that a passage in one of Hayley's juvenile poems, "Epistle from Mary to William," is "picturesque poetry, in its highest possible perfection—nor are any of Pope's lines more richly harmonious" (*Letters* 2:205). A person so generous in her opinions of favored publications, not to mention readiness to evaluate texts passage by passage, was not likely to endorse Johnson's habits of hasty reading and unvarnished responses.

Seward's two sonnets on Dr. Johnson's posthumous reputation distill multiple reiterations of her argument. "On Doctor Johnson's Unjust Criticisms" recapitulates her proof of Johnson's envious temperament, Boswell's reported admission when he visited Lichfield while researching his biography. Writing to Hayley in April 1785, Seward recalled Boswell's attempt to distinguish between "envy and literary jealousy." When she called his distinction "sophistic," Boswell argued that Johnson, a critic, would not likely have envied poets, especially dead poets. He proposed that Johnson's rigor "proceeded from real want of taste for the higher orders of verse, his judgment being too rigidly severe to relish the enthusiasms of imagination" (*Letters* 1:62). Seward's opportunity came, however, when Boswell proceeded "unawares" to acknowledge that "Johnson had been galled by David Garrick's instant success, and long éclat, who had set sail with himself on the sea of public life," adding that

> it was a little cruel in the great man not once to name David Garrick in his preface to Shakespeare! And base, said I, as well as unkind.—He was galled by Garrick's Prosperity, rejoined Mr. Boswell. Ah! Said I, you now, unaware, cede to my position. If the author of the Rambler could stoop to envy a player, for the hasty splendour of a night of obscurity, must, in the end, prove as the meteor of an hour to the permanent light of the sun, it cannot be doubted, but his injustice to Milton, Gray, Collins, Prior, &c., proceeding from the same cause, produced that leveling system of criticism, "which lifts the mean, and lays the mighty low." Mr. Boswell's comment upon this observation was, that dissenting shake of the head, to which folk are reduced, when they will not be convinced, yet find their stores exhausted. (*Letters* 1:63)

Seward's account is worth quoting at length because it records what she believed to be her rhetorical triumph over Johnson's champion. According to Seward, she trapped Boswell into admitting that Johnson was motivated by envy, not only toward Garrick but all the poets he had disparaged in his *Lives of the Poets*. We

now agree that Johnson's criticism was not disinterested; that, for example, his
aversion to Milton's political principles influenced his remarks on that poet.
While we may not agree with Seward and may find her diatribes tedious, she was
justified in protesting that Johnson was not an irreproachable human being or
critic. In this reported conversation, she thought she got the better of Boswell,
reducing him to speechlessness after he gave her an opening, "unawares," to introduce her clever analogy comparing Garrick and Johnson to a meteor and the
sun. Boswell, by implication, acceded to her logic in claiming that, if Johnson's
"cruelty" to Garrick resulted from envy, then his critical analyses of Milton, Gray,
Collins, and Prior proceeded from the same cause. Her final (mis)quotation of a
line from James Thomson's *Agamemnon* (4.2.54) completed her argument by
implying the hubris of a man who had taken on the role of a literary god, damag-
ing posthumous reputations with impunity.[2] Here, Seward demonstrated her
ability to prevail in debate against the acolyte of a man famed for his propensity
to "talk for victory." Of course, if Boswell indeed shook his head as she describes,
the gesture may not have indicated defeat. Boswell may have shaken his head in
disbelief at Seward's conviction. Or he may have shaken his head to indicate that
further discussion was impossible with someone so adamant. Seward interpreted
Boswell's head shake as capitulation, however. The remembered triumph must
have cheered her when, in the early 1790s, her published criticism of his *Life of
Johnson*, accompanied by further asseverations of the great man's malignancy,
evoked from Boswell a sarcastic, dismissive printed response.[3]

"On Doctor Johnson's Unjust Criticisms" offers a succinct version of the memorable 1785 conversation. Seward begins in medias res following Boswell's "off-
stage" excuse that Johnson had little taste for the arts. Seward scoffed at such
comments, believing that Johnson's sublime writing style proved the contrary:

> Cou'd awful Johnson want poetic ear,
>   Fancy, or judgment?—no! his splendid strain,
>   In prose, or rhyme, confutes that plea.—The pain
>   Which writh'd o'er Garrick's fortunes, shows us clear
> Whence all his spleen to GENIUS.—Ill to bear
>   A Friend's renown, that to his own must reign,
>   Compar'd, a Meteor's evanescent train,
>   To Jupiter's fix'd orb, proves that each sneer,
> Subtle and fatal to poetic sense,
>   Did from insidious ENVY meanly flow,
>   Illumed with dazzling hues of eloquence,

And Sophist-Wit, that labor to o'er-throw
    Th' awards of AGES, and new laws dispense
    That lift the *mean*, and lay the MIGHTY low.

While the letter preserves an exchange, undoubtedly pruned to emphasize Seward's victorious role, the poem reenacts Seward's argument as a dramatic speech. From the indignant opening question and her adamant reply, Seward confronts readers with verse meant to demonstrate her own capacity for both logic and eloquence. Her use of the exclamation and question, of dashes, italics, and small capitals demand vocal performance (and probably received it, by the poet herself, in her drawing room). The sinuous "s" and "w" sounds of the octet imitate Johnson's supposed "writhing" in jealousy over Garrick's success, while other uses of consonance, such as "plea" and "pain" in the third line, support her dismissal of Boswell's excuse. Among examples of assonance, the drawn-out "e" sound centered in line 5 skillfully highlights her accusation that Johnson reacted with spleen to genius. Her careful placement of caesuras after "no," "plea," and "GENIUS" mark the progress of her argument toward the supposedly irrefutable claim that surely Johnson must have understood the difference, like that between a meteor and a planet, between his and Garrick's achievements and therefore should have refrained from envying the actor's fame. Her original metaphor for Johnson's reputation, "the permanent light of the sun," has become "Jupiter's fix'd orb," emphasizing the doctor's colossal status and his position as veritable father of Britain's literary gods. At the heart of the sonnet, the metaphor reinforces the paradoxical coexistence within Johnson of intellectual greatness and small mindedness. As the eighth line turns toward Seward's denunciation of Johnson's envy, persistent "s" sounds reinforce the "sneers" associated with his criticism. The sonnet concludes with the phrase that supposedly left Boswell shaking his head, incapable of further reply. Seward does not specify Johnson's critical depredations within the poem, consigning her examples to a footnote. Instead, she denounces Johnson's abuse of his capacity for the "splendid strain" (l. 2), turned instead into "eloquence, / And Sophist-Wit" employed to blacken the reputations of some poetic "ancients" while extolling others who little deserved such praise (such as Yalden and Blackmore) at their expense. The reference to *Agamemnon* now reinforces the earlier comparison of Johnson to Jupiter, as well as the implication that the doctor was a false god, subject ultimately to the same critical vicissitude he inflicted on others.

Seward's "On the Posthumous Fame of Doctor Johnson" likewise took its genesis from letters (and presumably conversations) in which she insisted that justice demanded acknowledgment of Johnson's flaws. Sonnet 76, "The Critics of Dr. Johnson's School (*Original Sonnets* 78), originated in a comment she made to Whalley in a letter dated February 1, 1786: "Critics are also starting up, producing books abounding with the spawn of Johnsonian envy, unsupported with Johnsonian ability, and unadorned with Johnsonian wit" (*Letters* 2:123). The corresponding sonnet opens with a dramatic verbal gesture: "Lo! Modern Critics emulously dare/Ape the great Despot" (ll. 1–2). Seward probably decided that the rhetorical repetition of "Johnsonian," clever in her letter, was insufficiently vivid for her sonnet. The sestet instead invokes multiple images to convey her point that Johnson's current imitators lack "the great Despot's" brilliance:

> Spirit of Common Sense! Must we endure
>> The incrustation hard without the *gem*?
>> Find in th' Anana's rind the wilding sour,
> The Oak's rough knots on every *Osier's* stem?
>> The dark contortions of the Sybil bear,
>> Whose inspirations never meet our ear?   (ll. 9–14)

Here, Seward has delayed the sonnet's turn until the beginning of its sestet, a calculated delay followed by a peroration as dramatic as the sonnet's exclamatory opening. As Seward piles up her metaphors, she enforces them with assonance, as in "endure"/"incrustation," "find"/"rind," and "Oak's"/"Osier's." Her by now inescapable point, that Johnson's followers reproduce his harshness without his knowledge or cleverness, culminates in the final image of a writhing but uninspired Sybil. Although Johnson was, and is still, viewed as an oracle by admirers, Seward insists his putative inheritors have no wisdom to share, despite their adoption of his magisterial style.

Today, few readers instinctively associate sonnets with critical battles such as Seward's. In Milton, however, she would have found her precedent. Milton's sonnet 11, "On the Detraction which Followed upon My Writing Certain Treatises," defended his authorship of *Tetrachordon*, one of several publications questioning England's stringent divorce laws. Assailed by conservative, and in his opinion, ignorant, critics, Milton "wished he had not wrote this work in English," according to Warton's note in his edition (342). Seward, similarly embattled and as self-righteous as Milton, followed him in crafting several sonnets of critical assault rather than of amour. The majority of Seward's sonnets, however, develop more traditional themes. Picturesque landscapes, for example, were among her passions. Seward delighted in scenery, even glimpsed vicariously through letters such as Whalley's descriptions of his continental rambles. Some of her sonnets seem ripostes to Smith's gloom. Sonnet 15, "Written on Rising Ground near Lichfield" (*Original Sonnets* 17), for example, extols the consolations of nature. Where Smith consistently found in the natural world an inadequate mirror of her suffering, Seward found compensation even for woes greater than her own:

> The evening shines in May's luxuriant pride,
>   And all the sunny hills at distance glow,
>   And all the brooks, that thro' the valley flow,
>   Seem liquid gold.—O! had my fate denied
> Leisure, and power to taste the sweets that glide
>   Thro' waken'd minds, as the soft seasons go
>   On their still varying progress, for the woe
>   My heart has felt, what balm had been supplied?
> But where great NATURE smiles, as *here* she smiles,
>   'Mid verdant vales, and gently swelling hills,
>   And glassy lakes, and mazy, murmuring rills,
> And narrow wood-wild lanes, her spell beguiles
>   Th' impatient sighs of Grief, and reconciles
>   Poetic Minds to Life, with all her ills.

Like Smith, Seward fails to specify her cause for woe, although the date appended to the sonnet, May 1774, suggests her continued suffering over Saville, compounded by the departure of Honora Sneyd after her marriage less than a year before. If accurate, the date makes it impossible for this sonnet to have been a response to Smith's, published ten years later. The contrast between the two women's reactions to nature, however, is striking. Seward's poem does not claim despair, as do Smith's poems; her grief is not even obdurate. Read with Smith's in mind, the sonnet questions how a poet who claims a passionate affinity with the natural world could fail to experience consolation amid its beauties. Truly "poetic Minds" are reconciled "to Life, with all her ills" through communion with nature.

Seward describes a glorious but familiar scene of a spring evening near her home. The setting is emphatically beautiful in comparison with the wild, tempestuous locales favored by Smith. The setting sun gilds surrounding hills, and brooks punctuating the valley glisten as well. As the speaker contemplates the landscape spread out before her, she wonders momentarily what her grief might have been had she no "Leisure, and power to taste," the changing attractions of the seasons. In a spot so lovely, the natural world itself supplies a balm otherwise unattainable. Seward describes her gentle native landscape, with its green valleys, low hills, lakes, and streams, as the antidote to fruitless grief. For Seward, it is the landscape itself that is her healer, whereas for Wordsworth it is memories of past excursions that spur comforting memories as he gazes out upon the Wye Valley in "Tintern Abbey." Unlike Smith, who in sonnet 31, "Written on Farm Wood, South Downs, in May 1784 " (31), describes a spring vista that can delight only "the hind—whom no sad thought bereaves/Of the gay season's pleasures!" (ll. 7–8), Seward wonders how "poetic Minds" can fail to find some pleasure in the scene, despite life's ills. She repeats her initial description in the sestet, as if inviting readers to contemplate the scene themselves and emulate "poetic Minds" by experiencing its healing power. Seward's confidence in nature's ability to assuage grief might therefore set her apart from Smith and other Romantics such as Wordsworth whose emphasis was often on their own minds and indeed on the impossibility of fully escaping the boundaries of the ego. Even Keats, the prophet of negative capability, confessed in "Ode to a Nightingale" his inability to escape, more than momentarily, from his "sole self" (l. 72). In sonnet 15, Seward assumes that sensible or "waken'd" minds can be beguiled or enchanted by nature, healed of their woes while feasting visually on seasonal glories. Her attitude reminds us of Anne K. Mellor's observation that women Romantics often rejected their male Romantic-era counterparts' preoccupation with such concepts as the autonomous self and the transcendent imagination, extolling instead the rational (female) mind and domestic relationships (*Mothers* 86–87). From Mellor's perspective, Seward's sonnets may have more in common with the writings of many contemporary women than do those of such a recognizably "Romantic" writer as Smith.

Another appealing landscape sonnet anticipates Wordsworth's descriptions of his boyhood in *The Prelude*. Sonnet 7 describes Seward's early childhood rambles around Eyam, Derbyshire, from which her family moved when she was seven. Like the boy Wordsworth, she was evidently permitted to roam. She imbibed the magnificent scenery, which became her lifelong passion:

> By Derwent's rapid stream as oft I stray'd,
>   With Infancy's light step and glances wild,
>   And saw vast rocks, on steepy mountains pil'd,
>   Frown o'er th' umbrageous glen; or pleas'd survey'd
> The cloudy moonshine in the shadowy glade,
>   Romantic Nature to th' enthusiast Child
>   Grew dearer far than when serene she smil'd,
>   In uncontrasted loveliness array'd.
> But O! in every Scene, with sacred sway,

Her glances fire me; from the bloom that spreads
    Resplendent in the lucid morn of May,
To the green light the little Glow-worm sheds
    On mossy banks, when midnight glooms prevail,
    And softest Silence broods o'er all the dale.

Very much like Wordsworth's descriptions of himself roaming the Lake District, Seward's memories portray a child exploring the riverbanks, gazing "wildly" at the surrounding peaks before education or maturity intervenes between the setting and her pure wonder. As also in Wordsworth's verse, nature acts as a supplemental mother, the "Romantic" setting encouraging Seward's blossoming enthusiasm or sensibility. Seward claims to have been nurtured on the sublime: the "vast rocks," "steepy mountains," "umbrageous glen" and mysterious, moonlit glade, are all manifestations of nature at its most terrific or impenetrable. The sonnet's octet recalls this precious seed time, when rugged sublimity, going beyond the beautiful, the serene, or the simply lovely, endeared itself.

Seward's sestet, however, confesses that all natural scenes fire her imagination. Early-morning blooms and midnight glowworms alike are precious. The sonnet's close implies that nature acquired a godlike power over Seward's mind during those infant rambles. Nature's "sacred sway" carries some of the sense of divine immanence or natural transcendence proclaimed by her younger contemporaries, although the Anglican Seward most likely intended only to assert the powerful sensibility infused in her by frequent experience of sublimity. "Sacred sway" may also imply that God acts through nature to inspire Seward's imagination. Her final image suggests a continuum of nature from the beautiful to the sublime. The just-opened blossom, shining in the clear morning air, is juxtaposed with the tiny glowworm shining in the obscure "midnight gloom." Today, it is difficult to read this poem without thinking of Wordsworth's "Intimations of Immortality" ode. In a classic reading, Geoffrey Hartman describes the ode as a poem about the poet's fear of "a decay of his 'genial' responses to nature" and his fear "that this decay has affected his powers of renovation" (274). Hartman explains that by the ode's conclusion, the poet has achieved regeneration of his response to nature, the prerequisite to mature love of man (277). "To me the meanest flower that blows" evokes "Thoughts/that do often lie too deep for tears" (ll. 205–6), confides the relieved poet. In her sonnet, Seward expresses no sense of diminishment from her childhood intimacy with nature. Rather than loss, she experiences gain as a result of maturity—appreciation for the beautiful as well as for the sublime. The blossom and the glowworm inspire equal fascination, comparable joy. The sonnet portrays

Seward as a complete poet, still alive to childhood visions of splendor but also capable of minute discernment. To invoke yet another Romantic poet, one more her contemporary, she like Blake can "see a World in a Grain of Sand / And a heaven in a Wild Flower" (ll. 1–2). The craggy heights that thrilled her as an infant have instilled as well her love of the evanescent and minute.

Sonnet 7 perfectly illustrates Seward's remark that such poems should have a "harmonious and impressive close, provided it be not epigrammatic or detached, but connected with the subject" (*Letters* 4:145). This sonnet's conclusion does not carry the reader back into the poet's mind but outward into the natural world the poet inhabits. While Seward portrays herself as a privileged being, an "enthusiast" from infancy, her sestet illustrates her comprehensive love of nature by invoking the blossom and the glowworm, not her psychological processes or memories. Seward is at once an eighteenth-century poet of sensibility and an incipient Romantic, but more the former than the latter. She despised Wordsworth's "I Wandered Lonely as a Cloud," for example, remarking to Walter Scott in 1807, "Surely if his worst foe had chosen to caricature this egotistic manufacturer of metaphysical importance upon trivial themes, he could not have done so more effectually." More pleasing to her was Wordsworth's "Sonnet upon Westminster Bridge," which she found "beautiful, unaffected, and grandly picturesque" (*Letters* 6:367). Two further examples illustrate Seward's distinctive approach to landscape; one is a personal meditation like sonnet 7 and the other resembles a landscape painting, the artist herself removed from the scene.

Sonnet 11 describes the pleasures of shady retreats on summer days:

> How sweet to rove, from summer sun-beams veil'd,
>> In gloomy dingles; or to trace the tide
>> Of wandering brooks, their pebbly beds that chide;
>> To feel the west-wind cool refreshment yield,
> That comes soft-creeping o'er the flowery field,
>> And shadow'd waters; in whose bushy side
>> The Mountain-Bees their fragrant treasure hide
>> Murmuring; and sings the lonely Thrush conceal'd!
> Then, Ceremony, in thy gilded halls,
>> Where forc'd and frivolous the themes arise,
>> With bow and smile unmeaning, O! how palls
> At thee, and thine, my sense! — how oft it sighs
>> For leisure, wood-lanes, dells, and water-falls;
>> And feels th' untemper'd heat of sultry skies!

Here, Seward exploits well the potential opposition of sestet to octet. She revels in the tempting description of shady retreats, delaying the sonnet's turn until the abrupt address to Ceremony in the ninth line. She also uses the floating pause to advantage, as her lines "rove" like the poet's memory into the valley and along the brook, feeling the breeze, hearing the bees' hum, catching the scent of honey. All her senses are alive to the scene, and the sonnet's break, after she seems to invite us to listen to the thrush's song, is even more jarring. Seward also uses onomatopoeia to great effect, as when describing "the pebbly beds that chide," the consonants here stuttering like the ripples themselves as they splash over the stones. Likewise, the smooth "w" sounds in "west-wind," followed by the low-register vowels and "m" muted by "sh" in "cool refreshment" emulate the wind's effect, while the fifth line's consonants, framing the elongated sound of "creeping," captures the slowly approaching breeze. Seward's sestet turns not only from this appealing scene but also from its specificity to the abstracted "Ceremony" in metaphorically "gilded halls" that surely dominated the lives of the poet and most of her genteel readers. The vague but no doubt perfectly understood description of "bow and smile unmeaning," the rituals of formal visits, throw a pall over the sonnet even as they numb the poet's and reader's senses, so recently alive to natural beauty. The sonnet's final lines invoke the pleasures of a leisurely stroll even as the poet "feels th' untemper'd heat of sultry skies" in the stuffy drawing rooms of "gilded halls." We read with sympathy, sharing the poet's distress and longing. The sonnet does not boast the poet's unparalleled suffering or unique horror in mundane company. In fact, the poem depends rather on shared memories of the relief offered by a cool dell on a sunny day. The very choice of abstraction for the contrasting drudgery of "Ceremony" presumes a community of readers likewise enchained to social rituals and longing, fruitlessly, for escape to spontaneous pleasures. We might think of Wood's emphasis on Seward's devotion to sociability even while we read her sonnet about wandering alone in the shaded glen. The sonnet's very longing for solitude requires, of poet and readers, the counterexperience of society.

Another sonnet removes the poet from the landscape altogether. Soon after reading the *Lyrical Ballads*, and not long before publication of her sonnets, Seward described Wordsworth as "a poetic landscape painter—but his pictures want distinctness" (*Letters* 5:61). Sonnet 18, "An Evening in November, Which Had Been Stormy, Gradually Clearing up, in a Mountainous Country" (*Original Sonnets* 20), offers Seward's version of a poetic landscape:

> Ceas'd is the rain; but heavy drops yet fall
> From the drench'd roof;—yet murmurs the sunk wind

Round the dim hills; can yet a passage find
Whistling thro' yon cleft rock, and ruin'd wall.
The swoln and angry torrents heard, appal,
    Tho' distant.—A few stars, emerging kind,
    Shed their green, trembling beams.—With luster small,
    The moon, her swiftly-passing clouds behind,
Glides o'er that shaded hill.—Now blasts remove
    The shadowing clouds, and on the mountain's brow,
    Full-orb'd, she shines.—Half sunk within its cove
Heaves the lone boat, with gulphing sound; and lo!
    Bright rolls the settling lake, and brimming rove
    The vale's blue rills, and glitter as they flow.

Writing to a Mrs. Gell in December 1797, Seward remarked that "a flooded valley, beneath the cloudy lour of a wintry moon, is one of those terrible graces in
scenery, which the survey of danger, and the consciousness of protection, always
form to people of imagination. I gaze with pleasing awe on the swoln, the extravagant, and usurping waters, as they roll over the fields, and, white with turbid foam,
beat against the bushes." Unfortunately, she added, such "solemn luxury I can
seldom taste" owing to physical debility. But "I have been in situations . . . when
my mind could thus luxuriate in the prospect of scenic desolation" (*Letters* 5:27).
"An Evening in November" no doubt resulted from such an experience.

   "An Evening in November" describes the interstitial moment between storm
and calm, the interval when the poet might best survey danger with the consciousness of protection. The poem opens on a pause, a caesura between the
downpour and its moonlit aftermath. The verb "ceas'd," emphasized by Miltonic
inversion, captures the rain's stopping as both act and absence. Once more,
Seward exploits floating pauses and run-on lines to connote the storm's departure,
its lingering drip and whining wind. The scene is one of Burkean sublimity, complete with winds moaning through the "cleft rock, and ruin'd wall," as in a scene
from Rousseau, Goethe, or Radcliffe. A kind of pause within the pause, or caesura
within the poem, occurs in the sixth through ninth lines, when a handful of stars
"shed their green, trembling beams" through the parting clouds.[4] Seward uses her
customary technique of running her lines' sense together, here for the purpose of
emphasizing the moon's gliding passage to the top of a hill. Because these run-on
lines end the octet and begin the sestet, the sonnet seems to glide along with the
moon. As strong winds blow away the last clouds, a full moon emerges trium-

phantly over the scene. As the poem closes, we hear the "gulphing sound" of a boat half-sunk in the late storm. "Heaves" is another masterful word placement, thrusting us into the twelfth line even as the little boat is pushed upward by the waves. Our last view is of the lake brimming from the late downpour, its waves glittering as they rush along in the moonlight. The pause is almost over. The storm has past and the night's next phase succeeds. The lone reminders of the tempest are the half-sunk boat and the glittering, restless waves caused by the heavy rain. When the boat stops heaving in the brimming waves, when the moon shines on a placid lake, the interstice between storm and calm will have ceased like the recent rain.

"An Evening in November" perfectly fulfills one of Seward's early statements about suitable topics. "An appearance in rural nature, a thrill of the spirit from affectionate recollections, or a sentiment, or a reflection, strikes us. It would do little towards the composition of an extensive poem, but it happily, perhaps, occupies the dimensions of a sonnet" (*Letters* 2:226). She captures a fleeting phenomenon, the interval between the cessation of a storm and the restoration of complete peace. Parting clouds, rising moon, dripping raindrops, and brimming waves occupy but a few minutes, the perfect "dimensions of a sonnet." Yet Seward manages to endow her miniature landscape with a rising and falling action, from the heavy drops pouring from a roof to the subsiding waves. The sonnet even features a climax, when the moon rises between octet and sestet. The poet herself all but disappears except as the witness or verbal painter of the scene. We are not invited to regard, as in one of Smith's or Wordsworth's or even many of Seward's other sonnets, the image as a metaphor for the poet's state of mind. We might suspect that the poet felt an affinity for the scene she describes, but Seward does not claim or even suggest as much. There is no trace of ego in this poem; it is simply a record of profound observation. Although Seward projected her emotions onto the landscape in other poems, she refrains from doing so here. The resulting sonnet is a gem, perfectly free of the quality Seward detected when she called Wordsworth an "egotistic manufacturer of metaphysic importance upon trivial themes" (*Letters* 6:367). We experience the beauty of the moment with the poet, but she makes no attempt to impute human motives or meaning to the spectacle. For a rare moment in eighteenth-century and Romantic-era poetry, nature is permitted to speak for itself.

Seward was, of course, far from self-effacing, either in life or in most of her sonnets. Sonnet 5, "To A Friend, Who Thinks Sensibility a Misfortune" (*Original Sonnets* 7), celebrates her capacity for strong feelings. She makes an analogy to a

person who lives near a river and who complains that she would rather live in a
desert, because occasional floods follow heavy rains. The poet demurs.

> Seldom the wild and wasteful Flood extends,
>   But, spreading plenty, verdure, beauty wide,
>   The cool translucent Stream perpetual bends,
>   And laughs the Vale as the bright waters glide.   (ll. 11–14).

Despite periodic incursions of "wild and wasteful" emotions, sensibility is more
often the "cool translucent Stream" nurturing imaginative creation. Sensibility,
here, is nearly synonymous with fancy or genius, enriching its surroundings with
the "plenty, verdure, beauty" of art. We glimpse Seward's temperamental difference from Smith in the sonnet's final line. When Smith describes a flood, in
sonnet 44, "Written in the Church-Yard at Middleton in Sussex" (44), the tide rips
corpses from their graves. She then envies the corpses because, although exposed
and ravaged, they are dead and so no longer suffer the ongoing humiliation and
pain to which she is exposed. Seward imagines waves glittering in the storm's aftermath, in "Evening in November," or here, in the valley cleft by "bright waters,"
seeming to laugh or rejoice in the sunshine after the flood recedes. Seward's emphasis on "laughs," secured by the line's Miltonic subject-verb inversion, epitomizes her sonnet's perspective. Sensibility is the source of deep joy, not only for
the artist but for those enriched by her creations. We recognize that the nourish-
ing stream is also the artist herself, reflecting the storms and calms of her environment but also brightening her culture as she glides through life. Seward cherishes
sensibility because although her feelings are deeply painful at times, they constitute her distinction, her genius. We note, too, that the stream is not isolated but
"plac'd 'mid fair domains" (l. 5), an intrinsic part of the valley. The role of the
outcast wanderer is not for Seward. Her stream moves perpetually, but it glides
amid fields conscious of, and presumably thankful for, its gifts. Coleridge and
Byron evidently found in Smith the precedent for personae such as the ancient
mariner, Childe Harold, Cain, and others torn by peerless suffering. Seward offered a consoling alternative, perhaps the only justification possible for a staunch
Anglican, but her persona was less attractive to late-century iconoclasts, each of
whom preferred Smith's pose of sublime anguish. By reconsidering Seward's sonnets in light of her principles and practices and in the context of late-century
competition, however, we can appreciate the scope, artistry, and originality of her
magnificent contribution to the sonnet revival.

CHAPTER TEN

The "Lost" Honora

O f one hundred sonnets, it is difficult to do more than generalize. Seward personally defined the sonnet in Miltonic terms and produced masterful renditions of the "legitimate" sonnet, and at the same time she anticipated her Romantic-era successors in certain ways but also differed from them in eschewing the model of poet as outcast. Still, Seward was a poet of sensibility and therefore occasionally composed in the melancholy vein identified today with Charlotte Smith and the major Romantic-era lyricists.[1] Seward rehearsed the pose of indomitable melancholy in several sonnets paraphrased from a translation of Goethe's *Sorrows of Young Werther* (sonnets 88, 89, 90). Another, sonnet 84 (*Original Sonnets* 86), expresses the sorrowful mood she sometimes described in later letters, when she contemplated her lost youth and the deaths of family and friends. Sonnet 84 perhaps originated in Shakespeare's sonnet 72, "That Time of Yeeare Thou Maist in Me Behold," with its famous image of yellow leaves clinging to "those boughs which shake against the could" (l. 3). Seward compares her life, sans "Youth, Health, and Hope" (l. 8), to a November day, "while one sere leaf, that parting Autumn gilds, / Trembles upon the thin, and naked spray" (ll. 1–2). Here we might also find an echo of Smith's plaints, in the sonnet's conclusion, that while the dying year reflects her current plight, Seward finds memories of spring more painful "than Winter's grey, and desolate domain, / Faded, like my lost Youth, that no bright Spring renews" (ll. 13–14). Memories of health and youth remain, perhaps in the form of the pale light that "gilds" her as the day declines. But her memories seem to mock the poet, who declines like the year but will not experience its annual rejuvenation. Sonnet 85, "To March" (*Original Sonnets* 87), however, reintroduces her characteristic note of hope. Seward describes the month as "bleak, grey," harsh (l. 6). Nevertheless, she declares, we do not "shun" its cold winds:

> But, with blue cheeks, and with disorder'd hair,
> Meet its rough breath;—and peep for primrose pale,
> Or lurking violet, under hedges bare.   (ll. 10–12)

This image of the late-middle-aged Seward, blue cheeked, her hair disarrayed, stooping to search for primroses under a bare hedge, seems a more accurate representation of the poet who claimed sensibility as a gift rather than a curse. Enthusiasm apparently renders her indomitable, compelling her to seek out the first pale buds despite lingering winter. As the wood pile dwindles, she anticipates "the thrift of stinted grate, and sullen flame" (l. 14). The short, muted "i" sounds of the phrase's opening cut like a knife and also like the chill due to the thin flame inadequately heating her parlor. Seward seems prepared to endure.

But while Seward characteristically reverted to hope after bouts of sorrow, passionate emotions were her boasted distinction. Indeed, the hallmark of sensibility, and hence of genius, was capacity for extraordinarily keen emotional responses. Yet as Paula Backscheider reminds us, amorous passion, the sonnet's traditional subject, presented a dilemma for genteel women poets. She speculates that Smith may have chosen melancholy, the fashionable mood of sentimental writers (as well as of their heroes and heroines) as an alternative to erotic love for the theme of her sonnets. Smith thus selected a topic both fresh and appealing while avoiding one that was at best hackneyed and at worst indecorous (326). By creating a sonnet cycle on "the great mood of the poetry of her century," Smith identified herself as the exemplar of that state of mind, achieving iconic stature (Backscheider 326). Seward, too, faced the dilemma that sonnet topics posed to women writers. As we have seen, she solved the challenge partly by claiming Milton as her precursor. Milton's occasional sonnets covered an array of subjects, including religion, friendship, commendation, mourning, politics, and literary criticism. Seward wrote on all these topics and expanded her repertoire to include numerous poems on landscapes and translations. Seward was not only a poet of sensibility, however, but also a woman of strong emotional attachments. Since her chief complaint about Smith's sonnets was their derivative quality, she by implication valued originality and genuineness. But, like Smith, she faced the limits imposed by decorum. For her, a spinster and clergyman's daughter, the bounds were arguably stricter than they were for Smith, who was married with children. Smith might at least be acknowledged to have experienced adult heterosexual love, no matter how chimerical, tenuous, and disappointing. As the mother of numerous children, she might express maternal love, fast becoming almost the sole passion ladies might frankly acknowledge. Seward had neither husband nor children to extol or mourn.

Seward nevertheless drew on her personal attachments for sonnets expressing such traditional love themes as yearning and remembrance. Some of these poems take up the other unexceptionable subject of women's love, filial devotion. As with her other topics, we may often trace in Seward's correspondence the progress of her emotions throughout her father's final years. Sonnet 78 exemplifies her emotional tug-of-war between duty and sociability, resolved at least fictionally in favor of duty as her father's health deteriorated. Sonnet 84 captures a mood she often described to correspondents following her father's death in 1790. Her immediate family members and most friends now dead, she often recorded desolate feelings that intensified after John Saville's death in 1803 robbed her of all intimate relationships. She then resembled "one sere leaf . . . upon the thin, and naked spray" (ll. 1 -2). Saville, however, is never named in the sonnets; even had Seward been at liberty to write about heterosexual love, her scandalous attachment to a married man would have been a forbidden topic. Saville may well figure as the wished-for visitor in sonnet 41, "Invitation to a Friend" (*Original Sonnets* 43), "who always canst inspire / The soul of cheerfulness" (ll. 3–4). If Saville, the vicar choral, is indeed her addressee, the sonnet's final lines gain additional poignancy. She often described him as singing for her or for small gatherings at the Bishop's Palace. Here, she closes her sonnet in the hope that her friend will hurry to dispel the gloom of a December evening: "Come, that I may not hear the winds of Night, / Nor count the heavy eave-drops as they fall" (ll. 13–14). Presumably, Saville's vocal rendering of a tender ballad, or of her favorite Handel, will distract her from the howling winds outside.

But Saville was not to be identified or even distinctly alluded to if Seward wished to preserve her already tenuous reputation. To demonstrate her mastery not only of Milton's variants but of the entire sonnet tradition, however, she evidently determined to describe moods associated with other kinds of love besides filial. She therefore had to choose a relationship sanctioned by propriety. Without husband or children, Seward had few options. For the focus of at least fifteen sonnets, Seward chose a relationship that, instead of maintaining decorum, has perplexed readers since the poems' publication. Seward memorialized one of the chief emotional dramas of her life: her passionate attachment to Honora Sneyd, followed by Honora's betrayal, desertion, and death. The story of their broken relationship is scattered throughout the volume, but seven sonnets (4, 6, 10, 12, 30,

33, and 44) allude directly to Honora, while eight (13, 14, 19, 31, 32, 34, 58, and 77) and possibly others (such as 25) are associated with the story. Some contemporaries evidently found the sonnets inappropriate because they knew the principals and were disturbed by Seward's accusation, in sonnets 31 and 32, against Honora's husband, Richard Edgeworth, whom she held responsible for Honora's death. "I am sorry that you disapprove the publication of such [of the sonnets] as breathe those sorrows which flowed from the cruel alienation of my forever loved Honora's affection," Seward remarked to Mary Powys in a letter dated October 17, 1799 (*Letters* 2:257–58). After describing Romney's picture of Serena as the exact image of Honora when she used "to fold her night-robe around her lovely limbs," Seward added, "I believe that neither man nor woman, ever loving Honora, could cease to love her" (*Letters* 2:259). Such statements, in the context of Seward's elegies and sonnets about Honora, have led many scholars to conclude that Seward's was an erotic, lesbian passion.[2] Backscheider is the most recent to have arrived at that conclusion. In light of her review of the scholarship to date and her exhaustive reading of Seward's published letters and poems, she argues that Seward's elegies indeed denote her same-sex desire for Honora (296–312). Acknowledging the many permutations of affection and its expression, she nevertheless believes "it is clear that Seward's love for Honora is in some ways 'transgressive'" (300).

While I differ from Backscheider in her conclusion, I am indebted to her for making the most thorough, well-researched argument based on evidence available at the time. Barnard's recent biography, however, contradicts Backscheider's and others' assumptions by correcting the facts regarding Seward's and Honora's quarrel and clarifying the nature of Seward's and Saville's attachment as well revealing its endurance. Barnard studied two previous collections of Seward's unedited letters, to Mary Powys and Dorothy Sykes, that detail the progress of Seward's relationship with Saville, which began in 1766, throughout the 1770s (*Anna Seward* 74–76). Seward persisted in her attachment despite repeated confrontations with her parents and the alienation of many friends (*Anna Seward* 87). Throughout this period, an independent-minded Honora remained Seward's staunch supporter and confidante (*Anna Seward* 75). Seward, in turn, championed Honora and Edgeworth when the pair encountered Honora's father's resistance to their marriage (*Anna Seward* 81). Although the cause of Seward's estrangement from Honora remains mysterious, the break occurred not before but well after Honora's marriage and was somehow caused by Sneyd's father (*Anna Seward* 81, 105). In this chapter, I offer an alternative interpretation of Seward's relationship to Honora as recounted in the sonnets, grounded in the facts that Barnard has provided. My analysis suggests that the relationship Seward describes was shaped at least in part by the purposes of the sonnet medium. Much as Smith has not been credited with the full artfulness of her sonnets, Seward has not been recognized for her creativity in transforming the married Honora's ending of the friendship into sonnets mourning a sudden and dramatic break before the marriage. Because in the sonnets Honora deserts Seward before her wedding, Seward creates the impression that the marriage caused the break, which in turn has misled critics and biographers into misunderstanding the source of Seward's grief. Seward indeed meant to convey the depth of her anguish and created, or suggested, a scenario that dramatized her loss. Paradoxically, because her sonnets so powerfully conveyed her anguish, she has shared Smith's fate of having the full extent of her artfulness overlooked. If Thomas J. McCarthy is correct and contemporaries routinely "presumed that the feelings, experiences, and events in a work of literature were those of the author himself," Seward's earliest readers overlooked the subtle ways Seward changed the incidents recorded in her sonnets to suit her poetic vision (40).

Any account of Seward and Honora's relationship must start with the fact that they met when Honora was temporarily adopted into the Seward home following her mother's death (Ashmun 9). Honora was six and Seward nearly fourteen. According to Seward herself, she and her beloved sister Sarah, then twelve, folded Honora into their routines, practically superintending her education. Sarah died tragically at twenty, and thereafter Honora took her place in Seward's affections, sharing her bed and providing companionship in all her daily activities. Seward adored Honora, and her foster sister returned her affection. Seward cherished memories such as when Honora, who suffered from chronically poor health, went to Bath with a neighbor's family but missed Seward so much that she returned early. Seward encouraged John André's hapless courtship of her protégée, seemingly more disappointed than the noncommittal Honora when her family discouraged the attachment. Honora's father welcomed her home at nineteen. Seward and Honora remained close when Edgeworth proposed marriage to Honora in 1773, shortly after his first wife's death. Although Honora's father disapproved, Seward applauded her choice and happily served as Honora's bridesmaid after Mr. Sneyd relented (*Anna Seward* 80).

Seward and Honora exchanged letters and visits for several years. A brief but profound emotional conflict seems to have ensued; perhaps Mr. Sneyd relayed to Honora the imprecations Seward was directing toward Edgeworth, whom she thought neglected his wife's disintegrating health (*Anna Seward* 82). For whatever reason, Seward was rebuffed, and the two friends remained estranged until Sneyd's death in 1780. The intense, fruitless struggle that caused their break forms the background to one group of Honora sonnets. A second group evidently followed the occasion of Honora's death several years later. The depth of Seward's response to these events has perplexed everyone who has written about them. Ashmun, who thought that Sneyd broke with Seward before her marriage, suggests that "in more than sisterly fashion, [Seward] had centered her hopes and ambitions upon the growing Honora" (60). Her remark seems to hint at possible lesbian attachment. Reviewing the women's conflict, Ashmun asks, "Did [Seward] perhaps desire to marry Edgeworth herself?" (61). She dismisses that possibility, however, because she assumes that Seward disliked Edgeworth throughout their acquaintance.

Seward herself found nothing unseemly in either her devotion to Honora's memory or her publication of sonnets recording their relationship. Given recent readings of Seward's attachment as an instance of same-sex desire, her lack of reticence would seem bold indeed. But since Seward refrained from mentioning her known attachment, to Saville, in print, we should ask whether it is likely she would have thus trumpeted an illicit passion for Honora. As Backscheider and others have observed, the fact that Seward and Honora shared a bed after Sarah's death proves nothing; siblings of the same gender usually shared beds even in well-to-do households. Shared embraces, affectionate tears, and kisses, all of which figured in Seward's relationship with Honora, were also perfectly acceptable expressions of women's friendship (Backscheider 299–300). Women, after all, were considered the more emotional sex. Their sentimental endearments modeled a more refined standard of behavior for their constitutionally violent male counterparts.

The circumstances Barnard has revealed, moreover, suggest another reason for what might appear to be excessive grief over the loss of Honora. 1773 was a critical year for Seward not only because of Honora's marriage but also because of Seward's father's efforts to estrange Seward from Saville, who, according to Barnard, was banished from the Bishop's Palace at about the same time (*Anna Seward* 71). Having been informed of Seward's and Saville's secret attachment, Seward's father ordered the pair to separate. Years later, Seward guardedly described these simultaneous catastrophes in a letter to Mrs. Temple, wife of a former suitor, dated June 19, 1796. During the same period when she lost her chief confidante to marriage and departure for Ireland,

> family discontents combined to increase the pressure of that bosom-woe. Another friend, scarcely less dear to me than Honora, was injured, was unhappy, — and those misfortunes were of a nature, that, though my sympathy might sooth, it could not remove them. By that deprivation, and by those regrets, were the precious established habits of my life broken, and the native gaiety of my spirit

eternally eclipsed, however time might restore constitutional cheerfulness. (*Letters* 4:218)

Honora's was therefore not the only cherished friendship of which Seward was deprived at this time. Her cryptic reference to a dear friend who "was injured" surely indicates the circumstances of Saville's separation from his wife. Since he chose to avoid the scandal of divorce, Seward could only commiserate; she could not "remove" his suffering by becoming his second wife. Because her father was concerned to end Seward's connection with Saville, her sympathy could only be expressed in attenuated fashion, to her lasting regret. Saville's distress thus combined with Honora's departure to eclipse Seward's spirits.

Another dimension of Seward's relationship with Honora also points toward a different explanation for her grief after Honora's marriage. As we observed in chapter 3, the plot of *Louisa* might have been motivated by Seward's need to control, at least on paper, the circumstances of her life following her father's discouragement of two suitors. In the poetical novel, she achieved fictional retaliation against her father and maneuvered her heroine to the marriage of her choice. I submit that Seward's bitter anger over Honora's estrangement was exacerbated by her inability to control her friend's physical decline by persuading her to remove herself from the marshy environs of Edgeworthtown. All accounts of Honora's childhood stress Sarah's and Anna's command. In the letter explaining the dual loss of Honora and Saville, Seward described the critical juncture at which Honora became her bedmate and substitute sister:

> When my attachment to General, then Cornet V[yse], sunk in the snow of his altered conduct, Honora Sneyd, educated in our family from five years old, was commencing woman, and only eight years younger than myself; more lovely, more amiable, more interesting, than any thing I ever saw in the female form. As a child, I had loved her with the extremest fondness. Death had deprived me of my beloved and only sister, in the bloom of youth, who had shared with me the delightful task of instructing our angelic pupil; and, when disappointed love threw all the energies of my soul into the channel of friendship, Honora was its chief object. The charms of her society, when her advancing youth gave equality to our connection, made Lichfield an Eden to me, from the year 1766 to 1771. Her father then recalled her to his own family. . . . In May 1773 she married. (*Letters* 4:217)

Seward transmuted her romantic feelings for Vyse into friendship. If Honora was a kind of consolation prize for a woman denied the opportunity to marry, her

eventual loss would have been bitter, a reenactment of the original disappointment. Honora entered the Seward household the very year that Saville was engaged as her music instructor (Barnard, *Anna Seward* 83) and departed at about
the time Saville was dismissed. Honora, whom both tutored, might even have
seemed like the child Seward and Saville would never have. In retrospect, the
sonnets' re-creation of the break with Honora resonates with the double anguish
of simultaneous losses and may even serve a metonymic function in conveying
the grief associated with both.

In a later letter, Seward commiserated with Anna Rogers Stokes on the anniversary of her daughter's death, which was also the birthday of her own late sister,
Sarah. But, she adds, Mrs. Stokes has since had a second child. "Honora Sneyd
was my child of recompense, as your little Anna is of yours—yes, through nine
happy years; she then became lost to me, body, mind, and heart, although not to
life till seven years later" (*Letters* 5:327). When the two letters are put together,
Honora emerges more as Seward's adopted child, the child she would never bear
herself, but a child given in recompense for her failed courtships. Since contemporaries were beginning to celebrate maternal love, Seward's passion for her
"lovely, amiable, interesting," and "angelic" foster sister, raised more as her foster
child, would have seemed less extreme than it does today, especially if viewed in
the context of her lost suitors and deceased sister. Even Seward's bitterness is more
explicable in these terms. Betty Rizzo's *Companions Without Vows*, although
about a different kind of domestic relationship, illuminates Seward's predicament.
Rizzo observes that when eighteenth-century ladies had the opportunity to act in
the role of "spouse"/employer, as they did when they engaged companions, they
sometimes failed to establish anything like the dignified, respectful relationship
they claimed to long for in marriage. Instead, they replicated the controlling behaviors to which they were subject as wives because it was their sole model for
relating to a dependent, even if socially equal, associate.[3]

Seward may have adopted an analogous, controlling posture toward her beloved Honora. Writers often note that when André courted Honora, Seward apparently took the lead, encouraging him and writing to him and chaperoning
their meetings. Seward romanticized the impecunious young émigré, insisting
years later "all the dark colour of André's fate took its tint from disappointed and
unconquerable attachment to [Honora]" (*Letters* 5:259). Backscheider suggests
that Seward was courting Honora herself, through André (301–4). But an equally,
if not more, plausible interpretation of their triangle is that Seward was sponsoring Honora's courtship by a young man who was as penniless as her own youthful
suitors but far more charismatic. Through Honora, she might relive those affairs

but achieve a satisfactory conclusion. When Honora demurred, accepting her family's disapproval, Seward clung to the fiction of André's tragic love. Since she had manipulated the couple's romance from the start, she proceeded to turn the young man's rejection and ultimately, his death, into a grand tragedy. Likewise, Honora's decision to marry a man whom Seward grew to dislike caused permanent heartache. Honora, her "child of recompense," first removed herself physically and then broke the emotional and intellectual bonds that had sustained Seward after Sarah's death. Honora was truly lost "body, mind, and heart." Her mythical status was established by the epithet Seward habitually referred to her by; she became "lost Honora." Since young women were usually described as "lost" after a sexual scandal ruined their reputations, Seward's formula acquires the regretful tone of a mother's eternal mourning for a disgraced, estranged child. Her many incantations of the epithet function throughout her letters somewhat like the phrase "Oh lost" in Thomas Wolfe's twentieth-century novel *Look Homeward, Angel*. Like Wolfe, Seward invokes the hopelessness of her own loss and the poignancy of Honora's early death and makes clear her despairing recognition that neither the young woman nor their shared youth can ever be restored through sentences that resemble his refrain, "O lost, and by the wind grieved, ghost, come back again" (1). Since Honora was one of the few people Seward trusted, her sudden rejection would have been devastating. On Honora's part, Seward must have seemed to have shockingly violated their friendship in her harsh criticism of Edgeworth, assuming that is what led Honora to break with her friend (and it is the most likely explanation in light of the one established fact in the break, namely that Mr. Sneyd played a part). Honora's beloved mentor might have seemed to have mutated into a sort of wicked stepmother, trying to harm her marriage. Seward's criticism presumed an authority she had long practiced but was not entitled to, particularly after Honora's marriage. Honora's anger would have been understandable.

Looked at from this perspective, Seward's sonnets about Honora become coherent if not quite conventional. In their representation of the drama of a self-nominated foster mother whose "child of recompense" turned against her, these occasional poems resemble Shakespeare's sonnets about his false mistress or unreliable friend or any sonnets narrating the permutations of unsatisfactory relationships. As Smith chose melancholy for her theme, Seward chose her thwarted friendship with an ungrateful young woman. Although the sonnets are scattered, they are thematically linked. Seward carefully arranged her volume for publication in 1799, so she could have placed the sonnets together as a cycle if she had wanted, but she preferred to follow Milton's practice of writing about discrete occasions (such as Honora's departure or final illness) rather than construct semi-autobiographical chains in the manner of Smith, Mary Robinson, William Lisle Bowles, and other competitors. She may have perceived what Esther Schor has observed about such narrative sonnet sequences: they severely test a poet's "ability to assimilate ethical and logical appeals to the task of arousing pathos" (61). In successive editions, Smith's prefaces note her continuing sorrow, implying her poetry's rhetorical inefficacy in moving her patrons to intervene in her legal battles with her estranged husband (Schor 64). Bowles's later sonnets lose confidence in the power of fancy to provide comfort on his spiritual journey and turn toward God (Schor 68–69). Seward might have noted how these two rivals' sequences strayed from their original confidence in the power of verse to provide solace or create sympathy. The attendant risk of failure to engage sympathy or achieve consolation could have dissuaded her from assembling her Honora sonnets into a sequence. The last thing Seward desired was to be perceived as an ineffectual manufacturer of "everlasting lamentables." Most likely, though, she preserved the occasional nature of her sonnets to conform to her Miltonic model. Nevertheless, embedded within her collection is a discernable narrative similar to Shakespeare's record of false friendship, which takes the poet from lyrical celebrations of his patron's masculine beauty to "Farewell! Thou art too deare for my possessing" (sonnet 87). Seward's sonnets move from a tender recollection of Honora's fragility (sonnet 4, "To Honora Sneyd, Whose Health Was Always Best in Winter") to plaintive expressions of regret for lost friendship (sonnet 77).

"To Honora Sneyd" (*Original Sonnets* 6) is dated 1770, the year when fear of possible consumption led the Sewards to send Honora to Bath. Seward often recalled to Mary Powys her delight when Honora returned early from her sojourn, although she was "at that instant, the toast of that gay city" (*Letters* 1:156). Writing shortly after Honora's death, Seward was already idealizing her memories, since Honora would have been about ten years old, too young for all the social engagements this letter implies. Nevertheless, Seward remembers how delighted she was with Honora "for having exchanged balls and plays, and malls and parades, for books and conversation with me, and with a few chosen friends!" (*Letters* 1:157). Even better, Honora returned with health restored, although she was frail throughout her brief life. Seward evidently wrote the sonnet during this period of assured and unclouded friendship. The sonnet begins as a delicate tribute to spring, invoked as a "youthful, gay, capricious" being that paints the sky with rainbows and "bids all her Warblers sing" (ll. 1, 4). While the lark and thrush carol, hedges burst into bloom and "young Cowslips fling / rich perfume o'er the fields" (ll. 8–9). Hav-

ing evoked all the sensory joys of the season in her octet, however, Seward turns
in her sestet to a paradox:

> —It is the prime
> Of Hours that Beauty robes:—yet all they gild,
> Cheer, and delight in this their fragrant time,
> For thy dear sake, to me less pleasure yield
> Than, veil'd in sleet, and rain, and hoary rime,
> Dim Winter's naked hedge and plashy field.   (ll. 9–14)

The sonnet opens with a personification, spring as the embodiment of youthful
health and joy. Its conclusion, however, connects Honora with winter, her fragility
somehow compatible with its precarious weather. To the robust figure of spring,
Seward opposes the bleak winter landscape and, by association, Honora's pale
face and slender figure. She may have been thinking of that evening when Honora, home from her Bath journey, joined her by the hearth and "exchanged balls
and plays . . . for books and conversations with me." That winter, indeed, held pleasures for Seward unsurpassed by her memories of following seasons. Sonnet 6,
"Written at Lichfield, in an Eastern Apartment of the Bishop's Palace, Which
Commands a View of Stow Valley" (*Original Sonnets* 8) is an incremental repetition of "To Honora Sneyd" in the traditional manner of sequences. Its octet even
features the same "-ing" rhyme. In this poem, Seward gazes at the view framed by
her window in the palace. The late-winter morning is pointedly uninviting: "chill,"
"wintry," "gloom'd and rainy," "sullen," and "stormy" (ll. 1–3). Somehow, however, the dreary view is as precious "as when it bloom'd in Summer's gale" (l. 7):

> —When Sorrows fling,
> Or slow Disease, thus, o'er some beauteous Form
> Their shadowy languors, Form, devoutly dear
> As thine to me, Honora, with more warm
> And anxious gaze the eyes of Love sincere
> Bend on the charms, dim in their tintless snow,
> Than when with health's vermilion hues they glow.   (ll. 8–14)

Honora's face metamorphoses into the landscape, her features becoming "tintless
snow" compared with the "vermilion hues" of health, which in turn resemble
a spring scene "ting'd by setting sun" (l. 8). As in "To Honora Sneyd," winter is
prized for its connection with Honora, but here Seward's emphasis is not on the
season, dear because it promoted Honora's health. Rather, just as a lover of the

picturesque appreciates early spring, so too do we gaze on the languid features of a friend, seeking "with more warm and anxious gaze" the signs of returning health. The landscape's dreary features recall memories of summer's pleasures, which we hope will recur with advancing spring. The sonnet offers a muted hope, suggested principally by its setting in a "wintry spring." These two sonnets prepare the scene for the ensuing conflict. They establish Seward's love but also voice her anxiety. Honora's fusion with Seward's sense of place and of the seasons confirms her importance to the poet, while her association with winter might connote a degree of emotional coldness and her physical fragility, a hint of her friendship's brittleness as well.

These two sonnets were supposedly written in 1770, but they may have been composed later and projected back into that halcyon era. Likewise, sonnet 10, "To Honora Sneyd" (*Original Sonnets* 12) is dated April 1773, four months before Honora's marriage to Edgeworth. Seward may have recognized the danger posed by Edgeworth's hasty courtship and responded with this apprehensive sonnet. Or she may have composed the poem in retrospect, as one of a number of sonnets recording their friendship's demise. This sonnet is closely related to the other two, confirming Honora's identification with both literal and metaphorical chill:

> Honora, shou'd that cruel time arrive
>> When 'gainst my truth thou should'st my errors poise,
>> Scorning remembrance of our vanish'd joys;
>> When for the love-warm looks, in which I live,
> But cold respect must greet me, that shall give
>> No tender glance, no kind regretful sighs;
>> When thou shalt pass me with averted eyes,
>> Feigning thou see'st me not, to sting, and grieve,
> And sicken my sad heart, I cou'd not bear
>> Such dire eclipse of thy soul-cheering rays;
>> I cou'd not learn my struggling heart to tear
> From thy lov'd form, that thro' my memory strays;
>> Nor in the pale horizon of Despair
>> Endure the wintry and the darken'd days.

Those who wish to construe Seward's love as transgressive might well describe this sonnet as the record of a lovers' quarrel, perhaps recording an occasion when Seward overstepped the bounds of propriety, alienating her more reticent beloved. The poem can be read more convincingly as a foreboding of the period when Honora rebuffed Seward. The sonnet reviews exactly the course of events Seward claims only to fear, her rejection followed by the alienation she describes in her letters. The nature of their quarrel and Honora's break from Seward is unspecified, but its substance is hinted in the sonnet's opening lines. Honora weighed Seward's "errors" against the her "truth" and cast her aside. The sonnet's date suggests a "truth" such as that life among loving friends and familiar "joys" was preferable to accepting Edgeworth's proposal and moving to Ireland. Since the real break occurred later, was that "truth" an unpalatable revelation about her husband or criticism of Edgeworth's apparent hesitation to seek medical help for his wife? Was Seward's error her failure to desist in or soften her criticism, a characteristic trait? Or might Honora have finally been convinced by her father of Seward's "error" in attaching herself to a married man currently embroiled in a scandalous separation, with little hope for Seward of a positive outcome? By predating her apprehensions, Seward diverts attention from the real offense and implies a conflict over Honora's marriage. The scenario resembles a typical, if brutal, parent-child separation crisis. Seward offended and Honora responded not with forgiveness but by recalling her quasi mother's errors.

The rest of this sonnet recapitulates the aftermath of their break, when Seward proved literally incapable of tearing Honora's memory from her struggling heart, even though the living Honora distanced herself from Seward. Her behavior confirmed Seward's association of Honora with winter, not because she was physically fragile but because her "love-warm looks" changed to "cold respect" when she and Edgeworth visited Lichfield. In the sonnet, Honora has withdrawn her "soul-cheering rays," leaving Seward struggling in a bleak landscape. In sonnets 4 and 6, Seward associates Honora with both spring and winter, hope and fear, but winter and fear dominated owing to Honora's poor health. Here, a different fear has prevailed, crippling Seward rather than her young friend. Honora gone, Seward beholds only "the pale horizon of Despair" and fears she cannot "Endure the wintry and the darken'd days." Since she previously cherished winter as Honora's avatar, her ascendant season, Seward's vision of life as an endless winter without Honora is despairing indeed given her generally friendless environment throughout the 1770s. Honora has withdrawn the rays that transfigured winter for Seward, leaving a doubly dark landscape, or life, in prospect.

Sonnets 12, 13, 14, and possibly 19, "To —— " narrate the period immediately after their quarrel, when Seward struggled to reconcile herself to the loss of her "child of recompense." Dated July 1773, the month of Honora's wedding, the first three sonnets explore, in typical sonnet-cycle fashion, the emotions associated with rejection. Sonnet 12 (*Original Sonnets* 14) asks why Seward cannot be thankful for the many privileges left her despite Honora's desertion. She concludes by resolving to appreciate her remaining blessings, including the newfound knowl-edge that "THE HEART ESTRANGED NO ANGUISH CAN REGAIN" (l. 14). Sonnet 13 (*Original Sonnets* 15) rehearses yet another mood. Far from expressing the stoic, if not Byronic, acceptance of sonnet 12, this sonnet confesses that sleeplessness and anxiety have haunted Seward since Honora's alienation. "Thou child of NIGHT, and SILENCE, balmy SLEEP" is invoked in the poem's opening and closing lines, the entire line in small capitals at the conclusion. The repetition, with the heavy emphasis conveyed by the small capitals, suggests the poet's desperation and the circular nature of her thoughts, preying endlessly upon her consciousness. The sonnet refers to but does not name Honora as "th' Enchantress" who formerly protected Seward from "Care, and anxious Dread" (l. 7). Seward blames her men-tal anguish on Honora's absence, which has caused ceaseless "thoughts of whence, or how/Vanish'd that priz'd Affection" (ll. 3–4). Since Honora is both cause and cure of Seward's woes, she is unlikely to achieve rest, a predicament captured by the repetitious final line: Seward's mind is caught in the loop typical of such fruit-less preoccupations.

Sonnet 14 (*Original Sonnets* 16) tests yet another response to friendship's cessation. "INGRATITUDE, how deadly is thy smart/Proceeding from the Form we fondly love!/How light, compared, all *other* sorrows prove!" (ll. 1–3). After at-tempting stoicism, then searching in herself for the cause, Seward defines the nature of the unnamed Honora's betrayal. This sonnet echoes King Lear's cry, "How sharper than a serpent's tooth it is, to have a thankless child!" (*King Lear* 1.4.288–89). Seward addresses a personified Ingratitude, but the human source of her suffering is implied throughout. "Thou shed'st a *Night* of Woe," she com-plains (l. 4). Ingratitude is a kind of murderer, robbing victims of their peace of mind. "O! thy dart/kills more than life, —e'en all that makes Life dear" (ll. 8–9). Trust, self-confidence, contentment, we may guess from the other sonnets, are among its victims in Seward's case. Worse, Seward is not a stoic; she has suffered "till we, 'the sensible of pain' wou'd change/For Phrenzy, that defies the bitter tear" (ll. 10–11). Even madness would be preferable to her daily anguish. Her poem closes with a horrific image, as she professes that rather than endure further torment, she is willing even "in kindred callousness, to range/Where moon-ey'd Idiocy, with fallen lip,/Drags the loose knee, and intermitting step" (ll. 12–14). This sublimely awful idea, the poet's readiness to exchange complete mental va-cuity for the torture inflicted by ingratitude, marks the nadir of the sonnets' ac-count of her misery. Here, Seward might have outdone Smith in claiming supe-rior anguish; to find life as an idiot preferable to her tormented existence surely fulfills at least her criterion of original imagery. That a person who boasted about her sensibility would express such a wish implies agony commensurate with Lear's tragic exclamation over his perfidious daughters.

If "To —— " (*Original Sonnets* 21) was inspired by the same occasion, as I believe it was, it concludes Seward's poetic investigation of the pains attending broken friendship. "Farewell, false Friend!" seems to echo Shakespeare's cynical leave taking of his patron. Honora has apparently written a letter that contains some "falsehood" (l. 8), perhaps a profession of continuing esteem. We can guess her identity because her resort to a lie concludes "scenes of kindness" (l. 1):

> To cordial looks, to sunny smiles farewell!
> To sweet consolings, that can grief expel,
>   And every joy soft sympathy bestows!
> For alter'd looks, where truth no longer glows,
>   Thou hast prepar'd my heart.   (ll. 2–6)

In this sonnet, Seward claims to achieve an indifference that was impossible in life. But the tone of this poem is scornful, from her staccato invocation of past endearments to her mock thanks for the lying missive that confirmed Honora's alleged shamelessness. Seward concludes with the wish that when the former friends meet, they will refrain from any reference to their past attachment, "nor one sigh / Flatter with weak regret a broken vow!" (ll. 13–14). Addressed to Honora, the lines express Seward's hope that she will not exacerbate her lie. Of herself, the same lines request stoic endurance. Dignity requires that she stifle any "consciousness of eye" (l. 11) or sigh of regret.

Sonnet 19, like the three preceding, rehearses a pose. In her rich discussion of Smith's sonnet cycle, Backscheider reminds us that the speaker of *Elegiac Stanzas* is partly Smith herself but also partly a conscious creation. Failing to recognize that fictional element, we fail to credit Smith for her artfulness in transmuting the walks and meditations of daily life into poetry. In Smith's case, some contemporaries including Seward refused to acknowledge Smith's use of incremental repetition, for example, in creating her sequence, and her fabrication of an isolated, wandering persona. Seward, likewise, exercised a great deal of artfulness in creating her Honora sonnets. Although her letters and elegiac poems reveal the origin of these sonnets in real-life experience, we must admire the degree to which Seward transformed her friendship's rupture into poems that capture different states of mind associated with loss and grief. Seward would be the first to claim these poems as autobiographical, but she introduced fictional elements when crafting her experience into sonnets. Seward's dating several of the sonnets to 1773, when we know from Barnard that her break with Honora occurred several years later, suggests that as in her sonnet about tending her father, Seward had taken liberties with her context. She may have backdated the poems because the idea that the friends' estrangement was instigated by Honora's projected marriage seemed more dramatic to her than the actual circumstances of the break, whose cause was less explicable or less sympathetic to Seward, after the marriage. Perhaps sonnets written in 1773 became a self-fulfilling prophecy: Barnard describes a cryptic letter to Mary Powys during that year confiding Seward's knowledge of Edgeworth's "baseness" (Anna Seward 82). This revelation, however, does not seem to have affected her happiness regarding Honora's wedding or their initial correspondence. We must be cautious, therefore, in reading into these sonnets or any of Seward's poems (or her heavily edited letters, for that matter) an accurate record of her life.

Honora's "betrayal" became the occasion for Seward to write a series of poems re-creating, and in part creating, her experience of desertion and recovery. Sonnet 30 (Original Sonnets 32) reminds us of the fictional dimension, because the scorn Seward professes never surfaces in her remaining letters or in her other elegiac poems. As the conclusion of a series of poems exploring the events of a friendship broken but survived, however, the scornful posture provides a satisfying resolution. The poems indeed suggest the plot Ashmun and others accepted as fact, that Honora defied the pleas of the friend who had raised her to resist a marriage arranged by her father. Certainly, the controlling impulse revealed in Seward's earlier effort to manage André's courtship may have led to a rupture later, when her impetuous insistence on telling "truth" became an irreparable "error." We have no record of Honora's thoughts, but having turned down Thomas Day's proposal and acquiesced in, rather than pursued, André's courtship, she evidently preferred Edgeworth to her other admirers and suitors.[4] Seward's criticism of Edgeworth's behavior may well have forced Honora to choose her husband over her friend. In any event, Seward was probably not forced to endure the pain of frequent meetings that she anticipated in sonnet 19. Edgeworth and Honora resided at first in Ireland, then in Hertfordshire until Honora's palpable decline brought them back to Lichfield.

The second group of Honora sonnets clusters around the events of her illness and death. They brim with pain but also with anger against Edgeworth, whom Seward held responsible for marrying a woman whose health was manifestly inadequate for bearing and raising children. What we know of Edgeworth's behavior exonerates him from Seward's charge. Jenny Uglow observes, on the contrary, his decision not to trust the skills of local physicians but to convey Honora to England instead. They visited London to consult Dr. William Heberden, among the most celebrated physicians in Britain. Afterward, they went back to Lichfield. Honora continued to decline, but at least now she would die among friends and family (Uglow 316–19). Seward, however, persisted in her adverse interpretation of Edgeworth's attachment and motives. She structured Honora's death into a tragedy, complete with villain. Sonnet 30 opens the drama. Seward may have composed the sonnet when news of the Edgeworths' impending return brought fond recollections. Or she may have inserted a sonnet written later as context for the four following. The sonnet's reference to "days long fled . . . Pleasure's golden reign" (l. 12) resembles her epistolary account to Mrs. Temple in 1796. But whenever composed, the sonnet evokes the mythic time when Honora's companionship "made Lichfield an Edenic scene" (*Letters* 4:217). After the tumultuous emotions recorded in the previous sonnets, this poem describes a mood of resignation, broken suddenly by a once-familiar melody:

That song again!—its sounds my bosom thrill,
    Breathe of past years, to all their joys allied;
    And, as the notes thro' my sooth'd spirits glide,
    Dear Recollection's choicest sweets distill,
Soft as the Morn's calm dew on yonder hill,
    When slants the Sun upon its grassy side,
    Tinging the brooks that many a mead divide
    With lines of gilded light; and blue, and still,
The distant lake stands gleaming in the vale.
    Sing, yet once more, that well-remember'd strain,
    Which oft made vocal every passing gale
In days long fled, in Pleasure's golden reign,
    The youth of chang'd HONORA!—now it wears
    Her air—her smile—*spells* of the vanish'd years!

The sonnet's octet carries its speaker back to a springtime Eden, a reverie so compelling it persists into the sestet. Seward turns her speaker, herself, into an exemplar of sensibility, her nerves "thrilling" to a melody. The song's notes glide through her "spirits," carrying the impulses that evoke her sentimental response. Perhaps, in life, Saville performed the nearly forgotten song that spurred her memory. Here, sensibility induces synesthesia, as nervous "thrills" produce a sweet mood comparable to the effect produced by a lovely morning. Seward details the visual pleasures of such a morning in a landscape familiar from her descriptions of Stowe valley. She admires the soft effect of dew on the contours of a hill. Her gaze wanders from sunlight slanting across the hills, down to fields divided by

brooks "gilded" by the sun, and on to the "distant lake" shining in the same gentle
sunlight. The soft light bathes not only the scene but Seward's recollection, demonstrating memory's power to "distill" experience of all but its "choicest sweets."
Seward's rhyme words, "thrill," "distill," "hill," and "still" enforce her description
of sensibility's power to evoke powerful, here placid and pleasurable, memories
in a listener. The delayed turn of the sestet suggests Seward's awakening from a
kind of song-induced trance. She begs to hear the song again, finally explaining its
significance. The recollected landscape is gilded because it belongs to a "golden"
past. Honora herself gilded the past before she "chang'd." As in sonnet 13, Honora
is figured as an enchantress, who cast her spell over their shared experiences during those "vanish'd years." Did Honora sing the song herself? Was it a favorite song
of Honora's that Saville sang for his companions? Was it simply a popular song of
the time that Seward now connects with that lost era? We learn only of the song's
power to evoke memories of a "golden" past. The sonnet's conclusion suggests, if
subtly, that the memories, too, are "gilded" by the sunshine of recollection. The
passage of time has transformed Honora's youth into "Pleasure's golden reign," a
spell renewed by the once-familiar song.

Sonnets 31, "To the Departing Spirit of an Alienated Friend," and 32, "Subject
of the Preceding Sonnet Continued" (*Original Sonnets* 33, 35), form the dreadful
catastrophe of Seward's plot. "To the Departing Spirit of an Alienated Friend"
contrasts her anguish with Edgeworth's callousness. While Seward spends her
sleepless nights hoping "that Morn's returning light/Shall dawn for THEE"
(ll. 3–4), Edgeworth socializes in London. Edgeworth is painted as a villain: "I
hear him, who shou'd droop in silent woe,/Declaim on Actors, and on Taste decide!" (ll. 13–14). The sestet juxtaposes the "glow" of Edgeworth's eyes with the
"woe" he should feel; his wife's "ebbing tide" with his petty conversations that "on
Taste decide." The sonnet is angry, and its accusation is repeated in the next sonnet, which presents Honora's death as the tragic outcome of her decision to trust
Edgeworth. Seward is vindicated but magnanimously pardons her late friend.
Edgeworth's callousness confirms the justice of Seward's fears:

> Behold him now his genuine colours wear,
>   That specious False-One, by whose cruel wiles
>   I lost thy amity; saw thy dear smiles
>   Eclips'd; those smiles, that us'd my heart to cheer,
> Wak'd by thy grateful sense of many a year
>   When rose thy youth, by Friendship's pleasing toils
>   Cultur'd;—but DYING!—O! for ever fade

The angry fires. — Each thought, that might upbraid
Thy broken faith, which yet my soul deplores,
    Now as eternally is past and gone
    As are the interesting, the happy hours,
Days, years, we shar'd together. They are flown!
    Yet long must I lament thy hapless doom,
    Thy lavish'd life and early-hasten'd tomb.

The poem constructs Honora's death as Seward's bitter triumph. Edgeworth's persistence in social activities during his wife's illness proves his hypocrisy. A man who truly loved his dying wife would never leave her, especially for London's distractions. Edgeworth's behavior proves that he won Honora by "cruel wiles," presumably pleading love that he did not feel. His persuasion was "cruel" because not only has marriage shortened Honora's life but he has deserted her on her deathbed. Seward tried to intervene, but her advice was rejected and she "lost [Honora's] amity." This version of their break sustains the reading of a rupture between quasi parent and child. Seward had expected gratitude for the many years of Honora's childhood when, channeling her hopes for marriage into friendship, she focused her energies on the "pleasing toils" of educating her foster sister. We might deduce that Seward considered herself to be investing in future companionship, or trying to escape future loneliness, by her efforts to cultivate Honora. But, as her letters and poems reveal, Honora chose marriage soon after their relationship blossomed into equality, or genuine friendship. Seward was at first pleased by Honora's marriage but their friendship was ruined, she hints, when she tried to warn Honora that Edgeworth's behavior was unworthy. The octet's succinct recapitulation addresses Honora, demanding acknowledgment of her husband's revealed nature ("Behold him") and of her folly in rejecting Seward's counsel. She also demands, indirectly, that Honora admit to ingratitude after years when her "smiles . . ./Wak'd by [her] grateful sense" of Seward's "toils" more than repaid those efforts.

The poem's turn, however, occurs when Seward recollects that Honora is dying or possibly even dead. Centered in the seventh line and printed in small capital letters, the word "DYING" precipitates the poem into its sestet just as the fact of Honora's death changed Seward's attitude, her cause of grief, her life. Justice demands recognition of Honora's "broken faith," but angry thoughts are no longer appropriate. They are "past and gone" like the "Days, years, we shar'd together." Seward's lament—"They are flown!"—is ambiguous. She seems to regret her wasted anger as much as her lost happiness. Both are part of Honora's story, conserved and mourned in these poems and for the rest of Seward's life. Seward describes Honora's early death as a "hapless doom." Honora has been unlucky in her choice of mate; marriage hastened her death. Instead of conserving her life, remaining in Lichfield, and enjoying the pleasures of healthful rambles, books, and conversation with Seward and other friends, she "lavish'd" her precious health on six children (two of whom were her own) and a careless husband. The epithets of the concluding couplet—"hapless," "lavish'd," and "early-hasten'd"—stress Honora's mistake, her luckless decision to waste herself on Edgeworth. Marriage, as well as early death, has been her "doom," or rather, she doomed herself to death when she married. However we read the lines, Seward continues to blame Honora even after she claims to have stopped blaming her. Her death itself seems a gesture of ingratitude, of "broken faith." Although Seward lamented the flight of "happy hours" in previous sonnets, it is as if she hoped that somehow Honora might be restored, that the ungrateful child would return and confess her error. Now, all recriminations are futile, but this sonnet conveys Seward's lingering anger toward both Edgeworth and Honora. A modern psychologist might deduce that Seward was mired in an early stage of grief, at least when she composed this sonnet. Oddly, however, Edgeworth vanishes after his brief appearance as the villain. Honora's marriage seems less important than her unfinished business with Seward, who remains as the real "hapless" victim. The passionate confrontation implied by Seward's command ("Behold") will never take place; her superior love will never be acknowledged. Seward has lost control of Honora.

Sonnet 34 (*Original Sonnets* 36) records the falling action of the tragedy. It is dated June 1780; if that is accurate, Seward composed the poem less than two months after Honora's death on April 30. In the aftermath of that event, and in the context of sonnets 31 and 32, sonnet 33 completes the narration of Honora's demise. Taken out of context, this poem might be read as the expression of transgressive desire, a nightly plea that Honora visit Seward's bed, if only in dreams. But in the context of previous poems about the circumstances of Honora's death and contemporary brain science that posited "the continual activity of the brain, even during sleep," the sonnet yields a different reading (Richardson 6).[5] In sonnet 31, Edgeworth deserted his wife's deathbed while Seward spent sleepless nights worrying about her friend's fate. In sonnet 32, Seward seems to regret that she will never be able to confront Honora and receive the justice of acknowledgment and apology. Anger is futile after her friend's death; all that remains is lament for Honora and for their pleasanter past. Now, her feelings still raw, Seward again wishes for a glimpse of Honora:

Last night her Form the hours of slumber bless'd
   Whose eyes illumin'd all my youthful years.—
   Spirit of dreams, at thy command appears
   Each airy Shape, that visiting our rest,
Dismays, perplexes, or delights the breast.
   My pensive heart this kind indulgence cheers;
   Bliss, in no *waking* moment now possess'd,
   Bliss, ask'd of thee with Memory's thrilling tears.
Nightly I cry, how oft, alas! In vain,
   Give, by thy powers, that airy Shapes controul,
   HONORA to my visions!—ah! Ordain
Her beauteous lip may wear the smile that stole,
   In years long fled, the sting from every pain!
   Show her sweet face, ah show it to my soul!

In earlier sonnets, Seward often referred to Honora's figure as her "form," her appearance. Sometimes that form was only present in memory. Here, Seward invokes Honora's form in a slightly different sense: Honora's "Shape" only can appear, her empty form, a dream vision. Seward begins by recounting the dream that "bless'd" her with Honora's visitation and especially with a glimpse of Honora's eyes. Seward's poem becomes an incantation, invoking the "Spirit of dreams" to repeat the previous night's delusion. Seward claims that the dream restored a pleasure never again to be experienced *"waking,"* the approach of her smiling friend. She ends the octet begging "with Memory's thrilling tears," a reference to the keen sensibility that caused her nerves to produce tears from even an imagined sight.

The sestet begins by revealing that Seward repeats her incantation each night, usually to no avail. She asks specifically that the form appear smiling. Seward's previous sonnets claimed the healing power of Honora's smile, and here, she begs to see that smile again. "Show her sweet face, ah show it to my soul!" Sadly, the smile can never greet her while waking. The smile that relieves all pain can no longer appear to her while she is awake. It will always be an illusion, a form, an airy shape. We gauge the depth of Seward's grief by her willingness to beg for an apparition, since Honora herself will never reappear. This poem does not seem to be about an erotic wish. We know, from the previous sonnets, that Seward was angry that the husband who might have seen Honora throughout her final illness chose not to do so, while she, who truly cherished her friend, could only wait for

news of her condition. Sonnet 33 continues the themes of absence and of longed-
for presence. In this poem, Honora herself completes the narrative by visiting
Seward, albeit as a ghost. In the previous sonnet, Seward longs to cry "Behold," to
demand Honora's recognition that her husband had been, in a phrase from sonnet 31, "Rashly-Chosen" (l. 7). She ends sonnet 32 in lament, mourning her friend
but also their friendship's lack of closure. Now, Honora has appeared with her
familiar healing gesture, the sweet smile that habitually "stole / . . . the sting from
every pain." Although an illusion, the dream Honora has administered the balm
enabling Seward's gradual recovery from Honora's death. By "seeing" Honora,
even in dreams, Seward achieves some peace after the tumultuous period of her
friend's death.

Sonnet 34 provides a denouement to Seward's version of Honora's demise.
Dated June 1780, it meditates on the pain of mourning and the rarity of true sympathy. "When Death, or adverse Fortune's ruthless gale, / Tears our best hopes
away, the wounded Heart / Exhausted, leans on all that can impart / The charm of
Sympathy" (ll. 1–4). We know from the previous poems that Seward considered
Honora's departure a hapless or luckless venture and her death the end of Seward's
"best hopes." Surely her father and Saville, and other confidantes such as Anna
Rogers Stokes and Mary Powys to whom she often wrote about Honora, must have
offered sincere condolences. They and many Lichfield residents knew Seward's
devotion to Honora and her devastation when Honora died. They would have
commiserated with her anguish. This poem, however, suggests that most sympathy is feigned. Perhaps Seward believed few could understand her exquisite misery and so pretended concern they did not really feel. The sonnet declares that
even artificial commiseration is helpful. The wounded heart finds any "mutual
wail / . . . soothing" (ll. 4–5). Pretended sympathy is better than "cold neglect, or
Mirth that Grief profanes" (l. 11). Seward concludes with an image that recalls
some of her loveliest landscape poetry: "Thus each faint Glow-worm of the Night
conspires, / Gleaming along the moss'd and darken'd lanes, / To cheer the Gloom
with her unreal fires" (ll. 12–14). Glowworms are not stars, but they provide a bit
of light for the foot passenger at night. Feigned sympathy likewise provides some
relief for the mourner otherwise enveloped in grief. Sonnet 34 confesses that
Seward has taken a step toward composure, that she has made a gesture toward
reclaiming herself from the depths of woe. Seward's personality emerges, for example, from the throes of self-pity, pain, anger, and other emotions informing her
previous four sonnets. Her acerbic nature reasserts itself; she is aware that most
acquaintances offer the pretense of a "mutual wail." Most revealing, however, is
the renewed musicality of the sonnet. Sonnets 31, 32, and 33 contain powerful

imagery and suggestive rhymes, but they are not dominated by musical patterns of assonance and consonance like so many of Seward's other sonnets. Here she seems again to take pleasure in orchestrating her verse. The long "a" sound is repeated not only in end rhymes but in "vain," "feign'd," "penetrate," and "sable" within the octet. Other phrases repeat vowel sounds, as in "mutual . . . soothing," "bleeding grief," and "Night conspires." This sonnet shares with others the characteristics of a performance piece. Although Seward may well have read her sonnets about Honora's death to a select audience, it is easier to imagine her reading, somewhat archly, this sly tribute to hypocritical condolers. In that sense, as well as in the poem's confession that sympathy is welcome and effective, sonnet 34 concludes the traumatic drama of Seward's Honora sonnets.

Several other sonnets, however, illuminate these poems, although placed elsewhere in the collection. Sonnet 44 (*Original Sonnets* 46) is apparently a companion to sonnet 33; Seward either wrote the pair soon after Honora's death or later reworked the theme as an exercise in incremental repetition. In sonnet 44, however, she invokes not the spirit of dreams but of "Rapt Contemplation." The sonnet is set not at night but in an "umbrageous vale" at noon, where breezes, shadows, flowers, and streams invite reverie. Like the dream spirit, however, Contemplation has the power of illusion:

> Give thou HONORA's image, when her beams,   .
>   Youth, beauty, kindness, shone, — what time she wore
>   That smile of gentle, yet resistless power
>   To sooth each painful Passion's wild extremes.
> Here shall no empty, vain Intruder chase,
>   With idle converse, thy enchantment warm.   (ll. 5–10)

Seward often suggests that Honora's function in life was to "sooth" her "painful Passions." Honora's gentleness was the antidote to Seward's fiery sensibility. (We hear as often of Honora's eyes brimming with sentimental tears, but her sensibility seems to have been of a complementary nature.) Honora seems to have had the power to calm Seward, smiling in a way that put experiences into perspective or rescued the poet from ill humor. Seward longs here, as in sonnet 33, for a glimpse of that restorative smile. We sense her impatience with those who offered a "mutual wail" in "idle converse," her longing to be alone in a shadowy spot that conceals her from society while prompting daydreams. Seward admits that, like the dream, Contemplation offers only a "persuasive, visionary Form," an empty shape, but as she concludes in the sonnet 33, with its plea for the simulacrum of "*waking*" experience, the vision is more precious than any that "real Life" can

provide (l. 13). Contemplation is now preferable to activity. Like Narcissus bending over the pool of the "bending flower" "trembl[ing] o'er the shadow'd streams"
(ll. 3–4), Seward longs to spend her time beholding illusory images. Seward's
confession of her feelings resembles Earl R. Wasserman's description of Percy
Shelley's adult skepticism: "When the inconstant world can no longer be a source
of hope, the solitary mind is driven to project itself as its own narcissistic object
. . . a 'ghastly presence' ever hovering 'Beside thee like thy shadow'" (9). Honora
has become, to some extent, Seward's "elusive Other Self that walks beside one
through life" (Wasserman 9) or at least the link in Seward's mind with her youthful self before adult vicissitudes of all kinds ruptured her happiness. Like Shelley,
however, Seward did not permit herself to languish indefinitely in narcissistic
self-pity.

Sonnet 44 links with sonnet 33 to portray Seward sleeping and waking in hope
of a healing vision. The sonnets illuminate her later revelation to Mary Powys that
she kept Romney's fictional portrait, *Serena Reading* (an illustration of Hayley's
The Triumphs of Temper) in her bedroom. The print, which she considered an
accurate image of Honora at sixteen—the height of their "Edenic" years—was
so placed "that it may be the last object I behold ere I sleep." She even took the
picture along for the same purpose when she traveled (*Letters* 3:173). Surely
Seward believed that gazing on Honora's image would induce the dream vision
she craved, convey the soothing effect of Honora's smiling gaze. Sonnet 58 (*Original Sonnets* 60) addresses another dimension of recollection. Seward describes
the appurtenances of mourning: the "slow Hearse," "Parian Statue," and "pomp
of sorrow" (ll. 1–2, 5). She declares all the fashionable parade of the funeral industry inadequate (ll. 5–8). We must remember the departed throughout our lives:

> —if, thro' each day,
> [Memory] with whate'er we see, hear, think, or say,
> Blend not the image of the vanish'd Frame,
> O! can the alien Heart expect to prove,
> In worlds of light and life, a reunited love?   (ll. 10–14)

Seward argues the rationale for what might seem to us a morbidly tenacious grip
on Honora's memory. An Anglican, firmly convinced that deceased family and
friends rejoined one another in an afterlife, she wonders whether those who forget
"the FOR EVER ABSENT" (l. 7) will be welcomed at their reunion. By continual
meditation on deceased loved ones (as, for example, in sonnet 81, "On a Lock of
Miss Sarah Seward's Hair, Who Died in Her Twentieth Year"), Seward thought
she was preparing a joyful reception for herself by Honora and her family after

death. The belief expressed in this sonnet helps to explain what would otherwise appear a fetishistic devotion to the Romney portrait, a copy of which she sent her friends the Llangollen ladies, who "enshrined" it in their parlor (which delighted her). Like Sarah's hair, the *Serena* print became a relic that Seward meditated on to refresh her memories so that after death, she would not feel estranged.

Sonnet 77 (*Original Sonnets* 79) provides a coda to the Honora sonnets. Like sonnet 58, it is a pious reflection. But where sonnet 58 urged continual mourning as her duty to the dead, with memory as a shrine, sonnet 77 seeks alternatives to constant recollection. Like sonnets by Smith or the later Romantics, Seward finds in the landscape an image of her state of mind. Less Romantic is her hope of finding relief from her distress in learning and religion:

> O! hast thou seen a vernal Morning bright
>> Gem every bank and trembling leaf with dews,
>> Tinging the green fields with her amber hues,
>> Changing the leaden streams to lines of light?
> Then seen dull Clouds, that shed untimely night,
>> Roll envious on, and every ray suffuse,
>> Till the chill'd Scenes their early beauty lose,
>> And faint, and colourless, no more invite
> The glistening gaze of Joy? — 'Twas emblem just
>> Of my youth's sun, on which deep shadows fell,
>> Spread from the PALL OF FRIENDS; and Grief's loud gust
> Resistless, oft wou'd wasted tears compel:
>> Yet let me hope, that on my darken'd days
>> Science, and pious Trust, may shed pervading rays.

Seward compares her youth to her favorite landscape, the lovely view she often described with its bedewed fields and gilded streams. Light, so often invoked as the source of transformative beauty in her sonnets, here evokes a "glistening gaze of Joy." The brimming tears of sensibility, moved by natural beauty, gleam like the gemmed banks, trembling leaves, and glittering streams. Youth seems blended with this magical place. When "dull Clouds" obscure the sun, they drain the scene of light and color. "Untimely night" robs the landscape of its beauty, so that sensibility's eye can no longer respond, just as Seward's youth was cut short by untimely deaths. Her central phrase, the "PALL OF FRIENDS," refers not merely to their draped coffins but to the "deep shadows" cast over her life by early losses. We might also include Saville's melancholy, the effect of his failed marriage, but this must remain a metaphorically buried inference.

For all its gloom, sonnet 77 is artfully composed. Her Miltonic structure here gives way to a more Shakespearian arrangement, as the octet is divided into two quatrains contrasting sunny and clouded landscapes. A third quatrain explains her metaphor, before a rare couplet that appears to turn, in a fashion Seward usually deplored, from the inevitable conclusion to be drawn from the landscape image toward alternative consolations. Seward prepares for the reversal by admitting that her frequent "gusts" of grief are useless. But the poem's dominant metaphor has identified Seward with the landscape, blending tears of joy with beams of light and tears of sorrow with gusts of wind. The couplet conclusion seems to extract Seward from the natural world, replacing it with intellectual and spiritual resources that might "shed pervading rays" through the gloom of identification with a blighted landscape. The natural sun may be supplemented with a metaphorical sun, the light of religion offering recourse from endless mourning. As Seward's final Honora sonnet, sonnet 77 turns rather dramatically, perhaps desperately, from repeated immersion in the natural world, and particularly in the Stowe Valley landscape, toward other sources of comfort and healing that the devout Seward would have endorsed. Here we feel her kinship not with Smith, who turned toward heaven but only in hope of relief after death, nor with the Shelley of "Adonais," but with the mature Wordsworth, who turned to Anglicanism as the surest protection against "individual or collective fanaticisms" (Hartman 334). This sonnet's abrupt and pious conclusion need not be considered facile. It is the gesture of a woman long used to finding comfort in nature but recognizing, at last, that nature is as likely to perpetuate her grief as to lighten it.

The fifteen sonnets I have assembled tell the story of Seward and Honora's friendship, its loss, and Seward's ensuing struggle for composure. Seward evidently thought her contemporaries would understand both the story and the special nature of her attachment to Honora. Today, it is difficult for us to imagine a powerful affection, amounting at times to obsession, without an erotic component. In centuries when privileged people lived to a great extent sequestered by gender, the continuum spanning varieties of same-sex friendship must have been much broader. We now find poetic sequences devoted to earlier same-sex friendships puzzling, whether Shakespeare's sonnets to the Earl of Southampton or Tennyson's In Memoriam about Arthur Hallam. Both those sequences have been studied for clues to the writers' sexual orientation. It is unlikely we will ever know for certain. But I have offered here a reading that makes sense to me and makes sense of the sonnets and that I believe would have been comprehensible to Seward's early readers. Seward's correspondence and her other elegiac poems confirm the autobiographical dimension of the sonnets, but she changed the date of Honora's break with her to give it a dramatic crisis, Honora's marriage. We can also see that Seward turned her fluctuating moods into variations on the theme of lost friendship. She invented her timeline and omitted episodes such as André's courtship that would have diluted her emphasis. She achieved enough distance to construct poems that, when read together, narrate a story, whose plot begins with the crisis of Honora's betrayal and then moves on to the climax of her death, which is followed by the poet's mourning and, finally, her turn to religion. Seward habitually boasted her capacity for feeling, and she mythologized her attachment to Honora as if the latter had been the ne plus ultra of young womanhood. But perhaps because of her capacity for self-aggrandizement, she recognized that her broken friendship was the stuff of sonnets, material apt for shaping into the sonnet form's traditional celebration of beloved, yet unattainable, figures. Eschewing, as she believed Milton had done, the "mistaken idea, that sonnets should be either amorous or gay" (*Letters* 2:306), she chose a doomed friendship for her recurring theme. She scattered the poems throughout her volume as if to obscure the coherent narrative I have detected, most likely to emphasize their sincerity as responses to particular instances rather than their artifice as links in a cycle or chain.

Transmuting Honora's rejection of Seward and her death into occasional sonnets provided an additional form of comfort for Seward. As we have seen, she seems to have struggled throughout her adulthood to wrest some control over her life and career. The Honora sonnets likewise fulfilled Seward's need to control or even transform her circumstances. Honora's persistent attachment to Edgeworth was apparently both surprising and ultimately humiliating. Seward's carefully nurtured "child" rejected her. We will never know the substance of their disagreement. Honora's point of view was never recorded. Did Seward hint too broadly at Edgeworth's "baseness," provoking Honora's defiance of the older woman's presumption? In the sonnets, Honora is first a traitor but then becomes a victim of her poor judgment and Edgeworth's neglect. Seward tailors the story to her specifications. Speaking throughout, she robs Honora of a voice: we never hear Honora speak, except for one reference to her "condolings." We see Honora's eyes and her lips, but her capacity to soothe is always conveyed through tears and smiles. Even when Seward associates a song with Honora, we are never told whether Honora sang the song herself. If Seward derives comfort from dreams of Honora, from her smiling but empty form, the beloved, living Honora she describes was always, to an extent, a form or shape rather than a human being. When the shape finally spoke, she evidently exchanged words with Seward that provoked their complete rupture. By muting Honora, Seward once again controls experience, if only in retrospect. Of course, sonnets are always about the poet's states of mind rather than about those of other individuals who figure in his or her relationships. For this reason, Paul Oppenheimer has called the sonnet "the first lyric of self-consciousness, or of the self in conflict" (3). The "Dark Lady" never defends herself to Shakespeare, Stella never explains her position to Astrophel, and Honora will never present her case for trusting Edgeworth, if that indeed caused the dispute. Seward chose the perfect vehicle for her poems exploring ruptured friendship. "Lost Honora" became the subject of a number of poems scattered throughout her volume of *Occasional Sonnets*. Assembled, they enrich our knowledge of Seward's emotional life and of the varieties of eighteenth-century friendship. They also demonstrate Seward's mastery of her cherished Miltonic sonnet form. Written in response to, and imaginatively dramatizing, various episodes of her friendship's decline, they testify to the power of the occasional sonnet.

CHAPTER ELEVEN

Memoirs of the Life of Dr. Darwin

Digging in The Botanical Garden

In my introduction, we glimpsed Seward in a characteristic posture in her auto-biographical "Lichfield, an Elegy." Traveling past Honora Sneyd's burial place to her present home and by implication into the future when she will write this poem, Seward nevertheless strains her eyes looking back to catch a last glimpse of her beloved's grave (1. 138). The image captures Seward's state of mind as she described it in many of her later poems and letters: attentive to daily events and ongoing cultural currents but yearning for the emotional attachments of her youth. The image also represents Seward's position as a writer. While alert to and often welcoming poetic trends such as interest in the sublime, in the gothic, in regional dialects, and in neglected forms like the sonnet, Seward remained attached to the prosodic and critical standards of her youth. Growing up in the middle of the century, she retained her belief in principles established and re-fined by poets like Milton, Pope, and Thomson. She welcomed the midcentury impulse to establish a British canon, participating in the debate over Dryden's or Pope's superior ranking and extolling the verse of contemporaries such as William Hayley. Her poetry exemplifies the sensibility inculcated in her youth to a degree deemed artificial or mannered soon after her death but prized throughout most of her lifetime. Seward's Janus-like pose in "Lichfield, an Elegy" thus embodies her position among late-century British poets. To a striking degree, Seward epitomizes eighteenth-century poetics at the moment when verse turned to Romanticism. Her writings, I hope to have shown, offer valuable perspectives on the new movement's organic development from previous traditions.

Her criticism reflects the strong belief she inherited in the importance of harmonious sound to verse destined for public performance. She boasted her study of British poets' techniques, which emphasizes how a poet might create sound effects for rhetorical purposes without distorting English usage. Such practice was common to early eighteenth-century poets like Pope but less adhered to by midcentury prosodists who, according to Paul Fussell, willingly sacrificed normal diction and pronunciation in order to achieve metrical regularity.[1] Seward's formal, polished, but "natural" versification resembled the acting style of her dramatic idol Sarah Siddons, although in Seward's case her preference was not prompted by a novel turn away from prevailing conventions so much as by adherence to an earlier style than that currently in vogue among poets.[2] Another belief following from the declamatory purpose of verse was the poet's role in public intellectual discourse. As we have observed, many eighteenth-century poets remained convinced of their important function in leading national patriotic discourse.[3] Seward intervened in public discussions following James Boswell's publication of *The Life of Samuel Johnson* and after Erasmus Darwin's death. In both cases, her assessments insisted on yet another set of "old-fashioned" models, the "beauties and faults" method of literary criticism and an approach that emphasized the moral function of literary and biographical studies. In an historic period obsessed with canonizing British literary worthies, Seward's practices could be construed by antagonists as mean spirited rather than balanced or principled. But while her practices often hark back to those of her early models and mentors, Seward also exemplifies the sensibility characteristic of her youth, in its senses both of swift responses to perceptual stimuli and of sympathy with the distressed.[4] When she rails against Johnson's cruelty to living poets, she is holding him to a standard of compassion embraced by her and Boswell's generation but not necessarily by Johnson's. Seward's admiration of sensibility sometimes appears at odds with her devotion to early-century critical values, but the combination marks her, like some of her admired contemporaries such as William Hayley, as the inheritor of a century's traditions and practices.

Seward's assumption of her role as British muse, even in literary-critical matters, invited conflict, particularly with some dismissive male writers. As Susan Staves observes in her *A Literary History of Women's Writing in Britain*, late eighteenth-century women writers found criticism an important vehicle for establishing their role in public intellectual discourse.[5] Staves takes as a model for her study some women critics' examinations of writings by other women, who took those publications seriously by describing "faults of substance or style they discerned" as well as commending their strengths (Staves 438). When Seward approached the writings of Johnson, Boswell, and, later, Darwin in the same spirit, however, she was publicly chastised for her presumption. Seward's attempts to revise literary history as written by these imposing male figures closes my study, because they confirm both Seward's eighteenth-century poetic and critical principles and make clear the obstacles placed in her way by gender constrictions, particularly as they were imposed by the end of the century. If Staves criticizes Seward for colluding, in *Louisa*, in the decadent sentimentalism of the 1780s (400) — an assessment with which I respectfully disagree — she would have to admire Seward's boldness in exerting her influence to correct Boswell's Johnsonian portrait. Yet no critic has offered a reading of Seward's criticism that accounts for her negative conclusions in other than personal terms. Seward, it seems, can only be exonerated for her temerity by the critic claiming that she was snobbish, jealous, or naïve.

The implication permeating older commentary on Seward's criticism is that her argumentative persona was unpleasant and therefore easily dismissed. I therefore end by considering other ways of construing Seward's critical publications: as efforts to practice on Darwin, Johnson, and Boswell the critical methods all four writers held in common, as exercises of her cultural influence, and as attempts to escape the dominion, real and imagined, of these powerful father and brother figures over her imagination and career. Seward manifestly failed in her efforts to modify future estimates of either Darwin (whose *Botanic Garden* has not proved immortal) or Johnson (whose character has not been deemed cruel). But many reactions to her criticism were in fact sexist. Neither a London bluestocking nor a "hyena in petticoats," Seward was nevertheless a woman in quest of authority. Now that studies by Anne K. Mellor, David Simpson, Markman Ellis, Mary A. Waters, and others have reexamined women's participation in late eighteenth-century literary criticism, we can appreciate Seward's contributions to their growing influence.[6] Like Simpson, who proposes that Mary Wollstonecraft's "unstable" style in the *Vindication of the Rights of Woman* resulted not, as has been assumed, from incompetence but from her effort to reach an audience likely "to respond to the appeals of an unstable style" (109), I argue that Seward's apparent vendettas against Darwin and Johnson did not emanate from insufficient self-control but from her wish to defend herself and other late eighteenth-century poets threatened by their assertions.

—◦᠎◦—

Among many examples of Seward's eighteenth-century poetic principles, one suffices to illustrate why her practice was praised by contemporaries but seemed old-fashioned by the time her collected poems were published. A recent study by Elspeth Jajdelska examines the evolution of reading in Britain at the turn of the seventeenth into the eighteenth century. Jajdelska traces the gradual change from spoken to silent reading, indicated partly by changes in printers' punctuation conventions. Texts meant to be spoken by readers tended to have heavier punctuation, indicating emphases and pauses, because they would presumably be acted out, to a degree, by a skillful reader (14). Jajdelska deduces a gradual shift away from such punctuation in printed texts by the mid-eighteenth century. Although Jajdelska's study is about prose, it supports my argument that Seward was a typical eighteenth-century writer, chiefly influenced by the poetry most valued in her youth. The musicality of Seward's verse was more characteristic of Milton's and early eighteenth-century poetry, such as Pope's, than of, for example, Smith's. Milton's verse famously bends English syntax to achieve the declamatory emphasis of Latin rhetoric. Pope, especially in his youth, believed that sound should echo sense and was rewarded by his enemies with epithets such as "tuneful Alexis" (Hill, l. 1). Seward labored to create mellifluous sound patterns in her verse, as we have observed throughout this study. When she delivered her poetic precepts to a Miss Cayley, she was chiefly concerned with the effects created by various combinations of English sounds, urging her young admirer to adopt some and avoid others.[7] Seward was preoccupied with the sound of her verse because she assumed poetry would be read aloud. She often read her own poetry and that of others aloud in drawing rooms, recording proudly her reputation as a dramatic performer.[8] But although novels and poems continued to be read aloud into the next century—in Jane Austen's *Sense and Sensibility* (1811), Marianne deplores Edward Ferrars's "spiritless" and "tame" declamation of Cowper (11)—silent reading was becoming standard. Charlotte Smith's sonnet speakers, musing in solitude about their loneliness and unshared grief, clearly resonated with readers beginning to practice private reading more often than the sociable, vocal reading for which Seward intended her "tuneful" compositions. Seward's techniques survived in poets such as John Keats, whose beautiful orchestration of sound in such poems as "Ode to Autumn" descend directly from prosody like hers. For his devotion to mellifluous effects, as Susan J. Wolfson has observed, Keats was accused of "effeminacy" of style, among the other charges leveled at him and his poetry by reviewers of the 1820s perturbed, among other things, by his manifest sensibility and aestheticism.[9]

Seward not only espoused earlier eighteenth-century poetic principles; she expounded on and promoted them. Many of her discourses must have been conversational, and many were included in letters such as her exchanges with Hayley and George Hardinge and her advice to Miss Cayley. But she also contributed criticism to the *Gentleman's Magazine* and published the first biography of Erasmus Darwin. Susan Staves has argued for the importance of women's emergence, in the second half of the century, as historians, translators, and literary critics (Staves 286–361). By publishing such writings, women established their intellectual prowess and claimed their right to help shape their culture. Staves observes the significance of Elizabeth Montagu's *Essay on the Writings and Genius of Shakespeare* (1769), a riposte to Voltaire's dismissal of the English bard (304–9). Montagu established herself not only as a capable defender of Britain's chief writer but also as a patriot rebutting the French insult to her nation's culture. Staves's discussion of bluestockings such as Montagu and Carter suggests their importance as a model to Seward. Twenty-two and twenty-five years her senior, respectively, Montagu and Carter published their chief works during Seward's teens and twenties, setting patterns for future women's participation in public intellectual discourse. In her chronological history, Staves groups the bluestockings together with sentimental novelists as the chief literary figures between 1756 and 1776, and certainly both influenced Seward's intellectual development. We have seen evidence of her sentimentalism throughout her poetry. To complete this study, however, attention is due to the critical writings in which Seward publicly argued her views about poetry and demanded her right to influence reception of important figures and publications. In her published criticism, as in her other writings, Seward upheld the poetic values and sensibility of her youth while attempting to carve a space for herself as authoritative female critic in a literary world that despite the triumphs of Montagu, Carter, Catharine Macaulay, Hester Chapone, and Hannah More, and the publications of many others still resisted acknowledging women's cultural authority and at times even attempted to efface their contributions.[10]

Seward recognized the importance of establishing herself as a critical authority as well as a poet. As I argued regarding her career choices in my second chapter, the fact that a great deal of vigorous criticism remained unpublished in her letters until after her death indicates not Seward's shyness but her choice to confine her readership in many instances to family and friends. Seward occasionally intervened in literary-critical debates, such as those over the relative superiority of Samuel Richardson or Henry Fielding, through periodical publications.[11] Neither was she apparently averse, at least in principle, to engaging in "professional criticism" in the sense of taking on regular assignments for pay. When in 1788, Thomas Christie invited her to become a regular contributor to the *Analytic Review*, Seward demurred, citing "feminine employments," which might to a hasty reader suggest her refusal to enter into a paid engagement. Her explanation to Christie, however, was that "feminine employments," such as a large household and myriad social obligations, had left her time to master only a small number of fields: English literature, music, painting, and moral philosophy (*Letters* 2: 4–6). Her excuse, then, was that "a stock of knowledge so limited" disqualified her from participating in Christie's plan for a wide-ranging "view of the present state of the polite arts" (*Letters* 2: 7). To her epistolary acquaintances, however, Seward had no compunction about sharing her opinions even on topics outside her boasted areas of expertise. As we have observed throughout this study, Seward imparted her views of events and figures political as well as literary in letters that sometimes seem like miniature essays rather than informal correspondence. It is quite understandable why she confined her reflections on Pitt and the wars against France in the 1790s to this sympathetic readership. But her literary discourses and debates reflect what Staves describes as the use of the familiar letter throughout the century to create networks of supportive, even if challenging, intellectual friendships (*Literary History* 23). Of course, Seward edited her letters, refining them for posthumous publication. The original letters, if less polished, were probably intended in many instances to be enjoyed and discussed not only by the intended recipient but by select friends of the sociable Hayleys, Whalleys, Llangollen ladies, and others. Seward thus established herself through her epistolary network as a literary authority in a medium understood by contemporaries to be among the alternatives to print publication.[12]

Another critical mode that Seward attempted late in her life was biography. Asked by Erasmus Darwin's son for anecdotes toward a biography, Seward responded by publishing a lengthy series of what Mrs. Thrale-Piozzi might have called "Observations and Reflections" on her early Lichfield mentor, who had subsequently moved to Derby and died in 1802. Appearing five years before her death, Seward's rather hastily composed *Memoirs of the Life of Dr. Darwin* (1804) contains personal memories, anecdotes communicated by mutual acquaintances, and criticism of his published treatises and poems. Ashmun agrees with the *Edinburgh Review* in damning Seward's valuable if unreliable record, the first published biography of Darwin (236–37). Today, it is easier to accept that Seward was, as she avows, emulating Hester Thrale-Piozzi's and James Boswell's biographical writings about Samuel Johnson by shaping her memoirs around striking anecdotes such as his cure of the Countess of Northesk (77–82) and the suicide of his eldest son (296–98). Her discussion of Darwin's great poem, *The Botanic Garden*, became an opportunity for detailed criticism of a work admired by many contemporaries, a lengthy analysis both appreciative and, where she deemed appropriate, corrective. Through her criticism, she attempted to achieve what she thought Boswell had neglected to perform in his biography of Johnson, an honest assessment of her subject's brilliant but flawed tour-de-force, composed in a genre in which she felt secure of her mastery. Those expecting pure biographical narrative were no doubt puzzled by the digression, but Seward may have been motivated by the opportunity to associate her critical acumen with a celebrated work deserving exhaustive assessment.

Indeed, Seward's analysis of *The Botanic Garden* occupies two chapters and 141 of the 313 pages of the *Memoirs*, nearly half the entire volume. (Since another chapter, 48 pages long, describes the eccentricities of Thomas Day, Seward's anecdotes and criticisms outweigh her memoirs.) One suspects that Seward stretched her rather meager biographical information as a pretense for publishing this "beauties and faults" study based on eighteenth-century principles such as the importance of harmonious sound and technical polish. Seward narrates the cantos of the poem, Darwin's epic account of creation and of the perpetuation of plant life in a series of fanciful images that blends ancient myth with modern science, particularly botany. Seward compares the poem favorably with Milton's *Paradise Lost* and Pope's *Iliad* while praising Darwin's ingenious accounts of such modern inventions as the steam engine, electrical power, submarines, and hot air balloons. She notes many contemporary figures whom Darwin cites, luminaries such as James Cook, James Watt, Matthew Boulton, Josiah Wedgwood, Benjamin Franklin, Joseph Priestly, and Joseph Wright of Derby. But she also makes lengthy comparisons with Shakespeare and living poets like Hayley, Robert Southey, James Beattie, and Francis Mundy, illustrating her criticism with multiple passages and even whole poems by favorite writers. Seward seems to be associating these poets with the scientific masters Darwin celebrates in the notes to his verse. Much as Darwin lauds all modern scientists but chiefly the British, Seward honors contemporary British poets as their counterparts in cultural importance. But she does not praise only poets and only men; she instances Samuel Richardson's *Clarissa* and *Sir Charles Grandison* as "novels no longer, but English classics" known in translation throughout the world (178). Lady Mary Wortley Montagu is praised for her "patriotic" introduction of the smallpox vaccine (43). Seward corrects Darwin's description of Mary Delany's paper flowers, devoting three pages to a description of Delany's life and techniques (229–31). Seward thus adds to Darwin's encomia an additional roster of British cultural worthies, a gesture typical of her generation's patriotism but extrinsic, in its lavishness, to the strict purposes of literary criticism.

Seward's analysis is chiefly admiring; she narrates each canto and comments, as if for those who have not read the poem or those who will appreciate "touring" the poem with a judicious commentator. Her infrequent criticisms are expressed

authoritatively even when they correct a single phrase. For example, of one passage she comments, "Alliteration is an edge tool in the poet's hand, improving or
injuring his verse, as it is judiciously or injudiciously used" (224). She then includes a three-page discourse on alliteration citing Milton, Pope, and Beattie,
concluding that "this digression . . . will not be thought irrelevant to the peculiar
theme of these pages, when it is considered that, for the presumption of censur-
ing, even in one instance, the eminently harmonious numbers of the Botanic
Garden, it was requisite to justify each censure" (227). Seward's discussion confirms her authority as a prosodic expert capable of discerning Darwin's occasional
blunders, the feminine descendent of Pope's critic who can censure freely because she has written well. "That a poetic simile should not be precise in its resemblance is certain, at least that it is more sublime, or more beautiful, for not
quadrating exactly; yet it ought to possess such a degree of affinity with the subject, that when the theme and its illustration are viewed together, we may feel,
though we cannot verbally demonstrate, the perfect justice of the similitude"
(239), she remarks in another place, claiming for metaphor an intuitive aptness
that cannot be scientifically proven ("verbally demonstrated") but that nevertheless exists. Seward thus insinuates that her personal critical acumen is comparable
to Darwin's prowess as scientist; she can discern unerringly the appropriateness
or inaptitude of a simile much as he can use scientific apparatus to diagnose an
illness or invent a new carriage.

Seward's attention to Darwin's techniques is intrinsic to her old-fashioned
"beauties and faults" critical method. She excuses her presumption in citing the
weaknesses as well as strengths of *The Botanic Garden*:

> Human ability never did, and probably never will, produce an absolutely per-
> fect composition. The author of this memoir has, from infancy, sedulously stud-
> ied and compared the writing of the distinguished Bards of her nation, together
> with the best translations of those of Greece, Rome, and modern Italy. She has
> presumed to descant upon what appeared to her the graces and defects of the
> Botanic Garden; induced by a conviction that the unbiased mixture of candid
> objection with due praise, better serves the interest of every science than un-
> qualified encomium upon its professors. (277)

Seward claims an expertise in her "science" based on lifelong study of poetry
in English. Darwin's epic is flawed, but after all, "no eminent Poet has so many
passages which are every way exceptionable, as . . . our great, our glorious Shakespeare" (279). The purpose of criticism is to weigh the strengths and weaknesses
of a literary text, and, "if, after a just balance of beauty and defect, the first out-

weighs the latter in immense degree, then attention, love, and applause is due to that work as a whole" (278). Having metaphorically weighed, as in a laboratory, the fable, characters, and techniques of *The Botanic Garden*, Seward concludes that the poem is destined for lasting fame. In concluding her analysis with Shakespeare's great and glorious name, Seward returns to an earlier passage favorably comparing Darwin's to Shakespeare's imaginative power: "The lavish magnificence of imagery in this work, genius alone, bold, original, creative, and fertile in the extreme, could have produced" (151). For Seward, Darwin's imaginative genius outweighs any incidental failures. While she observes scattered technical lapses (for example, "Personification is surely carried too far when . . . azotic gas is made the lover of virgin air" [156]), Seward considers Darwin a worthy successor not only to Shakespeare but to Milton and Pope, a triumvirate she venerated throughout her life.[13]

By placing herself in the role of Darwin's critic, Seward turned the tables on her first poetic mentor. Her lengthy technical digressions and occasional corrections of fact seem designed partly to prove that the pupil had now outstripped her master both in technical skill and sometimes even in knowledge, as in her description of Mrs. Delany's paper flowers. In one instance, Seward chastises Darwin for using, with no acknowledgment, forty-six lines written by herself for his exordium (258). While expressing near-worshipful admiration of *The Botanic Garden*, Seward manages to suggest her poetic superiority, in some respects, to the man who encouraged her verse writing at thirteen but later claimed her lines for his own and had earlier been credited by some with rewriting Seward's original draft of *Elegy on Captain Cook* (Ashmun 74–75). Teresa Barnard believes that Darwin probably collaborated in the Cook elegy when it originated as a manuscript exercise (*Anna Seward*, 118). Seward, as the chief writer, had later taken full credit for the poem, as was customary in such circles. After her initial, successful publications, Seward established herself as an independent poet (*Anna Seward*, 118). As Darwin's protégée, Seward, however, was ideally qualified to assess his work. Darwin evidently instilled in Seward her admiration of Pope and urged her study of his style. Her eventual mastery of Pope's craft thus became not only her source of authority but the critical "edge tool" with which she dissected Darwin's couplets. Unfortunately, both Darwin's and Seward's adherence to the technical virtuosity that dominated poetry of the early century, such as attention to sound effects, would shortly doom both to oblivion, or at least to excision from studies of both eighteenth-century and Romantic-era verse. In his reprint edition of *The Botanic Garden* — included in a Garland series of significant minor poetry between 1789 and 1830 — Donald H. Reiman quotes Leigh Hunt's explanation for why he was dismissed: Darwin "was of the school of Pope," and by developing Pope's "monotonous and cloying versification" to an extreme, he "gave the public at large a suspicion that there was something wrong in its nature" (1:xiii). Far from an immortal masterpiece, *The Botanic Garden* seemed to Hunt in 1815 a decadent exercise in the outmoded couplet form. Reiman concludes that although all of the early Romantic poets were surely influenced by aspects of Darwin's work (Blake, after all, engraved plates for the first edition), most considered his style a negative example (1:xii–xiii). Since Seward focused her critical discourse precisely on Darwin's style, the Popeian style she too had worked to analyze and refine, her elaborate study of *The Botanic Garden* had as little chance as the epic itself of impressing posterity. Her own poetry would fare no better.

It is important not to overstate Seward's negativism in the *Memoirs*. An earlier study of Darwin's poetry by James Venable Logan devotes several pages to the possibility that Seward may have written critically of Darwin because at one time she loved him but had been jilted (5–9). Logan weighs whether such an episode accounts for the "alleged malice in the *Memoirs*" (5) but fails to find support for either the love affair or the allegations, judging her biography "pronouncedly friendly" (6). Logan does, however, assert that Seward had "a good deal of spleen in her nature, as witness her attitudes toward Dr. Johnson and Edgeworth, and in her later years it vented itself on Darwin" (7). We encounter variations on Logan's diagnosis of Seward's "spleen" in observations from the eighteenth century until now, as various critics grapple with her propensity for judgmental evaluation. In *Erasmus Darwin and the Romantic Poets*, Desmond King-Hele describes Seward's biography as "often quite waspish" (15) but deems her review of *The Botanic Garden* "both discerning and magnanimous" (155).[14] King-Hele, however, believes that since Darwin likely wrote or heavily revised portions of Seward's *Elegy on Captain Cook*, he unconsciously borrowed lines of hers as a sort of repayment (153–54). His deduction supports the notion of a competition between the younger poet and her mentor; he considers their "literary relationship . . . incestuous" and assumes that each influenced the other (154). King-Hele's hint of a kind of family relationship, in which Seward began as a poet firmly under the tutelage of her poetic "father" but later wished to distance herself, while Darwin remained understandably oblivious to her rebellion, rings true. We have noted Teresa Barnard's discussion of the origins of the Cook elegy in a manuscript circle (*Anna Seward* 118), a practice that, as we also have observed, later Romantic-era poets disclaimed after they rose to prominence, according to Michelle Levy. Seward's transition from collaborative to individual poet was thus not untypical — or rather, it would soon resemble the career path of Coleridge, Wordsworth, Shelley, and other poets who worked to obscure the collaborative bases of their early publications. In each case, the writer's path to acknowledgment as "an original genius" was fraught with complexity owing to relationships with early collaborators (Levy 9). King-Hele's suggestion thus seems quite plausible and represents an advance over Logan's, which seeks an explanation in Seward's emotions and settles, if not on the resentment of a woman scorned, on the peevish "spleen" of an aging spinster. King-Hele acknowledges that Darwin wrote some of the lines in Seward's first, spectacularly successful, published poem but concedes her anger over his later plagiarism was justified. He considers Seward's criticism as that of a practicing poet, albeit a poet with an axe to grind.

Seward's critical remarks, dismissed as padding by Ashmun (236), in fact follow Samuel Johnson's precedent, in his *Lives of the Poets*, of including criticism within biography. Seward's analysis also suggests a good deal about her relationship with her first mentor. Much as she diverts veiled anger against her father into her portrait of Eugenio's well-meaning but destructive father in *Louisa*, so in the *Memoirs* she subtly avenges Darwin's professional slights by exposing his theft of her forty-six lines of verse not once but twice (94–96, 258) and criticizing his various poems incorporated into her narrative. She, moreover, chastises the impiety of his proposition, in the *Zoonomia* (1794), that animals have a share of reason rather than mere brute instinct. Darwin's ideas, of course, later became the groundwork of his grandson Charles's evolutionary theory, but to Seward, the idea that humans and animals were not completely different creations was, if not blasphemous, the result of such devotion to his theory of interrelatedness that he failed to recognize the barrier God had erected between species (61–68). Under the guise of an impartial, on the whole admiring, biographer, Seward insinuated her mentor's poetic and religious failings, suggesting in turn her personal superiority in those areas. In the end, then, Seward's *Memoirs of Dr. Darwin* is as much about herself, or about her relation to Darwin, as it is about the doctor. But Seward presented her biography as a model of indifferent observation, clearly intending a contrast between her "warts and all" portrait and the worshipful narratives Thrale-Piozzi and Boswell had written about Samuel Johnson.

Boswell and especially Johnson lurk throughout the *Memoirs* as Seward's unacknowledged models and adversaries in the art of biography. While the *Memoirs* are about Seward's relationship with Darwin almost more than about Darwin himself, they are also about Seward's relationships with Boswell and Johnson. Seward's need to outdo Boswell at his own, Johnsonian, biographical methods derived from a contretemps in the previous decade. She echoes Boswell's claim, in his *Life of Johnson*, that "had [Johnson's] other friends been as diligent and ardent as

I was, he might have been almost entirely preserved" (1:30). At the conclusion of her preface to the *Memoirs*, Seward remarks that another Darwinian protégé, a Mr. Bilsborrow, is writing the doctor's life, but Darwin left few biographical materials, Bilsborrow only knew him in his Derby years, and she is the only living authority on Darwin's Lichfield years who is willing to share her information about him. Between herself and Bilsborrow, therefore, "all will probably be known that can now with accuracy be traced of Dr. Darwin" (*Memoirs* xii). However, Seward, unlike Boswell, does not include letters and other documents in his biography, remarking that Darwin's letters were not exceptional and that he frowned on publishing inferior work (vi). Neither will she record conversations, "since Dr. Darwin constantly shrunk with reserved pride from all that candour would deem confidential conversation, and which the world is so apt to ridicule as vain egotism" (xi). Since Boswell's *Life* most memorably portrayed Johnson through conversations both public and confidential, Seward seems to imply that her own, much briefer study is in fact superior because she eschews recourse to letters and conversations. Seward, moreover, knew that Boswell had been selective in his anecdotes, refusing to use material he considered particularly unflattering. Her "beauties and faults" approach seems designed to counter his selectivity with her rigorous fairness, "precluding, on one hand, unjust depreciation, and on the other, over-valuing partiality" (xii). Her dependence on personal experience and the testimony of a few trusted witnesses contrasts with Boswell's effort to fill the gaps caused by his late acquaintance and long absences from Johnson. In short, *Memoirs of the Life of Dr. Darwin* represents Seward's last effort to settle scores with Boswell by crafting a biography more honest and fair, if obviously less complete, than his famous *Life*. By applying the critical values she imbibed from Darwin, as his pupil, and from Johnson, as his avid reader, she attempted to surpass Boswell in his own biographical medium.

Johnson is the third, perhaps the most important, professional rival looming over Darwin's biography. Seward first alludes to him in her preface in an ostensibly admiring remark about Thrale-Piozzi's and Boswell's portraits. Had they not portrayed Johnson as a genius flawed by "somber irritability . . . literary jealousy . . . party prejudice . . . [and] bigot zeal," readers would have believed all the invidious assessments in his *Lives of the Poets*. "Then, to the injury of our national taste, and to the literary and moral character of the great English classics, more universal confidence had been placed in the sophistries of those volumes" (ix). The chief accomplishment of Thrale-Piozzi and Boswell, then, is that they inadvertently exposed Johnson as an unreliable arbiter of British literary culture. Johnson himself appears only briefly in the *Memoirs* because he and Darwin felt "mutual and strong dislike" for one another (43). Pausing to consider for several pages Johnson's failure to acknowledge the many literary and learned inhabitants of Lichfield—including her father—Seward concludes that "Johnson liked only worshippers" and was averse to the society of his intellectual equals (53). Johnson overlooked Darwin, for example, because although the latter was "at least his equal in genius, his superior in science," his stammer disqualified him for Johnson's combative and sarcastic conversation (54). "[Too] intellectually great to be an humble listener to Johnson, he shunned him. . . . The surly dictator felt the mortification and revenged it, by affecting to avow his disdain" (54). Seward's observation of the antipathy between two great men, neither of whom would acknowledge the other's eminence, is quite plausible and reflects almost as poorly on Darwin as on Johnson. Yet Seward frames their aversion as entirely Johnson's fault, an example of his "literary jealousy" that she condemned whenever given an opportunity.

Seward's conviction of Johnson's rudeness and unfairness, based on personal experience and printed evidence, emerges early in her correspondence and culminated in a public dispute with Boswell. The exchange took place in a series of letters to the *Gentleman's Magazine* following Boswell's publication of his *Tour of the Hebrides* (1786) and again after the appearance of Johnson's *Life* (1794). In both instances, Seward's intention was to dissuade the public from lionizing a brilliant man whose flawed character rendered his guardianship of the British literary canon, not to mention his stature as a moral and intellectual exemplar, questionable. Seward's quest to dethrone Johnson has been considered at best naïve and at worst malicious but always puzzling. Ashmun cites Walter Scott's conviction that snobbery inspired Seward's contempt, although she admits that there were plenty of witnesses who corroborated Johnson's rudeness and disdain for other writers (117, 121–23). Seward's mystifying preoccupation (Ashmun describes it as "almost . . . an obsession" [123]) demands explanation and appropriately concludes this study. Johnson was another, perhaps the most significant, in the series of Seward's literary "fathers"; she shared more opinions with Johnson than otherwise, and her chief objections were not based on snobbery or ignorance but on justifiable principles.

CHAPTER TWELVE

Anna Seward, Samuel Johnson, and the End of the Eighteenth Century

The most surprising aspect of Seward's antipathy toward Samuel Johnson is that she shared a great many of his assumptions. Seward was twenty when, in 1762, the fifty-three year-old Johnson received a pension for his renowned *Dictionary*. More than a generation younger than Johnson, she devoured all of his writings and incorporated many of his literary judgments into her own theories. They also shared some personality traits. Both, for example, indulged in forms of "talking for victory," Boswell's term for Johnson's combative style. Many of Seward's letters exhibit a Johnsonian persistence in debating topics, especially literary topics, until her correspondents admitted the justice of her opinions. Likewise, her published criticism often appeared as debates: Gretchen Foster has edited her exchanges with Joseph Weston, in the *Gentleman's Magazine*, regarding the relative merits of Dryden and Pope. Besides attacking Boswell's writings, she also exchanged letters with Thomas Jerningham in the *Gentleman's Magazine* (1801) debating pulpit oratory. From the debates with Weston and Jerningham, it is clear that Seward enjoyed such epistolary contests, although by her own account she did not enjoy conversational wrangling. In their different ways, however, Johnson and Seward excelled in rhetoric designed to convince others of, and even to insist on, the justice of their opinions.

Both Johnson and Seward admired Augustan poetic standards such as respect for traditional rules of composition, a belief in the idea that artists had a moral responsibility, and the belief that art should reflect general truths about humans and the natural world. In *Rasselas*, for example, Imlac teaches such classical precepts as that the poet "does not number the streaks of the tulip" (63) but presents images of general nature, a belief Seward echoed in 1807 when after reading the *Lyrical Ballads* she exclaimed to Walter Scott that Wordsworth must have been mad to write about ten thousand dancing daffodils. An "egotistic manufacturer of metaphysic importance upon trivial themes," Wordsworth had turned the classical standard on its head (*Letters* 6:366–67). Seward also followed Johnson in adopting the "beauties and faults" structure of Restoration criticism, a method that, as Jean Marsden has observed, resulted in contemporary rejection of Johnson's preface when his edition of Shakespeare was published in 1765 (122). Marsden concludes that Johnson's preface appeared during the transitional period "when neoclassical attitudes toward literature and the poet became intermixed with those frequently termed romantic, when emphasis on individual emotional response began to overwhelm the common consensus called taste" (126). The new standard, which Austen parodied in *Sense and Sensibility* just two years after Seward's death in Marianne's certainty "that rapturous delight . . . could alone be called taste" (15), made Johnson's and Seward's efforts to balance praise and blame seem cold, even mean spirited. Since Marianne represents both sensibility and a discernibly "Romantic" perspective, Seward's method had become not only old fashioned but unattractive to many fashionable readers. Seward's persistence in approaching texts from this perspective probably accounts for some critics' impression of her malice, both in letters to friends like Hayley critiquing their latest publications and in published analyses like her chapters on *The Botanic Garden*. For Seward, as for Dryden, Pope, and Johnson, painstaking reflection on a work's graces and defects yielded a quasi-scientific assessment of its value. She may have adopted the approach to avoid the bias against women as supposed creatures of passion rather than reason, incapable of valid critical judgment. Whatever her reasons for a critical practice at odds with that of her contemporaries, and even with her own proclaimed sensibility, Seward's predilection for Johnsonian critical methods raises further questions about her violent rejection of his opinions.

Seward's antipathy to Johnson appears in a series of letters to Thomas Whalley in 1781. She describes Johnson's character as a compendium of antitheses: "at once the most liberal and the most ungenerous; the most dark, and the most enlightened; the most compassionate and the most merciless; the most friendly, and the least sincere; the best-humoured and the most acrimonious; the most soothing, and the most abusive; the most grateful, and the most ungrateful, of mankind" (Whalley 1:346). She defined each of the opposed traits, explaining that Johnson was literally generous to the poor but "ungenerous because he has no mercy upon reputation of any sort, and sickens with envy over literary fame; as his late work [*The Lives of the Poets*] sufficiently evinces" (Whalley 1:346). She found him a religious bigot whose superstitions were "malign and violent" and who was merciless to anyone whose political or religious views differed from his (Whalley 1:347). Although Johnson could be friendly and affectionate, "from the instant that the lightest opposition is made to his opinions, he exalts his voice into thunder, and 'don't talk nonsense', and 'sir' or 'madam, it is false', and 'if you think so, you think like a fool', becomes the language he uses, and with which he interlards his imperious dogmas" (Whalley 1:347). These impressions were based on Seward's observations of Johnson during his biannual visits to Lichfield, when he dined at the Bishop's Palace and was often in her company. There was probably more than one instance like one she recalled in which Johnson condemned her to "die in a surfeit of bad taste" for admiring *Lycidas* (*Letters* 1:66). Seward found Johnson's animosity toward Milton, as well as his sharp criticism of Cowley, Collins, Gray, Mason, Beattie and other poets she admired, unforgivable. Since Johnson had dedicated his *Dictionary* to the honor of his country, he was certainly aware of patriotic efforts to establish a British canon. As we have seen, Seward believed that Johnson's criticism threatened both the national taste and the "literary and moral" reputation of British literature (*Memoirs* x) and that she was not exaggerating his potential influence (Bonnell 134). When in 1785 Boswell asked her for anecdotes about Johnson, she reminded him that "the genuine lovers of the poetic science look with anxious eyes to Mr. Boswell . . . expecting . . . impartial justice " (*Letters* 1:42). Her disappointment with the *Life of Johnson* and determination to delineate the uglier aspects of Johnson's character—his literary jealousy and bigotry—were thus rooted in her wish to counter Johnson's denigration of British writers and to reinstate the "defects" amid the "graces" she found too prevalent in Boswell's account.

Seward's repeated claims that Johnson exhibited jealousy were, we have seen, the object of a sonnet about an occasion when she believed she tricked Boswell into admitting that Johnson's disparagement of David Garrick resulted from envy of the actor's early success. Boswell, on that occasion, had asked why a critic would envy dead poets. Seward's response assumed Johnson resented his many years of obscurity before achieving recognition and financial security. The opinion of neither was to change. Seward believed that *The Lives of the Poets* did not contain disinterested, balanced criticism but "sophistries . . . which seem to have put on the whole armour of truth by the force of their eloquence and the wit of their satire" (*Memoirs* x). Seward's belief that criticism was a quest for the "truth" about a work's value was another belief she inherited from predecessors, along with the assumption that criticism was a moral as well as intellectual exercise.

Marsden has observed, for example, that Johnson's disappointment with the lack of poetic justice in Shakespeare's plays was becoming anachronistic (124–25). Johnson believed Shakespeare's lack of concern with poetic justice indicated a moral failing. Similarly, Seward believed that Johnson's failure to comment justly on the nation's poets was a moral failure. His "gloomy bigotry" additionally undermined his critical reliability: religious prejudice made disinterested moral criticism unlikely. Seward proposed to dissuade Boswell's readers from "boundless veneration" of Johnson that would lead, in turn, to "injustice toward *many*" other writers (*Memoirs* ix). This task would require exposing the jealousy, sophistry, and bigotry she had witnessed from childhood but that Boswell had purged from his account. While Boswell and others accused her of malice, Seward believed herself to be enacting her proper role as British muse, exposing Johnson for the glory of British poetry. In her view, Boswell had failed, in both the *Tour* and *Life*, in his critical duty by not portraying Johnson's "deep . . . shades" as well as his virtues (*Letters*. 1:45). In letters published in the *Gentleman's Magazine* after each publication, Seward attempted to balance Boswell's account.

Seward's temerity in addressing Boswell is more remarkable in light of Barnard's revelation, in her recent biography, of a series of secret letters between Seward and Boswell in 1784. Boswell, enamored of the beautiful author of *Louisa*, initiated the correspondence in the guise of a literary admirer. Since his seductive intention was clear, Barnard concludes that Seward engaged in a brief exchange in hope of converting Boswell's physical attraction into an intellectual affinity. Seward, flattered by the attention of an influential man of letters (134), knew that Boswell was aware of her reputation, damaged by her relationship with Saville, and hoped to convert his salacious thoughts into friendship. The letters ended with Seward's definitive, yet flattering, refusal of an affair (138). Yet, as Barnard notes, the episode must have affected their public exchanges over Johnson (139). Seward undertook her public accusations knowing that Boswell could, if he chose, reveal a clandestine correspondence that, despite her refusal to permit his advances, showed her willingness to accept his addresses. An eighteenth-century woman already concerned about her reputation would have to have considered such a possibility, unrelated as it might have been to her critical purposes. In the secret letters, Boswell confirmed that, for him, Seward's sexual appeal took precedence over her literary ability (136). He might easily have chosen to end her critical attacks by exposing what would have been considered at least an impropriety. According to the period's logic, such an exposure would have doomed Seward's critical reputation. She chose nevertheless to persist in her campaign to adjust Boswell's portrait of his beloved mentor.

Seward's first letter to the *Gentleman's Magazine* appeared in February 1786 among a number of critical letters following Boswell's publication of his *Tour of the Hebrides* (59:125–26). Her main purpose of exposing Johnson's lack of benevolence is indicated by her choice of Benvolio as a nom de plume. Since, as we have seen, Seward defined Captain Cook as heroic owing to benevolence, she implied that Johnson was antiheroic because he lacked that virtue. Her letter first chastises the magazine for idolizing Johnson, whom Boswell's recent journal has revealed to be prejudiced and sophistical. She deplores Boswell's scenes recounting Johnson's pious respect for ancient Catholic ruins, particularly when he railed against Dissenting fellow Protestants. She attests that personal acquaintance confirms the accuracy of Boswell's recollections, although he "strives to spread a veil" over Johnson's "malignance" (59:125). She instances Johnson's insulting remarks about Scotland even in the company of his hosts, his claim that Cowley was more concise than Pope, and worst of all, his refusal to acknowledge Garrick's leadership in reviving Shakespeare's popularity. Garrick, she protests, revived Shakespeare by producing and performing his plays. Garrick, in fact, was "Shakespeare's best commentator, not excepting" Johnson (59:126). Seward questions Boswell's taste in recording Johnson's disparagement of Elizabeth Montagu's defense of Shakespeare and concludes by rebuking the magazine for claiming, in its review of Boswell's *Tour*, that "virtue was the best recommendation" to Johnson (59:126). The friend of Richard Savage and Oliver Goldsmith (whose veracity had been questioned) could not be described as a man who demanded virtuous companions. Toryism, she suggests, was a stronger criterion, leading him to praise Richard Blackmore, damn Thomas Gray, and declare "King William a rascal" (59:126). This first letter contains most of the themes in Seward's private correspondence: his religious and political bigotry, jealousy of fellow writers and of Garrick, and the sophistry with which he defended his absurd opinions.

Seward took most seriously her self-imposed mission to expose Johnson's failings before his biographies managed to establish him in the public consciousness as a kind of saint. She did not wait long before publishing, in April 1786, another Benvolio letter aimed more squarely at undermining Johnson's reputation for morality, as attested by Boswell in his *Tour* and Thrale-Piozzi in her *Anecdotes*. Benvolio is outraged by Thrale-Piozzi 's pronouncement that Johnson was "good beyond the imitation of perishable beings." In Benvolio's view, the "injustice and malice" displayed throughout *The Lives of the Poets* amply refute Thrale-Piozzi's accolade (59:302). Seward cites Johnson himself, in his *Rambler* 60 essay on biography, in defense of Boswell's disclosures of Johnson's less attractive remarks and actions. Accurate representation is a duty "paid to knowledge, to virtue, and to

truth" (59:303). Her own reflections perform that duty by observing, in Thrale-
Piozzi's memoirs, instances of unchristian rudeness and lack of charity. She adduces comments that Johnson himself must have known to be insincere or even
false, as in his remark that "any man, any woman, any *child*, might have written
Ossian's works" (59:303). She questions the superior virtue of a person "who delighted to destroy the self-esteem of almost all who approached him by the wound-
ing force of witty and bitter sarcasm" (59:304). "If it is possible," she concludes,
"that a man might have been pre-eminently excellent, who scarce ever conversed
without violating the rule of doing unto others as he would they should do unto
him . . . there may be sanity in the declaration, that Dr. Johnson was 'good beyond
the imitation of perishable beings'" (59:304). Exposed even by his admirer as having violated Christ's chief command, obedience to the "golden rule," Johnson
may have been "*one* of the greatest *geniuses*, and certainly the *most extraordinary*
being that ever existed" (59:302), but he was still human and liable to sin. By naming and illustrating his sins (besides pride, anger, envy, and untruthfulness, Benvolio also alludes to Johnson's sloth and gluttony), Seward tries to cut Johnson
down to mortal size after Thrale-Piozzi's apotheosis. Today her gesture would
seem irrelevant, but since, as we have seen, Seward adhered to the same tradition
of moral criticism expounded by Johnson, her effort to unveil his moral failures
was an intrinsic part of her campaign to undermine his critical authority. As we
have also observed, she was walking a literary tightrope, because Boswell might
have accused her of moral failings in turn if he had not maintained a gentlemanly
silence.

Seward's third Benvolio letter appeared in August and answered a response to
her previous articles charging her with malevolence for exposing Johnson's faults.
Once more she focused directly on her mission as moral witness. She comments
that if Benvolio's strictures of Johnson's malevolence are themselves malevolent,
then a judge who condemns a murderer is himself a murderer (62:684). She adds
that since evidence of Johnson's "jealous pride . . . irascibility . . . and envy" is
manifest in printed records, it cannot be malevolent to acknowledge his faults,
even if Johnson, in his published diary, confessed only to indolence (62:684).
Seward concedes that Johnson's personal failings do not lessen the force of his
moral arguments. But she insists that Johnson's lack of charity rendered him less
than Christian: "If Johnson walked humbly with his God, he did not walk obedi-
ently, since his life was one continued disobedience to the humility commanded
by Him in the Scriptures; and to his great precept, 'Do unto others, as ye would
they should do unto you'" (62:685). She concludes by defending herself against
the charge of malevolence, instancing published evidence of Johnson's injustice,

superstition, and unfairness. "To bear testimony against its corrosives, with a view to counteract their influence and baleful example, cannot render misapplied the signature of Benvolio" (62:685). By systematically dismantling her critic's argument, Seward reveals the false logic of the charge. Johnson's lack of charity, reflected in his bearing false witness against Milton, Gilbert Walmesley, Matthew Prior, James Hammond, and Gray, has the potential to damage their reputations as men and as writers owing to his "unjust influence and baleful example." She compliments her adversary for comparing Johnson to a pineapple while insisting that his rough exterior did not conceal inner sweetness but "internal bitterness . . . of which the generous mind is indignant" (62:685).

Seward's Benvolio letters attracted rejoinders, but they appeared among other *Gentleman's Magazine* reviews praising or lamenting aspects of recently published Johnsoniana. While adamant, they were among a number of reviews both friendly and hostile. Benvolio's perspective was that of a moral critic calling attention to Johnson's envy and injustice in order to undermine his literary judgments. Since Johnson routinely misrepresented his fellow writers' work, denying even the most characteristic aspects of their writings—"he . . . has denied to Prior ease, to Hammond nature, and to Gray sublimity" (62:685)—he cannot be trusted. Although the Benvolio articles selectively repeat ideas conveyed many times in Seward's private correspondence, they focus on her moral intention and argue logically from the evidence in Johnson's, Boswell's, and Thrale-Piozzi's publications. Benvolio's tone is indignant, expressive of "the generous mind" fearing Johnson's corrosive influence on national literary taste. Defending herself against the charge of malice, Benvolio claims to defend charity toward fellow writers, Dissenting Protestants, and former mentors. Johnson failed to treat them benevolently and thus requires chastisement lest others be misled by his unchristian example. Although she identified herself as Benvolio to friends, she did not publicly avow the letters until December 1793, by which time their clarity and logic had been obscured by an intervening controversy.

The March 1793 issue of the *Gentleman's Magazine* contained a series of extracts from letters between Seward and Hayley following publication of *The Lives of the Poets* in 1782 (73:197). As she explained in a letter to Anna Rogers Stokes, she had transcribed passages from their letters for correspondents who had been curious, at the time, about her and Hayley's opinions of Johnson's *Lives* (*Letters* 5:223). Ten years later, apparently capitalizing on public interest in Boswell's biography, one of those correspondents had anonymously submitted the extracts for publication. Anyone who remembered Benvolio would have recognized "his" opinions and style in Seward's remarks. The letters to Hayley, however, suggest a

personal element to Seward's antipathy that counters her pose as defender of justice. She describes entertaining Johnson during a visit to Lichfield and biting her
tongue when he disparages Beattie and Mason. When Johnson has little more to
say about Hayley than that he "is a man of Genius," Seward recalls, she mutters
to herself "And is that all that thou hast to say?" but *to his ear I kept an indignant
silence*" (73:198–99). Since Seward has already described how she recoils from the
vollies of sarcasm unleashed by Johnson on those who contradict him, her silence
throughout the conversation is understandable. But her anger toward Johnson
after he commends her friend as a "man of Genius" is confusing. Angry with him
for abusing Beattie and Mason, she is nearly as irritated by his failure to elaborate
on Hayley's brilliance, although he has confessed to reading only one of Hayley's
poems. Here we sense a more than professional animosity. It is as if Seward, having constructed her notion of Johnson, is disappointed by his failure to condemn
Hayley and thus confirm her image of his unfairness. Hayley's extracts are more
playful and disinterested; he compares Johnson to Milton's Satan and styles him
the Leviathan of criticism. Seward's excerpts are eloquent but reveal a personal
dimension that could be used to her disadvantage. Seward herself, however,
seems chiefly to have objected to the extracts' unauthorized publication because
she thought it might annoy Hayley. Her letter to Stokes describes mortification at
finding her exchanges with Hayley in print (*Letters* 5:224). In a letter to the *Gentleman's Magazine* in May, however, she corrected some transcriptions in her own
letters lest they seem "nonsense" (73:293) but otherwise expressed no reticence
about having her correspondence made public.

Seward's final published strictures of Johnson were part of an uncomfortable
exchange with Boswell in the late fall of 1793. Boswell had asked Seward eight
years previously for anecdotes about Johnson, and she had complied with stories
based not only on her personal observations but also on his mother's and Lucy
Porter's memories. "If he inserts them unmutilated . . . they will contribute to
display Johnson's real character to the public," she explained to her Quaker friend
Molly Knowles (*Letters* 1:47). When the *Life of Johnson* was published in 1791,
however, she was predictably disappointed: "What I foresaw has happened. That
ingenious pencil which so well fulfilled the biographer's duty, and painted the
despot exactly as he was, when roaming the lonely Hebrides, has, at the impulse
of terror, been exchanged for a more glowing one; and in this work almost everything is kept back that could give umbrage to Johnson's idolaters" (*Letters* 3:85–
86). She nevertheless believed that Boswell had recorded enough rude or contradictory remarks about living persons that Johnson's true character was exposed.
She paraphrases Johnson's "Vanity of Human Wishes": "Say thou, whose thoughts

at humble fame repine,/Shall Johnson's wit with Johnson's spleen be thine?" (*Letters* 3:87). She was further disconcerted at finding few of her anecdotes included and those few, edited to suit Boswell's version of his mentor. One incident she had narrated, for example, was a dispute she had witnessed between Johnson and Knowles about the conversion of a young heiress, Jenny Harry, to the Quaker religion; Johnson condemned Harry as an apostate despite Knowles's defense of Harry's right to obey her conscience. Johnson had persisted in reviling the "odious wench" for her disobedience to her father and desertion of the Anglican religion. Seward was incensed. She had not read the second volume, "but I hear it contains the memorable conversation at Dilly's, but without that part of it of which I made minutes, and in which you appear to so much advantage over the imperious and gloomy Intolerant" (*Letters* 3:74). Although she does not record her protest in her letters, she must have challenged Boswell about his omissions because he responded in notes to his second edition. These notes, too, disappointed Seward because he rejected some of her information, claiming it was based on unreliable sources. Boswell's repudiation spurred Seward to attempt a public intervention.

The October 1793 number of the *Gentleman's Magazine* opened with a letter from Seward complaining that Boswell had not only rejected some of her information but failed to state the reasons why she believed her facts were accurate. For example, Boswell "corrected" her testimony, gleaned from her mother and Lucy Porter, that the poem "On Receiving a Sprig of Myrtle from a Lady" was written for Porter by the adolescent Johnson. Johnson's longtime friend Edmund Hector had told Boswell that the poem was in fact written by Johnson on behalf of Hector after the latter received a gift of myrtle. Seward argues that Hector's contradictory story was easily explained by Johnson's probable reluctance to confide, when giving a copy to Hector, that his poem had originally been addressed to the daughter of the woman he eventually married. She adds that Johnson's many patently false critical assertions made plausible the "slight untruth" of such an evasion. Seward concludes by insisting that her letter be published in order to clear herself from Boswell's imputation of dishonesty, vanity, or prejudice (74:875).

After his silent reception of the Benvolio letters and the excerpts from the Seward-Hayley exchange, Boswell was roused by Seward's published complaint. He replied at length in the November *Gentleman's Magazine* in a letter calculated to embarrass and insult his antagonist. He begins by paraphrasing her October letter, in which Seward explained that she had obliged Boswell's request for information by "[covering] several sheets of paper" describing a few anecdotes (74:875). Boswell mocks her by admitting that Seward "did indeed *cover several sheets of paper* [with a] *few* anecdotes," but her stories were "not only poetically luxuriant, but . . . tinctured with a strong prejudice against" Johnson (74:1009). He proceeds to dismiss one of Seward's anecdotes, claiming the three-year-old Johnson composed a brief poem about killing a duck, as "utterly improbable . . . credulously related" by "good Mrs. Lucy Porter, among others" (74:1009). Another vignette, recounting Mrs. Johnson's stern conversation with her son about marrying Mrs. Porter, struck Boswell as "so strange" that he sought confirmation from the person whom Seward claimed as her source. That lady promptly repudiated the story, which Boswell then suppressed because "my book was to be a *real history*, and not a *novel*" (74:1009). Of the myrtle sprig poem, Boswell comments that since his version was originally published by Thrale-Piozzi and confirmed by Hector, he had no choice but to correct Seward's anecdote based on their "decisive evidence." He quotes the note in his second edition, which recounts Seward's information, adding that "she no doubt supposed [it] to be correct; but it shews how dangerous it is to trust too implicitly to traditional testimony and ingenious inference" (74:1010). Boswell thus neatly undercuts Seward's authority by rejecting her sources, her mother and the "credulous" Porter, in favor of Thrale-Piozzi and Hector. Having detected Seward's prejudice against Johnson, he suspects the motives of her "ingenious inference."

Boswell argues against Seward's assertion that the myrtle verses were written for Lucy Porter "as if good enough only for a schoolboy. They have been long and universally admired . . . and require no defence" (74:1010). He believes it more likely that Johnson wrote the poem for Hector and then, "with a pleasant economy, made them serve a second time for a compliment to her" (74:1010). Such conjecture, however, is irrelevant because "that they were written for Mr. Hector . . . is all that is necessary to be proved; and it has been proved" (74:1010). Boswell declares that Seward should not have felt her veracity questioned because "it is only a matter of argument upon evidence; and, I think, a very plain one" (74:1010). Having rejected her ability to construct a sound argument along with her evidence, Boswell proceeds to question Seward's grasp of context. She has accused Johnson of making false assertions but failed to grasp that his witty remarks were not intended to convey his serious opinions. Rather, they were instances of his "wonderful dexterity in retort" (74:1010). Seward, he implies, is incapable of appreciating that distinction, even as she is incapable of reading Latin; Boswell remarks that Johnson's conversational judgments "are evidently *ardentia verba* (glowing words—I ask her pardon for quoting a Latin phrase)" (74:1010). How could an unlearned woman appreciate Johnson's epigrams? Boswell defends his mentor from Seward's imputations of falsehood, suggesting that they proceed from malice. He concludes by implying that he chivalrously repressed Johnson's opinion of her, "thinking that she might not like it," and so now wonders if some-how she learned his estimate and was stung to retaliate on her venerable towns-man since his decease" (74:1011). What else could have motivated her various disguised attacks (he clearly intends the Benvolio letters) or the publication of her letters to Hayley, "impotently attempting to undermine the noble pedestal on which the public opinion has placed Dr. Johnson?" (74:1011). In a final flourish, Boswell renounces any effort to expose "the little arts which have been employed by a cabal of minor poets and poetesses, who are sadly mortified that Dr. Johnson, by his powerful sentence, assigned their proper station to writers of this descrip-tion" (74:1011).

Boswell's rejoinder is worth describing in detail not only because his wit is amusing but because he employs rhetorical strategies intended to destroy Seward's credibility. In her Benvolio letters, she relied on textual examples of Johnson's cruelty and falsehood, but Boswell implies that she either misunderstood the irony of his remarks, was motivated by malice, or both. Since wit or intelligence as well as learning were required to engage in ironic wordplay, a literary and conversational technique much admired in the late seventeenth and early eigh-teenth centuries, Seward has unmasked herself as an unworthy commentator on Johnson and his circle. Boswell sneers at Mrs. Seward and Lucy Porter as credu-lous old women retailing old traditions; his witnesses, the sophisticated Thrale-Piozzi and learned Hector, are, he implies, necessarily preferable. He regards their evidence as proof and Seward's anecdotes as worthless tales. Finally, Boswell confirms Seward's worst fears about Johnson's potential to destroy the reputations of British poets, living or dead. His reflection on the cabal of minor poets im-potently trying to lower Johnson from his pedestal responds to her repeated warn-ings, as Benvolio and in the "scraps of letters" to Hayley, that Johnson would succeed in lowering the public's estimate of the poets he dismissed, however wittily, in his publications and conversations.

Boswell's letter was, as Seward declared in her next and final published letter on the subject, "too invidious not to require some comments" (74:1098). The December *Gentleman's Magazine* carried her lengthy retort. She denies either embellishing any facts or expressing resentment at his suppression but just ob-serves she merely asked that her reasons for accepting the anecdotes be acknowl-edged. In her view, "they all convey as strong internal evidence of their verity, from characteristic turn of expression, as any that can be found" in Boswell's *Life* (74:1098). In his emendations, for example, Boswell had said that the story of the duck, although discredited, had invited the "ingenious and fanciful reflections" of Seward (Boswell 1:40–41n3). After quoting her reflections on the creative potential manifested in the four-line poem, Boswell concludes that Seward's ideas were too "beautifully imagined" to omit, but as they were based on fiction, they could not be included in the biography proper. In her letter, Seward explains that, urged by friends who resented Boswell's rude introduction of her remarks, she requested only that he state her grounds for accepting such anecdotes as genuine, instead of presenting her comments as mere "fanciful reflections" on fictional events. She reiterates her belief that Johnson wrote the verses to a lady with a myrtle sprig for Lucy Porter, having "too great a respect for Mrs. Porter's, and for my mother's, long and unvarying testimony, to *resign* it" (74:1098). Since, as Boswell admits, Johnson often asserted falsehoods purely to win conversational disputes, there is no reason to accept as true his explanation that he wrote the verses for Hector. She defends herself against Boswell's charge that her version attempts to disparage Johnson by assigning the poem to his youth. In fact, the verses are more admirable as juvenilia than as inferior mature work. Seward also defends the story of the duck verses as related by Johnson's mother herself to Porter: "It is more likely he should have forgotten what he said at three years old, than that either of those good women should invent a falsehood" (74:1099). After confronting Boswell's patronizing dismissal of her chief witnesses, however, Seward admits that the origins of certain anecdotes are uncertain because she heard them repeated by various people, such as "the late Mrs. Cobb." She accepted such stories because of their "Johnsonian spirit" (74:1099). As for Johnson's veracity, one has only to compare his praises of Thrale-Piozzi in his published letters with his insulting remarks about her in the *Life*. She protests that she has always defended Johnson's superior prose style but has equally inveighed against his injustice toward other writers (74:1099); in other words, she has adhered to the "praise and blame" structure of classical criticism. It is not presumptuous to speak of a person as he really was.

Continuing her self-vindication, Seward maintains that her intention has been to serve as moral critic and dissuade less attentive readers from Johnson worship. She disputes Boswell's argument that Johnson's pronouncements against other writers were not untruths but witticisms: such "unjust depreciation" was beneath Johnson as it would be for any speaker (74:1099). She answers Boswell's implication that she is presumptuous to criticize Johnson: "I have a better right to protest against the malignity of *my* intellectual superior, Johnson, upon recorded *facts*, than he had to degrade . . . the morality and piety of *his* superior, Milton" (74: 1099). She calls Boswell's bluff, so to speak, thanking him for suppressing Johnson's negative comments about her, saving her from the fate of "many of my superiors, through Mr. Boswell's rage of communication" (74:1099). Because she often remonstrated with Johnson when he railed against deserving writers, she has always assumed that Johnson disliked her. Although Boswell thinks that minor poets resent Johnson because he put them in their place, she argues that Johnson too often elevated mediocre poets like Savage and Blackmore above genuinely gifted writers like Prior, Collins, Gray, and Akenside (74:1100). She recalls reading Johnson's assertion that "[Isaac] Watts was one of the few poets who could look forward with rational hope to the mercy of their God," a sentence she finds outrageous (74:1100). Johnson himself had praised imagination as the faculty that "exalts us in the scale of rational beings" (74:1100). Since poets, more than any other people, continually exercise their imaginations, they stand acquitted from Johnson's supremely presumptuous remark. In fact, Johnson knew that others had surpassed him as a poet and was afflicted with "envious spleen" (74:1100). She, however, is free of envy. Warmly admiring Johnson's style, many of his writings, and his Christian faith, she simply seeks to dissuade others from idolatry. She admits writing the Benvolio letters and encourages readers to reread them before believing Boswell's characterization of her as malicious. When Johnson's character is weighed, however, he fails in the balance described in Corinthians 13, St. Paul's epistle enjoining charity (74:1101). She quotes Bishop Newton, who also found Johnson's *Lives of the Poets* malevolent. Resting her case, she promises to write no more on the subject because any further assaults by Boswell "must ultimately redound more to his dishonor than hers" (74:1100).

Seward attempted a point-by-point rebuttal of Boswell's letter. She answered his deprecation of her witnesses and his implication that she exaggerated her stories. She countered his logic regarding Johnson's early compositions with her own logical suppositions. She questioned his excuse that Johnson's insults were witticisms by remarking on the unworthiness of such conversation. She defended herself against the imputation of personal envy or spite, quoting a learned man (since Boswell had pointed out her lack of learning) to corroborate her accusation that Johnson's criticism was often malicious. She reiterated Benvolio's charge that Johnson was uncharitable, which rendered his literary judgments suspect. Having concluded her argument, she was unprepared for the vehemence with which Boswell responded in the *Gentleman's Magazine* for January 1794. Boswell's final letter is written in a sarcastic tone: he refers back to his original explanation about the verses with a myrtle sprig as sufficiently convincing to "all who are capable of reasoning and judging of evidence"—a group that does not, obviously, include Seward (75:32). He rebukes Seward for attacking "the great and good Dr. Johnson" on the basis of such an inconsiderable pretext (75:32). Boswell himself is not Seward's enemy. In fact, after discarding such anecdotes as the verses on the duck

("to which, for a woman's reason, she still pertinaciously adheres"), he nevertheless included her "ingenious reflections . . . on that idle tale" (75:32–33). We have
seen that Boswell's note, in the *Life*, exposed Seward to ridicule, but Boswell insists his inclusion was gallant before repeating that "Miss Nancy Seward's" criticism of Johnson was presumptuous, since no less an authority than Edmund
Malone had styled him "the brightest ornament of the eighteenth century"
(75:33). Seward's "republican" preference of Milton over Johnson reveals her mistaken esteem for a "great poet, who was the most odious character . . . that ever
lived" (75:33). He reiterates that he is not Seward's enemy: "She never did me any
harm, nor do I apprehend that she ever can" (75:33). He has no wish to combat
with ladies, "and I really must complain that my *old friend* (if she will forgive me
the expression) should represent me so unlike myself" (75:33). Here, Boswell resorts to outright insult, calling Seward by the name used by only her family and
closest friends instead of the formal address appropriate to a public argument.
After that breach of manners, he alludes to her age, implying that Seward's bitterness emanates from her status as a fifty-two-year-old spinster. His gross familiarity
reduces her from a worthy to a trivial antagonist and their contest from a public
debate to a private quarrel. But Boswell's italicized *old friend* might also be a
veiled reference to their long acquaintance, including the attempted epistolary
seduction of which only they were aware but that he might easily make public by
producing her letters in his possession. Seward has never done Boswell any harm,
but he might do her harm; at least, his private knowledge enables him to address
her in a manner that suggests little regard for her dignity.

The rest of Boswell's letter descends into an orgy of sarcasm. He mocks Seward's
failure to comprehend Johnson's wit. He catches her in a misquotation of Johnson that she could easily have found recorded correctly in his book; this is an especially problematic blunder given Seward's reliance on textual evidence. He
reveals that he asked Moll Cobb, whom Seward had cited as a source, for confirmation of an anecdote and had been told she had no recollection of the event;
moreover, Cobb told Boswell that if Boswell praised Johnson, "Miss Seward will
not love you" (75:33). Of her recalling Johnson's statement that Watt was among
the few poets who need not fear meeting God, Boswell retorts "that poets, and
poetesses also, have too often been not of the most exemplary lives, is universally
known," but Johnson never wrote or said anything of the kind about them (75:33).
The statement certainly refers to Seward's attachment to Saville and also perhaps
to his own attempted seduction of the poet, undermining her critical authority by
hinting at her vulnerable reputation. After that glancing blow, Boswell reverts to
her intellectual poverty. He corrects Seward's quotation of Bishop Newton, which

omitted Newton's praise of Johnson's genius, learning, and piety (75:34). Although Seward accused Boswell of implying her envy and prejudice, he protests he does "not even suspect that my fair antagonist, 'herself all the Nine,' envies any human being" (75:34). He next defends himself for having countered her accusations of his "Guide, Philosopher, and Friend." Having compared himself and Johnson to Pope and Lord Bolingbroke, Boswell mocks Seward's Benvolio as Drawcansir, the blustering hero of Lord Buckingham's travesty of heroic drama, *The Rehearsal* (1671). He assures her that he has well considered her complaints; "the verdict of ineffective ill-nature will never be set aside" (75:34). To end her dispute over "the mighty points of the *Duck* and the *Myrtle*, which have been the causes of this war," Boswell quotes Johnson himself, citing Porter as a witness, that his father and not he wrote the epitaph on a duck. He quotes a letter from Hector, who wonders why Seward will not "be convinced of her errors" but confirms that Johnson wrote the verses at his request (75:34). "Let the duck be changed into a swan, and the Myrtle into an Olive," exclaims Boswell. Excusing himself from further contention, he hopes that Seward's imagination "has men and things enough to employ itself upon, without vainly aspiring to be the judge of Johnson" (75:35).

Even if she had not promised to cease communicating on the subject, Seward would have found a response awkward if not impossible. A letter to Henry Cary thanks him for defending her from Boswell's "impertinent and invidious spite" (*Letters* 3:346); Cary and others sent letters to the *Gentleman's Magazine* vindicating her of Boswell's charges. For Cary, Seward corrects Hector's account of the origin of the myrtle-sprig verses, revealing to readers of her published correspondence that she had not completely denied herself the opportunity to rebuke Boswell. In his letter, quoted in full by Boswell, Hector stated that Johnson was unacquainted with the Porter family until after he wrote the verses. Seward questions Hector's "strange forgetfulness," since Lucy Porter's aunt was married to Seward's grandfather, Johnson's tutor, and Porter visited her Lichfield relatives. It is not at all unlikely, contrary to Hector's belief, that the young Johnson wrote the verses for his teacher's niece and later shared them with Hector (*Letters* 3:348). Not coincidentally, Seward's cousin Henry White had also published a letter in the March *Gentleman's Magazine* explaining Hector's error using some of the same phrases in Seward's letter to Cary (75:196–97). Seward either borrowed White's description or, more likely, since the italicized phrases are typical of her style, White sent a letter by Seward to the magazine as his own. Most galling to Seward, however, was her inability to locate Johnson's remark about Watts; she asks Cary's help in finding the damning quotation that Boswell had categorically denied. At the close of her letter, she rejoices that another friend has located in *The Lives of the Poets* a similar statement at the close of Johnson's biography of Gilbert West: "A stroke of palsy brought to the grave one of those few poets to whom the grave needed not be terrible" (*Letters* 3:349).[1] If Johnson slandered poets thus in his praise of West, she sees no reason why he may not have uttered a similar remark about Watts. Such was Johnson's pleasure in "malicious reflections" (*Letters* 3:350). Unsurprisingly, she avoids mentioning Boswell's personal insults in her letters to supportive friends.

Seward evidently received her information about West from Anna Rogers Stokes, to whom she replied in a letter dated the same day as her letter to Cary. Before thanking her friend for the reference and assuring her that "it is sent to the Gentleman's Magazine" (*Letters* 3:353), Seward replies to another of Stokes's suggestions. Stokes and her husband had asked her to compile a sort of anti-*Lives of the Poets*, a positive companion to Johnson's negative volumes. Seward declines, citing depression, poor health, and the fact that she foresees the critical result. Not only do more readers prefer "to see excellence degraded than exalted" but

> to what derision would I be exposed from a thousand quarters!—An unlearned female entering the lists of criticism against the mighty Johnson! No, I can never cease to protest against his envious injustice, but cannot be taught to hope that it is in my power to counteract its irreparable mischiefs to poetic literature. I saw the dark cloud descend, surcharged with pernicious coruscations and quench the golden day of its fame—I fear for ever. (*Letters* 3:351–52)

Seward proceeds to describe her "deep-seated malady" that precludes any intellectual or physical exertion. One wonders whether her illness, which resembles depression, resulted from the frustrating outcome of her contest with Boswell. Certainly his insults would have been grounds for a challenge if she had been a man. Seward is amazed to have found Boswell "capable of insulting any person who cannot inflict the punishment of corporal correction" (*Letters* 3:353). Fatherless and brotherless, Seward has nobody to avenge Boswell's virtual assault. It must have added to her grief to recognize that not only could John Saville not properly undertake her vindication but that their relationship had given Boswell grounds for his snide reference to poetesses' less-than-exemplary lives. In retrospect, she no doubt realized that by permitting Boswell's seductive letters, she had not only failed to convert him into her platonic admirer but had illustrated her propensity for clandestine, if innocent, relationships. Seward's letter to Stokes, although written during a flurry of published defenses on her behalf, describes a despairing state that could have resulted from loss of self-confidence following Boswell's public drubbing. Seward had spoken with the authority of her lifelong study of British poets and English translations, only to experience "derision" at the temerity of an "unlearned female entering the lists of criticism against the mighty Johnson." The dark cloud she perceives descending on the reputation of British poetry may have been reflected in the dark cloud shrouding her mind at this time. Although we know from other letters that Seward feared she had developed cancer following a blow to her breast, her mental torpor seems at least to have been augmented by what she perceived as Boswell's treachery.[2]

Seward, or White speaking for her, published a final reply to Boswell's attack. In September 1794, a well-intentioned writer who signed his name AE. V. wrote to the *Gentleman's Magazine* supposing that Seward's ire had been raised by disparaging remarks about her father that Boswell attributed to Johnson in the *Life*. To AE. V., it seemed understandable that Seward would have been angered by Johnson's description of her father bringing "himself to the state of a hog in a stye" (75:815), Johnson's witty reference to Mr. Seward's annual spa treatments. Since Boswell, like Seward, was a dutiful child, he should not have been surprised by her reaction. In October 1794, Henry White wrote again on behalf of his cousin. He explained that Seward's anger had not been roused by Johnson's recorded remarks about her father, which merely confirmed the justice of her settled opinion. Her Benvolio letters had been composed long before the *Life* "generously recorded" Johnson's insulting remarks about a man whose hospitality he had often enjoyed. Mr. Seward was "entirely free from grossness or indelicacy in his manners"; Seward concluded that her father had simply shared the fate of many Johnsonian acquaintances (75:876). White's letter is a quiet denouement to the Seward-Boswell exchange. One might have expected Seward to address, energetically, this evidence of ingratitude, hypocrisy, and unfairness expressed against her own father. Perhaps she realized that any retort would attract another Boswellian charge of obtuseness or draw from him the threatened revelation of what Johnson had said about herself. For whatever reason, Seward allowed this fairly terse explanation to close the battle. Boswell died in May 1795, preventing any possibility of renewed conflict.

Seward felt humiliated by Boswell's letters, and most writers have agreed he bested her in their debate. Margaret Ashmun, for example, declares her "no sort of match" for Boswell, "an easy and practiced writer and skilled disputant" (207). Since Seward herself was nothing if not a practiced writer and keen disputant, Ashmun's verdict is not necessarily accurate. Looking objectively at their exchange, we can see that theirs was partly an early example of the pitfalls of Johnson's biographical method. In *Rambler* 60, Johnson had declared that "the business of the biographer is often to pass lightly over those performances and incidents, which produce vulgar greatness, to lead the thoughts into domestick privacies, and display the minute details of daily life, where exterior appendages are cast aside, and men excel each other only by prudence and by virtue" (*Selected Essays* 111). Because public achievements reveal little about a person's character, "more knowledge may be gained . . . by a short conversation with one of his servants, than from a formal and studied narrative" (*Selected Essays* 112–13). In the opening pages of his *Life*, Boswell cites Plutarch's opinion that "very often an action of small note, a short saying, or a jest, shall distinguish a person's real character more than the greatest sieges" before quoting extensively from Johnson's *Rambler* 60 essay (1:31–32). Indeed, Boswell boasts of not only recording Johnson's conversation throughout their long friendship but of making every effort to obtain "materials concerning him, from every quarter where I could discover that they were to be found, and [I] have been favored with the most liberal communications by his friends" (1:26). Johnson's model, however, created a number of problems. Eyewitness testimony is only as accurate as the memory or proximity of its source. No perfectly accurate version of Johnson's conversations, even "a short saying, or a jest," was possible. In his introduction to the Heritage Press edition of the *Life*, Edward G. Fletcher stresses the artfulness with which Boswell reconstituted Johnson's conversations from shorthand notes and memories (1:x–xi). But others, such as Christopher Hibbert in his introduction to an abridged edition of the *Life*, have emphasized the degree to which Boswell edited Johnson's conversation, refining his expressions and even suppressing incidents that revealed Johnson's earthy or crude aspects (23–25).

Concern about accurate witnesses and transcriptions made Boswell's *Life* vulnerable despite his claim to have "almost entirely preserved" his friend (1:30). Boswell himself disparaged Sir John Hawkins and Thrale-Piozzi, his predecessors, for what he considered their use of indiscriminate, unfair, and inaccurate material (1:27–28; 3:343–347). Contemporary reactions, judging from those published in the *Gentleman's Magazine*, ranged from mockery of Boswell's idolatry to accusations that he portrayed Johnson too unfavorably. Few doubted the accuracy of his Johnsonian quotations, however; the myth of Boswell hovering behind Johnson with a notebook had probably already gained currency (Fletcher x).[3] Johnson's conversations as recorded in the *Life* were believed to reproduce his actual words; Seward, for example, never accused Boswell of distorting Johnson's language but instead complained about the harshness of what she accepted as Johnson's speech. Boswell, in turn, maintained his veracity and questioned the transcriptions of writers such as Seward. In his account of an evening in 1778 spent in company that included Seward and Mrs. Knowles, Boswell included a previously mentioned conversation between Johnson and Knowles concerning the conversion of Jenny Harry to the Quaker religion. In Boswell's account, Johnson holds forth, overwhelming Knowles's few interjections with his powerful defense of filial obedience and orthodox faith (Boswell 3:298–99). Seward, as we have seen, became angry when she read this published version because Boswell omitted her own transcription of the conversation, in which Knowles argued persuasively on Harry's behalf. Seward promptly sent her record to the *Gentleman's Magazine*, signed from "A Constant Reader of the *GM*" (70:798–99), but in his supplementary notes to the second edition, Boswell sarcastically dismissed her transcription. Although crediting Knowles "with the fame of reasoning better than women usually do," Boswell rejected the idea that the conversation had taken place as she suggested. He invites readers of the *Gentleman's Magazine* to decide "from internal evidence" whether her minutes, written "after many years had elapsed," were plausible, since he had no recollection of her rejoinders in his own notes (Boswell 3:299n)). Both Boswell and Seward claim throughout their argument to draw from textual evidence, yet all of their evidence is reconstructed and revised and thus flawed.

Boswell, as he admitted to Seward, destroyed most of the copious materials sent him by Johnson's acquaintances. We must assume that he deemed much of this evidence apocryphal or inaccurate, but some must have been simply too unflattering for inclusion. The problem with trying to reconstitute a human personality through reported speech is that humans are more complicated than even a large conversational sample can represent. From a vast number of examples, Boswell chose ones that if they did not invariably show his hero to advantage at least never portrayed him as irrationally cruel or harsh. Boswell's Johnson was, as he admitted, his "Guide, Philosopher, and Friend," "the brightest ornament of the eighteenth century"; he selected and polished Johnson's remarks to present him as such to others. Seward's Johnson, on the other hand, was a "gloomy tyrant," "the old literary Colossus" barring the gates of fame to fellow writers. Her most vivid memories of Johnson were of peremptory literary judgments that she rarely contradicted for fear of becoming the object of his wrath. Familiar since childhood with tales of Johnson's literary precocity, youthful poverty, rash marriage, and rise to national prominence, Seward sent Boswell information consistent with her vivid but partial image. Both Seward and Boswell had evidence for their versions, but the "paper war" episode reveals the impossibility of "almost entirely preserving" a person even using reams of evidence. If Boswell had succeeded, generations of writers would not have gone on to attempt more accurate portrayals of the multidimensional Johnson. Seward's Johnson, although far less nuanced than Boswell's, is not fictional. In his twentieth-century biography, W. Jackson Bate describes Johnson's remorse for his harsh, overbearing, contradictory habits of speech (586–87). Although she viewed Johnson only from this perspective, Seward might be credited with trying to add this acknowledged dimension of Johnson's personality to Boswell's portrait. His assertion that only malice could have evoked her anecdotes has decoyed succeeding critics from considering the degree to which her accusations were justified. Instead, scholars debate whether she was motivated by malice or merely by snobbery.[4]

Boswell's dismissal of Seward's testimony returns us to the gendered nature of Seward criticism, reviewed in my first chapter. Seward was courageous in seeking public critical authority because her chaste but unconventional relationship with Saville, and her effort to dissuade Boswell without insulting him, might easily have been used to destroy her moral, and therefore critical, credibility. But gender influenced other important aspects of Boswell's rebuttal. Boswell sneers at Seward's witnesses because they were "credulous" old women rather than a learned gentleman or cultured lady. Seward retorts that Johnson's mother, her own mother, and Lucy Porter had known Johnson far longer than Hector or Thrale-Piozzi and that their veracity was unquestionable. Since Boswell cannot call the ladies' veracity into question, Boswell must rely on his readers' assumption that the memories of old women, especially old women proud of their distinguished relative, cannot be trusted. Johnson himself had ascribed the duck epitaph to his father, thereby settling that dispute. As Seward observes, his own memory of an event that took place when he was three years old may not have been as accurate as his mother's, but Boswell declares the matter settled, and most scholars have accepted his "proof."[5] Seward offers plausible alternatives to explain why Hector may have been mistaken about the myrtle sprig poem, but Boswell rejects her reasoning, even though her point that Johnson may not have wanted to acknowledge his earlier composition of the poem for Porter is not incompatible with Hector's explanation. My point is not that Johnson probably wrote the myrtle poem for Porter as Seward claims but only that her version has been judged improbable based on Boswell's manifestly hostile objection. Seward's persistence and Boswell's public rejection suggest their competition for access to Johnson's private life. Boswell seems especially threatened by women's claims to such knowledge. Having disparaged Thrale-Piozzi's accounts, Boswell was not disposed to validate Seward's. Seward, in turn, was an ideal opponent because rather than acknowledge her arguments, he could dismiss her as an "unlearned," irrational woman.

Some of Boswell's gendered insults are more obviously unfair today. His ad feminam remark about the less-than-pristine lives of poetesses assumes that

Seward's devotion to John Saville invalidates her critique of Johnson's failings. His apology for a Latin expression ignores whether a classical education is needed for Seward's observations; Boswell assumes many readers will agree that an un-learned woman is ill qualified to accuse Johnson of literary injustice. Boswell's remark also disparages Seward's boasted knowledge of English poetry: since she has no classical training, with what authority can she speak, even of English verse? Although we can see that Latin is a rhetorical red herring, contemporaries who shared Boswell's ideology probably found it convincing. Another obviously gen-dered insult is Boswell's accusation that Seward failed to grasp Johnson's wit. Like late twentieth-century feminists, Seward is to be considered humorless, in her case because she takes Johnson's pronouncements too seriously. She must suffer a "defect in the reasoning faculty" because she mistakes for slander or untruth what was meant in jest (74:1011). Boswell berates Seward even for misquoting Johnson's sarcasms; if she is going to assault Johnson for his bon mots, she should at least remember them correctly (75:33). Why cannot Seward, a minor poet, ap-preciate Johnson's witticisms at the expense of minor poets? Boswell's rejoinder resembles the response of those who tell modern ethnic and gendered jokes to the victims of such jokes who object to them; then as now, the victim was accused of a poor sense of humor, or at least a failure to grasp irony, because she took Johnson's remarks as insults instead of as conversational gambits. Boswell's jeers call attention to similar gender biases implicit even in some recent references to Seward.

Boswell's insistence on Seward's humorlessness also recalls us to her position as a poet molded by both early and midcentury poetic values. Her moral emphasis and "beauties and faults" approach were derived from earlier models, but sensi-bility was characteristic of her generation. Boswell himself was not void of senti-ment, but his irony at the expense of Seward's failure to appreciate witty raillery revealed his own failure to credit Seward's repulsion of such harsh tactics. Seward framed her criticism in terms of sensibility. In her second Benvolio letter, for ex-ample, she asks how Thrale-Piozzi could have praised as exemplary a man who repaid his interlocutors with "rude retorts, which an amiable mind, if it could repay with equal severity, would, for the sake of the surrounding company, rather suffer than imitate;—who knew not how to pity the yearnings of affection which had lost its object; or allow for the infirmities of slow oppressive disease" (59:304). Her emphasis on courteous self-restraint, on sympathy for the sick and bereft, marks Seward as a proponent of sensibility and explains her inability to find humor in such remarks as "that ill-health generally made a man a scoundrel" (59:304). Today, we might find Johnson's wit a tonic against the mid-eighteenth century's taste for sympathetic tears, but Seward's recoil from his harshness was more typical of the era's ideal response to embarrassment, bereavement, and illness. When, in her next letter, Seward declares that "Sensibility must be disgusted" by Johnson's expressions of contempt for Scotland even while enjoying Scottish hospitality, her readers understood her reference to Johnson's failure to empathize with his hosts and to refrain accordingly from making rude comments at their nation's expense. Thirty years older and so less influenced by sensibility's dictates, Johnson persists in the conversational habits of an earlier generation that Boswell, loving him, records as faithfully as he can and that Seward, in turn, finds inexcusably cruel.

Seward was caught between the early eighteenth-century taste for wit and the early nineteenth-century rejection of sensibility's excesses, between early eighteenth-century preference for formal verse satire in heroic couplets and the Romantic turn to meditative lyrics in what Wordsworth called "the language of conversation in the middle and lower classes of society" ("Advertsisment"). Leigh Hunt may as well have mentioned Seward, Darwin's pupil who gloried in her refinement of Pope's musicality, when he decried Darwin's "poetical music" as "extreme" and affected (Reiman xiii)—epithets that, as Susan J. Wolfson has observed, would soon be applied to his protégé, John Keats (216–18). Seward was a late eighteenth-century poet in the sense both of her definitive allegiance and because she embraced Pope's Augustan principles as the vehicle to express sensibility. Her published criticism, surveyed objectively, is neither malicious nor naïve but expressive of her generation's tastes and concerns. Seward's argument, in the case of Johnson, is limited to exposing his wanton cruelty toward others, particularly poets, support of whom was a patriotic enterprise. When Boswell replied that Johnson was being facetious, Seward was not persuaded, because to speak what was not true in jest was still to lie, and moreover, Johnson's epigrammatic jests were memorable and influential. Such wit offended her sensibility because at best it needlessly embarrassed Johnson's victim; at worst it threatened the reputations of those assaulted. When Seward belabored her criticism, especially on behalf of British poets, Boswell accused her of malice and envy. But a good deal of his retaliatory argument is rhetorical sleight of hand: tactical maneuvers that defend his hero by making Seward appear unchaste, incompetent, malicious, and presumptuous. That both Seward and Boswell argued from unreliable (selective, reconstituted, revised) evidence meant that neither could definitively prove the other wrong, but Boswell's sarcasm has often been judged victorious over Seward's sensibility by later critics who ignore her premises but appreciate Boswell's manipulative prose.

At times, Boswell's attacks on Seward read like a nasty older brother's efforts to show up a rebellious sister, particularly when he resorts to using her family nickname as a way of undermining her dignity. The "brother" appears to battle for recognition of his superior, intimate knowledge of Johnson. Boswell revered Johnson as a father substitute, one of a succession of such figures in his life.[6] Particularly after Johnson's death, Boswell sought to defend his mentor from criticism derived from his remarks quoted in the *Life*, no doubt aware that critical objections to Johnson's manner partly owed to his own re-creation of Johnson's speech (Bate 365). Boswell thus had to rescue Johnson without admitting the degree to which Johnson's reported conversation was in fact his version of Johnson's style. Seward, in turn, believed Johnson's brusque judgments confirmed his dismissive remarks about some of Britain's greatest writers in the *Lives of the Poets*. Her personal memories of Johnson's conversation resembled Boswell's; she believed one bon mot valid because of its "Johnsonian spirit" and lamented that the *Life* contained so many "recorded proofs of his unprovoked personal rudeness" (*Gentleman's Magazine* 74:1099). When an anonymous contributor speculated that Seward resented Johnson's disparagement of her father, she denied the explanation except to allow that Johnson's insult confirmed her general complaint, published in her Benvolio letters years before publication of the *Life*, when Boswell's *Tour of the Hebrides* and Thrale-Piozzi's *Anecdotes* had inspired her to call attention to Johnson's reported flaws. Seward's readers today must account for both Seward's and Boswell's vehemence, especially when discussing her criticism, or her observations will continue to be dismissed.

If Seward was not driven to expose Johnson on behalf of her father, perhaps it was because Johnson was a father figure himself, one whom she particularly needed to confront. We have seen her expose the damage caused by a controlling father in *Louisa* and assert technical mastery in reviewing the work of her poetic "father" in *Memoirs of Dr. Darwin*. Of all the "fathers" controlling aspects of Seward's life, however, Johnson was professionally the most important. We have seen, for example, that she employed Johnsonian precedents, such as relying on living witnesses and including critical analysis, in her biography of Darwin. Nevertheless, as opposed to Boswell's "great and good" figure, Seward's Johnson was a malign patriarch guarding the portals of the literary canon. Unlike Johnson's other "daughters" such as Hester Thrale-Piozzi (who was one year older than Seward), Frances Burney, and Hannah More, Seward was never acknowledged as such and certainly never sought Johnson's approval. Instead, she expressed relief that Johnson rarely mentioned her poems while admitting that he had complimented her "Elegy on Cook" and had "spoke very handsomely" of her writings to a gathering at Porter's. She thanked Thrale-Piozzi for suppressing Johnson's remarks about her in her *Anecdotes*, disbelieving he had "[passed her] over in total silence" (*Letters* 2:44). Seward's letter seems contradictory: she is glad Johnson took no notice of her poems, although he did, even praising them, and happy not to find herself discussed in the *Anecdotes*, although she feels sure Johnson talked harshly about her. Perhaps Seward feared that Johnson had condemned her on account of to her relationship with Saville, as Boswell insinuated in the *Gentleman's Magazine* when he claimed that if she knew Johnson's opinion, "she might not like it" (74:1011). But Seward implies that she wishes Johnson had paid more, equally favorable, attention to her poems and granted her the consequence of talking about her. Having achieved some renown for her verse, Seward apparently wished for approval by the other literary star of Lichfield—the patriarch of British letters. Failing to attract his sustained notice, Seward protested his overbearing manner in her correspondence and, after Johnson's death, published her objections to the literary colossus in an effort to overthrow his authority. Her gesture was pyrrhic, pulling down on herself the ridicule of succeeding critics instead of rallying the British public on behalf of their poets. Johnson approved of few living poets, and Seward warmly admired many. Since Johnson and Seward shared many poetic principles, especially those prevalent in the earlier part of their century, there is rich irony both in their different conclusions and the fact that Seward's opinions have been virtually ignored. Today, with renewed critical interest in Ossian, Chatterton, Southey, and other Seward contemporaries, she does not look quite so foolish for defending British verse. But as British taste evolved in the early nineteenth century, her defense was ignored.

Today it is also easier to appreciate Seward's struggle to impose her critical views in a culture that did not easily accept women authorities (one thinks of Catharine Macauley Graham and of Mary Wollstonecraft as other examples of women who were ridiculed for their iconoclastic opinions). Following Nancy Chodorow, scholars have examined different eras' acculturation of women and the effects on women writers' personalities and careers.[7] In *Their Father's Daughters*, Elizabeth Kowaleski-Wallace has examined the consequences of the eighteenth-century maturation process for women, when severe restrictions on gender roles made attaining adulthood even more difficult. Women who overcame their mother identification, often because their mothers had died when they were very young, and strove for a role their society gendered "masculine"—that is, women who identified with their father's role—faced nearly insurmountable challenges. Kowaleski-Wallace examines the careers of Hannah More and Maria Edgeworth, women very different from Seward, who adhered to their fathers, figuratively in More's case, literally in Edgeworth's, "to obtain what [they] needed" (33). From Seward, we hear little of her mother, who seems to have been gracious and loving but who acquiesced in her husband's repression of their daughter's literary interests (Ashmun 83). We hear a great deal more of Mr. Seward, and much of what we learn must have created resentment (Barnard, *Anna Seward* 33–38). When finally permitted at last to devote herself to poetry, Seward spent the rest of her life establishing her literary reputation and living as much as she could on her own terms. She replaced her mother and, eventually, her father as host of the Bishop's Palace salon. It was important to Seward that she maintained her social as well as literary status, owing to her need to take over her parents' roles. That she did so while also maintaining her relationship with John Saville attests to Seward's strong will in carrying on her life as British muse and Lichfield social doyenne. Far from the shy provincial lady, Seward actively resisted the constraints on her behavior and, perhaps because she chose to remain in the town where her address and connections somewhat protected her status, overcame many of the obstacles erected by the father and "fathers" in her life.

Samuel Johnson might have been surprised to learn that Seward responded to him like a rebellious daughter. Johnson probably did not think or speak much about his Lichfield compatriot, as her half-expressed wish to have been included among his conversational topics intuits. Despite his occasional compliments, he was not generally impressed by the generation of poets to which Seward belonged and that she passionately defended. And, as Seward acknowledged, Johnson was not fond of those who contradicted his opinions. Johnson, of course, was soon canonized, and much of her generation's poetry was dismissed by the next. But her self-elected status as Johnson's rebellious daughter remains intriguing. Today, however, we can admire Johnson and his "son" Boswell without disparaging Seward. We can applaud her for trying to free herself, as far as she dared, from certain patriarchal restrictions and to control some of the circumstances of her personal life and literary career. In this she resembles Hester Thrale-Piozzi, Frances Burney, Mary Wollstonecraft, and other late-century women who made agonizing choices in order to fulfill themselves personally and as artists. As a poet, Seward imagined herself part of a great chain including Shakespeare, Milton, Dryden, and Pope, successively building on their achievements until the present day. She incorporated midcentury sensibility into the heritage of refined, public-minded verse, asserting, in a patriotic era, her generation's place as the current gems adorning that glittering chain. Critically, Seward tried to refine the practices of Johnson and Boswell, which they in turn inherited from predecessors who insisted on literature's moral imperative and the inextricable link between biography and criticism. Creatively, Seward embraced her role as "Queen Muse," protector of a tradition she strove to maintain and, within the limits of its poetics and adherence to sensibility, to expand. Seward's liminal status, born in the middle and writing at the end of the eighteenth century, made her an invaluable commentator on the turn to Romanticism. I hope that my readings have opened fresh perspectives on the writings of this dynamic woman, whose poetry and prose illuminate her precursors, her contemporaries, and those who followed her.

Notes

PREFACE

1. Stuart Curran discusses Seward in a number of articles and book chapters; see, for example, "Anna Seward and the Dynamics of Female Friendship."

INTRODUCTION

1. Seward was dropped from the second edition of David Fairer and Christine Gerrard, eds., *Eighteenth-Century Poetry*. She is not included in Fiona Robertson, ed., *Women's Writing, 1778–1838*. Among recent Romantic-era anthologies, Seward is not included in Deirdre Shauna Lynch, Jack Stillinger, and Stephen Greenblatt, eds., *The Norton Anthology of English Literature*, vol. D, nor in Charles Mahoney and Michael O'Neill, eds., *Romantic Poetry*.

2. Examples include Paula Backscheider's discussion of Seward's elegies and same-sex desire in *Eighteenth-Century Women Poets and Their Poetry*, 296–312, Sylvia Lorraine Bowerbank's chapter on Seward and environmental concerns in *Speaking for Nature*, 161–88, John Brewer's chapter on Seward as provincial poet in *The Pleasures of the Imagination*, 573–612, and Harriet Guest's chapter on Seward as a domestic muse in *Small Change*, 252–67. Recent articles on Seward and environmentalism are Donna Coffey's "Protecting the Botanic Garden," and Sharon Selzer, "Pond'rous Engines' in 'Outraged Groves.'"

3. I concur with Wheeler's thesis, although his article concerns a specific phenomenon, the use of place in Enlightenment and Romantic-era poetry, while my book reaches the same conclusion by investigating a range of poetic values and practices.

4. See Tim Fulford, *Landscape, Liberty, and Authority*, for a thorough discussion of eighteenth-century landscape poetry.

5. Brewer discusses the popularity of "tours" of London and of various British regions in *The Pleasures of the Imagination*, 50–51, 631–37. An example of a popular poetic "tour" was the title poem of Mary Chandler's *A Description of Bath . . . with Several Other Poems*.

6. Esther Schor analyzes the eighteenth-century evolution of the elegy and the watershed significance of Gray's "Elegy" in *Bearing the Dead*, 40–47.

7. See Thomas M. Woodman, *Thomas Parnell*, and Cecil V. Wicker, *Edward Young*.

8. Although "There Was a Boy" was included in both the *Lyrical Ballads* and the thirteen-book *Prelude*, the church is described as a "thronèd lady" only in the latter. See William Wordsworth, *The Thirteen-Book "Prelude,"* 402.

9. Marjorie Levinson describes Wordsworth's turn toward transcendence, which, she says, is what "makes [his poetry] Romantic" (45). Liu's reading is historicist, as is James Chandler's *England in 1819*, which encompasses a year of literary masterpieces written in the wake of the "Peterloo Massacre."

10. In *Romantic Ecology*, Jonathan Bate praises as "green" poems that name places, poems that sometimes are dedicated to loved ones whose names are "inscribed" (literally or metaphorically) on the landscape. Such poems indicate a poet's ability to be "lord of that which we do not possess," in the words of Edward Thomas (9).

11. Anne K. Mellor's two influential studies are *Romanticism and Gender* and *Mothers of the Nation*.

12. Janet Todd, *Sensibility*, Markman Ellis, *The Politics of Sensibility*, and Thomas J. McCarthy, *Relationships of Sympathy*. To these should be added Blakey Vermeule, *The Party of Humanity*, and Amit Rai, *Rule of Sympathy*.

13. Seward is mentioned in Nicholas Roe, ed., *Romanticism*, 3, 28, 32, 54, 184, 574, and in James Chandler and Maureen N. McLane, eds., *The Cambridge Companion to British Romantic Poetry*, 119, 157. Neither she nor her poems appear in the *Cambridge Companion*'s "Chronology."

CHAPTER 1: UNDER SUSPICIOUS CIRCUMSTANCES

1. Seward, for example, appears in the introduction to Carol Shiner Wilson and Joel Haeffner's *Re-Visioning Romanticism* amid a list of rarely taught women writers (6). Also symptomatic of Seward's neglect is that Adela Pinch refers to Seward's opinions throughout *Strange Fits of Passion* (45, 61, 68, 70, 72, 109) and lists her among the works cited but does not include her in the book's index, obscuring her prominence among contemporary critical voices.

2. Of the many books on Aphra Behn, see, for example, Heidi Hutner, ed., *Re-reading Aphra Behn*. Carol Barash reevaluates Katherine Philips's poetry in *English Women's Poetry*, and Donald J. Newman and Lynn Marie Wright's edited volume *Fair Philosopher* collects fresh scholarship on Haywood's *Female Spectator*. On writers closer to Seward's time, see Carrol Fry, *Charlotte Smith*, Deborah Kennedy, *Helen Maria Williams*, and Gina Luria Walker, *Mary Hays*.

3. See Richard Greene, *Mary Leapor*, Mary Waldron, *Lactilla, Milkwoman of Clifton*, and Ann Messenger, *Woman and Poet in the Eighteenth Century*. Messenger notes that Seward omitted Darwall from her list of seven noteworthy women poets in 1789 (1).

4. For example, Robert DeMaria Jr., ed., *British Literature, 1640–1789*, includes among mid- to late eighteenth-century poets Mary Collier, Mary Jones, Elizabeth Carter, Mary Leapor, Anna Laetitia Aiken Barbauld, Hannah More, Charlotte Smith,

and Anne Cromartie Yearsley but omits Seward. All of these poets deserve notice— and some are very important—but Seward surely is also worthy of attention.

5. For information about Scott's career, I consulted Edgar Johnson, *Sir Walter Scott.* For Scott's relationship with Seward and her writings, see 1:271–72, 312–13, 326, and 362.

6. Seward excelled at occasional verse; two good examples are her "Verses Inviting Mrs. C—— to Tea on a Public Fast Day, during the American War," an acerbic comment on the fast's, and war's, futility, and her "Admonition to Rosilda," warning a friend against her contemplated marriage to a dissolute man.

7. The phrase "the trough of the wave" is the title of an essay by Bertrand H. Bronson.

8. See Gretchen M. Foster, *Pope Versus Dryden.*

9. See Claudia N. Thomas, *Alexander Pope and His Eighteenth-Century Women Readers,* 110–17, 217–20, 227–29. See also Jacqueline M. Labbe's "Every Poet Her Own Drawing Master." Among other examples are the previously cited chapters by Guest and Bowerbank.

10. Barbara Schnorrenberg, for example, in her entry on Anna Seward perpetuates an incorrect birth date (281–82). Ashmun had corrected this mistake in her biography (5).

11. Besides McGann's, Todd's, and Ellis's previously cited books, see John Mullan, *Sentiment and Sociability,* and G. J. Barker-Benfield, *The Culture of Sensibility.*

12. See Linda Colley, *Britons.* Her book has inspired others, including Suvir Kaul, *Poems of Nation, Anthems of Empire,* and Dustin Griffin, *Patriotism and Poetry in the Long Eighteenth Century.*

13. See, for example, Marlon B. Ross, *The Contours of Masculine Desire,* and Carol Shiner Wilson and Joel Haeffner, *Re-Visioning Romanticism,* in addition to Mellor's and Colley's books.

14. Some examples, among many, include Donna Landry's groundbreaking *The Muses of Resistance,* Amanda Foreman's *Georgiana, Duchess of Devonshire,* and Moira Ferguson's *Eighteenth-Century Women Poets.*

15. Elizabeth Eger and Lucy Peltz's *Brilliant Women* accompanied an exhibition at the National Portrait Gallery devoted to the bluestocking phenomenon. Seward is mentioned in passing (45, 113) as poet and provincial salonnière.

16. Kelly's biographical preface to *Anna Seward* is more respectful than Ashmun's account but nonetheless borrows much from it. Compare, for example, Ashmun's "The Sewards . . . began to look about, in the furtive manner of prudent parents, for eligible young men, not averse to becoming bridegrooms" (17) with Kelly's "Like other parents, the Sewards began to look around for suitable husbands for their daughters" (xii). Likewise compare Ashmun's "She was gaining a reputation beyond Bath and Lichfield, and she did not shrink from sending her already sanctioned verse to the London journals" (74)—which refers to Seward's pursuit of publication following her Batheaston success—with Kelly's "Seward began to make quite a name for herself beyond the limits of Lichfield and Bath-Easton when she decided to send her verses, sanctioned by the Bath-Easton assembles, to London journals" (xv), or Ashmun's

"Immediately she reaped the reward of timeliness. In the *salons* of London her lines were read and quoted; and in distant country houses her name was repeated beside the hearth" (86)— referring to the reception of the *Monody on Major André*—with Kelly's "Her *Monody on Major André* . . . was timely . . . and Seward became a household name" (xvi). In other words, Kelly omits Ashmun's sneering tone but depends almost exclusively on *The Singing Swan* for her biographical narrative.

17. Other examples include Adeline Johns-Putra's "Gendering Telemachus."

CHAPTER 2: "FANCY'S SHRINE"

1. Indeed, provincial poets had long intervened in national debates. In "Political Verse and Satire," Kathryn R. King instances Katherine Philips as a Welsh gentlewoman who circulated poetry about national politics (203–6). Donna Landry in "The Labouring-Class Women Poets" notes the rural washerwoman Mary Collier's bid for national recognition (234).

2. In taking this position, I differ from a scholar such as Mary A. Waters, who in *British Women Writers and the Profession of Literary Criticism* explains that she defines as professional only those women critics who wrote "literary criticism for money under circumstances requiring that they meet the demands and offering them the support of a newly emerging literary profession" (7). She does not include ladies who published criticism with no consideration of pay or women who wrote professionally in other genres but only occasionally published criticism. Waters draws attention to the undervalued writing by paid women critics and thus insists on a strict definition. I am likewise drawing attention to a writer undervalued for other reasons, among them, that men and women who did not write for pay are liable to be dismissed today as "amateurs" in the sense of "unskilled," no matter how refined their writings.

3. For one example of Seward's many assertions of the poet's cultural significance, see her sonnet "On Reading a Description of Pope's Gardens at Twickenham": "This is the Poet's triumph . . ./. . . his consciousness of powers/That lift his memory from oblivion's doom" (*Poetical Works*, 3:141, ll. 9–11).

4. Horace Walpole remarked, "The poor Arcadian patroness does not spell one word of French or Italian right" (Hesselgrave 6).

5. Gittings also notes that "Laurel crowns were bandied about, both as figures of speech and in actual fact, in Hunt's circle" (145).

6. It is admittedly difficult to imagine Gittings making this statement in the wake of Anne K. Mellor's, Paula Backscheider's, and other more recent writers' emphasis on the domestic priorities and sociability of much Romantic-era, and especially women's, verse.

7. I am grateful to Jennifer Keith for directing me to this important discussion.

8. In *Hogarth*, Ronald Paulson, for example, discusses the ubiquity of signboards in eighteenth-century London, with their "symbolic representations" employing essentially "the same devices" that Hogarth used in his paintings and engravings (2: 335–36).

9. Seward admired Kauffman; witness her allusion to "ANGELICA's unrival'd hand"

in the "Invocation of the Comic Muse" (l. 31), which specifically praises an image of Thalia, crowned with roses and dressed in a blue robe, disarming Cupid. Kauffman's sportive nymphs were ubiquitous in reproductions, particularly on decorative porcelain, for which, as Malise Forbes Adam and Mary Mauchline observe, Kauffman's "Cupid designs monopolized the field," almost always portrayed cavorting with muses and nymphs (136).

10. In "Sensuousness in the Poetry of Eighteenth-Century Women Poets," Margaret Anne Doody discusses this ode in the context of women's flexibility in addressing the relation between human and animal, a theme men usually treated by affirming strict barriers between species.

11. See Adam and Mauchline, "Kauffman's Decorative Work," and David Alexander, "Kauffman and the Print Market in Eighteenth-Century England."

12. See David Alexander, "Chronological Checklist," 181.

CHAPTER 3: THE PROFESSION OF POETRY

1. For the feminization of sensibility, see John Mullan, *Sentiment and Sociability*, and G. J. Barker-Benfield, *The Culture of Sensibility*.

2. Mellor arrives at a different conclusion from Zionkowski in *Romanticism and Gender* based on the large numbers of women publishing in all genres by the late eighteenth century. In *Borderlines*, Wolfson, however, points to women's ongoing difficulties when exercising their "masculine" intellects in print.

3. Margaret J. M. Ezell examines why many past women writers have been ignored in *Writing Women's Literary History*. Her study is much broader than mine, but she demonstrates that women who wrote from a religious perspective and/or circulated their works in manuscript have been overlooked even by feminists rediscovering early modern women writers. In *A Literary History of Women's Writing in Britain, 1660–1789* Susan Staves likewise argues that women who wrote from a religious or often even a conservative point of view have been given less attention than women whose writings were more secular or rebellious.

4. Dustin Griffin in *Literary Patronage in England* concentrates on kinds of patronage featuring the exchange of financial assistance or church or government places in return for authorial dedications and professional services including entertainment. He does, however, note that "hospitality of one form or another" was among forms of patronage, including "'familiarity,' whereby persons of talent are permitted to cross a line, under controlled conditions, that normally separates the ranks of a hierarchical society" (18–19). "Encouragement," according to Griffin, was also a means of patronage and could range from "kind words and assurances of interest" to financial support (19). Since Seward was an independently wealthy gentlewoman, she no doubt referred to Lady Miller as her patron on account of the latter's hospitality and encouragement and the opportunity she provided to socialize with those of much higher rank. Lady Miller conferred these in exchange for the "entertainment" Seward provided at the Batheaston assemblies and the luster she shed on them when her poems became famous. Later in her life, Seward herself "gave a great deal of time and energy

to 'patronizing genius.' Her patronage of [William] Newton, the Derbyshire Minstrel, took the form of hospitable entertainment, social introductions, and solid cash
advances" (Ashmun 280). Seward's patronage of Newton was quite conventional compared with her "client" relationship with patron Lady Miller.

5. In *Anna Seward*, Barnard discusses Seward's expert management of her father's
business affairs; see, for example, 147–48. Barnard concludes that such employment—
rather than more "feminine" occupations such as sewing or caring for her ailing
father—constituted Seward's household duties.

6. See Steven H. Clark, ed., *Mark Akenside, James MacPherson, Edward Young*,
75–77, and Mary Waldron, *Lactilla, Milkwoman of Clifton*, 211.

7. Thomas Gray published only thirteen poems in his lifetime, often after Horace
Walpole had admired them in manuscript. William Cowper's writing was partly a
therapeutic diversion from his mental illness. William Mason's circumstances resembled Joseph Wharton's and William Lisle Bowles's; all three were primarily clergymen
as well as poets and men of letters. Thomas Wharton the younger was, like Gray, a
successful academic who was also recognized as an influential poet; he was poet laureate from 1785 to 1790. Seward resembles these male contemporaries in that she, like
them, was a serious, widely read poet but was never a professional in the sense of earning her living through writing.

8. Seward's *Elegy on Captain Cook* went through five editions between 1780 and
1784. Her *Monody on Major André* went through nine editions, including six in America, between 1781 and 1806. *Louisa* appeared in five editions in America and five in
Britain between 1784 and 1792. *Llangollen Vale, with Other Poems* merited three editions in 1796, and *Original Sonnets on Various Subjects* three editions in 1799. Jennifer
Kelly lists Seward's editions in *Anna Seward*, xxiii–xxiv.

9. Examples include the volume of women's tributes entitled *The Nine Muses*,
edited by Delarivier Manley, Elizabeth Rowe, "Upon the Death of Her Husband,"
included in the second edition of Pope's *Eloisa to Abelard*, and Mary Jones, "In Memory of the Right Honorable Lord Aubrey Beauclerk, Who Was Slain at Carthagena."

CHAPTER 4: BRITISH PATRIOT

1. Harriet Guest, argues, for example, that for critics of Catharine Macaulay, "patriotism is based in sensibility and local emotion, but these are feminized qualities
which, when removed from a private and familial register, are involved in the discourse of corruption employed in the narrative on the decline of the Roman empire"
(*Small Change* 219). Anna Laetitia Barbauld was praised, in contrast, because she
cloaked her patriotic interventions in the guise of a Roman matron upholding "household virtues" as the basis of the civic ideal (251).

2. In *Bearing the Dead*, Esther Schor discusses midcentury anxiety about the
sincerity of public elegies: "Critical qualms about sincerity reveal a residual uneasi-
ness about the manliness of publicizing displays of emotion" (47). Seward avoided the
latter issue by presenting herself as chief public mourner. In her elegies for André and
Lady Miller, she emphasized her personal grief for those she publicly mourned. Paul

Goring describes the function played by novels in modeling somatic behavior such as tears and fainting. By responding correctly to the trials of heroes and heroines, readers confirmed their membership in the polite reading community and, in effect, confirmed their polite status (142–47). It is probably not claiming too much to say that Seward's elegiac speakers modeled sentimental patriotic responses for her early readers.

3. Barnard regards it as equally plausible that Seward alone wrote the elegy on Captain Cook (123).

4. In *A Swan and Her Friends*, E. V. Lucas states that "to the [Batheaston] vase was due . . . two of her most serious and worthy effusions—the 'Elegy on Captain Cook' and the 'Monody on André'" (142). Margaret Ashmun cites the Cook elegy as among the "already-sanctioned" (by the Batheaston assemblies) poems Seward sent "to the London journals" (74).

5. See Claudia N. Thomas, "Masculine Performances and Gender Identity," for a discussion of Lady Beauclerk's choice of Mary Jones, a family friend, to write an elegy following her husband's death in the naval battle at Carthagena (169). An earlier example of a national elegy penned by a woman is Lady Mary Lee Chudleigh's "On the Death of His Highness the Duke of Gloucester."

6. Although some of Colley's details have been disputed—see, for example, Hannah Smith, "The Idea of a Protestant Monarchy in Britain, 1714–1760," which refutes Colley's argument that Britons felt no personal allegiance to the Hanoverians but instead were committed to the Act of Succession that established them—I accept the broad sweep of her argument as elucidating several cultural trends reflected in Seward's opinions and career.

7. See especially chapter 5, "A Culture of Reform," 215–86.

8. Beaglehole adduces exhaustion from the previous voyages as the main cause of the lapsed judgment that led to Cook's death (711–12). Glyn Williams states that "with hindsight . . . Cook should not have been approached" to lead his final voyage, given the "physically grueling and mentally exhausting" nature of his too-recent previous voyages (*Voyages of Delusion* 286).

9. See, for example, John Dryden's *Annus Mirabilis* (1666), Joseph Addison's *Spectator* no. 69 describing the Royal Exchange (1711), Alexander Pope's "Windsor-Forest" (1713), and James Thomson's *The Seasons* (1730).

10. Cook literally planted seeds on some South Pacific islands that he visited (Beaglehole 335, 536, 545, 552).

11. See Sandro Jung, "Susanna Pearson and the 'Elegiac' Lyric."

12. See Joshua Hett Smith, *Narrative of the Death of Major André*. An engraving of André's memorial is reproduced on the page facing 176. On the return of his remains, see Robert McConnell Hatch, *Major John André*, 276.

13. See Jennifer Kelly, *Anna Seward*, 320n12.

14. Indeed, Seward's threat coincidentally echoes the words of a British officer serving in America in a letter home describing the army's "shocked" reaction to André's death. "Both officers and men are so enraged by this business," he wrote, "that they swear they will have revenge whenever they can get an opportunity, and I make no

doubt that before this Rebellion is over there will be no quarter given on either side. . . . There never was so melancholy a thing" (qtd. in Christopher Hibbert, *Red-coats and Rebels*, 297).

15. Jennifer Keith discusses earlier women's struggles to define themselves as poets despite the traditional identification of women not with poets but with poets' source of inspiration (*Poetry and the Feminine from Behn to Cowper*, 51–79). Seward would seem to have resolved that struggle by identifying herself as both poet-speaker and muse.

CHAPTER 5: WARTIME CORRESPONDENT

1. In *Wordsworth's Great Period Poems*, Marjorie Levinson, for example, posits that the poet deliberately omitted mention of the abbey itself in Tintern Abbey, along with the British revolutionary associations of the date and site of his poem, because "the object . . . is to replace the picture of the place with 'the picture of the mind'" (5). Alan Liu in *Wordsworth* agrees that "Tintern Abbey" denies the history implicit in its place and date but argues that the poem is in fact about history, in opposition to "the sheer will and ambition of a poet" (217). Nicholas Roe finds it impossible to believe that Wordsworth was evading sociopolitical associations when he wrote "Tintern Abbey"; the Wye Valley contained several "republican" sites besides the abbey, and walking tours themselves were considered a "democratic" gesture (*Politics* 126).

2. On the conservatism of Seward's letter, see Kennedy, *Helen Maria Williams and the Age of Revolution*, where she describes Seward as speaking "like the nation's spokesperson, giving Williams one last chance to come home to London with her respectability intact and her rashness forgiven" (96). In "Benevolent Historian," Kennedy made essentially the same point by claiming that Seward addresses Williams "as a type of prodigal daughter" (321). Both comments align Seward's social conservatism with political conservatism, an identification I wish to complicate.

3. In *British Women Poets of the Long Eighteenth Century*, Paula Backscheider and Catherine Ingrassia include six poems printed between 1790 and 1800; all but one (an encomium on a British soldier by Joanna Baillie) deplore the French wars' carnage.

4. In her note to the poem, Jennifer Kelly supposes that Seward omitted the poem from both her *Original Sonnets* and posthumous edition because "she no doubt considered it too political" (325n10). Since Seward did not hesitate to publish her opinion of the American War, it is probably not accurate to suppose her generally averse to publishing on a political topic, but Seward may have been hesitant to perpetuate a poem that at best was an embarrassing reminder of a position she later reversed and at worst may have thought seditious a decade after its publication.

5. In *Poetical Works*, the poem is titled "Ode on England's Naval Triumphs in the Present War."

6. See, for examples, *Critical Review*, May 1799, 33–38, *European Magazine*, May 1799, 323–25, and *Monthly Review*, August 1799, 361–99. All focus on Seward's technique and style.

7. Lewis L. Turco, in *The New Book of Forms*, identifies the a-b-a-b stanza as a Sicilian quatrain, "a set form of the heroic stanza" (206).

CHAPTER 6: SEWARD AND SENSIBILITY

1. Other important sources on sensibility include Jean Hagstrum's classic *Sex and Sensibility*, Janet Todd's succinct *Sensibility*, Markman Ellis's *The Politics of Sensibility*, and Susan Staves's often pejorative analysis in *A Literary History of Women's Writing in Britain, 1660–1789*.

2. In her biography of Seward, Teresa Barnard notes this letter-journal as the earliest extant evidence of Seward's self-construction through writing (8). She observes the parallels between Seward and her heroine Louisa, who likewise mediates her life through correspondence with an absent friend named Emma (13–14).

3. I take my information about the reception and editions of *La nouvelle Heloïse* from Judith H. McDowell's preface to her abridged translation of *Julie; or, The New Eloise*.

CHAPTER 7: *LOUISA* AND THE LATE EIGHTEENTH-CENTURY FAMILY ROMANCE

1. I paraphrase Janet Todd's description of the plot of *The Wrongs of Woman* in *Sensibility*, 135. Todd describes Wollstonecraft's struggles to free herself from her fascination with Rousseau, evident throughout both her fiction and nonfictional prose.

2. It is worth mentioning that Seward herself attempted a translation of *Télémaque* later in her life; two books and part of a third are preserved in manuscript at the Johnson Birthplace Museum in Lichfield. In "Gendering Telemachus," Adeline Johns-Putra argues that Seward's epic fragment, revised according to her poetics of sensibility, was unpublishable because it contradicted the masculine values of traditional epic. Telemachus himself, in Seward's version, becomes the feminized object of Calypso's lust. Johns-Putra's observation suggests that Seward characterized Telemachus as she did Eugenio. Published when sensibility still prevailed as a model for masculine as well as feminine behavior, and without the epic's expectations of warrior-like traits, *Louisa*'s hero appears to have been quite acceptable to readers. I claim for the verse novel, however, the same subtle but unmistakably subversive quality Johns-Putra finds in *Telemachus*.

3. See Mary Laven, *The Virgins of Venice*, for a discussion of this phenomenon, which persisted until Napoleon disbanded the convents.

4. Ashmun comments snidely of Ernesto's request that "the idea of their being saved by energetic work seems not to occur to anyone" (127), an example of inattentive reading perhaps caused by her general prejudice against Seward's writings.

5. Saville's situation was a less dramatic version of Eugenio's. Divorce at the time was possible only when a wife's adultery could be proved. Few women were hardy enough to expose themselves to such a charge, even when a marriage was insupportable, and few men likewise were willing to accuse their wives of adultery. Eugenio is representative in his hesitation; he feels guilty owing to his failure to love Emira, which

has driven her into debauched behavior. Saville's wife, according to Seward was merely "shrewish, vulgar, and many ways unamiable" (Whalley 1:344), so that divorce was impossible and separation his only option.

CHAPTER 8: MILTON'S CHAMPION

1. In their introduction to *A Century of Sonnets*, Feldman and Robinson state that "Seward was the first woman sonneteer with any substantial impact upon the tradition" (10). They also state, however, that Charlotte Smith and William Lisle Bowles "set the tone for the Romantic sonnet and its emphasis on feeling" (12).

2. See, for example, Jerome McGann, *The Poetics of Sensibility*, 156–58, Judith Hawley, "Charlotte Smith's *Elegiac Sonnets*," and Christopher C. Nagle, *Sexuality and the Culture of Sensibility*, 50–55.

3. Staves, to take one example, quotes these phrases at her study's conclusion, disagreeing with Seward's opinion but endorsing her right to criticize Smith's writings (*Literary History* 439).

4. Barnard reveals that Seward's chief reason for remaining in Lichfield was her attachment to John Saville (*Anna Seward* 21).

5. One thinks of the sign Bill Clinton's campaign manager, James Carville, famously placed above the candidate's desk during the 1992 presidential campaign, reminding him to repeat his chief theme: "It's the economy, stupid!"

6. Kramnick's chapter on the cultural logic of late feudalism examines the canonization of Spenser, but many of his points apply likewise to contemporary discussions of Milton. Thomas Bonnell has recently disputed Kramnick's logic: since the bookselling trade was sales driven, it would not have made sense to emphasize Milton's and Spenser's inaccessibility (22–23). Academic critics like the Wartons were concerned about corrupt texts and wished to encourage the reading of correct texts. Bonnell's point is well taken, but for a consumer like Seward, anxious to prove herself a discriminating reader and critic, the argument that Milton was "caviary to the general" would have increased his appeal.

7. Melissa Bailes reflects on Seward's accusations against Smith despite her own plagiarism in "The Evolution of the Plagiarist." Bailes considers Seward's categorization of poets analogous to her preference for the Linnean system of botany. Seward emulated the Linnean approach, "minutely systematiz[ing poets] into classes" (119). She consequently despised Smith's "stylistic hybridity" (119) while sanctioning her own borrowings because they adhered to the established order of the legitimate sonnet, "distinct, situated in its designated place and closing gaps within the poetic taxonomy" (121).

8. The original French can be found in *Oeuvres poétiques*.

9. Fussell remarks that "one of the basic aesthetic principles of conservative metric in the eighteenth century is that the poet has not only the right but the duty to improve natural phonetic materials until they become fit for elevated uses" (75). Although the *OED* lists "complicate" as a synonym for intricate and complex, that use was evidently more prevalent in the seventeenth century. Poets such as Crabbe and Southey still

used "complicate" in that sense, however, and Seward probably chose to do so owing to the word's striking, and increasingly unusual, quality.

CHAPTER 9: CORRESPONDING POEMS

1. Margaret Ashmun sympathetically recounts Seward's exchanges regarding Johnson. She explains the familial connection that may have resulted in Seward's condescension toward her grandfather's poor student (110–23). She details the evidence that formed the grounds of Seward's disapproval (139–43) and the blistering public exchange with Boswell that ultimately resulted (201–8), concluding that Boswell prevailed and that the experience humiliated Seward (206–7). But she also provides plenty of corroborating evidence supporting Seward's impression of Johnson as a man who could be harsh, rude, and even cruel in company (121–23). I discuss this episode in the concluding chapter.

2. Seward's reference is the scene in which Cassandra warns the eponymous hero:

The gods of death will, soon,
Extend o'er me their all-protecting wing.
I shall not long, I shall not want protection;
But who, devoted prince, will give it thee?
Even while we talk the secret wheels are turning,
That lift the vile, and lay the mighty low.   (4.2.49–54)

3. Seward's initial remarks were published by the *Gentleman's Magazine* in February and April 1786 and August 1787. In October 1793, the same periodical published her letter regarding Boswell's *Life*, to which Boswell replied in the November issue. Seward replied to Boswell in the *Gentleman's Magazine* for December 1793, disavowing her intention to pursue the argument, but Boswell published a final, angry rejoinder in the January 1794 issue. Seward wrote to several friends and relatives asking their support, and her cousin Henry White published two defenses of the poet in the same periodical, in March and October 1794.

4. In her letter to Henry Cary of March 4, 1798, Seward disputed Coleridge's statement that Wordsworth's description of the glowworm's light as green was original. She observes that the glowworm's light is "stellar" and that Ossian had described starlight as green long before Wordsworth was born (*Letters* 5:61).

CHAPTER 10: THE "LOST" HONORA

1. In *Wordsworth's Profession*, Thomas Pfau explains the appeal of Wordsworth's "Tintern Abbey" as its invitation to "an urban, educated 'middle class'" to gain the "distinctive cultural capital" implied by their "expertise" in identifying with the speaker's "inward *pathos*" (138). Pfau's argument might be extended to all the early Romantic poets, whose poems, like Charlotte Smith's sonnets, "trained" their readers both to appreciate and to identify with their dramatizations of what Thomas J. McCarthy, in *Relationships of Sympathy*, calls the "inner life of feeling" (148).

2. In *Surpassing the Love of Man*, Lillian Faderman describes Seward's relationship as an "ideal romantic friendship" (135). She doubts it was a sexual relationship based on Seward's very public references to their attachment but believes it was the "most enduring and passionate attachment of her life" (132). In *Intimate Friends*, Martha Vicinus is less circumspect about Seward's sexual orientation, writing that "the poet . . . frequently wrote about her various romances with other women" (8).

3. In *Companions Without Vows*, Rizzo remarks that the model for companionate relationships was marriage: "The autonomous mistress had the same powers over her companion that the husband had over his wife. She could choose either to exercise those powers autocratically, as she had probably seen her father and husband do, or to work out an equitable arrangement such as she herself would have liked to experience in her dealings with men" (1–2). She instances Elizabeth Montagu, in her relationship with her companion Dorothea Gregory, as an example of a woman who became a "patriarch" (117), tyrannizing her young companion. Although Honora Sneyd was not Seward's "companion" but rather her foster sister, Seward's assumption of influence over the younger woman's relationships bears comparison with the phenomenon Rizzo describes.

4. Ashmun confirms that Honora turned down Thomas Day's proposal, while, beside André, Lord Greville and a Colonel Barry also expressed their attraction (50–51).

5. Richardson cites brain activity during sleep as among the tenets of Romantic psychology held by Erasmus Darwin, Seward's mentor.

CHAPTER 11: *MEMOIRS OF THE LIFE OF DR. DARWIN*

1. Paul Fussell argues throughout the *Theory of Prosody* for the importance of harmony or melody to eighteenth-century poets and prosodists. Early in the century, Pope played with metrical stress patterns to create effects such as irony as well as variety within a predominately regular iambic pentameter structure (54). By midcentury, however, conservative prosodists were arguing that verse must be strictly regular. While this idea prevailed, readers of poetry persisted in scanning lines as regular iambics even when doing so countered the sense or natural pronunciation of verse (56–67). Late-century poets began to rebel against slavish adherence to metrical regularity, experimenting with accentual scansion and other methods of achieving melodic verse (156–63). Because Seward was trained to emulate Milton and Pope, she never indulged in the extreme quest for metric regularity. Her preference for variety within heroic lines agrees with ideas promoted by contemporaries like James Beattie and Robert Burns in the 1770s and 1780s (144–45).

2. In *Look to the Lady*, Russ McDonald describes how Siddons "moved the standard of personation away from the conventional and toward the natural or verisimilar," although she remained well within the boundaries of what Pope described in his "Essay on Criticism" as "nature to advantage dress'd" (24).

3. See Dustin Griffin, *Patriotism and Poetry in Eighteenth-Century Britain*.

4. An example of the first sense can be seen in Seward's revision of a couplet in Pope's "Essay on Criticism" in 1806, in which she created a metaphor for how we re-

spond to imagery that compared that response to a visual reaction. For Pope's "What oft was thought, but ne'er so well express'd," she substituted "Sprung from strange images in contact brought,/The bright collision of an agile thought,/And when together struck like flint and fire,/We start delighted, ponder, and admire" (*Letters* 6:308).

5. See especially chapter 6, "Bluestockings and Sentimental Writers, 1756–1776," in which Staves describes the importance of publications such as Elizabeth Montagu's *Essay on the Writings and Genius of Shakespear* (1769) and Elizabeth Carter's translation of *All the Works of Epictetus* (1758).

6. In *The Politics of Sensibility*, Markman Ellis observes two instances of Seward's literary-critical interventions, one in the *Gentleman's Magazine* in 1786 (203) and the other in Humphrey Repton's *Variety* in 1788 (208). Anne K. Mellor notes women's extensive participation in the discursive public sphere and commends Seward's confidence in her published critical judgments in *Mothers of the Nation* (100). In a fine instance of revisionist, feminist reading, David Simpson proposes in *Romanticism, Nationalism, and the Revolt against Theory* that Mary Wollstonecraft's *Vindication of the Rights of Woman* was not written in an "unstable" style because she was incompetent but because she was trying to engage with a female readership she deemed unstable (109). Mary Waters studies only the writings of women journalists who wrote for pay in her in *British Women Writers and the Profession of Literary Criticism, 1789–1832*, in an effort to increase critical recognition of this overlooked professional group.

7. Seward's advice to Cayley was part of a letter to Richard Sykes of March 16, 1794 (*Letters* 3:316–27).

8. Seward read aloud in her own parlor at Lichfield; in a letter preserved in the *Journals and Correspondence of Thomas Sedgewick Whalley*, she described reading Whalley's *Edwy and Edilda* by turns with three other readers to five guests in the "blue region," her personal parlor, in August 1781 (1:328). In a letter to Walter Scott dated July 1803, she describes reading one of his poems to "a young soldier of genius," pleased that "his kindling countenance, always, and often his exclaiming voice, marked every beauty as I proceeded" (6:100). The more famous gatherings of the bluestockings in London seem to have been characterized chiefly by conversation and indeed were celebrated for encouraging conversation between gentlemen and ladies of various political opinions and intellectual achievements and interests; see Nicole Pohl and Betty A. Schellenberg, eds., *Reconsidering the Bluestockings*, especially Harriet Guest's "Bluestocking Feminism" and Emma Major's "The Politics of Sociability." Contemporary accounts mention guests quoting poetry, but although gatherings such as those at Mrs. Thrale's home often featured much discussion of literature, they did not seem to feature the kind of dramatic readings Seward performed.

9. Wolfson devotes a chapter to this phenomenon in *Borderlines*. See, for example, her discussion of an especially pejorative essay of 1822 in *Blackwood's* accusing Keats of an "'effeminacy of style' that is 'all florid, all fine,' . . . 'cloying in its sweetness'" (247).

10. Michelle Levy describes in *Family Authorship* how the contributions of women participants in the family authorship circles of the male Romantic poets were downplayed or denied as the poets pursued individual eminence.

11. Markman Ellis attributes to Seward two acerbic articles in the *Gentleman's Magazine* (1785) disputing Clara Reeves's preference for Fielding in *The Progress of Romance* (203) and also observes two essays in Humphrey Repton's *Variety* (1788) promoting the superiority of *Clarissa* over *Tom Jones* (208).

12. Margaret Ezell discusses the letter as an established genre in *Writing Women's Literary History* (34).

13. Since Darwin was widely regarded for both his vast knowledge as well as his accomplished verse, Seward can be forgiven for her high estimate. His biographer, Desmond King-Hele, describes him as "the most famous English poet of the 1790s" (13).

14. King-Hele rather amusingly remarks that Seward "analyses the verse [of *The Botanic Garden*], its accentuation, phraseology, mannerisms and weaknesses, with a skill that no one who is not an eighteenth-century poet can hope to rival" (155).

CHAPTER 12: ANNA SEWARD, SAMUEL JOHNSON,
AND THE END OF THE EIGHTEENTH CENTURY

1. In fact, Johnson had written that West was one of the few poets for whom the grave "might be without its terrors" (*The Lives of the Poets*, 4:118).

2. On July 31, 1794, for example, Seward confided to a Mrs. Jackson her fear that she had contracted breast cancer after a blow to her chest (*Letters* 3:382–83).

3. A good representation of this legend is an often-reproduced nineteenth-century painting by James Doyle (1851) of a meeting of Johnson's Club at Reynolds's house, in which Boswell is poised behind Johnson, pencil and tiny notebook in hand.

4. Bate approaches Seward's biographical reminiscences in an evenhanded manner, accepting some suggestions and rejecting others. For example, he dismisses her account of the myrtle-sprig poem as "crazily assumed by some to be an actual love poem of his own" (128) but accepts her account of Johnson's courtship of Elizabeth Porter as "by no means improbable" (144). He also finds shrewd her deduction that Johnson's affection for Thrale-Piozzi was "cupboard love" (388). Bate attributes Seward's many inaccuracies not to "deliberate deceit or delight in creative invention" but to passing on "as assured fact" what was "sometimes only speculative gossip on the part of her mother and older people" (144). Bate thus takes Seward seriously as a source even if he finds her sources, in turn, unreliable.

5. In his popular biography of Johnson, for example, John Wain simply records that "Michael even made up a quaint little set of verses, commemorating the accidental death of a duckling, and attributed them to Sam," without mentioning Seward's alternative version of the anecdote (25).

6. Many scholars have commented on this aspect of the Boswell-Johnson relationship. David Daiches, for one, remarks that Johnson "was aware of Boswell's search for a father-figure and was prepared to play that role for him" (2).

7. See *The Reproduction of Mothering* and *Feminism and Psychoanalytic Theory*. Throughout her works, Chodorow argues that women's maturation is more complicated than men's. While both genders must separate themselves from their mothers

in order to become adults, a man separates himself from the person closest to himself but whose gender is unlike his own and models himself on his father. Women must somehow separate themselves from the person who is not only closest to them but with whose gender they identify. To varying degrees in different cultures, they then have difficulty becoming autonomous adults because the opposite gender is a problematic model while their own gender is perceived to be inferior.

Bibliography

Adams, Malise Forbes, and Mary Mauchline. "Kauffman's Decorative Work." In *Angelica Kauffman: A Continental Artist in Georgian England*, edited by Wendy Wassyng Roworth, 113–40. London: Reaktion, 1993.

Alexander, David. "Chronological Checklist of Singly Issued English Prints after Angelica Kauffman." In *Angelica Kauffman: A Continental Artist in Georgian England*, edited by Wendy Wassyng Roworth, 179–89. London: Reaktion, 1993.

———. "Kauffman and the Print Market in Eighteenth-century England." In *Angelica Kauffman: A Continental Artist in Georgian England*, edited by Wendy Wassyng Roworth, 141–78. London: Reaktion, 1993.

Ashmun, Margaret. *The Singing Swan: An Account of Anna Seward and Her Acquaintance with Dr. Johnson, Boswell, and Others of Their Time*. New Haven, CT: Yale University Press, 1931.

Austen, Jane. *Letters*. Edited by Deirdre Le Faye. 3rd ed. Oxford: Oxford University Press, 1995.

———. *Sense and Sensibility*. Oxford: Oxford University Press, 1990.

Backscheider, Paula R. *Eighteenth-Century Women Poets and Their Poetry: Inventing Agency, Inventing Genre*. Baltimore, MD: Johns Hopkins University Press, 2005.

Backscheider, Paula R., and Catherine E. Ingrassia, eds. *British Women Poets of the Long Eighteenth Century: An Anthology*. Baltimore, MD: Johns Hopkins University Press, 2009.

Bailes, Melissa. "The Evolution of the Plagiarist: Natural History in Anna Seward's Order of Poetics." *Eighteenth-Century Life* 33.3 (2009): 105–26.

Bainbridge, Simon. *British Poetry and the Revolutionary and Napoleonic Wars: Visions of Conflict*. Oxford: Oxford University Press, 2003.

Ball, Margaret. *Sir Walter Scott as a Critic of Literature*. New York: Columbia University Press, 1907.

Barash, Carol. *English Women's Poetry, 1649–1714: Politics, Community, and Linguistic Authority*. Oxford, UK: Clarendon, 1996.

Barbeau, Alfred. *Life and Letters at Bath in the XVIII Century*. London: Heinemann, 1904.

Barker-Benfield, G. J. *The Culture of Sensibility: Sex and Society in Eighteenth-Century Britain*. Chicago: University of Chicago Press, 1992.

Barnard, Teresa. *Anna Seward: A Constructed Life*. Burlington, VT: Ashgate, 2009.

———. "Anna Seward's 'Terrestrial Year'. Women, Poetry, and Science in Eighteenth-Century England." *Journal of Literature and the History of Ideas* 7.1 (2009): 3–17.

Bate, Jonathan. *Romantic Ecology: Wordsworth and the Environmental Tradition.* London: Routledge, 1991.

Bate, W. Jackson. *Samuel Johnson.* New York: Harcourt Brace Jovanovich, 1977.

Beaglehole, J. C. *The Life of Captain James Cook.* Stanford, CA: Stanford University Press, 1974.

Benedict, Barbara M. "Publishing and Reading Poetry." In *The Cambridge Companion to Eighteenth Century Poetry*, edited by John Sitter, 63–82. Cambridge: Cambridge University Press, 2001.

Blair, Hugh. *Lectures on Rhetoric and Belles Lettres.* In *The Sublime: A Reader in British Eighteenth-Century Aesthetic Theory*, edited by Andrew Ashfield and Peter de Bolla, 213–23. Cambridge: Cambridge University Press, 1996.

Blake, William. "Auguries of Innocence." In *William Blake's Writings*, 2 vols., edited by G. C. Bentley Jr., 2:1312. Oxford, UK: Clarendon, 1978.

Blathwayt, Janice. "A Bluestocking Bibliography." In *Reconsidering the Bluestockings*, edited by Nicole Pohl and Betty A. Schellenberg, 39–57. San Marino, CA: Huntington Library, 2003.

Boileau, Nicolas. *The Art of Poetry.* Translated by William Soames. Revised By John Dryden. Glasgow: R. and A. Foulis, 1755.

———. "L'art poetique." In *Oeuvres poëtiques*, 239–40. London: J. Brotherton et al., 1730.

Bonnell, Thomas F. *The Most Disreputable Trade: Publishing the Classics of English Poetry, 1765–1810.* Oxford: Oxford University Press, 2008.

Boswell, James. *Boswell's Life of Johnson.* 6 vols. Edited by George Birkbeck Hill and L. F. Powell. Oxford, UK: Clarendon, 1934.

Bowerbank, Sylvia Lorraine. *Speaking for Nature: Women and Ecologies of Early Modern England.* Baltimore, MD: Johns Hopkins University Press, 2004.

Brewer, John. *The Pleasures of the Imagination: English Culture in the Eighteenth Century.* New York: Farrar, Straus and Giroux, 1997.

Brissenden, R. F. *Virtue in Distress: Studies in the Novel of Sentiment from Richardson to Sade.* New York: Harper and Row, 1974.

Bronson, Bertrand H. "The Trough of the Wave." In *England in the Restoration and Early Eighteenth Century: Essays on Culture and Society*, edited by H. T. Swedenberg, 197–226. Berkeley: University of California Press, 1972.

Burgess, Miranda J. *British Fiction and the Production of Social Order, 1740–1830.* Cambridge: Cambridge University Press, 2000.

Burney, Frances. *Evelina; or, A Young Lady's Entrance into the World.* Edited by Kristina Straub. Boston: Bedford Books, 1997.

Cary, Henry Francis. *Sonnets and Odes.* London: J. Robson and W. Clarke, 1788.

Castle, Terry. *Masquerade and Civilization: The Carnivalesque in Eighteenth-Century Culture and Fiction.* Stanford, CA: Stanford University Press, 1986.

Chandler, James. *England in 1819: The Politics of Literary Culture and the Case of Romantic Historicism.* Chicago: University of Chicago Press, 1998.

Chandler, James, and Maureen N. McLane, eds. *The Cambridge Companion to British Romantic Poetry*. Cambridge: Cambridge University Press, 2008.

Chandler, Mary. *A Description of Bath Humbly Inscribed to Her Royal Highness the Princess Amelia, with Several Other Poems*. 8th ed. London: H. Leake, 1747.

Chodorow, Nancy J. *Feminism and Psychoanalytic Theory*. Cambridge, UK: Polity, 1989.

———. *The Reproduction of Mothering: Psychoanalysis and the Sociology of Gender*. Berkeley: University of California Press, 1978.

Clark, Steven H., ed. *Mark Akenside, James MacPherson, Edward Young: Selected Poetry*. Manchester, UK: Fyfield Books, 1994.

Clifford, James. "The Authenticity of Anna Seward's Published Correspondence." *Modern Philology* 39.2 (1941): 113–22.

Coffey, Donna. "Protecting the Botanic Garden: Seward, Darwin, and Coalbrookdale." *Women's Studies* 31.2 (2002): 141–64.

Colley, Linda. *Britons: Forging the Nation, 1707–1837*. New Haven, CT: Yale University Press, 1992.

Curran, Stuart. "Anna Seward and the Dynamics of Female Friendship." In *Romantic Women Poets: Genre and Gender*, edited by Lilla Maria Crisafulli and Cecilia Pietropoli, 11–21. Amsterdam: Rodopi, 2007.

———. "Dynamics of Female Friendship in the Later Eighteenth Century." *Nineteenth-Century Contexts* 23.2 (2001): 221–39.

Daiches, David. "Boswell's Ambiguities." In *New Light on Boswell: Critical and Historical Essays on the Bicentenary of "The Life of Johnson,"* edited by Greg Clingham, 1–8. Cambridge: Cambridge University Press, 1991.

de Man, Paul. *The Rhetoric of Romanticism*. New York: Columbia University Press, 1984.

DeMaria, Robert, Jr., ed. *British Literature, 1640–1789: An Anthology*. 3rd ed. Malden, MA: Blackwell, 2008.

Doody, Margaret Anne. "Sensuousness in the Poetry of Eighteenth-Century Women Poets." In *Women's Poetry in the Enlightenment: The Making of a Canon, 1730–1820*, edited by Isobel Armstrong and Virginia Blain, 11–15. Houndmills, UK: Macmillan, 1999.

Dowling, William C. *The Epistolary Moment: The Poetics of the Eighteenth-Century Verse Epistle*. Princeton, NJ: Princeton University Press, 1991.

Eger, Elizabeth, and Lucy Peltz. *Brilliant Women: 18th-Century Bluestockings*. London: National Portrait Gallery, 2008.

Ellis, Markman. *The Politics of Sensibility: Race, Gender, and Commerce in the Sentimental Novel*. Cambridge: Cambridge University Press, 1996.

Ellison, Julie. *Cato's Tears and the Making of Anglo-American Emotion*. Chicago: University of Chicago Press, 1999.

Ezell, Margaret J. M. *Social Authorship and the Advent of Print*. Baltimore, MD: Johns Hopkins University Press, 1999.

———. *Writing Women's Literary History*. Baltimore, MD: Johns Hopkins University Press, 1993.

Faderman, Lillian. *Surpassing the Love of Men: Romantic Friendship and Love between Women from the Renaissance to the Present.* New York: Harper Collins, 1981.

Fairer, David, and Christine Gerrard, eds. *Eighteenth-Century Poetry: An Annotated Anthology.* Oxford, UK: Blackwell, 2004.

Feldman, Paula R., ed. *British Women Poets of the Romantic Era: An Anthology.* Baltimore, MD: Johns Hopkins University Press, 1997.

Feldman, Paula R., and Daniel Robinson, eds. *A Century of Sonnets: The Romantic-Era Revival.* Oxford: Oxford University Press, 1999.

Ferguson, Moira. *Eighteenth-Century Women Poets: Nation, Class, and Gender.* Albany: State University of New York Press, 1995.

Fletcher, Edward G. Introduction. In James Boswell, *The Life of Samuel Johnson, LL.D.* 3 vols, edited by Edward G. Fletcher, 1:vii–xxx. New York: Heritage Press, 1963.

Foreman, Amanda. *Georgiana, Duchess of Devonshire.* New York: Random House, 1999.

Foster, Gretchen M. *Pope Versus Dryden: A Controversy in Letters to "The Gentleman's Magazine," 1789–1791.* Victoria, BC: University of Victoria Press, 1989.

Fry, Carrol. *Charlotte Smith.* New York: Twayne, 1996.

Fulford, Tim. *Landscape, Liberty, and Authority: Poetry, Criticism and Politics from Thomson to Wordsworth.* Cambridge: Cambridge University Press, 1996.

Fussell, Paul. *Theory of Prosody in Eighteenth-Century England.* New London, CT: Archon, 1966.

Gentleman's Magazine and Historical Chronicle. Edited by Sylvanus Urban [pseud.]. London: St. John's Gate, 1736–1833.

Gittings, Robert. *John Keats.* Harmondsworth, UK: Pelican, 1968.

Goethe, Johann Wolfgang von. *The Sorrows of Werther: A German Story.* 2 vols. London: Dodsley, 1786.

Goring, Paul. *The Rhetoric of Sensibility in Eighteenth-Century Culture.* Cambridge: Cambridge University Press, 2005.

Greenblatt, Stephen, Deirdre Shauna Lynch, and Jack Stillinger, eds. *The Norton Anthology of English Literature.* Vol. D, *The Romantic Period.* New York: Norton, 2009.

Greene, Richard. *Mary Leapor: A Study in Eighteenth-Century Women's Poetry.* Oxford, UK: Clarendon, 1993.

Greer, Germaine. *Slip-Shod Sibyls: Recognition, Rejection, and the Woman Poet.* London: Viking, 1995.

Griffin, Dustin. *Literary Patronage in England, 1650–1800.* Cambridge: Cambridge University Press, 1996.

———. *Patriotism and Poetry in the Long Eighteenth Century.* Charlottesville: University of Virginia Press, 2002.

Guest, Harriet. *Empire, Barbarism, and Civilisation.* Cambridge: Cambridge University Press, 2007.

———. *Small Change: Women, Learning, Patriotism, 1750–1810.* Chicago: University of Chicago Press, 2000.

Guillory, John. *Cultural Capital: The Problem of Literary Canon Formation.* Chicago: University of Chicago Press, 1993.

Haeffner, Joel, and Carol Shiner Wilson, eds. *Re-Visioning Romanticism: British Women Writers, 1776–1837.* Philadelphia: University of Pennsylvania Press, 1994.

Hagstrum, Jean. *Sex and Sensibility: Ideal and Erotic Love from Milton to Mozart.* Chicago: University of Chicago Press, 1980.

Hartman, Geoffrey H. *Wordsworth's Poetry, 1787–1814.* New Haven, CT: Yale University Press, 1964.

Harvey, Arnold D. *English Poetry in a Changing Society, 1780–1825.* New York: St. Martin's, 1980.

Hatch, Robert McConnell. *Major John André: A Gallant in Spy's Clothing.* Boston: Houghton Mifflin, 1986.

Hawley, Judith. "Charlotte Smith's *Elegiac Sonnets*: Losses and Gains." In *Women's Poetry in the Enlightenment: The Making of a Canon, 1730–1820,* edited by Isobel Armstrong and Virginia Blain, 184–98. Houndmills, UK: Macmillan, 1999.

Hesselgrave, Ruth Avaline. *Lady Miller and the Batheaston Literary Circle.* New Haven, CT: Yale University Press, 1927.

Hibbert, Christopher. Introduction. In James Boswell, *The Life of Johnson,* edited by Christopher Hibbert, 7–28. London: Penguin Books, 1986.

——. *Redcoats and Rebels: The American Revolution through British Eyes.* New York: Avon, 1990.

Hill, Aaron. "The Progress of Wit: A Caveat." In *Popeiana X: The Dunciad and Other Matters, 1730,* 15. New York: Garland, 1975.

Hofkosh, Sonia. *Sexual Politics and the Romantic Author.* Cambridge: Cambridge University Press, 1998.

Home, Henry, Lord Kames. *Elements of Criticism.* 3 vols. New York: Johnson Reprint Corporation, 1967.

Hutner, Heidi, ed. *Rereading Aphra Behn: History, Theory, and Criticism.* Charlottesville: University Press of Virginia, 1993.

Jajdelska, Elspeth. *Silent Reading and the Birth of the Narrator.* Toronto: University of Toronto Press, 2007.

Jarvis, Simon. "Thinking in Verse." In *The Cambridge Companion to British Romantic Poetry,* edited by James Chandler and Maureen N. McLane, 99–101. Cambridge: Cambridge University Press, 2008.

Johnson, Claudia L. *Equivocal Beings: Politics, Gender, and Sentimentality in the 1790s: Wollstonecraft, Radcliffe, Burney, Austen.* Chicago: University of Chicago Press, 1995.

Johnson, Edgar. *Sir Walter Scott.* 2 vols. New York: Macmillan, 1970.

Johnson, Samuel. *The History of Rasselas, Prince of Abissinia.* Edited by Jessica Richard. Peterborough, Ontario: Broadview, 2008.

——. *The Lives of the Poets.* 4 vols. Edited by Roger Lonsdale. Oxford: Oxford University Press, 2006.

——. *Selected Essays from the "Rambler," "Adventurer," and "Idler."* Edited by W. J. Bate. New Haven, CT: Yale University Press, 1968.

Julius-Puiu, Adeline. "Gendering Telemachus: Anna Seward and the Epic Rewriting of Fénelon's *Télémaque*." In *Approaches to the Anglo and American Female Epic, 1621–1982*, edited by Bernard Schweizer, 85–97. Burlington, VT: Ashgate, 2006.

Jones, Mary. "In Memory of the Right Honorable Lord Aubrey Beauclerk, Who Was Slain at Carthagena." In *Miscellanies in Prose and Verse*, 36–44. Oxford, UK: Dodsley, 1750.

Jung, Sandro. "Susanna Pearson and the 'Elegiac' Lyric." *Studia Philologica* 78.2 (2006): 153–64.

Kaul, Suvir. *Poems of Nation, Anthems of Empire: English Verse in the Long Eighteenth Century*. Charlottesville: University of Virginia Press, 2000.

Keats, John. "Ode to a Nightingale." In *The Poems of John Keats*, edited by Jack Stillinger, 370–73. Cambridge, MA: Harvard University Press, 1978.

Keith, Jennifer. *Poetry and the Feminine from Behn to Cowper*. Newark: University of Delaware Press, 2005.

Kelly, Gary. "Clara Reeve, Provincial Bluestocking: From the Old Whigs to the Modern Liberal State." In *Reconsidering the Bluestockings*, edited by Nicole Pohl and Betty A. Schellenberg, 105–26. San Marino, CA: Huntington Library, 2003.

Kelly, Gary, et al., eds. *Bluestocking Feminism: Writings of the Bluestocking Circle, 1738–1785*. 6 vols. London: Pickering and Chatto, 1999.

Kelly, Jennifer, ed. *Anna Seward*. Vol. 4 of *Bluestocking Feminism: Writings of the Bluestocking Circle, 1738–1785*, ed. Gary Kelly et al. London: Pickering and Chatto, 1999.

Kennedy, Deborah. "Benevolent Historian: Helen Maria Williams and Her British Readers." In *Rebellious Hearts: British Women Writers and the French Revolution*, edited by Adriana Craciun and Kari E. Lokke, 317–36. Albany: State University of New York Press, 2001.

———. *Helen Maria Williams and the Age of Revolution*. Lewisburg, PA: Bucknell University Press, 2002.

King, Kathryn R. "Political Verse and Satire: Monarchy, Party and Female Political Agency." In *Women and Poetry, 1660–1750*, edited by Sarah Prescott and David E. Shuttleton, 203–22. Houndmills, UK: Palgrave, 2003.

King-Hele, Desmond. *Erasmus Darwin and the Romantic Poets*. New York: St. Martin's, 1986.

Kowaleski-Wallace, Elizabeth. *Their Father's Daughters: Hannah More, Maria Edgeworth, and Patriarchal Complicity*. New York: Oxford University Press, 1991.

Kramnick, Jonathan Brody. *Making the English Canon: Print-Capitalism and the Cultured Past, 1700–1770*. Cambridge: Cambridge University Press, 1998.

Kroeber, Karl. *Ecological Literary Criticism: Romantic Imagining and the Biology of Mind*. New York: Columbia University Press, 1994.

Labbe, Jacqueline M. "Every Poet Her Own Drawing Master: Charlotte Smith, Anna Seward, and *ut pictura poesis*." In *Early Romantics: Perspectives in British Poetry from Pope to Wordsworth*, edited by Thomas Woodman, 200–214. New York: St. Martin's, 1998.

Landry, Donna. "The Labouring-Class Women Poets: 'Hard Labour we most cheerfully pursue.'" In *Women and Poetry 1660–1750*, edited by Sarah Prescott and David E. Shuttleton, 223–43. Houndmills, UK: Palgrave, 2003.

———. *The Muses of Resistance: Laboring-Class Women's Poetry in Britain, 1739–1796.* Cambridge: Cambridge University Press, 1990.

Laven, Mary. *The Virgins of Venice: Broken Vows and Cloistered Lives in the Renaissance Convent.* New York: Penguin Books, 2003.

Levinson, Marjorie. *Wordsworth's Great Period Poems.* Cambridge: Cambridge University Press, 1986.

Levy, Michelle. *Family Authorship and Romantic Print Culture.* Houndmills, UK: Palgrave, 2008.

Liu, Alan. *Wordsworth: The Sense of History.* Stanford, CA: Stanford University Press, 1989.

Logan, James Venable. *The Poetry and Aesthetics of Erasmus Darwin.* New York: Octagon, 1972.

Lonsdale, Roger. "Anna Seward." In *Eighteenth-Century Women Poets: An Oxford Anthology*, edited by Roger Lonsdale, 311–13. Oxford: Oxford University Press, 1989.

Lucas, E. V. *A Swan and Her Friends.* London: Methuen, 1907.

Mahoney, Charles, and Michael O'Neill, eds. *Romantic Poetry: An Annotated Anthology.* Malden, MA: Blackwell, 2008.

Manley, Delarivier, ed. *The Nine Muses; or, Poems Written by Nine Severall Ladies upon the Death of the late Famous John Dryden, Esq.* London: Bassett, 1700.

Marsden, Jean I. *The Re-Imagined Text: Shakespeare, Adaptation, and Eighteenth-Century Literary Theory.* Lexington: University Press of Kentucky, 1995.

McCarthy, Thomas J. *Relationships of Sympathy: The Writer and the Reader in British Romanticism.* Aldershot, UK: Scolar Press, 1997.

McDonald, Russ. *Look to the Lady: Sarah Siddons, Ellen Terry, and Judi Dench on the Shakespearean Stage.* Athens: University of Georgia Press, 2005.

McDowell, Judith H. Preface to *Julie; or, The New Eloise. Letters of Two Lovers, Inhabitants of a Small Town at the Foot of the Alps.* University Park: Pennsylvania State University Press, 1968.

McGann, Jerome. *The Poetics of Sensibility: A Revolution in Literary Style.* Oxford, UK: Clarendon, 1996.

Mellor, Anne K. *Mothers of the Nation: Women's Political Writing in England, 1780–1830.* Bloomington: Indiana University Press, 2000.

———. *Romanticism and Gender.* New York: Routledge, 1993.

Messenger, Ann. *Woman and Poet in the Eighteenth Century: The Life of Mary Whateley Darwall (1738–1825).* New York: AMS Press, 1999.

Miller, Anne Riggs. *Letters from Italy.* 3 vols. Dublin: W. Watson et al., 1776.

Monk, Samuel H. "Anna Seward and the Romantic Poets: A Study in Taste." In *Wordsworth and Coleridge: Studies in Honor of George McLean Harper*, edited by Earl Leslie Griggs, 118–34. Princeton, NJ: Princeton University Press, 1939.

Mullan, John. *Sentiment and Sociability: The Language of Feeling in the Eighteenth Century.* Oxford, UK: Clarendon, 1988.

Nagle, Christopher C. Sexuality and the Culture of Sensibility in the British Romantic Era. New York: Palgrave, 2007.

Newman, Donald J., and Lynn Marie Wright, eds. *Fair Philosopher: Eliza Haywood and "The Female Spectator."* Lewisburg, PA: Bucknell University Press, 2006.

Oppenheimer, Paul. *The Birth of the Modern Mind: Self, Consciousness, and the Invention of the Sonnet.* New York: Oxford University Press, 1989.

Paulson, Ronald. *Hogarth: His Art, Life, and Times.* 2 vols. New Haven, CT: Yale University Press, 1971.

Perry, Ruth. *Novel Relations: The Transformation of Kinship in English Literature and Culture, 1748–1818.* Cambridge: Cambridge University Press, 2004.

Pfau, Thomas. *Wordsworth's Profession: Form, Class, and the Logic of Early Romantic Cultural Production.* Stanford, CA: Stanford University Press, 1997.

Pinch, Adela. "Sensibility." *Romanticism: An Oxford Guide*, edited by Nicholas Roe, 49–61. Oxford: Oxford University Press, 2005.

———. *Strange Fits of Passion: Epistemologies of Emotion, Hume to Austen.* Stanford, CA: Stanford University Press, 1996.

Pohl, Nicole, and Betty A. Schellenberg. "Introduction: A Bluestocking Historiography." In *Reconsidering the Bluestockings*, edited by Nicole Pohl and Betty A. Schellenberg, 39–57. San Marino, CA: Huntington Library, 2003.

Poovey, Mary. *Genres of the Credit Economy: Mediating Value in Eighteenth- and Nineteenth-Century Britain.* Chicago: University of Chicago Press, 2008.

Pope, Alexander. *Eloisa to Abelard.* In *The Poems of Alexander Pope: A One-Volume Edition of the Twickenham Pope*, edited by John Butt et al., 252–61. New Haven, CT: Yale University Press, 1966.

———. *An Essay on Criticism.* In *The Poems of Alexander Pope: A One-Volume Edition of the Twickenham Pope*, edited by John Butt et al., 143–68. New Haven, CT: Yale University Press, 1966.

Prior, Matthew. "Henry and Emma, a Poem, upon the Model of the Nut-Brown Maid." In *The Literary Works of Matthew Prior*, edited by H. Bunker Wright and Monroe K. Spears, 278–300. Oxford, UK: Clarendon, 1959.

Rai, Amit. *Rule of Sympathy: Sentiment, Race, and Power, 1750–1850.* New York: Palgrave, 2002.

Reiman, Donald H. Introduction. In Erasmus Darwin, *The Botanic Garden*, 2 vols., edited by Donald H. Reiman, 1:v–xiv. New York: Garland Publishing, 1978.

Richardson, Alan. *British Romanticism and the Science of the Mind.* Cambridge: Cambridge University Press, 2001.

Rizzo, Betty. *Companions Without Vows: Relationships Among Eighteenth-Century British Women.* Athens: University of Georgia Press, 1994.

Robertson, Fiona, ed. *Women's Writing, 1778–1838: An Anthology.* Oxford: Oxford University Press, 2002.

Robinson, Mary. *Sappho and Phaon.* Washington, DC: Woodstock, 2000.

Roe, Nicholas. *The Politics of Nature: Wordsworth and Some Contemporaries.* New York: St. Martin's Press, 1992.

———, ed. *Romanticism: An Oxford Guide.* Oxford: Oxford University Press, 2005.

Ross, Marlon B. *The Contours of Masculine Desire: Romanticism and the Rise of Women's Poetry*. Oxford: Oxford University Press, 1989.

Rousseau, Jean Jacques. *Eloisa; or, A Series of Original Letters Collected and Published by J. J. Rousseau*. 4 vols. 2nd ed. London: R. Griffiths, T. Becket, P. A. De Hondt, 1761.

Rowe, Elizabeth. "Upon the Death of Her Husband." In Alexander Pope, *Eloisa to Abelard*, 47–52. 2nd ed. London, 1720.

Runge, Laura. *Gender and Language in Eighteenth-Century Literary Criticism, 1660– 1790*. Cambridge: Cambridge University Press, 1997.

Schnorrenberg, Barbara. "Anna Seward." In *A Dictionary of British and American Women Writers, 1660–1800*, edited by Janet Todd, 281–82. Totowa, NJ: Rowman and Littlefield, 1987.

Schor, Esther. *Bearing the Dead: The British Culture of Mourning from the Enlightenment to Victoria*. Princeton, NJ: Princeton University Press, 1994.

Schweizer, Bernard, ed. *Approaches to the Anglo and American Female Epic, 1621– 1982*. Burlington, VT: Ashgate, 2006.

Scott, Walter. *The Letters of Sir Walter Scott, 1787–1807*. 12 vols. Edited by H. J. C. Grierson. London: Constable, 1932.

Selzer, Sharon. " 'Pond'rous Engines' in 'Outraged Groves': The Environmental Argument of Anna Seward's 'Coalbrookdale.' " *European Romantic Review* 18.1 (2007): 69–82.

Seward, Anna. *Letters of Anna Seward, Written between the Years 1784 and 1807*. 6 vols. Edited by Archibald Constable. Edinburgh: Archibald Constable, 1811.

——. *Louisa, a Poetical Novel, in Four Epistles*. Edited by Carolyn Franklin. London: Routledge, 1996.

——. *Memoirs of Dr. Darwin, Chiefly during His Residence at Lichfield, with Anecdotes of His Friends, and Criticisms on His Writings*. Philadelphia: Shaw and Shoemaker, 1804.

——. *Monody on Major André, to Which Are Added Letters Addressed to Her by Major André, in the Year 1769*. Lichfield: J. Jackson, 1781.

——. *Original Sonnets on Various Subjects; and Odes Paraphrased from Horace*. 2nd ed. London: G. Sael, 1799.

——. *The Poetical Works of Anna Seward, with extracts from Her Literary Correspondence*. 3 vols. Edited by Walter Scott. Edinburgh: Ballantine, 1810.

——. *The Swan of Lichfield, Being a Selection from the Correspondence of Anna Seward*. Edited by Hesketh Pearson. London: Hamish Hamilton, 1936.

Shakespeare, William. "That Time of Yeeare Thou Maist in Me Behold." In *A Collection of Poems, in Two Volumes; Being All the Miscellanies of Mr. William Shakespeare*, 2:40. London: Bernard Lintott, [1710?].

Simpson, David. *Romanticism, Nationalism, and the Revolt against Theory*. Chicago: University of Chicago Press, 1993.

Smith, Charlotte. *Elegiac Sonnets and Other Essays*. 8th ed. London: T. Cadell, 1797.

Smith, Hannah. "The Idea of a Protestant Monarchy in Britain, 1714–1760." *Past and Present*, 185 (2004): 91–118.

Smith, Joshua Hett. Narrative of the Death of Major André. New York: Arno Press, 1969.

Spencer, Jane. *Literary Relations: Kinship and the Canon, 1660–1830*. Oxford: Oxford University Press, 2005.

Starr, G. Gabrielle. *Lyric Generations: Poetry and the Novel in the Long Eighteenth Century*. Baltimore, MD: Johns Hopkins University Press, 2004.

Staves, Susan. "Church of England Clergy and Women Writers." In *Reconsidering the Bluestockings*, edited by Nicole Pohl and Betty A. Schellenberg, 81–104. San Marino, CA: Huntington Library, 2003.

———. *A Literary History of Women's Writing in Britain, 1660–1789*. Cambridge: Cambridge University Press, 2006.

Stewart, Susan. "Romantic Meter and Form." In *The Cambridge Companion to British Romantic Poetry*, edited by James Chandler and Maureen N. McLane, 67–69. Cambridge: Cambridge University Press, 2008.

Sutro, Alfred. *The Batheaston Parnassus Fairs: A Manuscript Identified*. San Francisco: Grabhorn, 1936.

Thomas [Kairoff], Claudia N. *Alexander Pope and His Eighteenth-Century Women Readers*. Carbondale: Southern Illinois University Press, 1994.

———. "Masculine Performances and Gender Identity." *Studies in Eighteenth-Century Culture* 25 (1996): 167–85.

Thomson, James. *Agamemnon*. In *The Works of Mr. James Thomson*, 1–90. 3 vols. London: R. Baldwin et al., 1802.

Todd, Janet. *Sensibility: An Introduction*. London: Methuen, 1986.

Turco, Lewis L. *The New Book of Forms: A Handbook of Poetics*. Hanover, NH: University Press of New England, 1986.

Uglow, Jenny. *The Lunar Men: Five Friends Whose Curiosity Changed the World*. New York: Farrar, Straus and Giroux, 2002.

Urban, Sylvanus [John Nichols], ed. "Biographical Sketch of the Late Miss Seward." *Gentleman's Magazine*, April 1809, 378–79.

Van Sant, Ann Jessie. *Eighteenth-Century Sensibility and the Novel: The Senses in Social Context*. Cambridge: Cambridge University Press, 1993.

Vermeule, Blakey. *The Party of Humanity: Writing Moral Psychology in Eighteenth-Century Britain*. Baltimore, MD: Johns Hopkins University Press, 2000.

Vicinus, Martha. *Intimate Friends: Women Who Loved Women, 1778–1728*. Chicago: University of Chicago Press, 2004.

Wain, John. *Samuel Johnson*. New York: Viking, 1974.

Waldron, Mary. *Lactilla, Milkwoman of Clifton: The Life and Writings of Ann Yearsley*. Athens: University of Georgia Press, 1996.

Walker, Gina Luria. *Mary Hays (1759–1843): The Growth of a Woman's Mind*. Aldershot, UK: Ashgate, 2006.

Warton, Thomas, ed. *Poems upon Several Occasions, English, Italian, and Latin, with Translations, by John Milton*. London: Dodsley, 1785.

Wasserman, Earl R. *Shelley: A Critical Reading*. Baltimore, MD: Johns Hopkins University Press, 1971.

Waters, Mary A. *British Women Writers and the Profession of Literary Criticism, 1789–1832*. Houndmills, UK: Palgrave, 2004.

Whalley, Thomas S. *Journals and Correspondence of Thomas Sedgewick Whalley, D.D., of Mendip Lodge, Somerset*. 2 vols. Edited by Hill Wickham. London: Richard Bentley, 1863.

Wheatley, Phillis. "On the Capture of General Lee." In *The Poems of Phillis Wheatley*, rev. ed., edited by Julian D. Mason Jr. 167–70. Chapel Hill: University of North Carolina Press, 1989.

Wheeler, David. "Placing Anna Seward: The 'Genius of Place,' Coalbrookdale, and 'Colebrook Dale.'" *New Perspectives on the Eighteenth Century* 5.1 (2008): 30–40.

Wicker, Cecil V. *Edward Young and the Fear of Death: a Study in Romantic Melancholy*. Albuquerque: University of New Mexico Press, 1952.

Williams, Glyn. *Voyages of Delusion: The Quest for the Northwest Passage*. New Haven, CT: Yale University Press, 2003.

Wolfe, Thomas. *Look Homeward, Angel: A Story of the Buried Life*. New York: Charles Scribner's Sons, 1929.

Wolfson, Susan J. *Borderlines: The Shiftings of Gender in British Romanticism*. Stanford, CA: Stanford University Press, 2006.

Wood, Gillen D'Arcy. "The Female Penseroso: Anna Seward, Sociable Poetry, and the Handelian Consensus." *Modern Language Quarterly* 67.4 (2006): 451–77.

Woodman, Thomas M. *Thomas Parnell*. Boston: Twayne, 1985.

Woolf, Virginia. *A Room of One's Own*. New York: Harcourt Brace, 1991.

Wordsworth, William. "Advertisement to Lyrical Ballads, 1798." In *Lyrical Ballads and Other Poems, 1797–1800*, edited by James Butler and Karen Green, 738. Cornell, NY: Cornell University Press, 1992.

———. "Lines Written a Few Miles above Tintern Abbey." In *Lyrical Ballads and Other Poems, 1797–1800*, edited by James Butler and Karen Green, 116–20. Ithaca, NY: Cornell University Press, 1992.

———. "Ode: Intimations of Immortality from Recollections of Early Childhood." In *Poems, in Two Volumes, and Other Poems, 1800–1807*, edited by Jared Curtis, 271–77. Ithaca, NY: Cornell University Press, 1983.

———. *The Thirteen-Book "Prelude."* 2 vols. Edited by Mark L. Reed. Ithaca, NY: Cornell University Press, 1991).

Zionkowski, Linda. *Men's Work: Gender, Class, and the Professionalization of Poetry, 1660–1784*. New York: Palgrave, 2001.

Index

Reiman, Donald H., 235–36
Relationships of Sympathy (McCarthy),
    27, 162, 277n1
Repton, Humphrey, 279n6, 280n11
Restoration criticism, 241
Richardson, Alan, 11
Richardson, Samuel, 58; Seward and, 129,
    231, 280n11. Works: *Clarissa*, 118, 134,
    141, 233, 280n11; *Pamela*, 129, 157; *Sir
    Charles Grandison*, 233
Rizzo, Betty, 206, 278n3
Robinson, Daniel, 163, 164, 276n1
Robinson, Elizabeth, 159
Robinson, Mary, 1, 2, 163, 165, 208
Roe, Nicholas, 11, 274n1
Romanticism: conception of art in, 161;
    and gender definitions, 16–17, 38, 192;
    and sensibility, 2–3, 10–11, 162; Seward
    and onset of, ix, 1, 11, 162–63, 235, 265;
    women writers and, 9, 16, 113, 115, 192
Romanticism and Gender (Mellor),
    114–15
Romney, George, 222, 223
Room of One's Own, A (Woolf), 57
Ross, Marlon, 39–40, 52
Rousseau, George S., 118
Rousseau, Jean-Jacques, 17, 137; and
    conception of virtue, 126; *La nouvelle
    Heloïse*, 117, 118, 120, 121, 125, 126–28,
    136
Runge, Laura, 168

Sappho and Phaon (Robinson), 163
Sarpi, Paulo, 55
Savage, Richard, 56, 244, 252
Saville, Elizabeth, 153–54
Saville, John: Boswell implications
    around, 260, 263; death of, 201; inability
    to divorce of, 155, 275–76n5; marriage
    of, 141, 205, 223; Seward relationship
    with, 22, 24, 28, 37, 55, 113, 152–53, 191,
    201, 255, 264; Seward's father and,
    152–53, 204, 205; as Seward's music
    instructor, 206
Schellenberg, Betty A., 28, 34
Schnorrenberg, Barbara, 269n10
Schor, Esther, 84, 208, 272n2
Scotland, 261

Scott, Walter, 11, 168; as bard of war, 98;
    critical preface to Seward works by,
    18–23, 27, 34, 71, 239; *The Lay of the
    Last Minstrel*, 18; Seward letters and
    remarks to, 194, 241, 279n8; as Seward
    protégé, x, 15, 18
Scottish ballads, 21
Scriblerians, 39
self-abnegation, x, 138
Sense and Sensibility (Austen), 134, 230,
    241
sensibility: chaste, 139–40; as cultural
    paradigm, 118; gendering of, 85–86,
    90, 98, 119, 120, 155, 157, 275n2; heroes
    of, 70, 75, 82–83, 84, 85–86, 95; and
    hypocrisy, 134; influence of, on social
    movements, 118; Johnson accused of
    lacking, 260–61; in *Louisa*, 13, 117,
    118–19, 122, 125, 132–33, 138, 139–40, 146,
    154–57, 229; as motivation for human
    behavior, 118–19; novels of, 129, 149,
    150–51, 154–55, 181; as out of style, 27,
    181, 261; and patriotism, 70, 272n11; Pope
    and, 121, 157; and representations of
    emotion, 171–72; and Romanticism,
    2–3, 10–11, 162; and sacrifice, 150–51;
    and sentimental fiction, 13, 74, 77, 85,
    87, 123–24, 136, 138; Seward as poet of,
    x, 2–3, 10, 16, 198, 199, 200, 215–16,
    227–28, 264; Seward differences with
    Smith on, 198; and sublimity, 77, 78,
    126; women and, 98, 119, 120, 121, 155,
    156, 157, 275n2
Sentimental Journey (Sterne), 123
Sentiment and Sensibility (Mullan), 119
Serena Reading (Romney), 222, 223
Seward, Anna, career of: attempt to
    control, x, xi–xii, 12, 13, 225, 264; and
    attentiveness to publishing process,
    61–62; Batheaston debut of, 12, 32,
    37–38, 40, 55, 59, 68–69; gendered
    criticisms of, 53, 229, 250, 259–60;
    individual recognition of, 54, 236–37;
    as literary critic, 13–14, 15, 53, 161, 231,
    232, 279n6, 280n11; mentoring of young
    poets by, 15, 60, 108; not writing for
    money, 34, 59, 231–32; parental
    discouragement of, 22, 55, 58; and

"Tintern Abbey" (Wordsworth), 7, 9, 10,
99, 114, 192, 274n1, 277n1
Todd, Janet, 11, 275n1
topographic poems, 4
Toryism, 244
To the Memory of Lady Miller (Seward),
53, 62–68
Tour of the Hebrides (Boswell), 239, 243,
244, 262
tour poetry, 4, 6, 267n5
transcendence, 8, 10, 268n9
transgressive love, 202, 210, 218
transposition, 48
Tuite, Eliza, 100

Uglow, Jenny, 18, 214
Urban, Sylvanus, 15

Van Sant, Ann Jessie, 136, 181
Variety, 279n6, 280n11
Venice Preserv'd (Otway), 88, 118
Vesey, Elizabeth, 36
Vicar of Wakefield, The (Goldsmith), 123,
148
Vicinus, Martha, 278n2
Vindication of the Rights of Woman
(Wollstonecraft), 106, 229, 279n6
Virgil, 86, 87
Voltaire, 231
Vyse, Richard, 205

Wain, John, 280n5
Walmesley, Gilbert, 246
Walpole, Horace, 36, 270n4, 272n7
Walpole, Robert, 52
Warton, Thomas, 114, 170, 182–83
Washington, George, 83, 87, 88, 90
Wasserman, Earl R., 7, 222
Waters, Mary A., 229, 270n2, 279n6
Watt, James, 233
Watts, Isaac, 252, 254–55
Wedgwood, Josiah, 233
West, Benjamin, 75, 86
West, Gilbert, 255, 280n1
Weston, Sophia, 183, 184, 185–86
Whalley, Thomas S., 28; at Batheaston,
36, 65; *Edwy and Edilda*, 37, 74, 279n8;

Seward correspondence with, 101–2,
104, 165, 167, 190, 241–42; Seward
friendship with, 37, 56
Wharton, Joseph, 60, 272n7
Wharton, Thomas, 60, 272n7
Wheatley, Phillis, 86
Wheeler, David, xi, 2, 267n3
Whigs, 90
White, Henry, 114, 164, 174, 254, 256,
277n3
Wigley, Edmund, 103
William (prince), 95
Williams, Glyn, 273n8
Williams, Helen Maria, 2, 34, 104; *Peru*,
74; Seward and, ix, 15, 60, 100, 274n2;
Seward letters to, 27, 106
Wolfe, James, 95
Wolfe, Thomas, 207
Wolfson, Susan J., 16–17, 38, 271n2; on
Keats, 40, 230, 261, 279n9
Wollstonecraft, Mary, ix, 2, 119; and
challenges facing women writers, 263,
264; literary career of, 56, 59, 104, 264;
and Rousseau, 137, 138, 275n1. Works:
Vindication of the Rights of Woman,
106, 229, 279n6; *Wrongs of Woman*,
138, 156, 275n1
women: denial of agency to, 22; education
of, 106; maturation of, 263, 280–81n7;
as "more emotional" sex, 204; and
politics, 52, 90, 93, 105, 112; and
sensibility, 98, 119, 120, 121, 155, 156,
157, 275n2. *See also* gender
*Women and Ecologies of Early Modern
England* (Bowerbank), 29
women writers and poets: and amateur-
professional gendering, 51–52, 53,
56–57; at bluestocking salons, 39; and
difficulties establishing themselves,
39–40, 55, 57, 171, 263, 264, 274n15;
emergence and growth of, 231, 271n2;
and funeral panegyrics, 62–63, 272n9;
lack of acknowledgment of, 54, 186,
271n3, 279n10; as literary critics, 39,
228, 229, 231, 279n6; pen names of, 17,
45, 244; political and social involvement of, 9, 100, 112, 114, 274n3; as